"Evil People"

STUDIES IN EARLY MODERN GERMAN HISTORY
H. C. Erik Midelfort, Editor

"Evil People"

*A Comparative Study of Witch Hunts
in Swabian Austria and the Electorate of Trier*

JOHANNES DILLINGER

Translated by Laura Stokes

University of Virginia Press   *Charlottesville and London*

Originally published in German as *"Böse Leute." Hexenverfolgungen in Schwäbisch-Österreich und Kurtrier im Vergleich,* © 1999 by Paulinus Verlag/Spee, Trier, Germany

University of Virginia Press
Translation and new material © 2009 by the Rector and Visitors of the
University of Virginia
All rights reserved
Printed in the United States of America on acid-free paper

First published 2009

9 8 7 6 5 4 3 2 1

LIBRARY OF CONGRESS CATALOGING-IN-PUBLICATION DATA
Dillinger, Johannes.
  [Böse Leute. English]
  "Evil People" : a comparative study of witch hunts in Swabian Austria and the Electorate of Trier / Johannes Dillinger ; translated by Laura Stokes.
      p.   cm. — (Studies in early modern German history)
  Includes bibliographical references (p.   ) and index.
  ISBN 978-0-8139-2806-7 (cloth : alk. paper) — ISBN 978-0-8139-2838-8 (e-book)
  1. Witchcraft—Germany—Swabia—History. 2. Witchcraft—Germany—Trier—History. I. Title.
  BF1583.D5513 2009
  133.4'309434313—dc122

                                                          2008055272

Contents

Acknowledgments

When I was a little boy, I knew that a witch lived in a little house in the wood on the edge of which my parents' house stood. When I grew older, I learned that witches supposedly had danced in that wood. A little later still, I found out that some of my ancestors had been among the suspects.

I owe a great debt of gratitude to numerous people who helped me to write this book on the witches I have known for so long. Without the unfailing help and the friendly interest of Erik Midelfort, the American who became the nestor of German witchcraft research, this book would never have been written—neither the American version nor the German original. Alison Rowlands, Wolfgang Behringer, Richard Golden, and Robert Walinski Kiehl helped me greatly with practical support. Laura Stokes wrote a brilliant translation that helped me to understand my own text better. Dick Holway and Mark Mones demonstrated unusual interest and patience as editors. My academic teachers and colleagues in Tübingen, Washington, D.C., Trier, and Oxford aided me in innumerable ways. My students helped me to see things I thought I knew in a different light. Abraham and Victor, my old friends, were examples to me. I thank all of them profoundly.

I dedicate this book, like everything else, to my mother and the memory of my father.

Johannes Dillinger
Hoxberg/Oxford, April 2009

"Evil People"

Introduction

Comparing Witch Hunts

WITCHCRAFT RESEARCH AND HISTORICAL COMPARISON

A student protest was part of it. The students demanded a thorough investigation of outrageous rumors about the university president. They knew that public protest could force the authorities into action. A group of students gathered in front of a house where they knew the president of the university was. Soon, children joined the students. Even they had heard about the scandal involving the elderly professor. After a while, the students became impatient. They started shouting slogans that reverberated through the narrow streets of the old town. When the president of the university finally mustered the courage to leave the house, the students did not attack him. But the children ran after him. They yelled accusations in the old man's face: "Wizard! Wizard! Wizard!"

Somebody had attached a piece of paper to the castle's gate during the night. Since the castle stood on the edge of the town, it was not long before early passersby noticed the paper. Some nodded approvingly; others looked shocked. They all talked about the paper they had seen. The news spread rapidly through the town and into the neighboring villages. Before the lord of the castle could give the order to tear down the piece of paper, the whole countryside knew what it was: a crude sketch of a person burning at the stake. Everybody knew that the person in the picture was supposed to be the lord of the castle himself.

The two scenes just described took place in 1589 in the cathedral city of Trier and in 1594 in the town of Rottenburg. Both have to do with the belief in witchcraft and the persecution of so-called witches. In both cases, the supposed witches came from the upper strata of society. In both cases, the suspects were male. Otherwise, there is no obvious connection between the two scenes. Diederich Flade, a high-ranking official, professor of law, and president of Trier University, was executed weeks after the students' protest. Christoph Wendler von Bregenroth, the head of the administration of the Habsburg County of Hohenberg and lord of the castle of Rottenburg, escaped a witch trial. What do these scenes mean? What was the significance of these unusual rumors accusing two influential men of witchcraft? How were they related to each other? And what do they teach us about the witch hunts in general?

One way to understand these two episodes more fully would be to integrate each into an individual regional study about witchcraft in Trier and in Rottenburg, respectively. A great number of regional studies of that kind have been written in the past thirty-five years. Particularly in the case of the German heartland of the witch hunts, we can safely say that as a rule witchcraft research takes the form of a regional or local study. These studies have been most profitable, and we now know a great deal more about witch beliefs and magic than we used to. However, do these regional studies really connect with one another? In recent years, some historians have felt uneasy about the regionalism of witchcraft research. Karen Lambrecht and Monika Neugebauer-Wölk contend that the profusion of regional studies in the historiography of witchcraft has created a multiplicity of mutually unintelligible interpretive models. They claim that regional studies are often at odds with more general explanations of the great witch hunts of the sixteenth and seventeenth centuries. Interpretations that work in one region do not work in neighboring regions. Neugebauer-Wölk goes so far as to claim that instead of cutting a path through the enormous mass of source materials and tentative interpretations, witchcraft studies have created an ever growing pathless wilderness of their own. Malcolm Gaskill argues that the examination of individual trials demonstrates that sweeping sociological interpretations can never explain witch hunts. Gaskill's assumption questions the value of regional studies of witchcraft, to say nothing of transregional studies. Other historians, such as Wolfgang Behringer or Franz Irsigler, have tried to identify the general factors that came together in most of the more intensive witch hunts: an acute crisis, demonological knowledge at the popular level, willingness on the part of the people and their rulers at least to tolerate witch trials, and the catalyzing role of prosecution-minded jurists.[1] But in what ways did these factors interrelate during actual witch hunts in any given area?

In this book, I suggest taking a middle way between local studies and a generalizing European or even global view of witch hunts. I will compare the witch hunts in two territories that witnessed severe persecutions. For reasons I will explain later, I have chosen areas situated in the west and southwest of today's Germany: the lands of the archbishop of Trier and the western territory of the Habsburgs. Comparison will enable us to study the witch trials of each territory in great detail. At the same time, careful investigation of similarities and differences between the persecutions in these areas will help us to arrive at a deeper understanding of witch hunting in general.

The comparative method lends itself to research into witch trials, and witch trials present good objects for comparison. The elaborate witch concept was the basis of the witch trials. Theologians authoritatively formulated the main features of this doctrine in the fifteenth century: the pact with the Devil, sexual relations between the Devil and witches, night flight, the witches' Sabbath, harmful sorcery, and the notion linked to pact and Sabbath that the witch was acting not alone but as a member of an organized group. Recent research, especially the work of Hans Peter Broedel and of the Lausanne research group on early witch trials, has shown that the witch doctrine was no mere "invention" of theologians or demonologists. It was instead an attempt to theologically formulate and interpret elements of popular beliefs in harmful magic, night flight, and contact with spirits. Nevertheless, in this way a largely homogeneous demonological theory of witchcraft came into being.[2] This theory affected diverse social and judicial milieus. The different forms of its reception in various contexts—through legislators, administrations, courts, religious institutions, and ordinary people—provide objects for comparison. This is particularly true for the Holy Roman Empire, where the 1532 imperial criminal code of Emperor Charles V (hereafter called the *Carolina*) presented a legal framework for handling magical crimes during an early phase of the witch hunts.[3] The princes and magistrates of the hundreds of territorial states and independent cities of the empire had been powerful enough to force Charles V to include the "salvatory" clause in the *Carolina*. According to this clause, the legislators of princedoms and free cities could choose whether to accept the norms of the *Carolina* in their respective lands or to replace them with their own laws. Nevertheless, the imperial code set a standard no prince or city council could ignore. Thus, the *Carolina* and the witchcraft doctrine present a twofold point of comparative reference in relation to which we can examine the witch hunts in particular regions. The fact that the *Carolina* did not handle magical crimes in the way that the demonological-judicial witchcraft theory required presents a particular opportunity; we have a bipolar structure as the reference point for the comparison. Thus, historians do not need to construct the point of comparative reference. It was already apparent to contemporaries as a twofold structure of orientation. It will be of particular interest to find out in what ways the witch doctrine and the *Carolina* influenced the persecutions under the specific circumstances of different regions. In this way, witch hunts suggest themselves as objects of comparison.

Recent witchcraft research itself has been shaped by both implicit and explicit comparison. Contemporary witchcraft research—that is, research into historical witch trials since Erik Midelfort's new approach in 1968—is deeply indebted to ethnology and cultural anthropology. As Helga Schnabel-Schüle has shown, apart from the particular interest in women's studies, this is the most important reason why witchcraft research established itself as an independent field within early modern historiography. Edward Evans-Pritchard's study of magic among the east African Zande gave historical witchcraft research a decisive stimulus. The question of magic and witchcraft accusations and their function or dysfunction in society came into focus. After a preliminary attempt by Julio Caro Baroja in 1961 and Midelfort's program of 1968, Keith Thomas used the ethnological approach for the first time in a comprehensive work on early modern European magic in *Religion and the Decline of Magic* (1971). While Thomas's work succeeded beautifully in integrating witch trials with other manifestations of magical thought such as the saints' and relic cults, astrology, and belief in ghosts, he paid scant attention to concrete and potent regional and local factors and avoided all forms of quantification. Starting from a comparison of history and anthropology as disciplines, in a dialogue with Evans-Pritchard, Thomas reduced the fundamental differences between the two sciences to the essence of their methods: the cohabitation of the ethnologist within the studied society in contrast to the archival work of the historian. Thomas imported the framework and the objectives of anthropology into historiography. In doing so, he established magic as a major topic for anthropological history. A new field and a new direction of historical research emerged through comparisons with a sister discipline. However, neither historians nor anthropologists have since dared to cross the threshold to an elaborate comparison of non-European and European magic. Since 1970, such a comparison has become urgently necessary. The witch hunts of contemporary Africa and Asia show marked parallels to the witch trials of early modern Europe. Preliminary work in this extremely difficult field has already been done. The debt that history owes to ethnology could be repaid via methodologically responsible comparisons with new insights that might be fruitful for the ethnology of modern persecutions.[4]

The comparative method is thus suited to witchcraft research, especially for researching the German heartland of the witch hunts. The state of research here, however, is sobering. No monograph of historical witchcraft research has ever been produced, either before or after the publication of the original German edition of this book, that decisively compares witch hunts in two or more regions. Historical witchcraft research in Germany is still stuck in the mode of regional analysis. Dependence on the anthropological approach has given a decisive advantage to exclusive concentration on a single area of examination. Gerd Schwerhoff has at least acknowledged with admirable clarity that comparisons within and between regions are an indispensable means of avoiding the limitations of local history. Wolfgang Behringer has called for using "comparative regional studies" to correct and refine hypotheses and general statements about the witch hunts. Of course, many regional studies glance briefly at the secondary literature on other territories. For regional studies as such, that might be sufficient. Some authors have concentrated on regions that were so diverse in themselves that at least implicit comparisons were necessary to describe them. Behringer himself, and Midelfort before him, as well as Karen Lambrecht, Ronald Füssel, and others, have provided if not explicit comparisons, at least deliberate synopses of the extremely diverse histories of witch hunting in the various political territories that made up their areas of study. Anthologies on German regions or German and neighboring territories, however, almost always abstain from concluding with any comparative comments. Disappointingly enough, works by Harald Schwillus and Rolf Schulte that deal with clerics and other men suspected of witchcraft in a transregional approach do not attempt any comparison of the regions and territories studied.[5]

Even though comparative work on the regional level still needs to be done, some historians have used deliberate comparative approaches on the national level. This is in keeping with the general development of comparative historiography that has long had a predisposition to international studies based on nineteenth-century concepts of the nation-state. William Monter provided an early example of an "entangled history" with his comparison of witch trials in Scandinavian and Anglo-Saxon regions.[6] Peter Burke's "Comparative Approach to European Witchcraft" describes the comparative method as a third road between the all too simple and sweeping interpretations of nineteenth-century antiquarianism on the one hand, which were not grounded in the sources, and contemporary studies within local, regional, or even national boundaries on the other, which he criticizes as being too limited in outlook. Accordingly, he develops a handy center–periphery model, which illustrated the slow and incomplete reception of the elaborated witch concept on the margins of Europe. Comparison has thus led to a simple typology of the witch hunts that avoids the isolation of case studies as well as meaninglessly broad generalizations. It should be noted, however, that recent research on Scandinavia has questioned whether this comparison was not too quick to interpret the peculiarities of the "peripheries" as "deficient" products of the discourse of the "center."[7] We still await a comprehensive classification of the European witch hunts through comparative work.

In conclusion, historical comparison has already been applied to witchcraft research. As a means to understand better the peculiarities of individual territories as well as the overall development of the witch hunts, it appears unusually promising. Until now, however, historians of witchcraft have implemented the comparative method only in a few exceptional cases. So far, there has been hardly any theoretical discussion about the possibilities of comparison in the historiography of witchcraft. It is high time to turn to comparative work.

Even though this approach appears to have eluded historical witchcraft research, in recent years historians have paid increasing attention to the comparative method. What makes a historical comparison work? What are the limits of comparability? Certainly, we cannot pick just any historical item we fancy and compare it with anything else. It would be foolish to underestimate the work load a historical comparison implies. For a full comparison we have to work with—at least—two phenomena, two regions or maybe two epochs, and two sets of source materials instead of just one. Under what conditions are comparisons worth the historian's effort? What can comparisons really teach us about the past?

In 1929, Marc Bloch presented the first concise theory of comparison in historical scholarship.[8] His definition of historical comparison integrated the reciprocal effect of the "phenomena" and their "milieus"—that is, the comparanda and their contexts. According to Bloch, the main responsibility of the comparative historian is "to select from one or more different social milieus two or more phenomena which ostensibly exhibit certain analogies at first glance, describe the course of their development, establish similarities and differences, and explain these so far as is possible." Bloch stressed that comparisons are well suited to providing explanations for specific elements, reciprocal effects, and common substructures of large historical phenomena.

Theodor Schieder has described the comparative method essentially as a means for developing terminologies or typologies and thus anticipated a precept of the new global history: Comparisons can help us order the plethora of information about the past so that the essential factors and basic lines of historical developments become visible.[9] However, comparisons are not necessarily, or even mainly, about macro-phenomena and global categories. Heinz-Gerhard Haupt and Jürgen Kocka distance themselves from Schieder's position when they suggest a catalogue of the possibilities for comparative historiography. They argue that it leads to a deeper understanding of historical problems. Rather than erasing differences, comparative historiography highlights the peculiarities of individual phenomena. It analyzes how they are affected by general and specific conditions. Comparison thus becomes the most valuable tool for testing hypotheses.[10] Like Bloch, however, Haupt and Kocka warn against isolating a phenomenon from its context in order to compare it with seemingly similar phenomena. Such an ahistorical perspective would lead the historical comparison *ad absurdum.* Haupt and Kocka's criticism notwithstanding, the creation of typologies is among the most attractive functions of historical comparison, as Charles Tilly and Antoon van den Braembussche have pointed out.[11] Earlier, Durkheim described an analogy between the experimental method of the natural sciences and the comparative method of the social sciences and the humanities. On the basis of this analogy, Chris Lorenz has claimed that comparative studies are the historian's true answer to the question of causality. Given a pool of factors that might have caused a certain historical phenomenon, the most likely are those found among the factors that caused very similar phenomena.[12]

We must keep in mind the basic difficulties of comparative historiography. Thomas Welskopp argues that sheer similarity between certain historical phenomena is not sufficient to justify a comparative approach. He points to the importance of a common reference point. Any meaningful comparison needs "an exemplary *tertium comparationis*"—that is, a yardstick or a basic category to which all objects of the comparison are connected.[13] Michel Espagne's criticism is more encompassing. He states that comparing similar cultural phenomena from societies with more differences than similarities would suggest a symmetry that belied the fundamentally asymmetrical structure.[14] The construction of comparative objects—Espagne thought mainly of nation-states—tends to isolate these objects and take them out of context. It thus implies that there are *"aires culturelles closes,"* or closed cultural spaces. However, such do not exist in history. Espagne suggests that historical comparison should at least be complemented with research into cultural transfers. The question of reciprocal effects between objects of comparison has been the primary focus of recent comparative research. Here the comparative method of history begins to integrate questions of cultural transfer and moves toward a global history.[15]

So far, we have been speaking of historical comparison as a method. Strictly put, this is not entirely correct. A historical method is a specific way to approach and evaluate a particular kind of data—for example, a sophisticated statistical approach for working with a series of tax lists. Historical comparisons deal with and correlate multiple phenomena. The comparative method never specifies the nature of its objects, the questions posed, or the ways in which we might try to answer these questions. The means of gauging the comparison is also altogether variable.[16] Thus, it might be more appropriate to call the comparative method a "meta-method."

OBJECTIVES

Up to this point, we have made the following observations. Witch hunts always interrelated the more or less homogeneous witchcraft doctrine with the concrete situation in any given region. This constellation calls out for historical comparisons. The explanatory frameworks found in regional studies are often general—for example, the acculturation thesis or the indirect influence of the worsening climate (see chapter 4) and coincide substantially in different regions of investigation. And yet there were local peculiarities and often pronounced differences between the persecutions in certain regions, even between neighboring regions, that seem to defy general explanations. We require a decisively comparative examination of two areas of the central European heartlands of the witch hunts as a critical test of these explanatory frameworks and an opportunity for their revision. This is not a total deviation from regional analysis but its logical continuation. The regional approach in witchcraft research is by no means at its end, yet fortunately it is also no longer just beginning. Thus, an initial comparative reach beyond it appears possible. As a prerequisite for comparison, we must perform a comprehensive description of the objects of comparison.

To keep this work within reasonable limits, I have confined myself to two regions of investigation. The function of the comparison to be performed follows the definition of Bloch and of Haupt and Kocka, with a recognition of Espagne's criticism. Thus, I will view the objects of comparison here in light of their historical conditions and prerequisites. I will analyze and explain their commonalities and differences. The comparison further investigates reciprocal effects between the comparanda. I will avoid sweeping generalizations and refrain from the construction of typologies, as these should not be derived from only two objects of comparison. I will employ a specific comparative method following van den Braembussche: the system-forming comparison, which contrasts two points within a system with reference to their function for that system. From this, conclusions may be drawn about the whole system. In the application undertaken here, I will compare two regional studies on witch hunts with reference to witch hunting in general. The comparison will help to interrelate the regional studies with one another and with the witchcraft trials as a social macro-phenomenon in early modern Europe. Through comparison, a higher level of abstraction is possible than would be reasonable in a single regional study. Consequently, I will arrive at conclusions about the witch hunts that are both concrete and general. Simultaneously, the comparative approach will allow specific developments in the two territories to be described more clearly and more thoroughly. By means of a responsible narrative—that is to say, an analytical presentation based on the sources—the study will recognize the critical warning of Haupt and Kocka regarding the dangers of "ahistorical comparison." A narrative representation of the phenomena, however, is obviously insufficient; one also needs to analyze their contexts. Thus, for the present work I have consciously chosen to combine a narrative firmly based on the source materials with statistical quantification as well as analytical and comparative discussion.[17]

Ever since Bloch, comparative historiography has taken for granted the existence of structural commonality between the objects of comparison—or, at least, an apparent similarity.[18] Maximum contrast between the comparanda necessarily leads either to the simple observation of categorical and unbridgeable dissimilarities or to blanket statements that fall short of utilizing the potential of the sources. Hence, for this study, witch hunts have been chosen for which the archival preparatory work and the secondary literature indicate a generally similar form and a roughly similar level of intensity: Swabian Austria, the Habsburg possessions in what is today Baden-Württemberg, and Bavaria in southwestern Germany; and the ecclesiastical lands of the archbishops of Trier, called the Electorate of Trier, situated in the westernmost parts of today's Germany, directly bordering on Luxembourg (see map 1). Both regions experienced unusually severe witch hunts. The persecutions came "from below," the driving force being the average people in villages and rural towns. The form and appearance of these regions were also similar. They were both mid-size Catholic territories with largely parallel socioeconomic and political structures. Nonetheless, profound differences existed between the regions of investigation. Swabian Austria was a secular territory; the Electorate of Trier was ecclesiastical. Swabian Austria was a geographically fractured territory; the Electorate was relatively cohesive.

One prerequisite for a responsible application of the comparative method is to define the objects of comparison clearly and on the basis of the same criteria. The Midelfortian school of witch-trial research—first called that by Sönke Lorenz[19]—takes as its starting point the political realities of the particular regions of the Holy Roman Empire. This school describes the witch hunts in relation to the actual laws in force and the concrete structures of the court administration in the respective territories of the empire. This approach has proved itself exceedingly fruitful. Accordingly, I will use political

Map 1   Territories in the West of the Empire, 1650 (simplified overview)

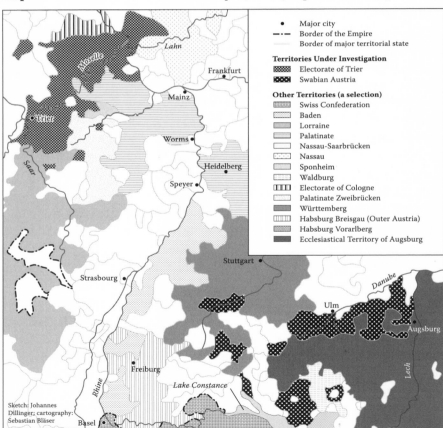

and jurisdictional criteria to define the territories under investigation. The territorial states of Swabian Austria and the Electorate of Trier form the regions of investigation. This means that I will discuss only those witch trials that were tried in places where an officer of the territorial government of Habsburg Swabian Austria or the Electorate of Trier, respectively, was the high judge or, at the very least, had a decisive voice in the proceedings of criminal justice. Of particular interest are the stances of the respective regional governments on witch trials and their ability to steer the trial proceedings. Thus, I will look at the norms the respective governments accepted as well as at the reality of the judicial systems. To avoid any lack of clarity, I will examine shared, mediated, or forfeited domains only if the concrete influence of the Habsburg or electoral administrations can be demonstrated. If one considered the shared domains and forfeited territories, one would have to deal with a great number of foreign territories with widely varied modes of organization, both ecclesiastical and secular. The comparison would thereby lose its precision and explanatory power. Because of this necessary limitation, I will not discuss any co-ruled territories of the Electorate of Trier or the enclaves of the monastic territories near the city of Trier that were not ruled by the prince elector.[20] In the case of Swabian Austria, a number of shared and mediated territories have similarly been left out. Among these are the five Danube cities—Mengen, Munderkingen, Riedlingen, Saulgau, and Waldsee—which because of nominal Habsburg overlordship are commonly considered part of Swabian Austria. Similarly the study does not examine Ehingen and Schelklingen, because the Habsburgs had lost jurisdiction over the courts of those cities.[21] I will not overlook the fact, however, that politically and jurisdictionally defined territories cannot be described without reference to their external relationships. Accordingly, a chapter will be devoted to the interactions of Swabian Austria and the Electorate of Trier with other territories on the subject of witch trials.

The objective of this study is a not an implicit, partial, or diachronic comparison but a "holistic" comparison—that is, a comparison that takes account of the phenomena in the entirety of their respective elements, aspects, and changes over the course of time.[22] The objects of comparison have fundamentally equal weight. With regard to the circumstances and function of the witch trials, the examination brings the same questions to bear on both territories in the same manner. This does not mean that the results are prejudiced toward similarity. To avoid repetition as much as possible, the chapters have been arranged as follows: When very similar answers are found for a given question, I will handle Swabian Austria and the Electorate of Trier together in a single section. When the answers show fundamental differences, however, the two territories will first be described separately. I will then provide a comparative conclusion in a separate section.

In accordance with the holistic comparison, the study aims at a holistic description of the witch hunts, which examines their folkloristic-anthropological, political, social, and economic aspects. After an overview of the state of research and the sources, one must describe the concrete conditions in the regions under investigation, taking into account administration, court organization, legislation, economy, and demographics as a framework for the witch hunts. I will undertake an approach to the witch trials in the manner of Thomas. I will not only examine the specific content of witchcraft fantasies, but also investigate elements of the popular belief in magic with regard to those elements' context and social meaning. Furthermore, I will scrutinize the means by which witchcraft suspicions arose against particular individuals within the context of magic beliefs. The next thematic focus encompasses the translation of these suspicions into trials, the nature of the proceedings, and their judicial and administrative conditions. In doing so, I will specifically discuss the respective roles played by the princely government, the local officials, and the populace. After a glance over the borders of the territories under investigation to their interactions with neighboring states, the study will examine the nature and causes of the end of the witch hunts. In the appendix, there follows a short survey of the chronology of the persecutions and analysis of the gender, marital status, and social status of the victims.

Swabian Austria and the Electorate of Trier: State of Research and Sources

Until the 1970s, the entire literature on the witch trials in Swabian Austrian was limited to a few brief notes in works on local or regional history. This historiography dealt with Swabian Austria not as unit of its own but, rather, with its individual provinces separately. In 1861, the Germanist Anton Birlinger published a faulty partial transcription of witch trials from the city of Rottenburg. Transregional studies included neither Swabian Austria nor any of its provinces, aside from a few cities. Wilhelm Gottlieb Soldan and Johannes Janssen mentioned that Rottenburg and Horb experienced intense witch hunts.[23]

Midelfort was the first to critically examine, reconcile, and assess these older publications, along with chronicle sources and some pamphlets, for an overview of the Swabian Austrian province of Hohenberg. Midelfort was also the first to describe the timing and social dynamics of the Hohenberg witch hunts. In accordance with his general approach, Midelfort understood the end of the trials as a function of their having reached into the ranks of the elite and of the growing influence of the law faculty of the University of Tübingen in neighboring Württemberg, which was critical of the persecutions. A study by Karl Kempf depends largely on a visitation protocol from 1604, representing a very important yet quite small selection of the Hohenberg witch files. Kempf deepened Midelfort's insights into the abovementioned concentration of the Hohenberg persecutions on members of the upper social strata. He was able to demonstrate for the case of Hohenberg's administrative center, Rottenburg, that there were interrelations between political conflicts in the city and accusations of witchcraft.[24] The works of Midelfort and Kempf, however, drew only on a narrow base of sources; large selections of the city and parish archives as well as the state archives in Karlsruhe, Stuttgart, and Innsbruck were left unexamined. The present work is a regional study that evaluates for the first time all of the available sources for the city of Rottenburg and the County of Hohenberg as a whole. Until the end of the twentieth century, the historiography of witchcraft barely touched the remaining areas of Swabian Austria.[25] In the original German edition of this work, I presented the first overview of the Swabian Austrian witch hunts.[26]

In 1806, Swabian Austria was dismantled, and its provinces were integrated into Württemberg and Bavaria. The Habsburg states in southern Germany vanished from the map and—at least for a time—from the awareness of historical scholarship. The historical territory of Swabian Austria was and remains disadvantaged due to the poor condition of the sources. Following the administrative hierarchy, there were two large groups of records relating to criminal justice in Swabian Austria: texts the central government in Innsbruck had prepared that were preserved at least in copy, and texts the local and regional officers of the governmental institutions and the municipal authorities wrote within the towns of Swabian Austria themselves. The latter contain most of the witch-trial records themselves. After the dissolution of Swabian Austria in 1806, the Innsbruck government released extensive collections of the first group of records to the archives of Bavaria and Württemberg. Today, they are preserved in the state archives of Augsburg, Karlsruhe, and Stuttgart. Here, the copy-book series "Vorlande" and "Hohenberg" are particularly helpful. They contain copies of the letters of the government to institutions and individuals in the respective territories. They each cover the greater part of the sixteenth and seventeenth centuries, encompassing the period under examination for the present work. The dissolution of the Innsbruck archival collection destroyed the most important body of sources. The division of the files among receiving archives was often arbitrary and incomplete, and further losses were incurred during transport. Moreover, the largest individual collection of documents remained in Innsbruck, where it is still part of the Tyrol archives. The many case records there and the Innsbruck copy books are of particular interest. Early on, a second group of sources that had remained in the towns of former Swabian Austria suffered considerable losses. Through poor archiving, fires, war losses, and substantial culling, great parts of the materials were destroyed. The remaining files are generally incomplete. As a rule, only the usually extensive confessions of alleged witches were kept, from which we can frequently draw conclusions about the social relationships of the trial victims. Apart from a few exceptions, testimony from witnesses is absent. Partially preserved town council proceedings provide information on the practice of witchcraft slander.

Surviving chronicles from Swabian Austria offer an important supplement to the archival sources. The journal entries of the Tübingen classical philologist Martin Crusius, which stretch from 1573 to 1604, as well as his "Annales Suevici" of 1595/96, frequently mention the witch hunts in Hohenberg. Dependent on Crusius are the annals of the monastery of Thann, written in 1724 by Malachias Tschamser. Because of the archival losses, Crusius and Tschamser are often the only sources for whole series of trials. Early modern news sheets and pamphlets paid scant attention to the witch trials in Swabian Austria.[27]

Research concerning the Electorate of Trier has been much more extensive than that for Swabian Austria. The early mass witch hunts in the Trier area drew the attention of contemporary authors, demonologists and journalists alike, to the region. The Suffragan Bishop Peter Binsfeld (1546–1598) of Trier wrote one of the most influential works of witchcraft doctrine in 1589, the *Tractatus de confessionibus maleficorum et sagarum*. Unless otherwise noted, all of the quotations that follow are drawn from the 1590 German version of Binsfeld's tract, published by Heinrich Bock in Trier. I will mainly read Binsfeld here as a witness to the demonological concepts current in the Electorate of Trier. I will use Binsfeld's work as a source for actual witch hunts only to provide a critical contrast with the trial records themselves.[28]

The substantial attention that contemporary authors paid to the intense witch hunts in the region of Trier led to short descriptions of the trials in survey works on the history of Trier as early as the seventeenth century. In the *Gesta Trevirorum*, Johann Linden, a monk from St. Simeon, sketched a first overview in 1620. In their *Libri Antiquitatum,* Christoph Brower and Jacob Masen still praised the witch hunts in 1670. Early historiographical surveys on the witch hunts, such as those of Wilhelm Gottlieb Soldan and Heinrich Heppe and of Johannes Janssen, also dealt broadly with the witch hunts in the region of Trier. Bernhard Duhr's description of the role of the Jesuits in the German witch hunts, still a standard work, remained true to the sources when depicting events in Trier and integrating them into the broader framework of the debate over the witch hunts within the Jesuit order.[29] Despite the early recognition of the unusual severity of the witch hunts in the Electorate of Trier, however, the trial records themselves long remained insufficiently exploited and scarcely analyzed. Historians repeatedly described spectacular cases, especially the witch trials against three elite men of the Electorate of Trier: Dr. Diederich Flade (1589), the president of the university, professor of law, sheriff (*Schultheiss*) and former vicegerent, and the jurors and former Burgomasters Niclaus Fiedler (1591) and Hans Reuland (1592/94). Yet earlier historians did not contextualize these trials within the course of the witch hunts; nor did they place the victims within the social and political order of the Electorate with any accuracy. In addition, there have been local histories of varying quality.[30] As a rule, the authors of these works did not distinguish the persecution-intensive monastic territories near the city of Trier from the Electorate with any clarity. Ignoring court districts and political borders, they dealt with all of them together.

Although in 1959 Wolfgang Krämer mentioned the Electorate of Trier in the title of his regional study, he dealt mainly with shared domains where the prince electors of Trier were but one of several territorial lords. Krämer mentioned in passing that committees of villagers had organized the witch trials in his region of study. Even before Krämer mentioned these committees, they had been noted in histories of the Moselle area, but nobody had paid any further attention to them. In 1991, Walter Rummel was the first to point out emphatically that it was peasant communities who led the witch hunts in the Trier region, establishing their own witch-hunting committees for this purpose. These witch committees investigated suspects, collected witness testimony, and hired jurists as legal consultants. Their relationships to their respective overlords were often quite strained. Rummel characterizes the witch hunts in the region as "popular movements with an insurrectional character." At the same time, Rummel emphasizes that witch hunts presented their organizers with opportunities for social advancement. It was the legal authorities who brought about the end of the trials. The territorial government had never been more than moderate in its support of witch hunts and ultimately adopted a stance critical of the trials; yet for a long time it could not persevere against the villagers, who vehemently demanded witch hunts. Prince Elector Karl Kaspar von der Leyen (1652–1676) forbade witch trials. The source base for Rummel's study consists of eighty-five trials against individuals who were not from the Electorate of Trier itself but from the co-ruled territories. In a later study, Rummel provides a brief overview of the course of the witch trials in the Electorate along with their sources. We now know that witch-hunting committees existed not only in the vicinity of Trier but, as other historians have shown, throughout the region from Luxembourg in the west to the Nassau territories in the east, from the territories of the Saar region in the south to the Electorate of Cologne to the north.[31]

Rummel concentrates on the political and social circumstances in the villages of his region of investigation, allowing beliefs in magic to fade entirely into the background. This theme has attracted the attention of Eva Labouvie. Not only does her work omit the political and administrative aspects of the witch trials, however, but her investigation of the modern German federal state of Saarland touches on only part of the Electorate of Trier.[32]

A regional history workshop in Trier follows Rummel's approach. Working together with the University of Trier, the "Arbeitsgemeinschaft Hexenprozesse im Trierer Land" has published a number of studies about witch hunts in the region and beyond in the series *Trierer Hexenprozesse*. The workgroup sets great store in an idea that Rummel proposed: that witch hunts should be interpreted fundamentally as "instruments" that were cynically and intentionally employed to expand spheres of political influence and to "eliminate" economic competitors and personal enemies.[33] This line of argument would have to be proved through detailed local and family history. However, no reliable sources for such intentional instrumentalization can possibly exist, and this problem is insurmountable. The present study therefore does not attempt to describe the social meaning of witchcraft accusations according to nineteenth-century rationality. Instead, it does so according to the magical worldview of the early modern period. We cannot understand the witch-hunts if we do not accept the fact that they were part and parcel of a specific pre-modern cultural framework which had its very own "rationality."

Recent witchcraft research has thus touched on the Electorate of Trier many times, but so far it has hardly dealt with the territory as a whole. The main cause for this is the desperate condition of the sources. The greater part of the Electorate's witch-trial records were probably already discarded in the seventeenth century. Even records in the individual towns of the Electorate have been lost, aside from a few remnants in the city of Trier itself. In 1784, an official in Münstermaifeld, one of the Electorate's major towns, destroyed a number of the surviving trial records. Two years after the last legal execution of a witch in Europe, he was embarrassed by the fact that his home country had witnessed a large number of witch trials.[34] At the end of the nineteenth century, George Lincoln Burr obtained the original copy of the witch trial against Diederich Flade for Cornell University; the city archive of Trier has only a copy. Even so, the remaining fragments of the Trier witch-trial records—some of which are quite extensive—can be supplemented considerably by references to trials in the Electorate of Trier found in the records of neighboring and co-ruled territories. These documents, some of them including transcriptions of Trier trials, are today in the Landeshauptarchiv Koblenz, the Landesarchiv Saarbrücken, the Hessian Hauptstaatsarchiv Wiesbaden, and the Bistumsarchiv Trier.[35]

Along with the Trier chronicles mentioned earlier, I will evaluate the annals of Neuss and a chronicle from Limburg. The German edition of this study was the first to systematically evaluate the yearly reports of the Jesuits of Trier and Coblenz. I have also examined the so-called witch card file of the Nazi Schutzstaffel (SS) for both of the territories under comparison. That examination has demonstrated, however, that the results of this megalomaniacal drudgery are unreliable.[36]

Map 2 Swabian Austria: immediate and undivided Habsburg territories in 1600

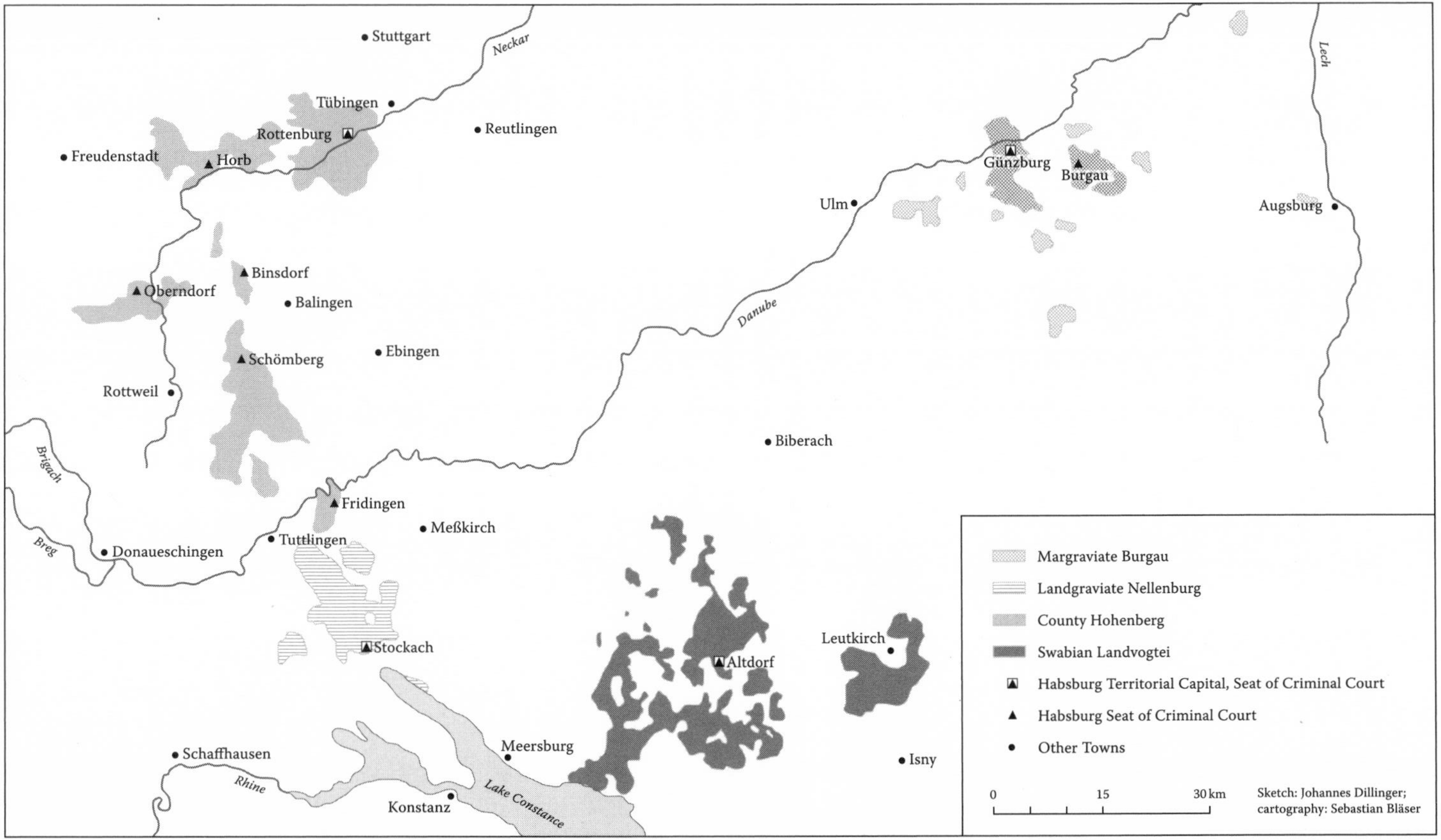

Lech

Augsburg

Burgau
Günzburg

Ulm

Biberach

Isny

Leutkirch

Altdorf

Neckar

Reutlingen

Stuttgart

Danube

Meßkirch

Tübingen

Ebingen

Meersburg

Rottenburg
Horb

Binsdorf

Balingen

Schömberg

Fridingen

Stockach

Lake Constance

Freudenstadt

Oberndorf

Rottweil

Tuttlingen

Konstanz

Donaueschingen

Schaffhausen

Rhine

Brigach

Breg

Margraviate Burgau

Landgraviate Nellenburg

County Hohenberg

Swabian Landvogtei

Habsburg Territorial Capital, Seat of Criminal Court

Habsburg Seat of Criminal Court

Other Towns

0   15   30km

Sketch: Johannes Dillinger;
cartography: Sebastian Bläser

1

"Authority and Liberties for the Country and the People"

Administration, Legal and Social Circumstances

SWABIAN AUSTRIA

The term "Swabian Austria" refers to those Austrian lands in the south of the Holy Roman Empire between Vorarlberg in the east and the older Outer Austria in the west (see map 2).[1] Until its dissolution in 1806, Swabian Austria consisted of four provinces under immediate and exclusive Habsburg jurisdiction: the Margraviate of Burgau, the Swabian Landvogtei, the Landgraviate of Nellenburg, and the County of Hohenberg. Similar to Vorarlberg, Swabian Austria was under the direct control of the Tyrolean government in Innsbruck until 1752. In this it was clearly distinct from the Habsburg possessions to the west; the government of Ensisheim administered the older Outer Austria, consisting of Alsace, Breisgau, Ortenau, and Hagenau.

The territorial sovereign of Swabian Austria was the Habsburg archduke of Tyrol. The Innsbruck administration comprised two leading institutions: the Austrian high government and the treasury. The treasury dealt with taxation and all other financial matters. In addition to the executive functions, the government claimed for itself the highest judicial review; all petitions were to be sent to it.[2] The appointment and dismissal of officials had to be approved by the government. In addition to this, the government in Innsbruck had jurisdiction in feudal matters and served as an adviser to the territorial ruler in military matters and foreign policy. Thus, the government was entitled to comprehensive oversight of the executive and judiciary. Its directives were binding for all subordinate offices. Courts and local officials could present active judicial questions to the government for a decision. Thus, the government also functioned as a court of appeals. In this capacity, the government received complaints alleging invalid trials or improper trial proceedings. Thus, the Innsbruck government was the final authority for complaints regarding witch trials. Its jurisdiction extended across Tyrol, Vorarlberg, and Swabian Austria. The analogous government in Ensisheim had corresponding jurisdiction only over the western territories of Outer Austria.[3]

After the emperor had outlawed Duke Friedrich IV of Habsburg in 1415, the imperial estates administered his possessions, including Swabian Austria, for many years in the emperor's name.[4] The territorial policy of the Habsburgs thus experienced a setback that they could never completely make good. It was no longer possible to combine the Habsburg territories in southwestern Germany administratively. The provinces of Swabian Austria were each subordinated directly to the archduke of Tyrol and to the Austrian high government and treasury in Innsbruck.

Swabian Austria had a complex internal structure. It will pay to look at the political and legal administration of the four provinces separately.

The County of Hohenberg

In 1381, Duke Leopold the Pious of Habsburg purchased the County of Hohenberg from Count Rudolf III of Hohenberg.[5] From the beginning, Hohenberg held a special position in Swabian Austria. With the county, the Habsburgs could control a territory with almost entirely clear boundaries. Hohenberg was burdened neither with intermediary lords nor by duties as a protector or steward vis-à-vis imperial monasteries.

The head of the Hohenberg administration was a territorial governor, officially the *Landvogt* or *Hauptmann*. As the governors of Hohenberg were almost universally represented by vicegerents, they played no role in practical administration. The governor appointed the vicegerent in consultation with the archduke. The vicegerent answered directly to the Innsbruck authorities, whose directives he implemented locally. The vicegerent resided in a castle in Hohenberg's administrative center of Rottenburg. In practice, officials in the other towns of Hohenberg almost always circumvented the vicegerent; they sent enquiries and complaints directly to the government in Innsbruck. The vicegerent possessed immediate influence only in the town where he resided. A marshal and scribes managed the treasury. The responsibilities of the vicegerent and the treasury officials were mirrored in bailiwicks (*Obervogteiämter*), each overseen by a bailiff (*Obervogt*). The bailiff was responsible for supervising judicial matters. There were bailiffs in residence in Horb, Oberndorf, and Fridingen. The agents of the territorial tax administration in the villages were local sheriffs (*Vögte* or *Dorfschultheissen*), who were nearly indistinguishable from the peasant population. In 1688, the government transferred the upper Hohenberg bailiwick of Fridingen to the more conveniently located city of Spaichingen. The vicegerent administered the office of the Rottenburg bailiff in the sixteenth and seventeenth centuries himself.[6]

Subordinate to each bailiff was a sheriff (*Schultheiss*). The sheriffs were named by the Austrian high government in consultation with the bailiffs. Sheriffs held office in Fridingen, Schömberg, Binsdorf, Oberndorf, Horb, and Rottenburg. The Rottenburg sheriff, however, was directly subordinate to the vicegerent. In Binsdorf and Schömberg there were no bailiffs; there the sheriff held all rights of governance. In Hohenberg, the sheriff served as high judge in the criminal courts.[7] Each place with a sheriff had its own criminal court.

The town councils of Rottenburg, Fridingen, and Horb each consisted of a great council and a privy council. In Rottenburg, the great council had 48 members, of whom 24 met separately as the privy council. In Horb, the great council consisted of 60 members; the privy council again consisted of 24. The smaller, undifferentiated form of the town council with 24 seats existed in Oberndorf clear into the eighteenth century. A Policeyordnung (ordinance for public decency and order) of 1607 mentioned a council with 18 members in Binsdorf, one with 24 in Schömberg, a great council of 18 and a privy council of merely 8 members in Fridingen. In Horb and Rottenburg, the council elected four burgomasters each year from the ranks of the privy council. They served in pairs for half a year each. In the other towns, the councils elected two burgomasters to serve a full year. Each year, the town councils co-opted their members. The town councils of Hohenberg did not exclusively represent a consolidated elite clearly distinct from the rest of the populace. The scale of the town councils alone ensured that they represented the communities as a whole more than just an economically defined upper class. A comparison of the names of council members from Rottenburg and Horb against census registers from the early seventeenth century reveals that their numbers included members of the middle class.[8]

Members of the town councils filled a crucial role: that of judges in the urban courts.[9] In both Rottenburg and Horb, the councilors chose twelve judges from the privy council. Similarly in Oberndorf, the council selected twelve of its members to serve as judges. The urban courts held the lower jurisdiction. The sheriff and council of judges decided criminal trials, with the sheriff as presiding officer and chairman of the proceedings. The jurisdiction of the sheriff as head judge had one exception: in inquisitorial trials in which the sheriff acted as prosecutor, the oldest member of the council of judges—a member of the town council—acted as chairman. The authority of the Hohenberg town councils extended to investigations. Town council members served as interrogators. They oversaw questioning with and without torture, although officially the sheriff was to be present. At least in Rottenburg during the period under investigation, the court delegated the unpleasant and time-consuming task of criminal interrogations to the two youngest council members.[10] Thus, the members of the town councils, even though they lacked particular administrative or judicial knowledge and often did not even have court experience, played a key role in criminal justice.

The Landgraviate of Nellenburg

Johann von Tengen sold the Landgraviate of Nellenburg to Duke Sigismund of Tyrol in 1465. The head of administration and guardian of the Habsburgs' rights was officially a noble governor (*Landvogt* or *Hauptmann*). Since the beginning of the sixteenth century, however, the representative of the territorial lord was a district commissioner (*Amtmann*) with broad authority living in the city of Stockach. This commissioner was simultaneously the account keeper. After the mid-sixteenth century, a second and coequal official appeared: the acting governor, who maintained contact with the government in Innsbruck. In 1726, the government merged the office of the acting governor with that of the territorial judge.[11]

A charter from 1502 mentions a town council in Stockach that purportedly consisted of the mayor (*Stadtammann*) and at least five other men. Possibly this was the minimum complement for quorum or the privy council. After 1615, the sources mention a twelve-member council, without any detectable differentiation into great and privy councils. The council functioned simultaneously as the town's court. The head of the court was the mayor, who was also the head of the town administration. As a rule, the district commissioner only communicated indirectly with the town council through the mayor. The governor appointed the mayor. After 1510, however, the governor was limited to choosing from among three candidates who were nominated by a special body of twenty to twenty-four persons, overlapping with the town council in membership. There is no information about the means of election for this special body, its composition, or how it came into existence. The mayor swore his oath of office to the Habsburg archduke. In 1532, the central government in Innsbruck inquired of the Nellenburg territorial scribe who it was that selected the mayor of Stockach, as well as how the town council, town court, and the territorial court were filled and by whom. Thus, even when the German southwest must have been of particular interest to the Habsburgs, the Habsburg central government was entirely uninformed about the details of authority and judicial power in its own territories. The archduke was obviously content when the territories of Swabian Austria respected his overlordship. Even though regional historiography often mentions "Habsburg hegemonic efforts" as a key political factor in southern Swabia, the real situation was much more complicated. The Habsburgs did indeed seek hegemony in the southwest of the empire. However, in the face of political competitors on all levels, extremely strained resources, and a multitude of problems engaging the meager governmental apparatus of the archdukes, jurisdictional quarrels in Swabian Austria were often simply not important enough to receive more than fleeting attention.[12]

The territorial court had met since 1400 in Stockach. A Habsburg official served as the head of the court and as territorial judge. During the period under investigation here, the mayor of Stockach was usually also the territorial judge. Following a reform of the territorial court by Archduke Ferdinand II, in 1562, at the latest, as a rule six townsmen of Stockach and six men from the landgraviate acted as jurors. The governor together with the Stockach territorial officials appointed these twelve; the territorial judge was to be consulted as well. The officials in Stockach enforced citations to appear before the territorial court.[13] It becomes evident here that the personnel of landgraviate and territorial court were interwoven despite formal divisions. This state of affairs caused some uncertainties of jurisdiction. The territorial court met twelve times each year. If delay posed a problem, however, an extra hearing could be arranged. The reform of 1562 required written records of all proceedings. The territorial court was an institution of Habsburg authority. It had jurisdiction over criminal matters. Unlike in Hohenberg, the town council did not have any authority in matters of criminal justice. An examination of the oldest remaining lists of jurors in the territorial court from the years 1658, 1663, and 1666 shows that, in this sample, five or six of these jurors filled territorial offices such as mayor, local commissioner (*Pfleger*), or sheriff. The Stockach schoolmaster appears twice. Only in 1658 did the lists designate two of the jurors as members of the Stockach town council. The court complement differed in each of the above-cited years. As most jurors were lowly members of the Habsburg administration, it is not surprising that conflict never arose between them and the powerful territorial judge.[14]

Unlike Hohenberg, the other parts of Swabian Austria were burdened with extremely complex legal circumstances and constantly disputed jurisdictional boundaries. Numerous exclaves and enclaves hindered the

consolidation of the Habsburg territories. For decades, Nellenburg found itself in conflict with neighboring lesser nobles, the Swiss Confederation, and
the County of Fürstenberg, in addition to having some disputed borders with
Württemberg.[15]

The Margraviate of Burgau

In 1301, after the line of the lords of Berg-Burgau had died out, the Margraviate of Burgau fell back as an imperial fiefdom into the hands of King Al-
brecht I of Habsburg, who bequeathed it further within the family. After the
Habsburgs had mortgaged the whole territory to other noble families to pay
their debts—not an uncommon way for major princes to quickly improve
their finances—Emperor Ferdinand I was able to establish his son Archduke
Ferdinand II of Tyrol as the Margrave of Burgau in 1559. As in Hohenberg
and Nellenburg, the noble governor of Burgau had almost no influence on
administrative practice. The acting governor directed official functions in
Burgau. He stood in direct contact with the government in Innsbruck. The
seats of the high courts in the margraviate were in the administrative center Günzburg and the town of Burgau, where the Habsburg territorial judge
resided. He was endowed with extensive jurisdiction over civil and criminal
matters. He was also, however, directly bound to the Burgau town council.
The twelve Burgau councilors made up his council of jurors, and the territorial judge himself served as chair whenever the city council met. His purely
judicial functions consisted of duties similar to those of a territorial bailiff.
The Burgau executioner stemmed from the Vollmayr line of executioners, of
whom several members exercised a profound influence on the witch trials in
Ellwangen and in the Prince Bishopric of Augsburg.[16]

The administrative center of the Margraviate of Burgau and seat of the
acting governor was Günzburg. The personnel of the town court and town
council were identical. In the strictest sense, then, Günzburg could be excluded from this study, which only considers Habsburg courts. Nonetheless,
one should not rule out the town, because Habsburg officeholders always
dominated the administrative and judicial practice of Günzburg. From the
beginning of the sixteenth century onward, it can be verified that the town
council had twelve members. Elections took place each time a new governor
took office. The governor selected two members of the old council, whom he
appointed as members of the new council. These immediately took an oath
to the sovereign and to the city. The first two councilors then selected two
more, and so on, until after a complex process of co-option the number of
twelve council members was reached. As opposed to the territorial sovereign,

the community had almost no influence on the composition and activities of the council. The governor appointed and removed the mayor. The mayor conducted investigations into criminal matters. Arrest and release from imprisonment lay within his authority alone, and in ex officio proceedings, the mayor acted as the accuser. Thus, although jurisdiction over capital cases officially rested with the city, in actuality Habsburg officeholders administered that jurisdiction. The bailiff (*Landammann*) in Burgau exercised a function analogous to that of a Hohenberg bailiff (*Obervogt*).[17]

The Margraviate of Burgau serves as an example of failed state-building not only because of complex internal divisions of jurisdiction. More than any other province of Swabian Austria, the region was constantly burdened by conflicts over jurisdiction with nearly all its neighbors. Lesser nobles and monasteries who claimed independence from Habsburg overlordship and a host of enclaves and exclaves tore the Burgau territory apart. Even a "summary extract" of complaints regarding enclaves' jurisdictional claims lodged in 1583 included 108 individual complaints.[18]

The Swabian Landvogtei

The Swabian Landvogtei possessed "legally and geographically the most entangled of circumstances."[19] By means of the imperial governors (*Landvögte*) whom he appointed, Rudolf von Habsburg had attempted to secure or win back the legal claims of the king that had been thrown into question or usurped during the interregnum. The Swabian Landvogtei was originally not a territorial state with an administrative center and clearly defined boundaries but a region in which an official representative of the king was entitled to a number of privileges. These rights had always been diverse, and they were in part contested. The Habsburgs managed to expand on these privileges and to form a territorial state, but they were not entirely successful. They had to relinquish altogether their claims for the lordship over Lower Swabia. In Upper Swabia, the Landvogtei was consolidated by taking over the splintered territorial rights around Markt Altdorf that the Guelph dynasty had formerly held. With their possession of the Swabian Landvogtei, the Habsburgs constructed a claim to the heritage of the Hohenstaufens and thus to sovereignty over all of the lords and towns of Swabia. Naturally, the Swabian prelates, nobles, and towns opposed this line of reasoning. Not despite but, rather, directly because of the imperial rights inherent in the Swabian Landvogtei, Habsburg sovereignty in the region could not be fully realized. The far-reaching claims that derived from the possession of the Landvogtei did not lead to administrative concentration or the development of the Habsburg rule in the Landvogtei itself. During the fourteenth and fifteenth centuries, the Habsburgs were unable to establish themselves. The possession of the Landvogtei was disputed within the Habsburg family and had to be mortgaged many times. When it finally came under the lasting control of the archdukes of Tyrol in 1541, the Swabian Landvogtei was further than ever from being a cohesive territory. Enclaves and the dwarf states of neighboring petty nobles refused to acknowledge Habsburg sovereignty. Their jurisdictional boundaries riddled the Landvogtei and blurred its borders. The Swabian Landvogtei remained forever "a territorial skeleton, the perpetually unfulfilled site of a Swabian-Habsburg principality."[20]

The administrative center of the Landvogtei and seat of the criminal court was Altdorf (today, the town is called Weingarten). In 1377, Charles IV had granted Altdorf the privilege of a weekly market and the selection of a twelve-member council that would also serve as the court. The German kings, however, never bestowed a town charter on Altdorf. The abbots of Weingarten disputed the sovereignty of the Habsburgs over Altdorf. The governor functioned as the vicegerent of the Habsburgs. He was the head of the whole administration. In addition to him were the accounting and chancellery officials (*Landweibel* and *Landschreiber*). The mayor of Altdorf played a central role in judicial matters. In the middle of the sixteenth century, a complicated compromise was developed. The abbot of Weingarten appointed the mayor, but in so doing he could only choose from among three of his subjects presented to him by the governor. The governor had to select the three candidates whom he proposed from among seven provided to him by the council of Altdorf. The governor had to confirm the abbot's selection. As the governor alone enjoyed the right to remove the mayor from his office, however, one can say that the Habsburgs had the greater voice in the process. Conducting trials before the high court in Altdorf required the cooperation of the council and officials of the territorial sovereign. The governor had the right to conduct investigations. The council and mayor functioned as judges. Once the verdict was reached, the governor had to confirm it before the council could have it carried out. This ponderous compromise, which had to take the rights of all parties into consideration even at the central criminal court of the province, thus revealed the weaknesses of the Habsburg Swabian Landvogtei.[21]

The Landvogtei found itself in jurisdictional quarrels with most of its neighbors, particularly the imperial free city of Ravensburg, the abbey of Weingarten, and the powerful noble dynasty of the high stewards (*Truchsessen*) of Waldburg. The officials in Altdorf as well as the Innsbruck government were incapable of employing an active policy toward these competing territories in the sixteenth and seventeenth centuries.[22]

In conclusion, we have seen that each of the four provinces of Swabian Austria was under the direction of a pair of governing officeholders: the governor and acting governor/vicegerent. Altogether, the positions of the mayor of Altdorf and Günzburg appear substantially similar to that of a Hohenberg sheriff. The administrative structure of the bailiwick was a peculiarity of Hohenberg. All in all, the Habsburg administration in Hohenberg appears to have been better organized and burdened with fewer competing claims. In Burgau and the Landvogtei, at least, the officials of the sovereign seem to have been dependent on the cooperation of the town representatives. The entire administration had an air of compromise about it. It existed in a state of equilibrium—maintained only with difficulty—between the interests of the sovereign and the town, or even between the sovereign, town, and neighboring states. Generally, the Habsburgs had great difficulties establishing their sovereignty over Swabian Austria. Until the nineteenth century, the saying "It is good to live under the two-headed eagle" was well known in southern Swabia. The two-headed eagle, the symbol of the Habsburgs, stood for a weak administration that conceded some flexibility to towns and villages. In the Swabian Landvogtei, the Margraviate of Burgau, and the Landgraviate of Nellenburg, there were each only one or two Habsburg criminal courts. In Hohenberg, conversely, there were six. The ratio of council members to the populace of the Hohenberg councils, as opposed to those in the rest of Swabian Austria, is notable. Although the respective towns did not proportionately have more residents, the councils of Hohenberg contained two to five times as many members as the others in Swabian Austria.

The Habsburg Court of Appeals in Swabia made the judiciary landscape of Swabian Austria even more complex. This Habsburg Court was an appeals court with universal jurisdiction.[23] In principle, criminal cases were not handled there. The possibility existed, however, to address procedural complaints about any trial to the Habsburg Court of Appeals. In function, the Habsburg Court of Appeals in Swabia was similar to the imperial appeals court, the Reichskammergericht. In contrast to the Reichskammergericht, however, the Habsburg court was located in the nearest proximity of the territories of Swabian Austria and enjoyed the sustained support of the government in Innsbruck. The Innsbruck government also used the Habsburg Court of Appeals to control the territories of Swabian Austria more tightly.[24]

One cannot discuss the witch hunts of Swabian Austria without taking their legal and socioeconomic framework into consideration. Witch trials often involved very serious miscarriages of justice, but they were no lynchings; they had a least a formal obligation to respect the law. It goes without saying that the witch hunts did not happen in a social vacuum. To understand the dynamics of persecution, one has to be familiar with the overall social situation.

The Tyrolean Territorial Ordinances of 1499, 1525, and 1532 recognized the crime of sorcery. In 1573, a new Territorial Ordinance combined "sorcery" and divination. It did not handle them as capital crimes but, rather, explicitly prescribed the same punishment as for blasphemy—namely, a fine. This remarkable legal traditionalism was the result of the Innsbruck government's deep dependence on the *Carolina*. The imperial law had not adopted the elaborated witch concept with its emphasis on the Devil; only harmful magic was to be punished with death.[25]

In 1569 and 1584, the provincial laws of Nellenburg and Burgau adopted the regulations of the *Carolina*.[26] For the Swabian Landvogtei and Hohenburg, the archduke never passed a law against magic, so the *Carolina* remained fully in force. Only in 1637, thirty years after the end of the main phase of the Swabian Austrian witch trials, did the central government in Innsbruck issue a directive on conducting witch trials in Tyrol and all of the provinces titled, "Instruction and Conclusions, under What Circumstances Persons Can Be Proven Witches." The Innsbruck chancery attorney Dr. Volpert Mozel composed this instructional directive at the order of the government, after witch trials had begun to increase in the Tyrolean heartland and criticism of the trials had grown loud in Swabian Austria. The decree was presumably sent to all courts in Tyrol and the provinces. It continued the old line, basically reiterating the *Carolina*. However, the directive cited Martin Delrio as well as the Jesuit theologian Adam Tanner (1572–1632) as new authorities.[27] It adopted word for word the restrictive measures of the *Carolina* regarding the evidence required for arrest and torture in witch trials. The directive emphatically called on judges to put witnesses under oath, review witness testimony and confessions critically, and actively seek out material evidence. It recommended that before a verdict was reached the trial records be submitted for review, but without specifying whether that meant to law faculties, private lawyers, or institutions of the government. On the question of torture, the document referred to Tanner's sharp warnings. Based on Tanner, but without adopting his fundamentally skeptical view, the directive warned against the use of denunciations and rumors as evidence.

Statements regarding the population of Swabian Austria are problematic. An early, unreliable count from 1591 registered 2,548 men in Hohenberg (not including the territory of Oberndorf) as capable of military service. Of them, 550 were registered in the administrative center Rottenburg and 332 in Horb. In 1615, a similar register counted 632 men in Rottenburg, 374 in Horb, and 3,088 in the county excluding the bailiwick of Oberndorf. In 1628, there were 365 taxpayers in Oberndorf and associated localities.[28] In 1700, a tax list registered a total of 3,102 taxpayers in all of Hohenberg.[29] The survey from 1615 listed 82 persons in Stockach, a total of 648 in Nellenburg. A fiscal record from 1680/82 counted only 480 taxpayers—certainly a decline resulting from the Thirty Years' War. By 1700 this dip had balanced out; the tax list for that year indicated 650 persons, of whom 55 lived in Stockach.[30] Information on the population of the Landvogtei first becomes available for the period of the Thirty Years' War. In 1632, some 532 citizens and residents could be mustered to the defense of Altdorf. Three years later, as a result of the military conflict and an epidemic, that number had dropped to 325. A tax list from 1700 counted 1,932 households in the Swabian Landvogtei, of which 180 were located in Altdorf.[31] The Margraviate of Burgau collected the hearth tax, a basic tax payable by all householders, from 2,467 persons in 1605, a summary figure that also included several mediated villages. For the administrative center of Günzburg and some neighboring villages, the number of deaths between 1610 and 1633 hovered around an average of 70 per year, which increased by a factor of four during the plague epidemic of 1634/35 and decreased to 18 in 1641. This indicates that the population of Günzburg had been reduced by three quarters because of the war. In 1680, there were 329 taxpaying households in the city, 797 for the Margraviate of Burgau altogether.[32] For all of Swabian Austria there were a total of 6,481 taxpaying households in the year 1700.

The territories of Swabian Austria profited from interregional trade to quite differing degrees. Hohenberg, without any tie to an important interregional trade route, remained relatively isolated. Günzburg lay on the post road and near the navigable Danube. Stockach lay near a number of important trade roads. Altdorf and the Landvogtei had access to the good trade network of the neighboring imperial city of Ravensburg. Nellenburg and the Landvogtei both profited from their proximity to the waterways around Lake Constance.[33]

The administrative centers of the provinces of Swabian Austria were agricultural towns. There was no culturally, politically, or economically dominant city within Swabian Austria. The southern regions near Lake Constance were proportionately stronger economically than the more heavily populated area of Hohenberg. Places with town charters in southern Hohenberg were

entirely rural in economic and cultural terms. Viticulture dominated the
northern part of the county, Lower Hohenberg, with the centers of Rottenburg, Oberndorf, and Horb. In 1615, after almost a century of ongoing crisis
in wine production, 28.5 percent of Rottenburg's male population still worked
in the vineyards. These winegrowers mostly worked in small enterprises and
belonged to the lowest income bracket.[34]

From the high Middle Ages into the second half of the sixteenth century,
viticulture in Hohenberg had continuously expanded. Then a structural shift
set in, which caused wine prices to sink and the area under cultivation to
shrink rapidly. At the end of this transformation came the abandonment of
viticulture in Hohenberg at the beginning of the eighteenth century. In chapter 4, I will discuss further the causes and attendant circumstances of this
development and its possible connection to the witch hunts. It was profitable
to cultivate grapes in the climatically milder parts of Nellenburg as well as
in the higher reaches of the Hegau hills. A detectable crisis in this mode of
cultivation was not yet apparent in 1600. A break in Nellenburg viticulture
first appeared, as it did for the rest of the Lake Constance region, with the destruction of vineyards during the Thirty Years' War. For the general economy
of the landgraviate, however, wine lacked the importance it held for Lower
Hohenberg. Grain cultivation dominated agriculture in Nellenburg. Viticulture impacted the Swabian Landvogtei more significantly. Yet the good soil
and milder climate of the Lake Constance region ensured that the damages
of the Thirty Years' War did not result in a lasting slump. In contrast to the
other territories of Swabian Austria, Burgau never engaged in viticulture.
In 1753, a description of the Margraviate of Burgau spoke of its "superabun-
dance" of grain due to the unusually good soil. In addition, from the fifteenth
century onward textile production played a significant role in Burgau.[35]

The Electorate of Trier

The territorial lord of the Electorate of Trier was both archbishop and prince
elector. The cathedral chapter elected him. The council of the prince elector
was first created as the highest administrative authority in the mid-sixteenth
century.[36] The council included both noble and bourgeois jurists. In 1569, the
territorial high court (*Hofgericht*), the highest court of appeals in the Electorate, split institutionally from the council, of which it had previously been a
part. As a court of appeals, the territorial high court did not have jurisdiction
over criminal justice, and it never dealt with witch trials, even in the context
of complaints concerning invalid trials. As of the fifteenth century, evidence

exists for a chancellery in the Electorate. The chancellery performed the paperwork for the government of the prince elector. It was headed by a legally trained member of the council. The chief financial officer of the Electorate was also always a member of the prince elector's council. An institutional division of executive and financial administration first took place at the beginning of the eighteenth century.[37]

In the fourteenth century, Prince Elector Balduin of Luxembourg divided the territory of the Electorate (see map 3) into districts (*Ämter*). In each district, a noble commissioner (*Amtmann*), appointed by the prince elector, served as his agent. It was entirely normal for a single commissioner to administer multiple districts. This district commissioner was the military commander and head of administration. He also had authority over finance and forest management. Beneath him worked a series of accountants and scribes. The district commissioner functioned as official prosecutor, and either the commissioner or a sheriff (*Schultheiss*) beneath him served as high judge of the provincial criminal courts.[38] The sheriff or district commissioner served as head of the jury court in each official district. The decisions of the jury, based on the results of investigations by the sheriff or district commissioner, gained the force of law only when he published them. The Administrative Decree of 1574 attempted to resolve a problem that was to have an impact on the witch trials and their aftermath: The local officials performed their role poorly as a link between the sovereign and the subjects in the towns and villages. On the one hand, they tended toward inactivity and redirected litigants even in petty cases to the central authorities. On the other hand, they accepted bribes and formed partnerships with their subordinates out of personal interest.[39]

Overall, the rulers of the Electorate of Trier were able to suppress much of the influence of the councils of the smaller towns. The prince electors ignored the privileges of chartered towns.[40] Although the court in the administrative center of an district might be filled only with men of that town, it was the district commissioner who selected the jury from the candidates proposed by the citizens,[41] or else the jury was filled under the direct supervision of the Electorate's officials. As a rule, the court had fourteen jury members. The jurors belonged to a relatively consolidated elite, beholden to the territorial sovereign. The court of the administrative center of every district could hear criminal cases.[42]

The criminal courts of the cities, composed exclusively of the sheriffs and the urban jurors, existed alongside the criminal courts of the high court districts. There, the reeves (*Zender*) of the villages that belonged to the district served as jurors. The high courts also had a district commissioner or sheriff of the Electorate as high judge.[43]

Coblenz and Trier held special positions. Trier, arguably Germany's oldest city, had been the capital of the Western Roman Empire in the third and fourth centuries—to this day, the town boasts more Roman ruins than any other place in Germany. In the early modern period, however, Trier no longer had any international significance whatsoever. The town was not even undisputed as the capital of the Electorate. In competition with the old cathedral city of Trier, which had often stood in conflict with the territorial rulers, Coblenz emerged at the end of the Middle Ages as the residence city of the prince elector. In the fourteenth century, Prince Elector Balduin of Luxembourg had divided the Electorate of Trier into the Lower Electorate north of the Eltz River and the Upper Electorate to the south. Correspondingly, the two cities had developed into centers of their respective regions: Trier dominated the south; Coblenz, the Lower Electorate in the north. In

Map 3 Electorate of Trier

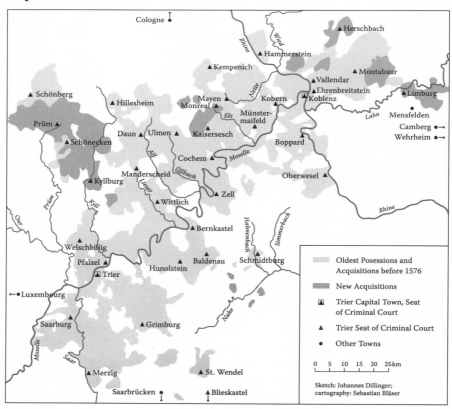

A view of Coblenz from the mid-sixteenth century. On the left is Ehrenbreitstein castle, the fortress of the prince electors of Trier.

this process, Coblenz surpassed Trier in status until the eighteenth century.[44] In 1537, the Lower Court Ordinance attempted to establish stages of appeal. Thereafter, the village courts were to turn to the courts of the districts for legal advice. For their part, the districts were only bound to the high courts (*Schöffengerichte*) of Coblenz and Trier. Coblenz was responsible for all of the districts of the Lower Electorate and for the small town of Cochem; Trier was responsible for the Upper Electorate. Citing the *Carolina,* the Lower Court Ordinance explicitly required the referral of complicated cases to these high courts. According to the wishes of the territorial sovereign, the lower courts had to send the files of such cases only to the high courts, not to the law faculty of the University of Trier.[45]

The district commissioner supervised the city council of Coblenz. The prince elector strongly influenced the great council of Coblenz, called the Whole Council (*Ganzer Rat*). Only eight citizens and eight guild masters sat on the Whole Council. Eight noblemen were also part of the council. They traditionally leaned toward the prince elector. In addition, there were fourteen jurors, freely appointed by the prince elector, and the sovereign's sheriff. From the Whole Council, a small committee called the Changing Council (*Wechselrat*) emerged as the actual ruling body. Here the influence of the territorial sovereign was even greater: Four citizens and four guild masters faced the sheriff, seven jurors, and eight noblemen. The fourteen jurors of the Whole Council simultaneously constituted the jury court that functioned both as criminal court and high court. The sheriff presided over it.[46]

The prince elector brought the city of Trier definitively under his control only in 1580, after a civil war and a long trial. The head of the city administration of Trier was the vicegerent, appointed by the prince elector himself. This office was first held by Johann von Schönenberg, who would later be archbishop, and after him by Diederich Flade. Apart from the electoral sheriff, the city council included five jurors. The prince elector named the jurors. They also sat on the secular high court, together with five guild members whom the territorial lord appointed similarly. There were also fifteen other representatives of the guilds in the Trier city council. The vicegerent took part in council meetings; he established the agenda and enjoyed a de facto veto of council decisions. The vicegerent and the sheriff held the high jurisdiction. The jurors of the criminal court made all decisions regarding torture and the confiscation of goods from condemned persons. The prince elector selected the fourteen jurors from among the members of the city council.[47]

Of course, the overwhelming majority of the population of the Electorate did not live in Coblenz and Trier or in the about twenty towns of middling size. Most of the prince elector's subjects lived in rural villages. These peasant subjects were far from being the loyal, apolitical, and somewhat timid, "obedient Germans" that nineteenth-century Prussian historiography has taught us to expect. The peasant communities of the Electorate defended their control of the local courts against the claims of the sovereign in late Middle Ages.[48] In the fourteenth century, the community courts in the region of Trier still possessed substantial jurisdiction over criminal and civil matters. In the course of conflicts with the prince elector, nobles, and clerical lords, the communities lost their legal jurisdictions, gradually and unevenly. Finally, mainly at the beginning of the sixteenth century, the territorial courts assumed authority in all criminal matters. Thus, jurisdiction over criminal cases, which held central significance as the essential right of sovereignty in the development of the early modern state, had remained in the hands of the subjects for a long time in the region of Trier. In this context, the consolidation and regulation of the district structure in the sixteenth century was a significant success for Trier's territorial government. After that, only the district commissioners and the jurors of the provincial administrative centers would have the right to investigate criminal matters.[49] As a basis for further discussion, two facts need to be emphasized: subjects lost their jurisdiction over criminal law late, and the process by which they lost that jurisdiction was rife with conflict.

The old jurisdictional rights of the communities in the Moselle-Hunsrück-Eifel region were part and parcel of local structures of self-administration. A reeve (*Zender*) served as the head of each community.[50] The responsibilities of a reeve could encompass more than a single village. Generally, his tenure in office would last a single year. In some communities, however, the reeve was elected for life. There were considerable local differences concerning the franchise, the voting procedures, and the influence of the territorial government. In some villages, community assemblies conducted the elections; in others, juries did. In some of the communities in the Moselle area, noble and ecclesiastical officials had no influence whatsoever on the election of the reeve. By contrast, he might be selected by the territorial ruler or his representative, based on the suggestions of the communal jurors. Sometimes the territorial sovereign simply appointed the reeve. Often the reeve was responsible to two authorities, and after the Middle Ages this shifted always further to the disadvantage of the subjects. The appointment of the reeve by the prince elector began to dominate in the sixteenth century. The reeve represented the community to the outside world in all judicial matters. Internally, he had oversight of the common fields and the authority to punish trespassing and enforce community ordinances. The reeve also presided over communal assemblies; as a rule, he was answerable to these bodies. Before the jurisdiction over criminal cases passed to the territorial districts, the reeve supervised arrests and executions. He was the head of the criminal court, but the communal jurors determined the verdict.[51]

Similarly to the reeve, with whom they cooperated very closely, the jurors took on a mediating role between sovereign and community. The community originally selected the jurors freely. Later, the village jurors fell under the influence of the sovereign. Their field of activity was the lower courts that lacked authority over capital cases. The lower courts had been communal and corporative institutions. The territorial legal administration slowly assimilated them into its own structure. By 1537, a Lower Court Ordinance of the Electorate had sought in vain to eliminate the sort of abuses that often characterized the witch trials. The ordinance forbade the jurors to hold expensive meals together during proceedings at the plaintiff's or defendant's expense. The Administrative Decree of 1574 repeated the ban on these expensive "court dinners."[52]

The power of the village communities of the Electorate rested in the community assembly. These assemblies either met regularly, based on the rhythms of the agrarian year, or ad hoc in exceptional cases. The community assembly still met as a deciding body alongside jurors and council even in places with urban charters. Such was the case in Bernkastel until the end of the sixteenth century and in Saarburg into the eighteenth century. Communal committees held central importance in the administration of communities in the Moselle-Hunsrück-Eifel region during the late Middle Ages and early modern period. The committee phenomenon was widespread, found throughout the area under investigation and beyond, in Luxembourg in the west, the Nassau region in the east, along the Saar River to the south, and along the Rhine to the north. These committees were bodies established ad hoc by the communities, each for a specific purpose. A village might form a committee, for example, if it needed a new regulation for the use of pasture lands. A community could create a committee to check the reeve's account books. Often, such committees represented a peasant community in court. In such cases, the committee appeared as the plaintiff before the court in the name of the community.[53] The communal committees that investigated witches were part and parcel of this more general committee phenomenon. I will discuss them extensively in chapter 5. As mentioned earlier, Swabians thought it good to live under the two-headed eagle of Habsburg. In the rest of Germany, it was proverbially good to live under the bishop's crozier. Contemporaries ridiculed the governments of ecclesiastical territories for being unable to exercise strict control over the towns and villages. At least as far as Trier in the sixteenth and early seventeenth centuries was concerned, they were right.

One has to take a look at the legal and social framework of the persecutions in the Electorate, too. On December 18, 1591, Prince Elector Johann VII von Schönenberg passed a Witch Trial Ordinance for the Electorate of Trier.[54] He bound the judges and officials to the provisions of the *Carolina*. Johann forbade witch committees called into existence by the subjects without the control or approval of the authorities. He did expressly permit the subjects, however, to bring accusations against persons suspected of witchcraft to local officials, as long as they could offer surety. Thus, bad reputations and suspicions were to be investigated ex officio according to the rules of the *Carolina*. Officials of the Electorate were to conduct interrogations only in the presence of two jurors. They were to control the executioner carefully in his use of torture. The ordinance clearly required that records from witch trials be submitted to the high courts of Coblenz and Trier. Decisions about arrest and torture, as well as the verdict, would be made there. In this respect, Johann's Witch Trial Ordinance simply echoed the Lower Court Ordinance of 1537. Denunciations of accomplices, however, were no longer to be read out publicly at the execution along with the confession; they were to be kept secret. In another reflection of the 1537 ordinance, the Witch Trial Ordinance devoted much space to the regulation of trial costs. Prince Elector Johann obviously intended to rein in rampant expenses. Daily pay rates were set for witnesses, notaries, and the executioner. The conflicting parties were to pay the official court personnel fixed honoraria.

The requirement to remit the trial records essentially would have centralized trial proceedings in the territorial high courts. If the local courts had carried out this rule consistently, circumstances in the Electorate of Trier would have been similar to those in the Palatinate or Württemberg. There the princes had placed witch trials under the constant control of their central governments. Trial records underwent a process of review that was frequently very lengthy. This process of critical review involved jurists who did not have any contact with the local communities where witchcraft panics might hold sway. As a result, in the Palatinate and Württemberg, the execution of witches was relatively rare.[55]

Johann's moderate Witch Trial Ordinance took an unmistakable position against the harsh stance of his Suffragan Bishop Peter Binsfeld, whose witch tract had first appeared in 1589. Johann implicitly rejected the witch tract by demanding careful proceedings in accordance with imperial law, insisting on procedural caution instead of Binsfeld's aggressive zeal for witch hunting. Moreover, the Witch Trial Ordinance established a clear distinction between witchcraft and folk magic. Following the demonological tradition, Binsfeld understood all magic as diabolical.[56]

A decree from Johann on October 1, 1592, forbade a practice that had developed in the city of Trier: it was unlawful to exclude the children of executed witches from city offices, guilds, and confraternities.[57]

On February 2, 1630, Prince Elector Philipp Christoph von Sötern renewed Johann's Witch Trial Ordinance and supplemented it with a substantially expanded list of trial expenses.[58] To rein in abuses, fixed daily rates for the members of witch committees now appeared alongside those for officials, jurors, notaries, and court personnel. This implied acknowledgment of the committees' activities should not be seen as a deviation from the line taken by Johann. Johann had banned only the witch committees not overseen by the territorial authorities.

The entire secular legislation on witch trials in the Electorate of Trier focused exclusively on the subject of trial proceedings. No law described the crime of witchcraft. It was clearly not the intention of the prince electors to initiate or force witch trials. Rather, the intention was to regulate them.

As archbishops, the lords of the Electorate of Trier also dealt with crimes of magic in church ordinances. A circular ordinance enacted by Archbishop

Johann VII in 1589 prescribed the punishment of folk magic but, as with the Witch Trial Ordinance, did not identify it with witchcraft.[59] Magicians were to be punished according to the severity of their crimes, no doubt in accordance with the *Carolina*. The ordinance required clients of folk magic "experts" to pay a fine. In this ordinance, Johann VII was again significantly less rigorous than Binsfeld. Archbishop Lothar von Metternich placed a different emphasis during his renewal of the circular ordinance in 1599. For him, the most pressing concern was to punish superstition, not to fight diabolical magic.[60]

A hearth list from 1563 counted 11,364 households in the territory of the Electorate of Trier. In 1684, the authorities re-counted the hearths in the Electorate; the total count was 15,087 households. The total population of the city of Trier around 1600 was about 6,000; that of Coblenz, about 5,000.[61] The Electorate, with its agricultural towns, was economically dominated by the urban centers of Trier and Coblenz. Despite being well provided with a trading hall and five markets of at least regional significance, the economic development of the city of Trier essentially stagnated in the sixteenth and seventeenth centuries. Lack of capital and a reluctance on the part of the established elite to take risks, combined with the repressive tax policies of the prince electors, limited the economic activity of the city. To this was added the loss of the princely residence to Coblenz in a long process that lasted into the eighteenth century. The city produced principally for its own needs; as a market base for urban production, the Upper Electorate was too poor and too thinly populated. Despite this economic stagnation, the populace of Trier was better off economically than that of the surrounding countryside.[62]

The transportation networks of the cities in the Electorate were insufficient. Trier and Coblenz profited from the Moselle, Saar, and Rhine as waterways. The regional road networks in the heights of the Eifel and Hunsrück uplands were in poor condition around 1600 and impeded trade. Only Bernkastel lay directly on a significant trade route.[63] The contrast between fertile valleys with mild climates (along the Saar, Moselle, and Rhine) and low but rough mountain ranges (in the surrounding Eifel, Hunsrück, and the foothills of the Westerwald) marked the economy of the Electorate of Trier. The slopes of the Moselle valley enjoyed a typical viticulture climate and were intensively cultivated. But up on the Hunsrück and Eifel, the rural population practiced almost no viticulture at all. Grain cultivation and pastoral agriculture dominated the economic structure of this comparatively poor part of the Electorate.[64] As with the winegrowing regions of Swabian Austria, the Electorate of Trier suffered the results of worsening climatic conditions following the crop failures of the 1580s. Numerous storms and damaging frosts in the 1580s and 1590s created very unstable prices for food and especially wine. A similar crisis struck the Moselle region around 1630. In parts of the Electorate, the once flourishing viticulture disappeared altogether in the mid-seventeenth century. The worsening climate affected viticulture particularly but not solely. For the 1580s and the 1630s there is evidence of unstable and frequently high grain prices. The inflation thus unleashed further worsened the situation of the underprivileged classes.[65]

OVERVIEW AND COMPARISON

The efforts of the princes and governments of Swabian Austria and the Electorate of Trier to bring all of the towns, villages, and courts of their respective territories under their control did not succeed. Sovereign control did not penetrate the territories fully. In comparison with other German early modern state administrations—for example, Württemberg, Bavaria, or the Palatinate—the administrative apparatuses of Swabian Austria and the Electorate of Trier were weak. Still, there were differences between the two.

In Swabian Austria, the Habsburg officeholders could never fully prevail against the council elites of the court towns during the period under investigation. The constitution of the court system represented a compromise between the sovereign and the towns in which the latter party kept important rights and competences. The government of the Electorate of Trier was at an advantage in this regard. In addition, the Electorate had at least attempted to organize judicial matters under two territorial high courts with extensive authority and clearly defined districts. The territorial courts of Swabian Austria failed to establish a similarly strict structure. The Habsburg officials, however, did not have to deal with criminal court districts composed of rural communities that had long been able to defend their jurisdiction over criminal cases. In Swabian Austria, there were no village committees functioning as structures of self-governance as there were in the Electorate of Trier. Such strong and active communal structures were not a part of the regional tradition. Neither of the two areas ever had witch commissioners or territorial tribunals that specialized in witch trials. The legislation on witch hunting varied. While the legislation of the prince elector of Trier twice attempted to rein in abuses during the height of the witch hunts, that of the Habsburg archduke was not specifically aimed at actual witch hunts in Swabian Austria. Swabian Austria simply had to follow the same general regulations designed for the Tyrolean home territory. The territorial sovereigns, however, always insisted on the imperial law of the *Carolina* in the attempt to subject witch hunts to sovereign control. Similarities ensued from this. In both cases, ordinances forbade the abuse of torture and the acceptance of denunciations as incriminating evidence supporting arrest or torture. The laws demanded that the local criminal courts remit the files of witch trials to higher courts or legal experts to receive the advice of learned jurists. Laws in both regions remained dependent on the *Carolina* as a pragmatic guideline. The legislation in both territories ignored radical theological positions entirely, such as that of Binsfeld, or only incorporated them in a moderated form, in the manner suggested by Tanner. The ecclesiastical territory of the Electorate of Trier showed no greater affinity for demonological concepts than did Swabian Austria. Thus, the framework of laws and government institutions in both territories actually were a hindrance to, rather than an impetus for, witch hunting.

The population of the Electorate of Trier was about twice as great as that of Swabian Austria. Both territories experienced an economic crisis at the end of the sixteenth century in conjunction with failed harvests. This had an especially intense effect on the regions dominated by viticulture. Strong urban production and structures of long-distance trade—which might have provided a balancing factor during crises—were absent in both regions, as was any trade center with significance beyond the region.

2

Golden Goblets and Cows' Hooves

Witchcraft and Magic

Scholars who look beyond witchcraft into the broader field of magic face the problem that sources on magic employ a multitude of terms in often ambiguous ways.[1] It is therefore necessary to begin by clarifying the definitions of the most important terms.

In sources from both Swabian Austria and the Electorate of Trier, the word *"Aberglauben"* appears as a term used by both secular and ecclesiastical authorities. It is used as the German equivalent of the Latin *superstitio:* mistaken beliefs condemned by secular and ecclesiastical authorities. Such "superstition" included religious and quasi-religious concepts·and practices that did not accord with the theologically educated church leadership's view of proper (in Swabian Austria and Trier, this meant Catholic) belief and practice or with that of the political leadership of these territorial states. I will only use the term "superstition" in quoting the views of this elite minority, as a concept with its own historical meaning. One cannot employ the term "superstition" as a category of interpretation or analysis, because in historical and ethnological scholarship there is no satisfactory definition of the term that distinguishes it from folk religiosity or erroneous natural knowledge.[2] Moreover, Enlightenment elites burdened the term with such pejorative connotations as "primitive," "unscientific," and "irrational," and such prejudices have persisted in anthropological and historical literature until recent times. Thus, we can no longer use the term in a neutral and strictly descriptive way.

For practical reasons, however, a generic term is necessary. I will use the concept of "popular belief" here. Popular belief includes everything that the majority of the population believed, including religious belief in a modern sense as well as belief in fate or a God-given world order, belief in spirits or in the efficacy of magic and its immediate consequences. The concept of popular belief, as the belief of the majority, does not imply a particular social position of the people involved. It does not exclude the participation of religious, political, or economic elites. It is also indistinct, which is useful, since I will use it to describe a comprehensive, heterogeneous phenomenon with variations between individuals and also between different social groups.[3]

I will use the term "witchcraft" only in the strict sense of the elaborated witch concept of late medieval demonology, according to which it consists of a pact with the Devil and apostasy, sex with the Devil, night flight, participation in the witches' Sabbath, and harmful sorcery. Accordingly, I will consider only those judicial proceedings directed against the crime described in the elaborated witch concept to be "witch trials." Proceedings against harmful magic that lack these elements will be termed "sorcery trials."[4]

For many early modern people, simple forms of magic were a part of everyday life. I will refer to this ordinary magic, which was not necessarily performed by a magic specialist with expert knowledge, as folk magic. Any activities and associated ideas that depended on the belief in the immediate efficacy of Catholic liturgical or quasi-liturgical rituals in everyday reality I will term "church magic." For example, the idea that some special prayer would function like medicine to alleviate physical pain would be church magic. The belief in the consecration of the elements of the Eucharist would not be magical, as it bestows purely spiritual qualities to these elements that affect the transcendent properties of human beings rather than the physical ones. This church magic thus included elements of a *do ut des* cult ("I give in order that you should give") that was attached to the theologically defined Christian high belief but nevertheless—at least, on a fundamental theoretical level—alien to it. The assumption that God could be put under obligation in this way was, from a theological perspective, a denial of God's sovereignty. Recourse to the church as an institution did not facilitate an entirely clear separation of religion from magic; church magic was also practiced within the priesthood.

POPULAR DEMONOLOGY: WITCHCRAFT IDEAS IN SWABIAN AUSTRIA AND THE ELECTORATE OF TRIER

During the sixteenth century, authorities adopted an increasingly elaborate notion of diabolical witchcraft. In Swabian Austria, one can perceive no distinctive "warm-up phase," in which a gradual shift took place from older sorcery concepts to the elaborated witch concept. In the oldest documented case from 1493, a certain Ulrich Schaller was accused in Burgau of having made hail—the typical, senselessly destructive crime of witches that was so alien to more traditional sorcery that served the magicians egoistic interests.[5] That the authorities raised this accusation, even though it was atypical against a man, may reflect the early witch trials in Ravensburg under the leadership of Heinrich Kramer ("Institoris"). Here, weather magic had played a dominant role.[6] A case of witch slander from Stockach in 1521 lacked any specifics. Later trials around 1530 in Burgau, Nellenburg, and Hohenberg already involved groups of suspects, including people from the upper strata of society. The court files even mentioned that witches had a human leader—that is, the witches were regarded as an organization. This argues for a reception of the learned notion of witchcraft as a collective crime. Unlike sorcery, witchcraft was a kind of "organized crime." The rural populace already actively supported these trials.[7] From this we may conclude that the demonological witch concept had already found its way into popular belief in Swabian Austria by the first third of the sixteenth century and was being drawn on for the interpretation of concrete situations.

The appearance of the witch concept and the transition to prosecuting witches as groups of conspirators occurred considerably earlier in the Electorate of Trier, at the latest in the 1490s.[8] The early wave of trials in the district of Boppard, to which thirty individuals fell victim between 1492 and 1494, must have been based on denunciations within an elaborated witch model that included the idea of the Sabbath. It is unclear whether this was a delayed result of the preaching of Kramer, who in at least one sojourn in the Moselle region in 1488 sought to provoke the people and the authorities to hunt witches. At any rate, it is notable that during the trials in Boppard officials took care to prevent the imprisoned witches from touching the earth. Kramer had mentioned the same safety measure in the *Malleus* and emphatically recommended it, and witch committees in the Trier region still occasionally employed this practice during the 1580s.[9] Whether Kramer actually inspired a tradition here, the practice was acquired from the *Malleus,* or these were simply independent applications of a generally customary practice remains an unanswerable question.

By 1497, the confession of a witch executed in Trier contained elements that would characterize the confessions in the sixteenth and seventeenth centuries, as well. The witches met for the Sabbath at the Hetzerath heath. They intended to destroy the harvest through collective weather magic. The ringing of church bells, however, dispersed the witches. The only source for this trial is the chronicle of the monastery of Eberhardsklausen, which mentioned this confession as a memorable incident from that year. We should note that the chronicler—a cleric influenced by demonological literature—emphasized that he was reproducing the exact statements of the condemned.[10] It is probable, however, that the monastery was only hearing the echoes of ideas that it had previously helped to disseminate. Wilhelm of Bernkastel, the chronicler of Eberhardsklausen, had read the early demon-ologists Nider and Kramer and had taken it upon himself to warn the popu-lace of the menace of witchcraft in sermons and pastoral counseling. The earlier diffusion of the elaborated witch concept in the Electorate of Trier was thus the result of a clerical-theological infrastructure superior to that in Swabian Austria.[11]

Detailed descriptions of the crime of witchcraft first become available from Swabian Austria in the 1560s and from the Electorate of Trier in the 1570s.[12] At this time, as should be expected, they reflected the demonologi-cal concept of witchcraft in every way. There were no significant differences between the witchcraft ideas in the two regions. The witch concept had not been modified significantly in either of the regions under investigation.

Confessions followed a fixed pattern that was rarely broken. The accused confessed to a first encounter with the Devil under circumstances of emo-tional or economic need. The confessions did not exceed the scope of the or-dinary; they did not create exceptional circumstances for the appearance of the Devil. Usually he appeared as a stranger whom a woman met by chance. The stranger inquired as to the cause of her sadness in a friendly and seem-ingly helpful manner. Once she had provided information, he offered her monetary assistance. Here the narrative of the confessions operated within the realm of popular storytelling. The sudden appearance of a stranger who offered material assistance to the protagonist in his or her difficulties and who was later revealed to be a friendly spirit, usually a fairy, was a widely dis-persed element of folk tales.[13] The Devil was usually portrayed in this narra-tive form. Thus, storytelling in confessions was formulated along the lines of traditional narrative structures, which were not only easily available as they were generally well known, but were also categorized as fundamentally be-lievable. It was easy to assimilate the repertoire of ordinary fantasy available in legend motifs to the figure of the Devil as required by the witch concept.

In Swabian Austria, the names given to the demons in the witch stories reveal the application of fairy motifs to the Devil. The names of evil angels known to learned demonology were almost entirely absent from witches' confessions. Infrequently names appeared that referred directly to the char-

acter of the bearer, such as Hans Feind (Jack Enemy), Misgünstler (the Envi-
ous), or Luget (Liar). In addition, there were grotesque names such as Dr.
Virivanz—probably a parody of Latin considered appropriate for a demon
with a doctorate—or Kharfunkhen Kechele (Little Diamond Cook). Such
names appeared only in a single trial. In a whole series of trials, however,
names appear such as Gütlin (Little Good One) and Hemmerlin (Little Hammer), which were associated with brownie spirits who assisted various occupations. Similarly frequent were such names as Grünling (the Green One)
and Kreutlin (Little Herb), which indicate a vegetation spirit. Greslin, by far
the most commonly appearing name of the Devil, belongs among these. Presumably it is a derivative of the word for grass, thus meaning "Little Grass."
The name was explicitly appended with "the green one." The Devil here
was usually dressed in green and gray, colors that were also associated with
fairies.[14]

That the witches in Swabian Austrian confessions nearly always claimed
to have met the Devil for the first time in a meadow, garden, or grove may
also argue for the adoption of narrative elements from fairy legends. Thus,
the description of the first meeting between witch and Devil, which provided the basis for their future relationship, transferred to the Devil some
of the names, appearance, and modes of behavior from friendly spirits—or,
at least, not demonic ones—taken from popular stories. When the stranger
revealed his true identity, however, he turned out not to be a friendly fairy as
described in folk tales but a demon instead.

In the Electorate of Trier, the ideas of demons were further removed from
fairy motifs. Here exclusively grotesque names appeared for the Devil, such
as Bontenkübel (Colorful Bucket) and quite frequently Feder Hans (Jack
Feather) and Federbusch (Tuft of Feathers).[15] Feder Hans was originally a
derogatory name for mercenaries, feared for their brutality and plunder-
ing. Being itinerant, mercenaries were marginal in premodern society and
often scarcely differed from despised vagrants. Considering this context, it
makes sense that a word for mercenaries might be transferred to demons.
Hans Reuland testified in 1594 that the demon he had met called himself
Knipper Thullingh. This was probably a distortion of the name of the Ana-
baptist leader of Münster, Bernd Knipperdolling, who had been executed in
1536.[16] In the Electorate of Trier, it was claimed in a number of cases that,
following the sealing of the pact, the witch had received a new name from
the Devil.[17] This renaming was a repudiation of baptism, but the motif was
not maintained—it appeared in only a minority of cases in the Electorate
and is absent altogether in Swabian Austria. This suggests that the people of

Swabian Austria and the Electorate did not have a thoroughgoing conception of witches as a diabolic sect.

At the moment that the Devil revealed himself, the motifs borrowed from folk tales became distorted. The stranger qualified his promise of help; he offered the money only in exchange for sex. Prostitution or seduction narratives, however, did not exist among the accused men in Swabian Austria, and demons were never imagined in female form. In the Electorate of Trier, only Diederich Flade confessed to having been seduced by a demon in female form. This he probably adopted from learned demonology. All of the other accused men in the Electorate—as with male trial victims in Swabian Austria—simply omitted all elements of seduction.[18]

The woman recognized the demon by his cold semen. Only then did he demand the pact that she was to confirm by renouncing God and all the saints. The woman usually acquiesced immediately, and without qualms. In Swabian Austria, the witch might set absurd conditions—for example, that the alliance could not harm her soul or that she be allowed to continue her veneration of the Virgin Mary.[19] The Devil regularly granted such requests. In only one case in either region was a written pact mentioned, in the trial of Anna Humlerin in Nellenburg in 1680. This trial was under the strong influence of a single official and an external consultant, who positively fed the accused details drawn from learned demonology.[20] Formulae of ritual renunciation were only mentioned in the Electorate, and even there only in isolated cases.[21] Again, we find an exception to this in the trial of Diederich Flade. The court compelled him under torture to provide the formula of his renunciation. He composed one in Latin that had no parallel in either territory, including a theological basis for his pact with the devil: "I renounce and reject God, believing that his omnipotence cannot save me; therefore I devote myself to the Devil."[22] The desire that this first trial of a prominent man nail down every detail probably explains the particular interest in Flade's pact. Otherwise the courts in both territories showed little interest in the pact.

The first meeting of witch and Devil ended in both territories with the Devil's monetary gift turning into rubbish. Here again we encounter an element borrowed from folk tales. There, it usually appeared in the reverse form, with the gift of a friendly fairy being transformed from dirt and worthless junk into some valuable material. The Devil's monetary gift in witch narratives of the Electorate did not connote prostitution, and hence it also appeared in the testimony of men.[23]

In both regions, the concept of witchcraft as a learnable "art" belongs to the oldest traceable elements of the fantasy. Witches stated that other witches had been their teachers. No one sensed any inconsistency between the narratives of the pact and that of having a teacher.[24]

After the pact-seduction narrative, the confessions in both regions lost their consistency as unfolding stories. They were reduced to curt descriptions of individual acts of harmful magic and witch dances. The rudimentary trial tactics of suspects dictated their confession narratives. Generally, the Devil appeared in order to provide direct assistance in traveling to the Sabbath or particular enchantments. At the witches' Sabbath itself, a circle of prominent witches took on a leadership role, while other witches often obeyed only hesitantly or after being beaten by their leaders or the Devil. Only in isolated cases did anyone confess to using sorcery at his or her own initiative or to satisfy a personal desire for revenge.[25] Trial victims were clearly attempting to minimize their own personal guilt. The fantasy of sorcery against the elite appeared sporadically only in the Electorate.

Given the high number of cases even at the beginning of the first wave, however, one could interpret this as the revenge of suspected witches for the witch trials. The witches apparently personally and directly threatened the abbot of St. Maximin, Vicegerent Johann Zandt von Merl, and Prince Elector Johann VII, whom the accused witches saw as responsible for the witch hunt. In 1595, at the end of the great wave of trials, a confession from the Electorate even says that the leaders of the witches were entertaining a plan to destroy the city of Trier as "retaliation" for the witch trials. In a bizarre variant of this revenge concept, the witches supposedly planned to destroy the forests by raising storms, so that no more witch burnings could take place for want of wood. Witchcraft thus was sometimes imagined as an instrument against people who were economically and politically stronger than the witches.[26]

Enchanted impotence and love magic played only a small role in Swabian Austria, and in the records available for the Electorate of Trier such elements are completely absent.[27] Shape-shifting also appeared only rarely in the two regions. Several men and women were accused of being werewolves. Here, the motif of the *"charmeur des loups"*—that is, a wizarding shepherd who was able to communicate with the wolves and thus to keep them away from his herd—may have played a role.[28]

One central charge against the witches was sorcery that caused sickness to man or beast, which they supposedly accomplished in a variety of ways. The diverse methods used suggest various degrees of distance between the witch and her victim. These conceptual elements must be briefly discussed, as they were vital for the genesis of concrete suspicions. One method, *veneficium,* could be either poison or harmful magic, and the boundaries between the two were fluid. The witch could administer a harmful material to her victim—man or beast—in food.[29] Another method was merely to touch the victim with a hand or with a stick or salve that the witch had obtained from the Devil.[30] Such a concept of harmful magic required only fleeting contact between witch and victim. This offered, however, room for a simple preventative measure against harmful magic: to avoid all contact with the suspect and to forbid him or her entry to one's house.[31] It was this idea that stood behind the tendency in both territories to suspect witchcraft rather than theft if someone suddenly entered the barns or houses of his or her neighbors. Contact could be dangerous. If a person forced his or her presence on another or established contact secretly, contemporaries expected a magical assault. Finally, with the possibility of accomplishing harmful magic by merely breathing on the victim, the required contact was reduced to mere physical proximity.[32] It goes without saying that, to name a specific victim of harmful magic and a specific responsible witch, an accusation or confession narrative simply could not do without at least the physical proximity of perpetrator and victim. Contemporaries believed that witches were only capable of causing harm over vast physical distances by means of weather magic. Then, of course, it was no longer a single, specific individual but rather the whole community that was the victim of the sorcery. In both of our regions, precisely this kind of magic, which turned ominously from the goal of harming individuals to the devastation of entire regions, was considered the most dangerous and the most prevalent form of witchcraft. In 1590, a suspect in Rottenburg supposedly claimed of herself: "Even if she were a hundred miles from here she could harm Swabia in a way that would make people wring their hands in agony."[33] The witches of Trier purportedly planned to destroy all plant life or—a motif that was absent in Swabian Austria—to spread the plague.[34]

Weather magic stands at the center of the confessions and hence at the heart of the witch concept in both Swabian Austria and the Electorate of Trier. In particular, in the persecution-intensive areas of Hohenberg, the populace directly associated storm damage with witchcraft. The Rottenburg vine dresser Peter Kniess complained about the mild proceedings against witches in the following terms: "We have great grievances regarding the evil women, which are dealt with inadequately. The poor citizenry are thus afflicted with hail and storms, such that no one knows anymore where he can feel at home."[35] Crop-damaging storms repeatedly became catalysts for witch hunts in Swabian Austria and the Electorate of Trier. In both territories, weather magic became the central event even at the Sabbath, which appears frequently to have taken place for just this purpose. Weather magic was always imagined as a collective act of the witches and resulted in intensified persecutions. In Swabian Austria, weather magic was consistently depicted as ordinary sympathetic magic: the witch filled a pot with her urine, spilled it, and a thunderstorm, hail storm, or frost resulted. As the liquid poured out of the pot, so rain, hail, or hoar-frost were supposed to fall down from the sky.[36] The leaders of the witches, who mostly came from the upper class, were said to be eager to knock over the "weather pot." In this way they were characterized as particularly malicious.[37] People in the Electorate of Trier similarly imagined collective weather magic of the witches as sympathetic magic, but they considered weather magic the exclusive province of women. In Trier, the witches supposedly damaged the harvest not only with weather magic, but also with magically summoned vermin. Flade was even said to keep a barrel of snails ready in his cellar for the purpose of damaging crops.[38]

Confessions in both territories scarcely mention night flight. In the juridical context of the trials, the flight had hardly any significance. It could be used neither as evidence nor as a chargeable act of harmful magic by itself. Night flight was only discussed in more detail when the means of flight functioned as a status symbol. Wealthy witches arrived at the Sabbath on horses or in coaches. The witch concept in both territories concentrated on stories of flight more for testimony about the social structure of the witches than on "technical" questions regarding the witches' flight. The witches flew on staves they had coated with a magical salve. They received the salve from the Devil or—in the Electorate of Trier—made it themselves from the corpses of children. In neither region is there the slightest indication that the accused in the witch trials had used hallucinogenic drugs in the form of a salve and might thus be describing the experience of intoxication as night flight.[39]

In most cases, abandonment of the church and the renunciation of God were explicitly formulated in the original pact with the Devil. This meant withdrawal from the Christian community, from the religiously conceived and founded political order, and ultimately from Christian culture. In place of marriage and family appeared the sexual relationship with the Devil. In place of the political, social, and religious order appeared the community of witches, actualized in the witches' Sabbath. Descriptions of the Sabbath show how people in the two regions imagined the witches' assembly and the inner structure of the witch group. In both the Electorate of Trier and in Swabian Austria, deponents and interrogation personnel did not imagine the witches' assembly fundamentally as a congregation of a heretical sect. In neither region did the church or state attempt to impose cultic, counter-religious elements on the witch concept. In Swabian Austria, neither church visitations nor territorial religious ordinances ever mentioned witchcraft, even though these were born of massive Counter-Reformation objectives.[40] Peter Binsfeld of Trier, of course, understood the witch as a heretic. Yet he neither styled witches as a concrete satanic cult nor mentioned anything about quasi-liturgical ceremonies at the Sabbath. The Devil resembled a violent lord or husband; he was not an object of worship.[41] Only a single child from Wehrheim, a shared domain of the Electorate and Nassau-Dillenburg, testified in 1684 of a sermon being held at the witches' Sabbath.[42]

In both territories, only a minority of confessions mentioned any desecration of the Eucharistic host. Burgau witnessed a major scandal when the Innsbruck government discovered that petty aristocrats working as Habsburg officials not only employed folk magicians and soothsayers on a regular basis but were also members of a ring that bought and sold consecrated hosts. They were abusing the hosts as protective charms. The ringleaders, however, were punished for sacrilege, not for witchcraft. Only in two witch trials in Swabian Austria do we find the Devil making statements with which he intended to dissuade the witches from the Catholic faith. But Niclaus Fiedler from Trier testified that the Devil reviled the saints as "seducers." In his trial, as in many others in the Moselle region, Mary was berated as a whore. In another trial in the Electorate of Trier, the accused testified that her accomplices had told her that neither heaven nor hell existed. Diederich Flade, whose testimony was considerably more theologically elaborate than that of any other trial victim, even said that he "had his doubts about many articles of the faith," and that he was hence susceptible to the Devil's snares. Yet he never claimed that the Devil had brought him to question his faith. None of the above-cited statements provoked follow-up questions from the interrogators. They had no significance in the remainder of the confessions.[43]

Thus, in neither Swabian Austria nor the Electorate of Trier was the congregation of the witches imagined as a religious ceremony. The central elements were not rituals and worship but communal meals and dances as well as the collective planning and execution of harmful magic. Religious elements of the witches' Sabbath, which some demonologists had described in exhaustive detail, were absent, and this fact is crucial to understanding the conceptualization of witchcraft in these regions. The witch society of the Sabbath constituted a corporative festive event rather than a religious one. Here again, it is clear that in structure and function the witches' society was analogous to the rural or urban community rather than the parish. Sometimes individuals seized the opportunity to form specific Sabbath narratives that reflected real social circumstances rather than the canon of motifs determined by learned demonological literature. This has two consequences for the historian's interpretations of Sabbath stories. First, it is pointless to dissect descriptions of the Sabbath in witch-trial case records in search of theological concepts and (older) popular ideas. The witches' Sabbath does not lend itself to interpretation when presumed to be a condensation of older traditions. It is also insufficient to view the pact and Sabbath as a radical abandonment of the real world, to conceive of the world of the Sabbath merely as other and strange, or to identify it simply with the spirit world of popular belief.[44] People described the Sabbath as a system of human interactions, and as such it fulfills the sociological criteria for a society.[45] A second consequence of the trial victims' narrative strategies is obvious: The witches' Sabbath must be interpreted for its potential as a depiction of a society. The Sabbath was an imagined alternative society that contemporaries believed to coexist with the social structures of everyday life.

At the Sabbath, witches discussed and carried out harmful magic together; they danced and sat down at tables for a feast. This was the outline of the typical Sabbath narrative in both territories. In some confessions, this outline was complemented with a list of other participants. In addition, in most confessions the Sabbath narrative was further amplified with details, grotesque elements, and motifs of reversal. Music at the witches' dance became a distinct theme in the Electorate of Trier. Precise details were recorded, such as that the music was discordant, that the musicians received payment, or that the pipers sat in the trees. They were variously said to have used cows' horns or horse skulls, cats, or simply staves as their instruments. "Witch-piper" developed as a specific accusation against men. In the Electorate, as in other territories, people said that the witches stole the corpses of children and devoured them at the Sabbath; this motif was absent in Swabian Austria. Demonologists—most notably, Delrio—had depicted the Sabbath as the world turned upside down. The attention of demonologists was accordingly concentrated on the blasphemous rituals of the witches as contortions—often literally reversals—of Catholic liturgy. In trials within our two territories, however, only non-religious reversal motifs appeared, such as a counter-clockwise round dance, in which the dancers turned their faces outward, or the absence of the most fundamental foodstuffs, bread and salt, at the witches' banquet. These elements also belonged to the basic stock of witches' Sabbath tales outside the Electorate of Trier and Swabian Austria.[46] When Flade was said to store a barrel of snails in his cellar, this was a reversal motif from the realm of harmful magic, almost poetic in the stringency of its

Thomas Sigfridus. The Witches' Sabbath of Trier, Leipzig 1594. Integrating horror and comedy, this picture was intended more to entertain than to inform. There are no striking parallels between the picture and the confessions of witches from the Trier region.

construction. The wealthy man stored in his cellar not food and drink for his own use but vermin with which to destroy crops to the detriment of all.

It is particularly significant that witchcraft narratives did not reverse or overturn social structures within the witches' Sabbath. In fact, the Sabbath appeared to be—true to the general absence of utopian elements in popular tales—an accurate reflection of real society. In Hohenberg, old women did not count for much at the assembly of witches, "The young are many and there are really enough of them."[47] In Swabian Austria, as in the Electorate of Trier, social divisions were clearly maintained at the witches' Sabbath. "Poor" and "rich," simplified binary code for perceiving social differences, pervaded and constituted depictions of the Sabbath in the Electorate and persecution-intensive Hohenberg. From the 1580s, when they first become available, throughout the height of the witch hunts, and on through the last of the trials, confessions in both territories report almost as a topos that "wealthy," "noble," and "rich" people participated in the Sabbath. They wore noble clothing; some officials even wore their chains of office, and a burgomaster of Trier was said to have flaunted his money purse at the Sabbath.

Witches' Dance. Rich witches in expensive clothes dance with demons while the musician sits in a tree. The scene resembles confessions from Trier. Illustration from Francesco Maria Guazzo, *Compendium Maleficarum* (Milan, 1608).

These external status tokens played a major role in witchcraft fantasies. Thus, a rich male witch might appear on a magnificent horse, with a coach, or even in a gold barouche. Wealthy witches in both territories brought their gold or silver tableware with them to the witches' banquet. In the Electorate this was contrasted with a grotesque element: the poor witches had to drink from cows' hooves. In Rottenburg and Trier, it was said that the leading officials of the territorial lords had presided over the Sabbath seated on thrones.[48]

Free from the constraints of archival sources, social romantics such as Jules Michelet and Emmanuel Le Roy Ladurie described the Sabbath fundamentally as a world turned upside down, a world that threatened real society with revolutionary downfall.[49] The Sabbath in the Electorate of Trier and Swabian Austria, which left social stratification with its hierarchical power structure firmly intact, clearly did not do so. Members of the upper class dominated the society of the Sabbath just as they dominated society in everyday life. If poor people arrived late at the Sabbath, no one waited for them; they were considered disposable in a society of witches ruled by the wealthy. According to confessions from both territories, rich and poor witches sat at separate tables at the witches' banquet, according to their social rank. "Some . . . went thither but kept to themselves and were fancy people"; "The fancy people had their own table and dance"; "The poor had to stand behind, just as always." It was put quite explicitly: "That place [the Sabbath] is like everywhere else in the world: the poor must give way to the rich and high-placed, and follow their wishes."[50] It should be noted that for Swabian Austria, this motif of the rule of wealthy witches over the society of the Sabbath is extensively documented only in Hohenberg.

Witches thus appear to have been divided into social classes analogous to those of real society. They had relationships of dominance and subordination that reflected the economic and political power structures of ordinary society. In both the Electorate and Swabian Austria, conflict between rich and poor witches over weather magic was a seminal moment in the Sabbath narratives. In both territories, it was categorically impossible for witches to protect their own property from the effects of weather magic. For this reason, poor witches, who feared for their own sustenance, were said to argue against weather magic at the Sabbath. The dominant witches from the upper classes, however, were always in favor of weather sorcery. If the poor did not immediately agree with them, they were beaten into compliance.[51]

This social arrangement of the witches was complemented in the Electorate of Trier with an urban–rural antagonism. The city of Trier was somewhat better off than the economically weak countryside. The antagonism was possibly an expression of peasant frustrations at the effects of inflation: they no longer earned the proceeds that they expected in the city market. In addition, some of the Trier elite provided credit to the rural populace.[52] Villagers from the area, when accused as witches, sweepingly referred to the leaders of the witches as the *Trierschen* (the people from Trier) in their Sabbath narratives. When people from Trier made their entrance to the dancing place using high-status horses and coaches, witches from the villages made room: "Make way! The *Trierschen* are coming!"[53] Peasants associated the city with oppressive social predominance and hence with particularly aggressive witches. These associations belonged together and mutually determined one another within a magical interpretation of the world.[54] Generally, the villages clamored for harsher proceedings against witches from the city. The confession of Margarethe from Euren brought the interpenetration of the urban–rural antagonism, subsistence fears, and harmful magic into focus. Margarethe claimed that at the Sabbath she had tried to prevent a famine by opposing the use of the weather sorcery planned by the Trier leaders, whereupon they beat her, saying, "Those from Trier will always have enough food."[55] No urban–rural differentiation with such a sweeping denunciation of townsfolk can be found in Swabian Austria. This can be ascribed to the fact that none of the little Habsburg territories had a city of Trier's importance, a city that confronted the villages of that area as a "significant Other." The reality in the Electorate of Trier differed from that in Swabian Austria and offered in this respect material for a different witch concept. Even the titles for particular officials of the city of Trier had analogues within in the society of the witches.[56]

The barb of hostility toward elites was a fixed part of the witch fantasy in both territories. When people from the upper echelons were brought before the court, they also described the witches' social arrangements as reflecting those of ordinary society.[57] In their confessions, members of the ruling class claimed that they had been dominated by even more highly placed people—or, at least, that they had never taken part in the practical execution of harmful magic themselves.[58] As reflections of reality, Sabbath fantasies in these two territories appear to have confirmed the existing social order while at the same denouncing it as corrupt. Thus, Sabbath narratives held great potential for social critique. This point in actual trials will be further discussed in chapter 5.

In Swabian Austria as in the Electorate of Trier, witches were conceived of fundamentally as female. Recent research has identified one of the well-springs of the witch trials in gendered forms of magic. In accordance with gender-specific social divisions of work, the entire compass of magic surrounding birth and death was unquestionably associated with women in both popular culture and demonological literature.[59] Typically male forms of magic can be identified on the margins of the trials in these territories: healing charms for man and beast, which could be directed against harmful sorcery, and magic aimed at material gain.[60] The only potential for surmounting this association of witchcraft with women lay in the conception of the witches' social organization as analogous to ordinary society. In the Electorate of Trier as well as in Swabian Austria, relatively more men were found among the powerful and wealthy leaders of the witches than among other social classes. Thus, the society of witches reflected real social relations not only concerning the power of different social groups, but also concerning the gendered potential for social influence. Consequently, although the concept of the Sabbath reduced the society it reflected largely to its female part, it did grant positions of power to a male minority. The far greater differentiation of the Sabbath concept in the Electorate (as compared with the Habsburg lands) may explain the fact that more men are found among the trial victims in the Electorate of Trier. The more developed image of the witches' society required more male witches.

As the Devil was described using elements from fairy legends, so also did the activities of the witches partially correspond to those of spirits in popular legends. They magically entered cellars and drank barrels dry; they rode horses to death.⁶¹ In Burgau and the Electorate of Trier, accusations combined the concept of the witch with that of the *Alp,* a malevolent spirit that torments sleepers, the embodiment of the nightmare. Especially in southeastern Germany, the *Alp* was conceived of not as a spirit but as a human being. Such persons were known as *Truden,* a German variant of vampire spirits. They allegedly entered the sleeping chambers of their victims magically and lay upon them, causing disturbed sleep. Moreover, the *Truden* were believed to weaken women and children by drinking their blood—or more often, the mother's milk—while they slept.⁶² Learned demonology did not accept the *Trude* concept. In 1627, the wife of one Melchior Walter of Günzburg believed that she and her newborn child were "plagued by *Truden*-craft." Female practitioners of folk magic explained to Walter that the *Trude* who threatened his family would ask him for a burning coal to light a fire. Using this oracle, Walter identified the young daughter of the locksmith Karl Karg as the guilty party. Walter then spread rumors that she was a "witch who had sucked and pressed his wife and child." This accusation combined *Trude* and witch. A whole series of witch trials in the Electorate of Trier and neighboring areas described activities of the witches clearly connected to this *Trude* motif. Both ordinary people and the court accepted such testimony as serious charges against the accused.⁶³

Poltergeists were not explained as ghosts or malicious house spirits but as witch magic. The claim to have seen a spirit was interpreted in both regions as self-incrimination for witchcraft.⁶⁴ One such story was the talk of the town in Rottenburg in 1604. One day, the burgomasters Nef and Schorrer were riding to Tübingen when Nef dropped behind. He briefly dismounted on Spitzberg hill, and his horse ran off. "After this, he became lost, went through a gap in a thorny hedge, and there found many women sitting near him in white clothing." The women's figures were entirely white. He recognized none of them and could not understand their speech. Nef crossed himself for protection. A nearby search party called to him, but he could not answer. The gathering of the white women ended suddenly after many hours when the clock struck midnight and Nef uttered a prayer. The entire narrative consisted of motifs from folk tales, but this was a folk legend told in the first person.⁶⁵ The only atypical element was that the white-clad women were not conceived of as fairies or ghosts, as folk-tale traditions would require, but as witches. The story did not change the material of the legend; it simply ascribed it to a different group of magical beings within popular imagination, that of the witches. Accusations of witchcraft grew out of this story, costing Nef his seat on the city council. A very similar narrative appears in the Electorate of Trier.

In 1592, the former Trier burgomaster Hans Reuland testified that he had lost his way and encountered a little brown man dressed like a peasant—a terse formula that often described a fairy. The little man offered him help but then revealed himself to be a demon. The source narrative was a fairy motif: the spirit who helps the lost wayfarer.[66]

The adaptability of the Sabbath concept went even further. The Rottenburg vicegerent, denounced as the leader of the witches, supposedly appeared at the Sabbath as a mounted hunter. Clearly, the head of the witches was being described as the leader of the wild hunt, a leader whom local traditions often identified as the ghost of an unpopular nobleman.[67] At the height of the witch hunts locals reinterpreted as the work of witches night noises on a particular mountain top, although in Hohenberg such sounds were traditionally explained as ghostly hauntings. The Tübingen scholar Martin Crusius felt obliged to remind his readers of the "correct" explanation.[68] In the Moselle region, people claimed that the ghosts of dead witches appeared at the Sabbath. These were principally thought to be witches who had escaped the judge and hence had to pay for their crimes after death.[69]

In both regions, autonomous, locally formulated witch ideas fused demonology and popular beliefs into genuinely new concepts. Thus, the witch or Devil could intrude into ghost stories and fairy tales and supersede traditional spirit concepts. The people of Swabian Austria and the Electorate adopted the elaborated witch concept too well. This demonological conception of witchcraft "expanded" into the realm of popular magic and spirit beliefs, to which it was essentially foreign. Through this process it became possible to transform popular narrative forms, which originally had aimed only at explaining and entertaining, into witness testimony relevant to criminal justice and social order. There is no evidence in the archival records that the Counter-Reformation battle against "superstition" forced this development when it reinterpreted the spirits of popular belief as demons, or that the development represented the reception of a Protestant explanatory model. The fact that witchcraft, unlike popular notions of spirits, was unreservedly acknowledged as real by religious and secular authorities no doubt facilitated this reinterpretation. However, the real strength of the "witchcraft" interpretation was that it made a witchcraft trial possible. Thus, it appeared to offer a means to fight the phantoms and misfortunes against which people otherwise saw no means of defense. But this expansion of the witch concept also amplified the fear of witchcraft present in society, as the witches were effectively granted new terrain. Clearly, we must address the expansion of the notion of witchcraft as a factor that promoted witch hunting.

POPULAR MAGIC AND CHURCH MAGIC IN SWABIAN AUSTRIA AND THE ELECTORATE OF TRIER

Historical research on magic has recently shifted its focus to magical folk beliefs.[70] I will now discuss these beliefs and their connection to the witch hunts.

In the Electorate of Trier and Swabian Austria, it was most often the very people who believed themselves or their possessions to be bewitched who called for the assistance of folk magicians and healers. Folk magicians broke illness-causing enchantments against man and beast. In both regions, healers determined whether illnesses were "natural" or caused by witchcraft. The function of the healer in so doing was not specifically diagnostic; he did not investigate symptoms. If the afflicted person already suspected witchcraft, the healer noticed this and provided confirmation. Or when the healer identified the witch supposedly guilty of the harm, he did little more than confirm a suspicion that, as a rule, the client already held.[71] Magic experts and oracles with the same mode of operation have also been found extensively outside of Europe. Peter Binsfeld, who rejected any kind of soothsaying as diabolic deception, felt obliged to warn repeatedly against witchcraft accusations obtained through divinations—probably the only case in which he was actually in full agreement with the *Carolina.* In this, he drew, as he rarely did, directly on his experience in the Electorate of Trier. In 1588, near Coblenz, a soothsayer had appeared who claimed to recognize a number of people as witches. The high court of Coblenz had to forbid local officials to proceed with torture based on his accusations. In Swabian Austria, the authorities frequently punished such witch accusations from folk healers as slander.[72]

We should not, however, underestimate the danger of identifying witches through popular magic. Even if the judicial authorities did not accept such accusations, a soothsayer could corroborate rumors circulating in the village communities and contribute indirectly to the genesis of witch trials. In Unlingen, for example, the folk healer Michael Stöckhlin cured multiple illnesses in 1619 that he interpreted as the witchcraft practiced by a certain Anna Michlerin.[73] When Anna Michlerin proceeded to bring charges of slander, another resident of Unlingen consulted a different folk healer, one Leonhard Fech. Fech was considered an expert at identifying witches. As the leader of a group of witch-hunting proponents in Saulgau, he had already successfully instigated the executions of three suspects. Fech used scholarly demonology in his arguments; he could learnedly expatiate on the abilities of witches before the court and explain the rather complicated question of why God permitted witchcraft. Here it can be seen that central theological positions from the background of the elaborated witch concept were known to some members of the middle class. Leonard Fech was merely a tailor and the owner of a farmstead. The advice of this "expert" tipped the scales, so that Anna Michlerin was charged and ultimately executed in Altdorf. I could cite other, similar cases.[74]

The identification of witches could apparently also be left open—that is, the procedure could succeed without the actual mention of a name. When the clergyman Wendel of Föhren was asked for his advice regarding a sick horse in 1615, he said that the horse should be sheltered in a particular place. The witches who had caused the illness would then pass by.[75] This was only ostensibly an identification, as it allowed the injured party to select from among the people who came near the horse the one whom he already suspected. In prophesying that the witch would show herself, the folk healer kept the selection from seeming arbitrary; he provided the preformed judgment with the air of "magic objectivity."

In the sources of Swabian Austria as well as those of the Electorate of Trier, most folk magicians were men. This finding aligns with that from other territories.[76] In just one case, from 1629, a Jew from Wittlich was asked to help with a case of bewitchment. Numerous executioners appear as folk magicians in both territories. Alongside activities analogous to those of other folk magicians, executioners also used magical methods in the torture of witchcraft suspects to compel the accused to confess. During the early chain trial in Boppard (1492–94), part of the usual treatment of the imprisoned was to soak their clothing and to "drug" their food with holy water. In addition, executioners often employed methods forbidden by learned authorities. According to Binsfeld, the "preparation of potions or drinks" for witchcraft suspects "to make them confess" approached witchcraft itself. A similar criticism against the executioner of Swabian Austrian Burgau was raised by the clergy in 1623. Presumably this case concerned a member of the Vollmair executioner family. Executioners from that family who served in Biberach were known as folk magicians and "experts" in the torture of witches.[77]

Not only executioners but also priests might act as folk healers and "witch finders" in both territories.[78] Binsfeld cited the ignorance of clerics and the ineptitude of ministers as one of the reasons the witch sect had been able to spread. He warned generally against the magical abuse of religious ceremonies. Yet Binsfeld did not explicitly address the question of priests as folk magicians. Perhaps the suffragan bishop and vicar-general Binsfeld was silent about such practices to avoid implicitly admitting a clerical failing. All examples of clerics' unorthodox practices in the sources of the Electorate come from the time after Binsfeld. Perhaps the reforms that he had promoted first brought attention to such occurrences. As late as 1783, clerics in the Electorate were still expressly forbidden to perform unorthodox blessings.[79]

In both regions, the courts more or less tolerated magic in the investigations against witches. The practice of local witch-hunting proponents was open to folk magic and hence was not in line with either the traditional demonological condemnation of all forms of magic or the Catholic Reformation criticism of superstition. Respect and authority as a folk magician could enhance one's career chances; at the end of the 1670s, an unpopular bailiff in Hohenberg appointed a well-known folk magician as sheriff to improve his own backing among the populace.[80] The new sheriff had supposedly already broken the enchantments of numerous witches, and so people esteemed him highly. The Innsbruck government protested against the appointment of a known sorcerer but was unable to prevail.

So far, I have shown that folk magicians and healers—contrary to the old theories of Michelet, Ehrenreich, and English[81]—were not categorically identified with witches but, rather, clearly functioned as agents of the witch hunts. All the same, there were some suspected witches who had worked as healers. The suspicion of witchcraft did not fall generally on folk healers as such, but in particular cases unsuccessful attempts at magical healing could be interpreted as harmful magic. An injured man asked Anna Schefer from Eutingen in Hohenberg to bless him to ease his pain. When a lasting paralysis resulted instead of the mitigation of his sufferings, the man interpreted this as the result of harmful sorcery on her part. In her trial in 1587, she confessed—reflecting the inversion motif typical to witchcraft—that instead of a blessing she had secretly whispered a curse, reversing the formula and calling on the Devil in the place of God. We can find similar cases in the Electorate of Trier.[82]

In both territories, people who believed that they were cursed not only sought out folk magicians but also went directly to the individuals they suspected as the perpetrators and asked them to withdraw the curse.[83] In such circumstances, suspects sometimes allowed themselves to be forced into the role of the witch who had imposed the curse. Under pressure, they reversed the sorcery and so indirectly confirmed that they had been responsible for the original spell. The magical healing that they performed drew on a ritual inventory of folk beliefs but was considered a confession of guilt. Here the social dysfunction of these witchcraft accusations is evident. In non-European societies infused with magic beliefs, witchcraft accusations could provide personal conflicts with a form that facilitated a settlement.[84] "Victims" and "perpetrators" established contact and arranged ritual "cures" as reconciliations. Due to the establishment of witchcraft as a crime in early modern European society, however, a "cure" performed by a suspect was always an implicit confession of a crime, which required punishment. The apparent neutralization of the curse was no longer accepted as the end of the underlying conflict.

In neither the Electorate of Trier nor in Swabian Austria is there any evidence of active counter-sorcery against witchcraft. If anyone used such practices, they must have been kept secret. We cannot explain the absence of active counter-sorcery against witchcraft, however, simply as a problem with the sources. The most active defense against witchcraft was, of course, the witch trial, so a defense against witchcraft was usually accomplished judicially, not by means of popular magic.

Folk magic, with its protective and healing sorcery, can only have offered a minor outlet for fears about witches. The isolation of village magicians and their relationship to church and state—which vacillated between rejection, toleration, and occasionally clandestine use by individual office holders—marginalized folk magic as a response to the menace of witchcraft. For church magic, however, different determining conditions applied. Not only the populace and occasional village priests but also the church leadership ascribed direct, quasi-magical efficacy to various ecclesiastical practices. They were sometimes conducted by clerics under direct episcopal control. In this respect, they differed from the practice of folk magicians, although popular healers also employed quasi-liturgical rituals and holy objects. The magical element of popular Catholicism was extremely polymorphic. I will examine three thematic areas here: simple forms of church magic in everyday life; wine and weather rituals; and pilgrimages and sermons. Finally, I will more closely examine the influence of the Tridentine reform in the form that Binsfeld promoted.

In Swabian Austria, as in the Electorate of Trier, one finds that the witches' Sabbath could be dispersed by the mere invocation of God's name. The mention of God's name functioned by its own power, entirely in the sense of popular church magic. As a magical word, it was efficacious independently of the speaker's intent. The sound of church bells had a similar effect. When bells could be heard ringing, the Sabbath was cut short. The witches in the Electorate even had their own expression for the ringing of the bells: "The dogs are barking." The banishment of demons and the storms they caused through the sound of bells belonged to the essential elements of religiously influenced popular beliefs. The ringing of bells was the only defense against witchcraft from popular belief that Binsfeld granted validity. Binsfeld's argument was so clearly distanced from popular beliefs that it almost seems to have had its roots in the Enlightenment: Church bells banish witches not simply because they are blessed, but because their sound focuses the thoughts of all who hear them on God. Thunderstorms are driven off by the bells because their movement ripples through the air and thus influence the "meterologica." Storm-ringing was forbidden in the Electorate of Trier in 1782. Emperor Joseph II decreed a corresponding prohibition for all Habsburg provinces in 1783.[85]

In both territories, people believed that blessed objects could ward off witches: holy water and blessed salt but, in the Electorate, also blessed candles and the Agnus Dei, a blessed wax medallion that was worn as an amulet around the neck or placed under the pillow. Not only did the church endorse these objects as means of protection, but they were also integrated into the system of popular beliefs.[86] The use of the Agnus Dei shows that we should not interpret church magic as part of popular or elite culture. Instead, we should analyze it as an integrative factor that extended beyond any one social class. Even Archbishop Johann VII wore such an amulet expressly to ward against witches.[87] We should not characterize the magic of popular religious beliefs as a means of initiating or spreading witch fears; the elaborated witch concept had long since been received, and the trials had begun. Indirect confirmation was no longer necessary.

In both regions, blessing was not only a "cure" for harmful magic but, most important, a common preventative method for protection against witches. At the same time, blessing is the best example of the ambiguity of church magic. Of course, blessing originated within the traditional ritual inventory of the church. In addition, there were many popular blessing formulas that employed liturgical language but that church leaders rejected as unorthodox and superstitious. Blessing was an ordinary, unspectacular practice. In both territories, the efficacy of protective blessings was assumed to vary.[88]

In the immediate vicinity of the Swabian Landvogtei lay the abbey of Weingarten, with the most significant pilgrimage site and the most important processions in the whole region. Weingarten's status was due to the reliquary kept there that, according to a legend related to the story of the Holy Grail, held blood from the wound in Christ's side. The cult of the Holy Blood underwent a twofold shift during the Middle Ages. In accordance with the Eucharistic connection between blood and wine, the monastery established a ritual relation between the reliquary of the Holy Blood and wine. The monks offered pilgrims wine in which they had immersed the reliquary. The wine thus took on the character of a relic of the second order: a quasi-artificial relic created by contact with the original relic. This may suggest a direct identification of the wine with the blood, although consecrated wine in particular was not mentioned. Differentiating between the blood of the human Jesus, Christ's blood as transubstantiated communion wine, and the wine as a relic of the second order was surely difficult for the laity. The Weingarten monks still bless wine with the reliquary today. In particular, the adoration of the Holy Blood was believed to guarantee good wine harvests.

The second focus of the Holy Blood tradition and the central ritual of the Weingarten relic cult was then, and still is today, the "Blutritt," or blood ride, a mounted procession in which the reliquary of the Holy Blood is carried. There is evidence of the Blutritt from 1529, but it may have had its origins as early as the eleventh century. From the beginning, the Blutritt was associated with a prayer for good weather. It contained all the characteristics of a weather procession, and it took place between planting and harvest. A priest blessed the fields with the relic and prayed for protection from hail and storms. The reliquary of the Holy Blood could be replaced with a Caravaca cross. Caravaca crosses, with double crossbars and frequently with characters and abbreviated blessings, were carried or kept in houses as protection against storms. Post-Tridentine Catholicism restricted weather processions in other places, but with the permission of the bishop, the abbey was able to promote the continuation of the popular and publicly effective Blutritt and its tradition of miracles and blessings as a demonstration of the Catholic Church's possession of the power of miracles as well as its control over the masses. In the context of denominational strife in the German southwest, the procession thus had political implications.[89]

Apart from the Blutritt, the monks held numerous other processions of the Holy Blood throughout the year, which one can consider weather processions. During bad weather, ad hoc processions and blessings also took place. In 1597, no fewer than ten such processions were held. The pilgrimage propaganda unabashedly preached a cause-and-effect relation between participation in the Weingarten rites and bountiful harvests. God would punish any neglect of the reliquary cult with damage from storms and failed crops. The pilgrimage literature even presented a Habsburg official as one of the guarantors of the Weingarten miracles.[90]

Weingarten dispensed a great many amulets. The monastery chiefly offered St. Benedict medallions and crosses, as well as St. Zacharias medallions and crosses.[91] These objects were "religious amulets" that as a rule were

Modern St. Benedict medallion. St. Benedict medallions were supposed to ward off weather damage and witches. The Weingarten monastery still sells St. Benedict medallions very like those of the early modern period.

intended to protect their wearers from all manner of evil, without further elaboration. Such amulets were well known. Benedict medallions were an integral part of the self-presentation of Benedictine monasticism. In Weingarten, these medallions and protective crosses appeared at the latest under Abbot Georg Wegelin (1587–1627). Other metal pendants, with the image of the reliquary, may have belonged to the earliest period of the relic cult. The Weingarten amulets were said to offer protection specifically against crop-destroying storms. Accordingly, they were usually buried in the fields, not worn on one's person, as was customary with religious protective symbols. Far from distancing itself from such practices as "superstitious," the Weingarten pilgrimage propaganda was still emphatically recommending them as late as 1735. The thinking thus advocated was so unorthodox and magical that some pilgrims from distant Catholic territories who buried the medallion in their fields found themselves accused of witchcraft.[92] In the second half of the sixteenth century, prayer tablets and pilgrim images appeared with the depiction of Weingarten motifs, blessings, and prayers against storm damage. No other church institution in either of the territories under investigation offered as complex weather a cult as did Weingarten. Naturally, the abbey of Weingarten received part of its income from the sale of the various church magical items that drew on the Holy Blood reliquary. In this respect, the abbey also had a material interest in propagating traditional religious methods for the defense against evil.[93]

In the Weingarten relic cult of the Holy Blood, a system of magical influence over the weather was created and endowed with the authority of the church. The idea that the weather could be positively influenced through participation in the rite of the Holy Blood became part of the religious-magical worldview of ordinary people. In the same way, people believed that, should the rites be abandoned, they would suffer divine punishment through storms. Thus, a self-affirming magical system was established that provided avenues for expressing needs and interpreting current events. The distinctiveness of Weingarten consisted in its emphasis on wine and weather.

Belief in witches did not destroy this system, which was based on medieval Catholic folk beliefs. The populace of both Swabian Austria and the Electorate of Trier frequently interpreted storm damage, particularly to vineyards, as witchcraft. This idea promoted the witch trials. Weingarten integrated witches into its array of protections for the (wine) harvest. Medallions or crosses blessed in the name of St. Benedict or St. Zacharias were said to ward off demons and especially witches.[94] A Weingarten prayer tablet with an image of these amulets said that they were reliable against witchcraft and would keep witches away. In 1735, a printed collection of reports about the miracles of Weingarten presented in a prominent position examples of wondrous assistance to man and beast against "the enchantments of evil people." As late as 1778, Weingarten prints still listed aid against witchcraft as one of the most important "miraculous powers" of the Holy Blood.[95]

The most impressive evidence of the self-promotion of Weingarten as a pilgrimage site against witchcraft is the ceiling fresco in the abbey church dedicated in 1724. Cosmas Damian Asam painted the apotheosis of St. Benedict in the central dome. This subject was naturally well suited to the self-expression of the Benedictine monastery of Weingarten. At the lower edge of the picture, Satan and the personifications of pestilence and the worldly ("Lady World") are plummeting down. Alongside, a witch is flying on a pitchfork, followed by a bat. As with the falling figures, the witch appears to want to flee out of the image. With one hand she covers her face protectively. Diagonally above the witch, two angels appear in the fresco, one wielding a St. Benedict cross, and the other a St. Zacharias medallion. Light shines from both objects. Clearly, the witch is fleeing from the amulets. As her symbol, the bat, shuns the light of day, so the witch shuns the light of the St. Zacharias medallion and St. Benedict cross.[96] Asam's picture had to conform closely to the abbot's wishes, so one can see it as pilgrimage propaganda. This late painting, created many years after the end of most witch trials in the region, was a conservative renewal and perpetuation of the witch concept. However, it called on the Weingarten tradition to employ only church magic against witches.

The fear of storm damage, particular to vineyards, was one of the most fundamental concerns of ordinary people driving the witch trials in Swabian Austria and the Electorate of Trier. One function of the trials was to

Cosmas Damian Asam. Apotheosis of St. Benedict, church of the Weingarten monastery. The witch, presented as a robust peasant woman flying on a pitchfork, flees from the amulets the angels wield.

prevent such damage in the future. Witch trials accomplished this by identifying and executing the responsible people through a criminal trial. The Holy Blood relic cult of Weingarten filled exactly the same functions—defense against witchcraft, prevention of storm damage, and protection of the (wine) harvest—within the framework of Catholic popular belief. In this case, the positive identification of the guilty was not necessary. The interpretation of good and poor wine harvests as a function of the proper performance of the Holy Blood rites thus created an alternative to understanding the failure of the harvest as a result of witchcraft. One of the sources of witch fears was thus dealt with differently. The cult nipped the demand for witch hunts in the bud. The secular government did not oppose this trend. Indeed, Habsburg officials supported the Weingarten cult and participated actively in it.[97]

In Rottenburg and Horb, confraternities of St. Urban existed that were more than simply associations of the winegrowers in honor of their patron saint. In the sixteenth and seventeenth centuries, the winegrowers sponsored processions through the vineyards on St. Urban's day as a means of praying for a good harvest. A magical ritual was also available that could be carried out ad hoc in reaction to the immediate threat of storm damage. The winegrowers showered a statue of St. Urban with water when hail or storms threatened to remind the saint of his duty to provide protection. This ritual of the Rottenburg winegrowers had no parallel in the Electorate of Trier or the rest of Swabian Austria, but similar practices are known from other regions.[98] Persistent crop failures, however, shook faith in the ritual of St. Urban in Hohenberg at the end of the sixteenth century, and Horb's Sheriff Johann Veser expressed his scornful distrust of the ceremony in 1599. After such crop losses, he said, "St. Urban [should be] drowned and the winegrowers hanged."[99] Veser was certainly not a representative of post-Tridentine purified Catholicism. Neither could nearby Protestant Württemberg have had a negative influence on the Catholic ritual, for even in Württemberg such practices were only slowly being repressed.[100] Veser's rejection of the St. Urban ritual was based exclusively on its lack of efficacy. Sheriff Veser, who here expressed himself so vehemently against traditional popular beliefs, was one of the most aggressive witch hunters of Swabian Austria in following years. Of course, that is not the whole story: His superiors compelled Veser to rescind his criticism, which had been perceived as abuse of the saint. Veser's derogatory comments were not the trigger for the Hohenberg witch trials, for these had long since begun. And they did not mark the moment when the winegrowers joined the ranks of active proponents of witch hunting. Rather, Hohenberg winegrowers were emphatic supporters of the witch hunts from the beginning. Crop failures heavily damaged winegrowers, and so they were supporters both of traditional religious protective magic and of the witch trials. These systems co-existed, but they also competed. Veser used the authority of his sheriff's office to demand an end to the St. Urban ritual. When he succeeded, the most striking, damage-specific alternative to witch trials disappeared from the public sphere, and criminal prosecution became accepted as the *only* appropriate response to storm damage.

Religious authorities in the region of Trier regularly denied the efficacy of church magic against witchcraft. A few unusually rich sources from the early period of the witch hunts in this region make it possible to observe how advocates of the witch hunts used aspects of daily religious life involving contact between lay and clergy to provoke the populace to pursue witches. In early 1488, the residents of Ediger parish requested the granting of indulgences for visitors to the stations of the cross that they had recently erected.[101] The parish noted in the request that the stations were to be used primarily for prayers for a successful harvest. The parish directed its written request to a papal legate who just happened to be in the Electorate at that time: the inquisitor Heinrich Kramer. Kramer complied with the community's request. In so doing, however, he added a new element: Indulgences would be granted only to those who prayed for protection from "the harmful works of the witches . . . the attacks of traitors and witches." Kramer explicitly constituted the indulgences at the Ediger stations of the cross in accordance with his inquisitorial responsibility to eradicate witches. In so doing, he re-dedicated the stations as a site for prayers against witchcraft.[102]

An initial difference from Weingarten consisted in the fact that Kramer spoke as an inquisitor. It might seem that Kramer was recommending a ritual defense against witches analogous to that of Weingarten, but he made it un-mistakably clear in the document that this could only be a secondary mode of defense against witchcraft. The pope's wish and Kramer's explicit assignment was the eradication of the witches. A year after the appearance of his *Malleus Maleficarum* in 1486, Kramer was using the construction of these stations of the cross to promulgate the newly elaborate witch doctrine, contrary to the intentions of the populace—and, quite possibly, to their surprise. Kramer's position on the Ediger case fully reflected the concerns that he had pursued in the *Malleus*.[103] The intention of that work was clearly to have witches pros-ecuted by ecclesiastical and especially secular courts; the entire third book consisted of specific directives for trial proceedings. Kramer's scrupulous investigation of the orthodoxy of popular religious defenses against magic received far less room in the text and reads more as a rejection of false prac-tices than as a recommendation of orthodox ones.

The Eberhardsklausen monastery showed similar tendencies at the be-ginning of the sixteenth century.[104] Here we find one of the greatest dissemi-nation points of the new witch doctrine in the Moselle area and insight into the history of the impact of the *Malleus* and Nider's *Formicarius.* The Eber-hardsklausen chronicler, the priest and monk Wilhelm of Bernkastel, had read both of these works and had adopted their belief in the threat of witches, with all of its consequences. Around 1510, Wilhelm wrote about parents who frequently sought him out because they suffered guilt over the death of a child. They reproached themselves for neglect, apparently because they had failed to employ the protections of church magic. They sought comfort and absolution from the confessor Wilhelm and, possibly, a special prayer or blessed object to protect their families in the future. Instead, Wilhelm offered them a demonological lesson that turned the situation entirely around and placed it outside the conventional religious framework: their children had been killed by witches. He even succeeded in helping the bereaved identify specific suspects.[105] These parents were not relieved of their guilt through prayer and penance. Instead, Wilhelm helped them project their guilt onto a third party. The resolution called for by the church authority was thus no

longer a traditional penance, the humble surrender to God's will, or the recommendation of a bit of church magic, but instead a secular criminal trial. It
is probable that Wilhelm and the monks around him spread similar ideas in
their sermons. The most obvious and necessary measure against witchcraft
was not a prayerful visit to Eberhardsklausen, church magic, and the hope of
a miracle from a merciful God. Wilhelm clearly called for the judicial prosecution of witches. His uncritical reception of demonology had suggested
this mode of action to him. In addition, and perhaps more important, the
use of criminal trials as a defense against witchcraft followed from the logic
of Wilhelm's argument. In light of the immediate threat from the power of
the Devil that he described, traditional religious interpretations and protections against evil could no longer suffice. Wilhelm threatened with God's
wrath any authorities who did not become involved in the battle against the
witch sect.[106]

During the period of reorientation from a belief in miracles and church
magic to the use of trials against witchcraft, transitional phenomena occurred that can no longer be observed in the later period. They were important to the initial acceptance of the witch trials as a course of action. Wilhelm mentioned two cases of innocent persons who had been imprisoned for
witchcraft in neighboring territories in 1451 and 1501 but were miraculously
freed.[107] With this, Wilhelm criticized hesitant authorities with an argument
that would later become a central axiom of demonology: one could proceed
against suspects ruthlessly, because God would not allow the innocent to be
condemned.[108]

In the sixteenth century, parish "hail festival" processions took place in
the Trier region that included prayers for the protection of crops from hail
and other storm damage. The decisive difference from the Weingarten cult
consisted in the fact that the hail festivals of the Moselle region were always
merely local festivals held by individual parishes. These hail festivals lacked
church recognition or affiliation with a regional institution, so regionally
important cults could not develop. The hail festival processions remained
strictly local phenomena, parochial in every sense. Other damage-warding
rituals, supported and propagated by church authorities, had degenerated
into ad hoc measures. They did not offer a viable alternative to a witchcraft
trial.[109] After Urban VIII had endeavored to limit and standardize festivals
with his 1642 bull "Universa," the archdiocese of Trier even tried to forbid
hail processions in 1678. But the populace of the Electorate opposed the restrictive position of their archbishop and clamored for weather processions.
The hail festivals only disappeared in the 1730s, presumably because the

Jesuit-supported cult of St. Donatus offered an alternative. In Weingarten, as we have seen, the papal bull remained unheeded.[110]

The discussion of church magic in the Electorate of Trier would be incomplete without a treatment of its most decided opponent, Suffragan Bishop Peter Binsfeld. Stricter even than Kramer, he described at length the magical rituals that he rejected, yet avoided giving positive examples of "orthodox" means of warding off disaster, examples compatible with post-Tridentine doctrine. He named only the sacraments as God-given sources of supernatural power.[111]

Binsfeld had a starkly different view from that of Weingarten—or, at least, that of the bishops of Constance, who were at that time uninterested in witch trials.[112] During the peak of the witch hunts in the Electorate, priests had to reckon with the scholarly authority of Binsfeld and his real power as vicar-general in their administration of religious protective charms. The suffragan's early practical activities with the implementation of the Catholic Reformation and his proceeding against Cornelius Loos demonstrate that he rigorously defended his position, and not just in scholarly discussions.[113]

Naturally, not all clerics in the archdiocese or in the Electorate of Trier shared Binsfeld's fundamentalist attack on popular abuses. It is striking that in Trier, the Jesuits—the education and reform order—promoted the efficacy of holy water and religious amulets, especially the Agnus Dei, against witches and demons. We should see this as more than just Counter-Reformation populism. Descriptions of the efficacy of prayer, confession, and church magic as protections against witchcraft and the predations of demons are a salient feature in the reports from Trier and Coblenz in the *Annuae litterae* of the years between 1585 and 1601, when so many witch trials took place. In the annual reports of 1590 and 1591, the Jesuits of the Electorate emphasized as one of their most important activities their travels through the countryside handing out a great number of Agnus Dei amulets.[114] The position of the Society of Jesus in the Electorate on witch hunts was ambivalent: From a 1589 letter of the general of the order in Rome, Aquaviva, it appears that the Trier Jesuits were pushing for witch trials. The Coblenz branch of the order distanced itself from them on this account. At the very least, the order must have become critical of mass witchcraft trials, or of the popular pressure for witch hunts, because denunciations of Jesuits and other clerics began to accumulate at the end of the 1580s.[115] At any rate, with their propaganda for traditional forms of church magic, the Jesuits promulgated an interpretation completely different from that of Binsfeld—one that implicitly contradicted him. Although a short obituary for Binsfeld in the annual report of 1598 referred to the suffragan as the "most loving patron" of the Trier Jesuit college, the *Annuae litterae* never mentioned his witchcraft treatise or his condemnation of Loos. Had the Jesuits recognized that they could reduce the popular demand for witch hunts by offering, in the form of popular piety, an outlet for witch fears other than criminal proceedings? Recent attempts to denounce the Jesuits once again as "propagandists" of the witch hunts are unconvincing because they condemn the order all too eagerly.[116]

MAGIC AND WITCH TRIALS: CONDITIONS AND CONSEQUENCES OF AN ALTERNATIVE

Keith Thomas has suggested that popular piety, with its diverse warding and protective rituals, offered a real alternative to witch trials. Thomas locates the shift to majority-supported mass witch hunts at the moment when the church renounced its popular magical inventory.[117] In different contexts, this renunciation might be the fruit of the Reformation or the Counter-Reformation, but also of the Catholic reform movement of the fifteenth century. The effect in any case remains the same. The populace was robbed of church magical protections against harm, whether from witches or from disasters that arose without agents. Of course, this was only a general trend that was locally realized at various rates and with varying severity. Neither the new Protestant denominations nor the old Catholic faith managed to eliminate the popular belief in church magic entirely. Nonetheless, an inventory of rituals for warding off disaster that the church had previously recommended, or at least tolerated, became so discredited that it was no longer available. The defense against witchcraft therefore became a battle against witches before the criminal courts. We can observe this development both in Hohenberg and in the Electorate of Trier. In the Swabian Landvogtei, however, the strong abbey of Weingarten worked against this trend. Witch hunts remained relatively rare anomalies in the Landvogtei and surrounding areas, while in Hohenberg and the Electorate of Trier the climate was perfect for the worst witch hunts.

The sources do not reveal a categorical dichotomy of church magic and witch trials as alternatives. The two systems co-existed and had shared elements, yet they also competed. Bronislaw Malinowski and John Beattie have argued that the investigation of the efficacy of magical acts is fundamentally foreign to magical thought. The desired effect is secondary; its absence can always be traced back to some erroneous execution of the ritual, thus confirming the system. For magical thought in general this may be correct. In actual practice, however, when multiple alternative means exist, we can certainly imagine that a technique that has repeatedly failed would be abandoned for another.[118] Whether it is a matter of a multiplicity of alternative magical techniques or of magical techniques in competition with non-magical ones is basically immaterial. Heinrich Kramer, Wilhelm of Bernkastel, Peter Binsfeld, and Sheriff Veser all strove to convince the populace that witch trials were the only effective measure against magical threats. So here we can expand Thomas's concept of the active role of ordinary people. Whether peasants and townspeople sought protection through the practices of folk beliefs or through criminal prosecution of witches was not merely a question of the choice made available by the church but also of the dynamically changeable acceptance of this choice by the populace.

If we accept a concern for efficacy as a part of early modern magical thought, we can see an explanation for the periodic ebb of the witch hunts. Of course, witch trials could not improve a strained social and economic situation. After some years, people must have turned away from witch hunting in disappointment. This experience may have contributed to the end of the great wave of trials in 1596 in the Electorate of Trier, or at least to the cessation of later intense persecution in Hohenberg in 1649.

Until this point we have silently assumed, as did Thomas, that religious protective magic can be considered parallel to witch trials. That they could functionally replace each other is questionable, however, as they were alternative actions from highly different realms: politically and jurisdictionally organized justice and administration on the one hand, and ideas and practices of popular beliefs rejected by some authorities and the church on the other. This contrast loses its clarity, however, if we consider the grounding of the early modern criminal-justice system in theology and popular belief. Schnabel-Schüle has shown that in the early modern period, "the system of penal sanctions had its ideational anchor in the figure of a punishing God."[119] Every breach of norms offended the divine order of the world. The wrath of God could be directed against the corrupt commonwealth in the form of storms, failed harvests, and plagues. To avoid such divine punishment, any violation of norms had to be avenged. Pressing for the punishment of a lawbreaker stemmed from a fear of God's wrath. The territorial sovereign guaranteed the equitable punishment of the delinquent and thus the accomplishment of God's will. This idea strengthened the authority of the territorial lord tremendously. Because they transgressed directly against God, witches in particular had to be punished with the utmost severity if one wished to escape the wrath of God.[120] In this way, the sphere of the divine (or diabolical) was supposed to be so influenced through the practice of criminal justice that this sphere retroacted in the desired manner on the visible world of ordinary life.

In this context it becomes clear how the concept of the Württemberg orthodoxy on witchcraft might function to inhibit persecution.[121] Proceeding from older religious interpretations, the Reformation preacher Johannes Brenz understood the work of witches as God's punishment for human sins, a punishment that was only indirectly realized through demons and men. From this he deduced that the proper response to harmful magic, especially storm damage, was not witch trials but individual prayer, contrition, penance, and reform. Pointedly, we could say that this was the Protestant alternative to Catholic Weingarten's response to the threat of disaster. Both solutions clearly worked against witch trials; they pointed away from legal persecution toward exercises of piety.

Witch trials attempted to influence an imaginary supernatural realm in a very immediate manner to effect consequences for society. According to demonology, the Devil remained forever dependent on the voluntary cooperation of people, the witches, in order to intervene in the ordinary world with harmful magic. This concept was known to proponents of witch hunting in the villages and rural towns of our territories.[122] If the authorities captured witches and executed them, the Devil had his tools taken from his hands. Unlike the rest of criminal justice, witch trials thus acted directly on the demonic sphere to accomplish an effect in the ordinary world. To this degree, witch trials actually could replace protective charms and counter magic. The witch trial was an administrative and judicial act that showed magical properties. One could even say that the witch trial was magic.[123] As a witch trial was nevertheless even more likely than the rest of criminal justice to suppress private and extrajudicial efforts to solve problems and resolve conflicts, this quasi-magical quality was the source of its extraordinary danger.

3

"If She Is Not a Witch Yet, She Will Certainly Become One"

Origins and Foundations of Witchcraft Suspicions

In June 1590, peasants from the villages of Obernau and Wendelsheim brought petitions to the vicegerent of Rottenburg, Christoph Wendler von Bergenroth. In the petitions, they asked him to have the noblewoman Agatha von Sontheim, who resided in the knightly territory of Nellingsheim, bordering Hohenberg, arrested for witchcraft. The peasants had held a meeting of the whole community, including the women, in which they had discussed and drafted the petition. A wide variety of circumstantial evidence supported their suspicions. Agatha von Sontheim was able to predict storms with precision. The peasants interpreted the reliability of her "weather forecasts" entirely negatively and saw them as implicit confessions of having used weather magic. Agatha's servants claimed to have overheard their mistress having sexual intercourse when she was alone in a closed room. Agatha threatened that she could cause harm to the peasants of the surrounding area from a hundred miles away. The petition also listed incidents of the noblewoman's life that at first glance do not seem like incriminating elements or indications of witchcraft. Agatha von Sontheim had introduced new taxes that people found unjust. Tensions were worsening between her and her peasants. Agatha had said that she hoped for crop failures and prayed for hailstorms so that the resulting shortage would inflate the price of grain. There is no reason to doubt the authenticity of these statements, given that peasants of different villages related them consistently and the accused herself repeated them after her arrest. Agatha knew that she was reputed to be a witch. When she and her aristocratic guests ran out of bread at a feast on her estate, she said ironically, "We could also eat like witches for once," reflecting the common belief that the witches' banquet lacked bread and salt.[1]

Here we gain direct insight into rural notions of witches and the circumstances surrounding the generation of witchcraft suspicions. The petitions touched on three motors of suspicion: first, individual events and the actions of the alleged witch; second, comments she made in response to suspicions; and third, long-term living conditions of the suspect and her relationship with her social environment. The aim of the following pages is to describe the genesis of witchcraft suspicions in Swabian Austria and the Electorate of Trier by examining these three elements. From the preceding it seems that certain activities did not so much create witchcraft suspicions as corroborate suspicions that already existed. Accordingly, we need to seek the primary sources of suspicion in the context of long-term tensions, social situations, and basic personal attitudes, whereas specific events and activities functioned only as secondary, corroborating factors in the emergence of witchcraft suspicions.[2] This analysis will start with an examination of secondary factors but will then expand its focus gradually to the underlying social structures that provided the foundations of suspicion.

Secondary Factors: Events

The *Carolina* identified certain actions as *indicia* (incriminating evidence) of sorcery. Among them were offering to teach others how to perform magic, threatening harmful magic that actually corresponded to damage that occurred some time later, and "using suspect objects, gestures, words and ways . . . that seem magical."[3] During the witch hunts in Swabian Austria and the Electorate of Trier, which were largely conducted by the townsmen and villagers, particular acts did assume the character of circumstantial evidence. These were not, however, necessarily clear instances of magic like those stated in the imperial law.

In both the Electorate of Trier and Swabian Austria, showing up unexpectedly or without a clear reason in another's house or barn triggered suspicions of witchcraft. Accusers and witnesses for the prosecution did not claim that the witch had entered the house or barn in a magical fashion. Her unexpected and unwelcome appearance itself aroused suspicion. Here, the practical concern for material property and security within the closed space of one's house and barn plainly combined with a mentalité that considered this area as intimately vulnerable. The invasion of this sheltered room of the home—a magical space—was seen as an act of aggression.[4]

The sudden appearance of a witch in a place where she was not expected was, in both regions, the most frequent form of inappropriate behavior to arouse the suspicion of witchcraft. It seems actively to have triggered suspicions even if there were no pre-existing rumors of witchcraft. If—regardless of the causes for it—a suspicion had already emerged and had spread through rumor, any extraordinary behavior could confirm it. An extreme example is that of a woman who dramatically strengthened rumors of witchcraft against herself because she wanted to do some shopping even as a massive fire was raging in the village around her. She was executed in a shared domain of the Electorate in 1583.[5]

As a rule, however, the activities that aroused witchcraft suspicions were far less conspicuous. If a suspect stared into empty space or seemed to converse with someone despite being alone, witnesses might interpret this as contact with invisible demons. Spending a night outside without a plausible justification, being outdoors just before or during a storm, a sudden disappearance, asking for fire at a neighbor's in the middle of the night, sketching crosses onto the floor with one's foot, loud howling or crying without any discernible reason, even sleeping in a strange posture: witch-trial testimony in both territories mentioned all of these acts as unusual and suspicious behavior.[6]

Once someone was suspected of witchcraft, the most banal "events" of everyday life became notable and worth mentioning. People believed that one might see demons in animal form in the vicinity of suspected witches. One might remember for years the ravens that had circled around the house of a suspect or the owl that had come to a witch through her window. Villagers took seriously the fact that a hare had shown itself during the bridal procession of a suspect woman and saw it as the appearance of her demon lover.[7] Although the modern reader finds common clichés of romantic witch stories and fairy tales confirmed here, to contemporaries these "events" were in themselves only tiny marginal notes in daily life.

What role did deviant religious behavior play in witchcraft suspicions? Binsfeld insisted that a lack of religious instruction was one of the "causes that direct a person to sorcery." In 1590, Archbishop Johann justified the intensification of catechetical instruction by citing the many witches who had confessed that they would not have formed a pact with the Devil had they only been taught as children to understand religious doctrine.[8]

In general, however, ordinary people did not pay close attention to religious behavior. Fast breaking was noted among the motives for suspicion only once.[9] In neither of the two regions under study is there evidence of a link between the witch hunts and Counter-Reformation measures, either against

Lutherans or against Anabaptists. In Hohenberg, heresy trials against Anabaptists had taken place in 1527-29,[10] but it does not make sense to assume that witchcraft accusations were being used as a way to take action against members of other denominations. Such an affiliation was punishable in itself, and the authorities needed no other offense to prosecute confessional dissenters. In a few isolated cases in Swabian Austria, people suspected of witchcraft were also called heretics, as in the case of a "Lutheran witch" in Altdorf in 1643. In his trial, Diederich Flade confessed to holding heretical ideas. But if he actually did, he had never mentioned them before. In the bill of indictment against Agatha von Sontheim, there is no mention of the fact that she had recently introduced the Reformation in her domain. Clearly, confessionalism and confessional strife were not elements of social life closely linked to suspicions of witchcraft. On the one hand, this was probably due to the proximity of other territories with long-established Lutheranism or Calvinism—for example, Württemberg, the County of Nassau-Saarbrücken, or the Palatinate. On the other hand, as we have seen, both Swabian Austria and the Electorate of Trier lacked the element of heretical assembly in their portrayal of the witches' Sabbath. As far as religious practice went, only grossly extraordinary behavior aroused suspicions of witchcraft, as, for example, when a woman in Burgau took the host out of her mouth after receiving the sacrament in 1599.[11]

In most cases, no one in either territory practiced the clearly magical actions that the *Carolina* considered incriminating evidence of witchcraft. Obvious magical acts did not immediately generate most witchcraft suspicions, but any deviation from the normal, even a most unspectacular one, did so. The socially vigilant rural community paid close attention to such actions. Among other things, intensive witch hunts occurred in both territories because of violations of village norms. Contrary to the law, moreover, unusual events were accepted as incriminating evidence in court.

Beyond extraordinary events and inappropriate behavior, any talk about witchcraft was apt to provoke suspicions. Contemporaries evaluated every comment as incriminating evidence if it seemed to imply some knowledge about the secret activities of witches. In the trial of Diederich Inich in Mayen in 1590, several witnesses reported an event they considered substantially incriminating. When Inich and some peasants were in a tavern discussing whether priests could forgive sins, the subject of the Tannhäuser legend arose among the assembled drinkers. One of the peasants said he had heard that it was supposed to be bright and light inside the Venus Mountain, the magical subterranean abode of Lady Venus where the knight Tannhäuser had supposedly dwelt. To the utter surprise of everyone present, Inich answered nonchalantly that one could hardly see anything inside the Venus Mountain as it was full of fire and steam. Then he drew the Venus Mountain on the table with chalk, claiming that it was near Naples and was guarded by an army of the emperor. Even though he said so, no one believed that Inich had merely heard all this from an itinerant mercenary. Anyone who could describe something so precisely must have seen it himself. Within a short time, Inich found himself in court as the defendant in a witch trial. It was not necessary to utter threats to arouse suspicion of witchcraft. Even if someone merely speculated about a threatening misfortune—such as a thunderstorm—that later took place, the courts were willing to consider this an indirect confession of having caused it.[12]

In Swabian Austria and the Electorate of Trier, if a person admitted to having expected to be formally accused, this was considered confirmation of the witchcraft suspicion.[13] Occasionally, suspects attempted to respond to slander by addressing it ironically. Contrary to the suspect's clear intentions, however, witnesses and judges never interpreted this as mockery and denial; they interpreted it as a confession and confirmation. The hearer not only filtered out whatever did not match preconceived assessments; with intellectual effort, even declarations of innocence could be turned into their opposite. In 1652, when a witchcraft suspect from the Electorate's shared domain of Mensfelden complained about the stress of having to work during the day while being a witch piper by night, this was taken as a confession. Even the crude joke of a suspect who claimed to have recognized a mysterious stranger as a demon by the infernal smell of his flatulence was recorded by the court as an implicit confession in a bill of indictment in Wittlich in 1629.[14] Witch hunters interpreted every comment of an alleged witch—often contrary to its unambiguous intention—as a confirmation of the suspicion and passed it on as significant. The alleged witch was often the victim of a conversation that masqueraded as real communication but actually served another purpose. She was admitted formally as a communicant, but the intent of her testimony was ignored. Witnesses interpreted all of the suspect's statements—corresponding to semantic convention but contrary to its logic in content and context—only as confirmation of earlier suspicions. Following Habermas, we can see this as an aggressive form of systematically distorted communication in which goal-oriented communicative action is disguised as communication-oriented.[15]

Yet judges and witnesses considered ignoring defamatory accusations of witchcraft as an indirect confession, too. This was of absolutely central importance to the corroboration and propagation of witchcraft suspicions. Most of the trial records from Swabian Austria and the Electorate of Trier repeated the stereotype that the person who simply accepted an accusation must be guilty. Witchcraft slander was a massive insult to the honor of the accused. Anyone who was not provoked to self-defense in such a case implicitly admitted that defense was impossible—that is, that the accusation was true. This was especially true for witchcraft suspects among the elite. The general sensitivity to witchcraft slander can also be seen from a list of fines in the shared domain of Mensfelden, which in 1618 suggested a fine of two florins for knocking someone down but a fine of six florins for calling a married woman a witch.[16]

A proper defense against the accusation of being a witch had to take place in court in the form of a libel suit against the accuser. The opposition of judicial and extra-judicial was of crucial importance. The extra-judicial communication of a witchcraft suspicion demanded that the slandered defend herself in court.[17] The slandered actively had to create distance between the judicial authority as an examining and deciding body and the defamatory communication. Judicial events had to be kept above the extra-judicial. Neither in the Electorate nor in Swabian Austria was a libel suit ever transformed into a witch trial such that the one who had brought charges of defamation found herself as the accused in a trial for magic. Why did so few suspects seize this possibility to confront the suspicion of witchcraft? Some must have doubted the efficacy of a slander trial. Moreover, the fact that suspicions of witchcraft circulated as rumors stood in the way of a slander suit. It was often difficult to identify any single person as the slanderer. Defamed persons who were socially superior to their accusers might consider a slander suit beneath their dignity.[18] On the one hand, confronting slanderers might not have seemed worth the trouble. But on the other hand, such a confrontation might be feared since it directed attention to the rumors of witchcraft. Many suspects believed that they could pretend the defamation had never happened. They failed to recognize that they thereby launched the mechanism of paradoxical communication—that is, that a rumor was confirmed by the obvious effort to keep it secret or to prove it false.[19]

PRIMARY FACTORS: EVERYDAY CONFLICTS AND STRUCTURAL CONFLICTS

In many cases, it is apparent that other tensions and conflicts aside from the witchcraft accusation strained the relations between the suspects and their

neighbors or relatives. The comparison of European and non-European beliefs in magic has directed the attention of witch research to exactly this area.
Ethnologists have mainly been interested in the strained social structures
that surrounded witchcraft suspicions. In the witch trials of the northwest-
ern German County of Lippe, Rainer Walz has been able to apply conflict
models from ethnological research as contexts for witchcraft accusations.[20]

Over and over again in Swabian Austria and the Electorate of Trier, witchcraft accusations grew from disputes that were initially quite ordinary. These
mostly personal conflicts might simmer for a long time before appearing in
the records. Occasionally, judicial officials provided information concerning
the pugnacious character of certain defendants. The conflicts behind charges
of witchcraft could be quite diverse. For example, Michel from Kommlingen
in the district of Saarburg had quarreled with the wife of Hans Hanf for a long
time. Michel had hurt the Hanfs' son, and Hanf's wife had called Michel a
thief. Furthermore, she was said to have threatened to harm Michel. When
one of Michel's horses died in 1589, he publicly accused Hanf's wife as a witch
and said that he would prove his accusation in court.[21]

In both territories, suspects were slandered by their spouses and relatives time and again. Frequently, one can discern family disputes in the background. Maria Springaufin from Stockach was considered a troublesome
woman. In 1617, she was accused of witchcraft by her brother and her own
daughter, with whom she had quarreled over an inheritance.[22]

Accusations of witchcraft arose from unspectacular conflicts over property and from ordinary neighborly and family disputes. "Unspectacular" and
"ordinary" do not, of course, mean "irrelevant." The affected people had been
suffering intensely from such disputes and their attendant circumstances,
often for years. The accusers and the witnesses had been experiencing the
defendants in a profoundly negative way.

In the Electorate of Trier and Swabian Austria, peasants and townspeople
frequently suspected the relatives of convicted witches of witchcraft. "Inheritance" through blood kinship was not necessary. Mere affiliation with a suspected family by marriage was enough for the emergence of suspicion. Thus,
the family was understood not as a (blood) kin group but unambiguously as a
social group.[23] Only if we consider that Diederich Inich came from a family of
witches we can understand why a woman could testify in Mayen in 1590 that
she had suspected him for forty years, even though he was only twenty-five
years old. He was suspected not so much as an individual but as a member
of a disreputable family. Dependents of witches were socially shunned and
constantly had to cope with the possibility of charges being brought against

them. This context explains why the rulers of the Electorate of Trier had to insist in 1592 that the children of executed witches should not be excluded from public offices.[24]

Unlike witch families, the incriminating detail that the *Carolina* referred to instead, maintaining contact with witches, hardly played a role in the genesis of suspicion in either of the two regions. It could gain no foothold. As shown earlier, witchcraft suspicions inspired both the strictest social control and wary distance.[25]

In addition, apart from the unspecific economic, neighborly, and family disputes of the sort mentioned earlier, there were specific areas of conflict that contributed to the emergence of a variety of witchcraft suspicions in both regions. These areas of conflict reflected broad fields of tension within society and genuine social problems.

The first one of these zones of social crisis was crime. The suspicion of witchcraft was often directed at criminals. In both territories, some suspects were accused of witchcraft and simultaneously of theft. All the same, the courts and the witnesses do not seem to have suspected that thieves were supplementing their criminal skills with diabolical magic, or even that thieves' folk-magic practices were diabolically inspired. Instead, charges of witchcraft were separate from accusations of theft. In the Electorate, there were analogous combinations of witchcraft accusations with accusations of fraud, counterfeiting, and arson.[26]

In both regions, contemporaries sometimes connected moral deviance and sex offenses such as adultery to witchcraft, as well. They took them as evidence for the depravity of the suspects, and they highlighted them in trials as incriminating elements. In this context, accusations of witchcraft against the "Pfaffenkellerinnen" (women who cooked for Catholic priests and who were often rumored to be their concubines) played a significant role.[27] Plaintiffs and the courts were not merely using accusations of witchcraft as a means of punishing criminals. All of these proceedings could, after all, have been conducted and concluded without the inclusion of the crime of magic.

The role that vagrants and beggars played in witchcraft trials in Swabian Austria was ambivalent. As is broadly verified in other regions, as well, both vagrant and local beggars often came under suspicion of witchcraft.[28] Almost forty years ago, Keith Thomas and Alan Macfarlane showed that the transformation of concepts of poor relief and household economy proved to be a factor in the origin of witch hunting. They argued that because of the adoption of Reformed doctrines of predestination, the pious works of popular Catholicism disappeared from the daily life of rural communities. They claimed that more prosperous peasants no longer accepted the religious duty to provide poor relief, the specific obligation to give alms to the marginal beggars and paupers of the village. According to Thomas and Macfarlane, the tensions that arose from this rather abrupt cessation of alms giving, which was neither expected nor tolerated by the socially weak, became a breeding ground for witchcraft suspicions. Moreover, they argued, this tension was activated in specific conflicts that in many cases directly caused witchcraft accusations. A wealthier peasant projected his guilty conscience onto a disappointed and angry pauper—who in turn might have publicly expressed this disappointment with curses—and then interpreted any subsequent misfortunes as the magical vengeance of the rejected alms seeker. Macfarlane himself later revoked the denominational element of his argument. We can find this Macfarlane-Thomas paradigm, which they derived from regional studies of England, in other areas of Europe, too, even in homogenously Catholic territories.[29]

In the Electorate of Trier and in Swabian Austria, the conflict situation described by Macfarlane played a distinct role. Yet the fear of magical revenge by rejected beggars could also yield a temporary advantage to the poor. In 1589, the cows of the knight von Kesselstatt supposedly got sick after his servants had turned away a begging woman. When she called at Kesselstatt's manor again, she received the alms she wanted. Yet beggars also often appear in confessions and witchcraft accusations in Swabian Austria as the victims of harmful magic.[30] The mistrust and latent fear that the rural populace and the townsfolk directed toward the barely controllable underclass of beggars thus found twofold articulation in witchcraft trials.

Strangers, people who did not yet belong to the village or town community, were also suspected as witches in both territories. A "stranger" was not only a person who had recently moved to the area but anyone who had not been born there. This was the case with the itinerant herdsmen who were executed as witches in the Electorate of Trier and Swabian Austria. Although personally known, they did not belong to the individual settled communities. The peasants observed them closely due to their responsibility for the herds. Peasants saw any serious failure of their herdsman as an instance of deliberate harmful magic. In 1652, people from Münstermaifeld accused a herder who had lost an unusual number of animals of being a werewolf who killed the very livestock he was supposed to look after.[31]

None of the socially problematic groups mentioned here were generally suspected as witches, however. In the descriptions of witches' Sabbaths from the Electorate and Swabian Austria, no one ever mentioned the appearance of groups of vagrants or "Pfaffenkellerinnen." In both territories, blanket suspicions and general denunciations of a whole group were directed exclusively at the "rich," the members of the upper classes.[32]

This was characteristic of the witch hunts in Swabian Austria and the Electorate of Trier: witchcraft *suspicions* were aimed disproportionately at members of the social and economic elite. As shown earlier, it is difficult to determine the extent to which these suspicions resulted in an equivalently high proportion of elite people among actual trial victims. In Swabian Austrian confessions, defendants generally claimed that the "rich" appeared at the Sabbath in disguise. That is why they were personally identified only in the rarest cases. In the Electorate, too, one occasionally finds this topos of the disguised "rich" at the Sabbath,[33] but there, as well as in the surrounding monastic territories, confessions usually identified the witches from the elite by name. Although this difference seems significant, it was of little importance to the trials. In the Electorate, denunciations of members of the elite had to accumulate before the courts brought charges. In Swabian Austria, the result was practically the same. Due to the public reading of confessions, the idea that "rich people" participated in the Sabbath became part of the witch concept in Swabian Austria. The entire elite were thus gradually incorporated into the notion of witchcraft, and social trust broke down. If at some point a defendant identified by name one of the "unknown gentlewomen" at the witches' dance, this denunciation was believable. It was not just credible; it satisfied expectations.

The phenomenon of witchcraft suspicions as an expression of social tensions and distrust among members of different urban strata can be observed in the accusations among the inmates and administrators of the Horb and Rottenburg hospitals. These hospitals (*Spitäler*) were not hospitals in our sense. They housed the well-to-do elderly and served as poor houses at the same time. At first, the hospital administrations of both cities were (rightly) accused of corruption. The transition from the criticism of selfish behavior to witchcraft accusations proceeded without difficulty. Members of the hospital administration fell under suspicion of witchcraft in both cities. The hospitals also reflected the social tensions of the towns. They were places of direct confrontation between different social classes, between "poor" and "special" inmates—that is, between poorhouse residents and affluent elderly pensioners. They were hotbeds of social envy. Status differences within urban society came into view nowhere so clearly as here, where they manifested themselves in separate lodgings and meals and different work requirements. Spatial proximity highlighted and intensified these differences. From

The hospital of Rottenburg. Numerous suspects lived here. The contemporaries saw the hospital as the site of witches' dances, which was wholly atypical given that it was an inhabited building within the city center.

the one side, envy might be expected; from the other, contempt toward the less privileged and an uneasy conscience. The hospital was a microcosm of the town. It was highly prone to controversies and the genesis of rumors. And it was far from being isolated. Since the hospitals, like public houses, offered meals for everybody, they attracted a variety of people day to day. They became centers of local communication. Numerous poor and wealthy hospital residents were accused of witchcraft in Hohenberg. The populace came to see the hospitals as the site of witch dances, which was particularly strange, given that they were inhabited buildings within the town walls. The emphasis on hospital residents was a prevalent feature in urban witchcraft. No evidence can be found in the fragmentary archival sources of Trier, however, that the people of Trier and Coblenz associated their hospitals with the witch hunts. In all, the hospital system was of only minor importance in the Electorate. Alternative poor relief offered by the monasteries mitigated the social situation in the hospitals.[34]

In Swabian Austria and the Electorate of Trier, we can find a fair number of similar or analogous elements that determined the social "image" of witch suspects from the elite. Suspicions of witchcraft fell on members of the upper classes who, in the eyes of the majority, had betrayed the social contract through corruption or especially through aggressive economic behavior. Elite witchcraft suspects had done very well financially during the economic crisis of the 1580s. Sheriff Diederich Flade and the suspected burgomaster Kesten of Trier had sold grain at inflated prices. At the time of his death, Flade had allocated more than 13,000 florins in personal loans of less than one hundred florins each to various citizens of Trier, as well as to peasants and winegrowers of the surrounding villages. He had acquired most of this credit during the crisis of the 1580s. Thus, Flade visibly benefited from the crisis and was reproached everywhere for his antisocial profit mongering; he was "notoriously avaricious." Other witchcraft suspects from the Electorate were also lenders, including one woman. Suspects from the elite had also allegedly used false weights and cheated the poor.[35]

People from the leading families of Swabian Austria who fell under suspicion of witchcraft were accused of ruthless avarice, as well.[36] Agatha von Sontheim not only raised the tax burden on her subjects but even admitted to hoping for crop failures for the sake of an increase in profit, so that "prices rise so much that the child in the womb must die of hunger."[37] Similar to Agatha von Sontheim, the vicegerent of Rottenburg, Christoph Wendler von Bregenroth, raised the feudal work requirements in his fiefdom and introduced new taxes. Wendler's interest in personal gain was notorious. He had come into money rapidly through three conspicuously "favorable" marriages. The vicegerent was repeatedly accused of enriching himself through currency manipulation. Villagers and townsfolk from Hohenberg also reprimanded Wendler for being "worse than Jewish" because of the usurious interest he took in granting loans. They baldly criticized Wendler's profiteering as a grievous offense against the social trust placed in him as a member of the social and political elite within the framework of the traditional order.[38]

The claim that certain members of the elite had damaged the entire local economy out of sheer self-interest enhanced the allegation of antisocial gain in both regions. Martin Gerber, merchant and burgomaster of Horb, for instance, purchased a large quantity of barley to brew beer. The city council complained that he thus not only displaced small-scale brewers but also triggered such a substantial price increase for barley that the price of bread made with barley became inflated as well. Gerber's economic activity depleted food supplies to the disadvantage of the poor. Because he had the best connections with the government in Innsbruck, Gerber was able to ward off attempts to bar him from brewing. The people of Horb felt that Gerber's behavior was especially objectionable because commercial transactions had already earned him a considerable fortune. Instead of supporting paupers with his money, he sought further, "superfluous" profit and rendered them poorer still. Strong witchcraft suspicions developed rapidly against Gerber's wife and daughter, who had warmly supported him.[39] It was quite common in these regions for the distrust of people who quickly achieved great economic success to develop into witchcraft suspicions. Indeed, such social tensions were one of the primary causes of suspicion.[40]

Among those suspect of witchcraft, the predatory pursuit of profit was usually connected with the desire for political power. Witch-trial victims from the elite were often typical parvenus. They were social climbers, people who had only recently entered the ranks of the local elite or who, although already members of leading families, were in the process of acquiring economic and political dominance. Due to lack of archival sources, however, we cannot determine when it was that witchcraft suspicions became linked to a striving for sociopolitical power within the two regions. In Swabian Austria, we find evidence for this as early as the 1530s and in the late 1550s, at the beginning of the persecutions.[41] In Swabian Austria, then, witchcraft accusations did not expand gradually into the political and economic ruling classes; nor did they reach the upper classes only at the height of the persecution waves. Instead, accusations against members of the upper classes already appeared at the beginning of the witch hunts. Thus, we cannot confirm Midelfort's thesis that accusations against members of the elite occurred late in southwestern German witch trials and produced a crisis of confidence that terminated the witch hunts.[42] Because of poor sources, we cannot tell whether denunciations against elites began as early in the Electorate of Trier. In the jurisdiction of St. Maximin, denunciations made against specific wealthy people, as well as general accusations against "the rich," collectively appeared in 1587—that is, in the year following the outbreak of persecutions in 1586. The first person to be executed in the Electorate of Trier who unquestionably ranked among the upper classes was convicted in 1588. With Flade's execution a little more than three years after the beginning of the witch hunt, witchcraft suspicions against social elites reached a super-regional peak. Social barriers to the prosecution of witches disappeared once and for all.[43]

The most important means of acquiring political influence was contact with the territorial lord—and, indeed, proximity to the sovereign was a characteristic of elite witchcraft suspects in both territories. They had connections with the central government, operated as its local agents, or held territorial offices directly. One of the first witchcraft defamations indicated in the records of Burgau was part and parcel of the troubled dependence of urban leaders on the territorial lord. The town of Günzburg had taken sides with the rebels in the Peasants' War in 1525. Following their defeat, the Habsburgs dissolved the old town council and established a new, sovereign-friendly council. In 1530, adherents of the old council brought charges of witchcraft against a woman whose family ranked among those represented in the new council. The bailiff Hipp von Remmingsheim of Horb had clashed with the town council over changes in the municipal law to the government's advantage. In 1594, he was murdered, and the perpetrator could not be caught. Hipp's wife, who had agitated for her husband's interests, had to flee Horb to avoid being arrested as a witch.[44] The matter of Martin Gerber and his connections with the government has already been addressed.

The incentive for favoring the interests of the territorial state, to which such council members as Gerber were predisposed, consisted in the opportunities it provided for career advancement and for gaining real power outside the sphere of the council's control. Offices, fiefs, exemption from specific laws, privileges, and frequent political contact with the authorities of the territorial state were the means to attain and express a new and higher status. In the service of the Habsburgs or through connections with the authorities in Innsbruck, the Hohenberg families Hipp, Lutz, Wendler, Gerber, and Precht obtained positions of power to which they could not have aspired before, despite their already favorable economic position. These social climbers did not seek careers in Innsbruck or Vienna, but they constructed local positions of power as agents of the central administration. Family ties developed quickly among such ambitious people. The Habsburgs even bestowed aristocratic titles on these parvenu families: A nobleman's "von" and the name of his most important possession was affixed to the family's surname (Hipp *von Remmingsheim*, Lutz *von Lutzenhardt*, Wendler *von Bregenroth*, Precht *von Hohenwart*, Liesch *von Hornau*). It is significant, however, that the Ifflinger dynasty of Fridingen in Hohenberg never fell under suspicion of witchcraft. This local elite family had assumed the office of the bailiff around 1600 but served in this position as agents of local interests and operated against the interests of the central administration.[45]

Most of the socially ambitious alleged witches in the service of the territorial rulers did not come from the old, established local elite. These strangers, who acted as agents of their territorial lords and competed for rank in a new social structure, like the French intendants in the seventeenth and eighteenth centuries, came under suspicion of witchcraft easily. In Hohenberg, this was true, for example, of Vicegerent Wendler and of the suspected Lutz and Hipp-Finintz families, while in Trier it was true of Diederich Flade, Niclaus Fiedler, and Hans Reuland. Flade's family, for instance, came from St. Vith in what is now Belgium. It was his grandfather who had come to the lands of Trier; when he arrived, he was already an official of the elector. The family soon managed to assume important offices in Trier and Coblenz, mostly as jurists in the service of the territorial sovereign. Diederich Flade studied in Louvain and Orléans; he first worked in Speyer as a jurist, then returned to Trier in 1557 and became under-sheriff (*Vizeschultheiss*) at the tender age of twenty-three. He advanced as a protégé of the elector. In 1559, he joined the prince elector's council; in 1567, he served as sheriff of the cathedrale's jurisdiction; and in 1571, he served as city sheriff and as a judge of the Coblenz territorial high court, the highest court of appeal. In 1578, Flade became a professor at the prince elector's university in Trier, and in 1586, he became its president. When the city of Trier fought in court for its independence against the overlordship of the prince elector, Flade served as a witness decidedly against the interests of the city. Flade represented the interests of the sovereign in another way, as well: He took action against the Reformation efforts of Olevian, who probably had the support of at least a large minority in Trier. In 1573, Flade clashed with the city once more when he usurped its jurisdiction. The prince elector rewarded his loyalty. After the city had lost its case for independence as an imperial free city in 1580, Flade became the prince elector's vicegerent in Trier in 1581. In chapters 5 and 6, I will examine the extent to which their connections with the territorial lord helped wealthy witches evade trials, effect acquittals, or even criticize the witch hunts generally.[46]

Taking the side of the territorial state, whether by assuming an office or aligning oneself with its political clientele, was possible only if one abandoned the competing local self-administration. Thus, one of the main areas of conflict during the early modern period affected the emergence of witchcraft suspicions in the two regions: the conflict between an aristocratic territorial state and an urban or rural community that was struggling for autonomy.[47] We do not know for sure whether the old elite of the city of Trier actively pushed for a trial against Diederich Flade and Hans Reuland. In the case of Niclaus Fiedler, however, people clamored for a trial against him "in the pubs and the guildhouses."[48] It is striking, furthermore, that between 1572 and his death in 1589, Flade served as a best man only once and only three times as a godfather; his wife served only once as a godmother, in 1574.[49] For a person of his position, this was a fairly small number, which may indicate early and persistently strained relations with his social environment. In Swabian Austria, unfortunately, a similar investigation is not possible. We do know, however, that there the old town-council elites proceeded rigorously against any agents of the sovereign who fell under suspicion of witchcraft.

The connection between witchcraft accusations and political competition also expressed itself in the countryside in both territories. The rural upper class of jurors and reeves was over-represented among the trial victims in the Moselle region. The electoral overseer of the Moselle fishery and the customs clerk of Pfalzel were prominent examples. They developed tense relationships with the populace because of their official duties. Many witches claimed to have seen both of them at the Sabbath.[50]

Beginning in the year 1604, the aristocratic dynasty of the lord stewards (*Truchsessen*) of Waldburg in the territory of Bussen had to deal with rural rebellion under the leadership of the Unlingen peasant Hans Edelin. The population of Unlingen was divided. Surprisingly, the party led by Edelin and a certain Hans Danfried gained broad support from both the government in Innsbruck and its officials in the Swabian Landvogtei, who hoped to suppress the local influence of the lord steward in the process. A group supporting the high stewards in Unlingen, including several members of the Michler family, worked against them. In the year 1619, Hans Danfried as plaintiff brought charges of witchcraft against Anna Michlerin. Not only the accuser and the accused belonged to the competing political parties; we can also identify most of the witnesses against Anna Michlerin as Edelin's supporters. It is significant that Danfried turned to the Habsburg court in Altdorf in the Swabian Landvogtei with his charges. The court of the lord steward actually had jurisdiction in criminal cases; that the insurgents did not want to plead their case there fit with the social logic of the conflict. The Habsburg court at Altdorf did not simply satisfy popular demands for witch hunting or for specific political changes. The court interrogated all witnesses extensively and even prompted some to retract their accusations. The judges also assigned an imperial notary as defense lawyer for the accused. Nonetheless, contrary to customary practice, the Altdorf court accepted the testimony of three witnesses for the prosecution as sufficient evidence for the use of torture. Anna Michlerin was burned in August 1619. Thus, in this case, political conflict was not merely the background for the genesis of suspicion; political strife was at the very heart of the suspicion and trial. As we saw earlier, however, the popular magicians Stöckhlin and Fech had significant influence over the accusation of Anna Michlerin as a witch. It is unlikely that they merely helped to conceal political interests. Once animosities—political or other—had helped to generate witchcraft suspicions against one or more persons, it followed from traditional conceptions of magic that a folk magician should help to identify the "culprits."[51] Just because witchcraft suspicions resulted from a political dispute does not mean that they were insincere.

While supporting the territorial lord brought some people into conflict with old urban elites, abusing positions of power obtained from such lords could lead to even greater conflicts with less privileged groups. Contemporaries condemned both the pursuit of profit and corruption as antisocial. At least one person who later denounced Flade as a witch had first come to know him as a judge who had twisted the law to his own advantage. In the fall of 1587, repeated complaints prompted an investigation of the secular high court in Trier, where Flade was serving as sheriff. At the end of the investigation, the prince elector explicitly admonished Flade. Early in 1589, just before the beginning of the witch trial, Johann VII seriously considered dismissing Flade as a judge because of his "avarice."[52]

Christoph Wendler, vicegerent of Hohenberg, worked ruthlessly for Innsbruck's interests. In some cases, however, he was willing to grant extensive concessions to the regional lesser nobility or to the town of Rottenburg. His contemporaries rightly accused him of corruption and saw many of his decisions as the result of self-interest. As a judge, Wendler was open to bribery. "The vicegerent [let] himself be stuffed like a boot bag. . . . There is no doubt that the vicegerent puts his own benefit before the commonweal." Wendler was even alleged to have introduced unjust taxes for his own advantage. Even in Burgau, where there were few trials, townspeople voiced witchcraft suspicions against a corrupt burgomaster. In both regions, suspicion of witchcraft and accusations of corruption went hand in hand.[53]

One of the ironies of the witch trials is that villagers and townsfolk suspected as witches those lawyers who had become rich quickly by prosecuting witches. Especially in the Electorate of Trier, rural witch hunters hired attorneys to draw up bills of indictment for them and help with the management of trials. The mass persecutions of witches constituted an excellent career opportunity for these jurists, and they rapidly accumulated material property as well as political power. This profoundly conflict-ridden advancement frequently resulted in the denunciation of these jurists as witches, and in at least one case, a trial followed.[54]

So what were the characteristics of upper-class witchcraft suspects? Suspicion of witchcraft was cast on members of the elite who had betrayed the social contract in the eyes of the majority through the political "treason" of alignment with the territorial lord through corruption or through their aggressive economic conduct. Witchcraft suspicions originated in daily encounters with the antisocial behavior of the elite. It was not so much the rich in general who were suspected as the economically predatory exemplars of early capitalism and other ambitious social climbers. Contemporaries interpreted as "avarice" any interest in profit on the part of the elite that went beyond the expectations of the general public. Villagers and townsfolk interpreted corruption and profit-oriented economic action interchangeably as signs of "avarice." Apart from the religious tradition that condemned usury and the mortal sin of *avaritia,* the negative impact that the behavior of a few members of the upper class had on large parts of the populace explains why ordinary people reacted so vigorously to this behavior. What was denounced as "avarice" could persuasively *justify* suspicions of witchcraft.

In both territories, this attitude is manifested in the sources. Several trial documents explicitly called the culprit *"geüttig* (acquisitive)" and saw that as an incriminating element in witchcraft accusations. These avaricious witches were economically active people from the middle and upper classes.[55] The court scribe of Rottenburg brought before a committee of inquiry his witchcraft suspicions against Christoph Wendler's third wife, who was actively supporting Wendler in his political and economic business: "Also *due to* her great avarice people believe [that Wendler's wife is a witch]. If she is not one yet, she will certainly become one." When Johann VII explained why he thought the witchcraft accusations against Diederich Flade were worth investigating, he asserted that often people "come into that bad state [of being witches] . . . because of their avarice. . . . Flade is notoriously avaricious." We continue to find such statements in the Electorate even in the late trials, after 1650.[56] Binsfeld had formulated the same idea theologically. He listed nine causes that could move someone to form a pact with the Devil: poor knowledge of religious doctrine, negligent authorities, lack of faith, curiosity, prurience, delight in cursing, unhappiness, desperation, and "avarice."[57] Binsfeld's list was based on his practical experience with witch trials, to which he explicitly referred. With the help of Binsfeld, we can explain the "avarice" motif further.[58] It was not a question of *aims,* not—as in earlier versions of the Faust story, such as Marlowe's—of contracting with the Devil to satisfy one's greed. Binsfeld, apparently in agreement with the Trier populace, did not interpret economic success as a gift from the Devil. It was avarice *itself* that brought a person into contact with demons. The line between sin and a pact with the Devil had become thin and indistinct, but it was precisely this line that critics of witch hunts insisted on drawing sharply. Binsfeld's opponent Cornelius Loos, for example, did not hesitate to present Flade's conviction as God's punishment for his greed. Loos criticized that greed severely but clearly rejected any necessary connection between such a sin and the crime of witchcraft.[59]

This provides a context for understanding the Sabbath narratives in both territories. As has already been mentioned, the antagonism between poor and rich witches and their recurring conflicts over weather magic dominated Sabbath fantasies in Swabian Austria and in the Electorate of Trier. Rich witches were always in favor of using weather magic to damage the harvest, while poor witches, worrying that they might not have enough to eat because they could not protect their own fields and vineyards, were always opposed to it. In both territories, witchcraft narratives consistently alleged that the "rich" inflicted their crop-damaging magic to raise the price of food by creating a shortage. The idea was applied to elites from Swabian Austria as well as to those in the Electorate: "The rich among them [the witches from Swabian Austria] are always eager for [weather magic], so that then the grain and the vines rot and they can gain more from their own." The "[rich witches from Trier] always wanted to spoil everything so that they might sell their grain and wine at the highest price."[60] Here, the concept of sorcery repeatedly reflected real economic conditions. Members of the upper classes frequently owned and cultivated areas at quite a distance from their residences; a storm (which contemporaries attributed to weather magic) might affect only a relatively small portion of all their fields and vineyards. Thus, weather magic could be profitable for them. Contemporaries had thought this idea through. In Swabian Austria, it was claimed in individual cases that rich witches had the ability to protect their property from harmful weather magic. Vicegerent Wendler acquired the vineyard of an executed witch from the lower classes of Hohenberg. The owners of the surrounding plots of land then proclaimed that this particular vineyard would no longer be harmed by weather magic, as it now had a "patron" in the witch Wendler. They had not thought the former owner capable of protecting her own crops from weather magic, although they had clearly considered her a witch. In the Electorate, one confession stated that only Flade and another rich witch from the Trier elite knew how to get rid of the snails that were ruining the crop.[61]

If "avarice" prompted witchcraft suspicions, the shape of "witchcraft" in turn came to conform to these expectations. Members of the elite who had come close to the Devil through their "avarice" continued to pursue this "avarice" after they had entered into a pact with the Devil.

The imaginary society of the Sabbath mirrored the conflict between different social strata caused by economic and social crises in real society, but in a simplified form. Because of that, however, social conflict at the Sabbath was more pronounced. As mentioned earlier, confession narratives claimed that Flade and Wendler presided over the witches' Sabbath like princes on thrones. In this they not only exceeded the social role they occupied in everyday society, but as lords of the Sabbath, as enthroned masters of the witches, they also assumed features of the Devil. The Devil on the throne presiding over the witches' Sabbath appeared in contemporary graphic depictions of the witches' dance.[62] One could scarcely think of an image that might more effectively amplify the wickedness and menace of the suspects Wendler and

Flade. Moreover, another interpretation presented itself that further destroyed social trust. If Wendler and Flade had status in the Sabbath society that not just equaled, but exceeded, the status they enjoyed in real society, this suggested that their position in ordinary society was but a consequence and a function of their role in the witch society.

These witchcraft suspicions aimed at the social elite deviated conspicuously in both territories from the stereotype of the witch doctrine. Kramer and Bodin both repudiated any involvement of the elite in the crime of witchcraft, apart from noble court magicians and supporters of learned magic. When later demonologists mentioned Flade as an example of a "witch master" from the upper class, this was the transformation of a new "fact" from the practice of witch hunting into theory. Binsfeld did not mention the existence of witches "of higher standing" in his theoretical introduction; he referred to it only in his specific advice for judges.[63] Although in this context Binsfeld did not mention the archdiocese, the region of the Moselle, or Flade as a prominent example, he clearly drew on his personal experiences with witch trials and the witch concept in the area of Trier. Confession narratives describing wealthy witches as dominating the Sabbath predated Binsfeld's treatise. Learned demonology was not the model for the Sabbath concept and trial events here; rather, it incorporated the details of specific events. That Binsfeld thus came into (tacit) conflict with the other leading theoreticians of the witch hunts shows how dominant the motif of social stratification at the Sabbath was in the Electorate. Delrio, who wrote after Binsfeld and depended on him without having any direct connection with similar trial events, described this problem briefly, but in the manner of Kramer and Bodin, he treated Flade as an exception that proved the rule.[64] Since Swabian Austria went largely unnoticed by the demonological and juridical literature, it does not offer an opportunity for comparison.

The wives of aggressive social climbers came under suspicion of witchcraft if villagers and townsfolk perceived them as assisting their husbands. They presumably shared the grasping methods and goals of their spouses. In doing so, they themselves became selfishly active, politically and economically. People from Rottenburg explicitly reproached Wendler's third wife and her mother for their economic activities. Wendler's wife was even accused of actively participating in her husband's corruption scandals. The wife and daughter of Martin Gerber from Horb had actively supported him. Independent and without spouses, Agatha von Sontheim and the widow of Bailiff Hipp from Horb aggressively had advocated their own claims. One could cite similar cases from the Electorate of Trier.[65]

Nevertheless, it was primarily men who had the opportunity to pursue their own advancement in a politically and economically aggressive way.[66] Among the witchcraft suspects from social elites were correspondingly many more men than among the suspects from all other strata. This skewed distribution of suspicions seems to have manifested itself in the trials themselves, if the surviving sources are representative. Trials against people from the upper strata of society had to overcome the gender-specific attribution of witchcraft to women, which unequivocally predominated both in popular belief and in demonology in the two regions.

People who did not have political or economical power could resolve conflicts with politically and economically superior antagonists only through the medium of the witch trial.[67] Neither greed nor corruption was the accusation that robbed Wendler, Flade, Agatha von Sontheim, and other "rich witches" of their support among their peers, their political comrades, and their territorial lord. Only the accusation of witchcraft could do this. The less privileged majority were not the only ones who harbored witchcraft suspicions against members of the upper classes. Given the latent suspicions of witchcraft against the elite generally, it stood to reason that members of this social group might also identify antagonists from their own stratum as witches. For them, the basic conflict that led to witchcraft accusations was not, as among the lower classes, concern over subsistence in the face of a socially aggressive elite, but instead economic and political competition within that elite. Thus, it would be inappropriate to describe witch trials simply as a weapon of "class struggle."

The notion of the wealthy witch who sought to profit through both magic and ordinary action can be partially explained by invoking George Foster's "image of limited good." According to this theory, members of agrarian societies acted as if all goods were available only in a limited and fixed amount (limited good).[68] Anyone who achieved personal gain was immediately distrusted by other members of society, who perceived such gain as being necessarily to their own detriment. Socially significant economic gain could be accepted if it was explained as a magical gift from outside the society—that is, as a treasure trove or as a gift from a spirit. Thus, in the traditional societies described by Foster, a nexus of the belief in magic and acquisitive economic behavior deflected or defused social conflict. However, in the Electorate of Trier and Swabian Austria, material gain became even less acceptable if it was attributed to magic. Even if contemporaries did not explain material gain as caused by the help of a spirit, the mere possibility of linking profit seeking with magic was apt to bring on social disaster. The idea of the limited good thus took on a new, devastatingly negative meaning. The nexus of magic and acquisitive economic behavior could no longer prevent the potentially explosive expression of latent social tensions, as it did in the traditional context described by Foster. Instead, it became a cause for suspicion in a criminal trial. As has been seen with folk healers, European witchcraft theory and the witch trial deprived magical beliefs of the pacifying effect that ethnologists have often found in non-European societies.

THE DESTRUCTIVE POTENTIAL OF VARIABILITY

As we have seen, in many cases witchcraft suspicions were embedded in older conflicts. Were witchcraft accusations and resultant witch trials merely tools of one party to eliminate another from the field of competition? Were they only a means to the end of "eradicating" a political or economic rival, a disagreeable neighbor? Such cases may have existed.[69] But it is absurd to suggest that witchcraft trials were regularly or often deployed (or "instrumentalized") in this fashion.

There is no evidence in the sources for a strict separation of magical from non-magical harm. The political and economic misbehavior of the elite, just like the sexual misbehavior of adulterers or the criminal misbehavior of thieves, was incriminating evidence of witchcraft. It justified suspicions of witchcraft. It makes no sense that a witchcraft accusation might have been deployed as an instrument against thieves or sexual deviants who had already been arrested and had confessed. But the fact that such charges were brought anyhow shows that socially unwanted behavior per se suggested the suspicion of witchcraft. Nobody was using witchcraft accusations here as an excuse to harm someone who was behaving antisocially. Rather, contemporaries concluded that a person was a witch from his or her antisocial behavior. Contemporaries did not allege or conclude that someone had a pact with the Devil. After considering his or her personality and way of life, however, they came to the conclusion that the individual in question would be likely to make a pact with the Devil. Witchcraft suspicions were not a matter of induction but of deduction. In both territories, the belief in witches and the fear of witchcraft were unquestionably and powerfully integrated into a worldview. It stood to reason to count one's opponent—anyone who seemed to present himself an enemy of oneself or the community—among the "enemy" par excellence—that is, among the witches. The confirmation of suspicions through the identification of specific suspects resulted from secondary grounds for suspicion, or, as in the case of Anna Michlerin, with the help of a folk magician. A comparative overview of the ethnological research of non-European societies with magic beliefs yields a very similar result. As has already been mentioned, elsewhere the belief in harmful magic has often been interwoven with various kinds of conflict. Yet in non-European societies, as well, there is no conclusive evidence for direct instrumentalization—that is, for allegations of witchcraft that were not actually believed by the accuser.[70] If the accusers and the suspects shared a history of harassment, rivalry, and aggression before the witch trial, this only means that witchcraft accusations were embedded in another field of conflict, not that they were disingenuous or insincere.

To summarize, in the Electorate of Trier and Swabian Austria contemporaries suspected the following sorts of people as witches: criminals, beggars, strangers, aggressive social climbers, relatives of convicted witches, belligerent and intolerant people, and those who came into lasting conflict with their families or neighbors. The common thread among these is fairly thin: suspicion of witchcraft was directed at those who seemed to have proved themselves untrustworthy or who stood outside of the community. The "enemy image" of the witch was a category of interpretation that absorbed everything negative. It was thus possible to identify as a witch any person whom one experienced as adversarial. People toward whom no social confidence ever developed or who had destroyed it through socially disapproved behavior became victims of witch trials. "Evil people (*böse Leute*)," a term that sources from both territories used as a synonym for "witches,"[71] thus serves as a commentary on the distribution of witchcraft accusations. Contemporaries could suspect any person with socially objectionable behavior as a witch.

Rainer Walz has emphasized that triggering elements for witchcraft suspicions were "diffusely" dispersed among all problem areas in society. Similarly, Gerd Schwerhoff has concluded that "*the* typical witch . . . did not exist." Robin Briggs has asserted that this variability prevents us from seeing that we cannot evaluate the characterizations of witches prevalent in the population as the key to the genesis of suspicion.[72] The power of the witch concept, however, lay precisely in the fact that it was so unspecific. The unspecific became the basis for positive interpretive statements in a multitude of situations. Witchcraft accusations functioned as almost universally applicable catalysts of conflict. Accusations offered material for the formulation and specification of social mistrust. In individual trials, various accusations resembled one another, and they were more or less in keeping with the general witchcraft doctrine. Nevertheless, they proved to be unspecific and thus extremely flexible with regard to the actual persons against whom accusatory statements were directed. Thus, even elite male officials, if they seemed to betray the social trust placed in them, could be successfully prosecuted as witches, even though they were extremely atypical victims. This development was due not to the uncritical adoption of learned demonology into the practice of trials but, rather, to an independent adjustment of the interpretive category "witchcraft" by the populace according to their day-to-day experiences. Ordinary people "creatively" adapted, expanded, and even distorted elements of the witch doctrine. They dissolved the social stereotype of the witch as a woman from the lower social strata. That this extension and adjustment of the witch concept was possible without making the resultant witch narratives dysfunctional in the judicial framework demonstrates that the "elasticity" of the idea of witchcraft was an essential part of its destructive potential.

The selection of witchcraft suspects during the initial genesis of suspicions was not the only highly variable element. In the process of confirming witchcraft suspicions, contemporaries also could understand a multitude of unspecific situations, activities, and statements as corroboration of suspicions. Witchcraft, unlike theft, arson, or murder, did not consist of a clearly defined act or sequence of acts. Comprising not only a hidden crime but also many different magical acts and miscellaneous contacts with demons, witchcraft could generate many possible causes for suspicion. It was impossible to limit them to any specific set of situations or actions. The central governments of Swabian Austria and the Electorate of Trier tended to think of this variability as a restraint on trials, for it was impossible to prove the crime of witchcraft positively. The process by which suspicions emerged was too open ever to be conclusive. The populace and local office holders, by contrast, thought of the "openness" of the crime of witchcraft in such a way that, for them, almost every act became magic and every statement a confession.[73] The premise for them was the concept that witchcraft was less a single act than, like heresy, a way of life. Unlike vagrancy, which was another criminalized way of life, witchcraft did not stand conspicuously outside of local society; it was so dangerous precisely because witches lived unrecognized within their urban or rural communities. Because witches remained integrated in society, there were many different actions and events that witch hunters could interpret as indications of witchcraft. The multifaceted forms the crime took, as well as the open, markedly variable distribution of suspicions, were characteristics of witchcraft that clearly distinguished it from all other crimes. The concept of witchcraft not only postulated that witches were a group but also contained a variability that allowed witch hunts to develop into mass phenomena.

4

"There Goes the Werewolf. We Thought He Had Been Caught Already"

Agents of Witch Hunting and the Management of Trials

GRAPEVINES: POPULAR DEMAND FOR WITCH HUNTING, ITS CAUSES AND MEDIUMS IN SWABIAN AUSTRIA AND THE ELECTORATE OF TRIER

The peasant population of the villages and the urban lower and lower-middle social classes constituted the greatest driving force behind the intense witch hunts in Hohenberg. Above all, winegrowers from Rottenburg and the surrounding villages demanded witch trials with increasing aggressiveness from Vicegerent Christoph Wendler and even threatened to lynch suspects. Villages acted collectively as witch hunters and accusers, and some proceeded actively against witches, driving suspects out of the area. Some villages acquired a reputation for being able to identify witches. The populace explicitly suggested that territorial officials take their advice. "At the urging of the surrounding villages," the town council of Rottenburg approached Wendler in 1596, demanding witch trials. In their demand for witch trials, the villagers were in agreement with the vast majority of the urban populace.[1]

Rottenburg and its surrounding areas depended on viticulture. About a quarter of the town's inhabitants worked in wine production. Barbara Lutz, Wendler's mother-in-law, fled because she feared that the winegrowers would lynch her. In 1605, after nearly two hundred trials in their town alone, the Rottenburg winegrowers still complained that "nothing is being done about people suspected of witchcraft, and their fruit keeps getting damaged." A winegrower even tried to stimulate a commission from the Innsbruck government—which in that year was only supposed to investigate corruption charges against Wendler—to take measures against witches in his village. Peasants and winegrowers in the rest of Hohenberg displayed similar desires for witch hunting.[2]

Local demands for witch hunts frequently led to explosive persecutions, usually limited to a single year and a single village. This distribution of trials reflected E. William Monter's "small panic" paradigm: short local witch hunts interrupted by pauses and with a victim count usually under ten people. "Small panic" witch hunts took place almost exclusively in persecution-intensive Hohenberg. In the remainder of Swabian Austria, there are clear indications of popular demands for trials. Yet a single-village outbreak of witch hunting occurred in only one case.[3] These different patterns of witchcraft trials suggest that the villagers' sense of being threatened by witches was stronger in Hohenberg than in the other Habsburg territories and that this fear had a larger impact on the courts.

Fear of weather sorcery was the primary motive driving proponents of witch hunting. The first trials in Swabian Austria were part of a small wave of witch hunts in the German southwest around 1530, trials that constituted a reaction to the economic crisis of the years 1528-30.[4] A chronological overview of the witch trials (see the appendix) shows that the agrarian crisis cannot sufficiently explain the timing and geography of witch hunts overall. Nonetheless, bad weather and associated crop failures influenced the fear of witchcraft and local demands for witch hunts significantly. A Rottenburg winegrower emphasized this in 1605. He and his fellow vineyard owners demanded that, "*because* they had so much hail, the authorities should arrest the witch-women."[5] Extremely vulnerable to thunderstorms, grapevines were particularly threatened by bad weather, which was then interpreted as sorcery. In fact, at the end of the sixteenth century, repeated storms further impoverished the already poor winegrowers of Hohenberg. Due to the economic predominance of small enterprises, viticulture in Rottenburg and Horb was extremely susceptible to crisis. The area of land being cultivated for wine began to shrink in Hohenberg, and in Rottenburg and Horb there was less wine cultivation at the end of the seventeenth century than there had been during the fifteenth century. Only merchants and wealthy landowners could profit from this production crisis. The decline of viticulture went hand in hand with inflation. The significance of this development can scarcely be overestimated. In the cases of Rottenburg and (within limits) Horb, a radical and fairly sudden restructuring of the entire economy took place. In 1604, it was said of Rottenburg: "Years ago this place was called a land of milk and honey [lit., the lard pit]; now it could be called the hunger pit."[6] The tendency to demonize people whose behavior was seen as antisocial erupted from this sense of crisis.

The rest of Swabian Austria did not experience a crisis like that in Hohenberg. In the Margraviate of Burgau, peasants planted more robust crops that did not suffer major damage due to climate change. Nellenburg did not practice viticulture as intensively as Hohenberg. The Swabian Landvogtei, by contrast, lay in a heavily viticultural region. Both of these regions, however, had decidedly favorable climates. The warming effect of nearby Lake Constance persisted despite the worsening climate. In addition, the trade network of that region was superior to that of Hohenberg, so no slump in the wine trade took place. All together, the shores of Lake Constance experienced only a few witch trials.[7] To understand the significance of the "Little Ice Age," it is hence necessary to observe its concrete influence in specific regions. The massive economic crisis that was the background and cause of the popular demand for witch trials in Hohenberg did not extend to the rest of Swabian Austria. Accordingly, no desire for witch hunting as strong as that in Hohenberg ever developed among the inhabitants of those territories.

The beginning and high point of the witch hunts in the Electorate of Trier in 1586 was clearly linked with failed harvests and the fear of weather magic. There unfortunately are no trial records remaining from this early phase of the witch trials in the Electorate. The Annals of Neuss, however, report that the 120 witches burned in Pfalzel had committed weather magic to damage the harvest. An unusually long, cold winter, prompting fear that spring would never come, must have daily increased the fear for survival. This formed the background for the eruption of mass witch hunts in the Electorate of Trier. If the agents of witch hunting had hoped that the 1586 trials would eradicate all of their enemies, then they must have believed that they failed. The agricultural crisis persisted. During the entire reign of Archbishop Johann VII (1581-99), only the years of 1585 and 1590 produced good harvests.[8] A protracted battle ensued against witches as weather sorcerers.

Walter Rummel's statement that there are no indications of economic crisis in the witch trials of the Electorate cannot be sustained.[9] The weather sorcery that was clearly central to popular notions of witchcraft was directed consistently against harvests, and particularly against the vineyards. We can thus find a correlation between agricultural profit margins and witch trials in the witch fantasy itself, which always had a connection to everyday life. Even in 1620, the chronicler Johann Linden saw the agricultural, and especially the viticultural, crisis as the source of the intense popular demand for witch hunts throughout the region of Trier. The situation may have been aggravated by the fact that in both the Electorate of Trier and Swabian Austria, the area of land under cultivation for wine was already relatively small. In addition to that, there were substantial differences in quality even among the vineyards of a single village, creating stiff competition among the winegrowers. The crisis arose during the late sixteenth century and was exacerbated generally during the Little Ice Age at the end of the 1620s.[10]

Large parts of the Electorate, however, were not dependent on wine cultivation. Why did persecutions of witches take place in those areas, as well? People actively carried rumors of witchcraft from one place to the next. The witch trials themselves generated further fears of witchcraft.[11] The early mass persecutions suggest that the menace of the witches was already felt very strongly. It followed from the concept of witchcraft as a collective crime and from the many different misfortunes that could be attributed to witchcraft that people would begin looking for witches in their own neighborhoods. A damaging storm set off the initial spark; a cluster of trials limited to a single locale followed. This, however, attracted much wider interest, and thereafter witch hunts could develop into a self-sustaining phenomenon and spread quickly through the region.

For comparison, we must examine the parts of Swabian Austria that had relatively few witchcraft trials. Why was it that no example of intense witch hunting functioned similarly there to overcome the impediments to witch hunting within the local economy? For one thing, the Habsburg territories did not exchange denunciations. Hohenberg, the center of explosive trials, was geographically isolated and did not maintain regular contact with its sister territories. No organizations of witch hunters like those of Trier existed that handled the flow of information regarding witch trials and denunciations. A cluster of witch trials on a scale similar to that in Pfalzel in 1586, a sensational "starting shot" for the witch hunts there, never took place in Swabian Austria. With the exception of the Fürstpropstei of Ellwangen, none of the persecution-intensive territories in the region of the Habsburg lands experienced such a trial cluster. In Ellwangen, as well as in the Prince Bishopric of Augsburg and in Obermarchtal, witch hunts were conducted primarily from the top down by the authorities.[12] Even if the trials there stoked fears of witchcraft in Swabian Austria, they provided no example with which ordinary people could have identified.

Recent research has identified the ordinary people of the Electorate of Trier, the vast majority of villagers and townsfolk, as the driving force behind the witch trials. As early as in the seventeenth century, historical descriptions of the witch hunts explicitly mentioned this aspect: "The *whole land* rose up to destroy the witches."[13] Historians have collectively confirmed the fact that the people of the Electorate and neighboring territories vehemently demanded witch trials from their governments and participated actively in witch hunting. Local "small panics" characterized the witch hunts throughout the region. The populace of the city of Trier shared the desire for witch trials with its rural neighbors. In light of this, we cannot speak of an urban–rural contrast. The "common man" was frequently mentioned in witch trials from the city of Trier as making explicit demands on the authorities for witch hunts.[14] The starting point was thus the same as in Swabian Austria with regard to who supported the demand for witch hunting and why.

In both regions, the popular demand for witchcraft trials was strengthened by the fact that people believed that the witch sect had recently grown substantially. The Devil and his allies seemed to be on the verge of a "revolution."[15]

The battle for God and against the Devil was, however, only occasionally put forth in the sources from the Electorate as the ideological motivation of the proponents of witch hunting. And in Swabian Austria, such a motivation was almost entirely absent. In both regions, the witch concept was in essential agreement with demonology, as has been mentioned, and the war against the witches was unquestionably also a fight for God's honor. However, in these regions we can identify neither an idealist religious interest nor an ideological confessional interest as the primary motivation for witch hunting, separate from the fear of harmful sorcery. The post-Tridentine rigor of Binsfeld's tract did not provoke witch hunting in the Electorate. Rather, it commented on it.

The Grapevine: Mediums of Witchcraft Suspicion in Swabian Austria and the Electorate of Trier

How were witchcraft suspicions transmitted? Through which mediums did a suspicion spread, and how was it brought to the attention of the courts? Witchcraft suspicions often spread in an unspectacular and ordinary manner: as gossip. Witchcraft defamations spread easily and more effectively via group discussions than in simple dialogue. In both regions, witchcraft suspicions were a favorite subject of conversation in informal groups and in neighborly and family encounters. The rumors against certain people were discussed "at the tables of the cathedral canons, in the festival hall of the city council, at the guild houses, and indeed, throughout the entire city."[16] As has been explicitly stated here, the fact that witch rumors crossed between social strata enhanced their validity. In the interrogation of witnesses, most of those questioned testified at least to knowing of rumors against a given suspect. As a popular saying had it, "even a child in its mother's womb" knew the rumors about particular individuals.[17]

Sermons played a special role not so much in spreading rumors against particular people as in spreading witch fears in general. In Rottenburg in 1594, just before the peak of the witch hunts, an otherwise unknown cleric spoke to this effect, saying that the town needed witch trials and that there was ample evidence against the witches. In Trier, only Niclaus Fiedler was explicitly denounced as a witch "from the pulpit, now and again." The Jesuit Jean Thierry (Macherentius), however, held a series of sermons in Trier in 1590 in which he dealt generally with the subject of witch trials. The texts of these particular sermons are lost, but it is likely that Thierry called for an intensification of the witch hunt. The Jesuit Superior Jakob Ernfelder subsequently forbade Thierry and other Trier Jesuits to speak about the witch trials anymore.[18]

In addition to the spread of witch suspicions via rumor, in which the suspects themselves did not take part, we also find the public formulation of witchcraft accusations in the suspect's presence. In its most direct form, an accusation "in the face," the suspected person was directly accused of being a witch in the presence of witnesses. The transition to proclaiming suspicions of witchcraft even more generally was fluid. Sometime before 1630, when Mebus Welcher from Limburg passed through the village of Heisenbach, someone called after him, "There goes the werewolf of Limburg. We thought he had been caught already! So now the witch-piper is coming." In Rottenburg and Trier, rumors alleging witchcraft of the leading territorial officials Christoph Wendler and Diederich Flade were articulated and propagated in a particularly intense and aggressive manner. Children and students followed Flade through the city and shouted accusations after him. At the end of 1594, a note with an image of the witches' stake drawn on it was hung on the gate of Wendler's residence. Posting such "shame notes" was a conventional method of making accusations public. Here the accusation was formulated in such a manner that all could understand it, and it was clearly placed in a public space.[19]

An accusation in the face before a third party was a serious insult to the honor of the accused, who was placed under immense pressure to vindicate himself. In neither of the two regions under study, however, is there any evidence that someone slandered in such a situation ever managed to refute the accusation convincingly on the spot. The proclamation of a suspicion in the face was a communication to and with the public, not with the suspected person.[20] The suspect was the victim of a pseudo-communication. He (or she) was made the object of a communication in his (or her) presence in such a way that it was nearly impossible for the suspect to take part in that communication. The particular context in which the accuser's speech act took place, and that simultaneously constituted the act, did not allow it.

Statements of dying people who felt that they were victims of magical illnesses also played a special role in both regions. When they named the person who had supposedly used sorcery to cause the illness, their families and the authorities always paid close attention.[21] The courts ascribed greater importance only to denunciations and self-incriminations.

Given how scrupulously witnesses and the authorities observed everything that might be construed as an admission of guilt, in both the Electorate of Trier and Swabian Austria self-incrimination always led to an investigation. In both of these regions it was extremely rare for adults to accuse themselves as witches. In the Electorate, four cases can be verified beyond doubt; they may have involved mentally ill people.[22] But none of these trials influenced the development of the witch hunts in the region. Things turned out differently with the earliest self-incrimination of an adult in Swabian Austria. A deranged hospital resident persistently claimed that she and another woman were witches. Although her statements were entirely atypical, her words seemed to confirm perfectly the correctness of all previous trials. In addition, the statements of this self-proclaimed witch kicked off further witchcraft trials. This self-incrimination by an adult stood at the beginning of the worst cluster of trials in Hohenberg. In 1586, there were forty-two executions in Rottenburg alone. No other place in Swabian Austria experienced a similarly intensive witch hunt.[23]

Voluntary self-accusations by children were one of the most widespread elements of the witch hunts.[24] For example, infamous trial series were sparked by self-incriminations by children in Württemberg at Calw (1683/84), Swedish Mora and Älvdalen (1669), and Salem Village in Massachusetts (1692/93). Children's confessions unfolded as variations on the witch/teacher motif: They claimed that allies of the Devil, often their own relatives, had tried to seduce them into witchcraft and had forced them to participate in the Sabbath. The children found themselves in the unique situation of being eyewitnesses to the witches' Sabbath but nonetheless innocent. As a rule, they needed to fear neither torture nor execution. Since they had voluntarily confessed and had broken away from the society of witches, these children were considered particularly dependable informants. Their childish "innocence" and "simplicity" were seen as guarantees of the validity of their denunciations.

In 1594, a child set off the longest chain of trials in the southern regions of Swabian Austria, which otherwise experienced relatively few trials.[25] Two children also considerably accelerated the Rottenburg witch hunts after 1594. Maria Ulmerin and her younger sister (whose name was not mentioned) were ten- and seven-year-old orphans who lived in the Rottenburg hospital. The children were believed to be possessed temporally by the Devil, but they also claimed that witches had taken them to the Sabbath. They denounced numerous people. The first trials based on the children's denunciations ended in guilty verdicts. In later years, the people of Rottenburg always cited the denunciations of the two girls as absolutely reliable. Maria Ulmerin and her sister also denounced numerous members of the upper social strata, including Vicegerent Wendler and his mother-in-law. The girls thus became the star witnesses for the prosecution against Wendler himself and the Swabian Austrian elites under his protection. After some months, the vicegerent was able to have Maria Ulmerin and her sister removed from Hohenberg. He turned the children over to the Jesuits of Constance, who were to exorcise them. Maria Ulmerin and her sister were indeed taken to Constance, where they lived with a woman who specialized in providing lodging in such cases. It seems that, following her successful exorcism, Maria wandered alone for years through the German southwest; her sister had died earlier.[26] The peak of the witchcraft trials in Hohenberg came in the nine years following the children's accusations, down to 1603.

A similar situation prevailed in the city of Trier after 1585. The *Annuae Litterae*, the yearly reports of the local Jesuits, were filled with accounts of demonic specters and possessions from this period. Naturally, the Jesuits attempted to present themselves to the Trier public and to the readers of their annual reports as successful exorcists. Every successful exorcism was interpreted as proof of the truth of the Catholic faith and the particular competence of the reform order. Nonetheless, these reports can be used as a source for the history of the Trier witch hunts. As competing religious orders and neighboring Protestants read these reports, too, everything that was said in them had to have some factual basis. Alongside numerous cases of demonic obsession, the *Annuae Litterae* mentioned not just two, as in Rottenburg, but an entire series of children who were considered temporarily possessed and were believed to have been abducted by witches and taken to the Sabbath. In 1587, the authorities sent a sixteen-year-old "witch boy" named Jeckel to the Jesuit college to be reformed. Jeckel was personally received by Johann VII, whose witch fears Jeckel confirmed by attributing the ailing elector's weakness to witchcraft. He also said that the life of Vicegerent Zandt was in immediate danger. The boy yielded numerous denunciations. The Jesuit Hermann Thyräus even reported to the general of the order in Rome, Aquaviva, that

Jeckel had denounced as witches people whom he just happened to see while walking to church. In 1588, further denunciations from an eight-year-old provoked trials: "There was no small fruit of damned witchcraft in [those] women."[27] Even after the executions of Diederich Flade and Niclaus Fiedler, the chain of denunciations by children who were possessed or had been abducted by witches did not cease. The example of Trier drew attention to witch children in neighboring territories, as well, and in 1590, the authorities of Diez brought a child to trial whose self-incriminations had been simply ignored for years. Binsfeld explicitly called for the testimony of "simple" and "innocent" children to be taken seriously.[28]

The children always simply repeated rumors already in circulation. In this way, they strengthened those rumors and appeared trustworthy themselves.[29] The children were vehicles for and distributors of witch suspicions that were rooted in deeper causes and often directed against the elite. As such, they had an immense impact in both Swabian Austria and the Electorate of Trier.

It has frequently been rightly observed that the normative provisions of the *Carolina* were largely disregarded in actual trial proceedings, even when the imperial law was officially binding in the territory in question. Yet it would be incorrect to speak of this imperial law as "ineffective." The Innsbruck government's evaluation of denunciations strikingly demonstrates how the promulgation of the *Carolina* in 1532 influenced judicial practice. In 1530 and 1531, Innsbruck still accepted single denunciations as sufficient evidence for torture in Swabian Austrian witch trials. In the government's next statement on witch trials in Swabian Austria, however, Innsbruck appraised the situation quite differently. In 1554, the government reprimanded Rottenburg officials for ordering torture based on a single denunciation and without consulting jurists. From that point on, the Habsburg government did not deviate from its basic support for the imperial law.[30]

In actual local persecutions, however, the courts disregarded the *Carolina*. Before the peak in trials in 1594-1603, about half of all denunciations in Rottenburg had remained without penal consequences. During the peak of the trials, however, only about a third of denunciations had no known consequences. Indeed, between 1596 and 1604, authorities often proceeded to torture on the basis of a single denunciation. The height of the persecutions in Horb, from 1598-1605, was similar to the rest of the witch hunts in that town. The courts identified a portion of all denunciations as believable. The criteria for this selection were the general reputation of the individual in question as well as primary causes and secondary, corroborating factors in the genesis of suspicion. In this way, the authorities prevented an "inflation" of denunciations and an accumulation of evidence that would have been difficult to process. There were no trial avalanches, but through this management of denunciations, chain trials and years of uninterrupted witch hunting became possible. Denunciations also bridged social distance. For example, a woman from Hohenberg's rural elite was arrested and tortured after two women of much lower social standing denounced her. There is, however, no evidence that trials were ever "exported" from one Hohenberg town to another through denunciations. Even in Hohenberg, denunciations in general never had the significance that they acquired, for example, in the ecclesiastical territories of Franconia.[31]

In Burgau, Nellenburg, and the Landvogtei, denunciations were recorded but never became grounds for initiating trials. Here also the acceptance of the *Carolina* was decisive.[32] At least as far as Nellenburg is concerned, we could perhaps see further grounds for this reserve in a legend spread by the nearby pilgrimage monastery of Reute. Supposedly, the Devil had once attempted to bring dishonor on the nun Betha, who was revered as a saint there, by appearing in her guise. Later, Adam Tanner was able to employ this story to "demonstrate" that the Devil could take on the form of an innocent person; for this reason, he concluded, denunciations should not be admitted in court.[33]

The relevance of denunciations in court constitutes only part of their possible effects. It was common practice in many territories to announce publicly the names of denounced accomplices when confessions were read at executions. In the manner of a self-fulfilling prophecy, these "publicized" denunciations directed suspicion toward the supposed accomplices. This suspicion was often so strong that it could coalesce into formal accusations. There is good evidence from the County of Hohenberg that denunciations came to be read publicly at executions because of the pressure the town councils exerted on the Habsburg officials. We cannot demonstrate the existence of a similar practice in Nellenburg or the Landvogtei. Judges in Burgau did have the confessions of some criminals read publicly, but the practice cannot be substantiated for witch trials.[34]

The fact that mass trials had taken place in the Electorate of Trier as early as the 1490s and more markedly in the 1580s indicates that the courts were accepting denunciations as evidence. The local witch committees of the Electorate and neighboring territories spent much time and money finding out whether anyone from their particular area had been denounced during trials in neighboring territories, and the local officials of the prince elector willingly provided the committees with this information. The courts of the Electorate and of neighboring territories kept special files in which they gathered denunciations. The Trier Witch Trial Ordinance of 1591 criticized the public reading of denunciations from confessions and forbade the practice. Even if the courts observed this prohibition, however, witch committees searched for denunciations and found opportunities to make them public.[35]

More than any previous demonologist, Binsfeld agitated for the acceptance of denunciations as evidence. A single denunciation, he argued, was sufficient to justify not only arrest but even torture in cases of witchcraft, because it was a *crimen exceptum,* a serious crime that was most difficult to prove. Moreover, a great number of denunciations, in his view, sufficed for a conviction without any further proceedings. Experience had proved that such harsh measures were appropriate. Here, Binsfeld probably had in mind the first mass witch hunts in the Electorate during the 1580s.[36] Unlike Binsfeld, Prince Elector Johann VII was uncertain about the significance of denunciations. On January 14, 1589, he requested an opinion from the theology faculty at the University of Trier regarding this problem in the Flade case. The written opinion no longer survives. Binsfeld's tract, which appeared in 1589, may also have been a response to the archbishop's request. It is impossible to know whether the suffragan wanted to correct an opinion that seemed too mild to him, whether he was putting the response of the faculty into book form, or whether he composed his short work instead of that response.[37] In any case, Johann VII did not accept Binsfeld's point of view. In the Witch Trial Ordinance of 1591, there was no trace of Binsfeld's extremely strict and naive faith in denunciations.

In 1603, Duke Maximilian of Bavaria requested a legal opinion from Nicholas Rémy, procurator-general of Lorraine, as well as from the Margraviate of Baden and the Electorates of Mainz, Cologne, and Trier, on how denunciations should be handled. As Behringer has shown, Binsfeld strongly influenced the Bavarian debate about witch trials. In this case, however, Maximilian did not defer to Binsfeld's demonological tract. Instead, he inquired specifically about denunciations in the *actual* trial proceedings in the Electorate. The jurors of the Trier high courts made no mention of the Witch Trial Ordinance in their answer. Denunciations, they wrote, should be subjected to critical scrutiny. Even multiple denunciations were insufficient indication for arrest and torture if they were limited to the assertion of having seen a given individual at the Sabbath. One could only proceed to torture if the information in three or four denunciations agreed in such details as particular acts of harmful magic or the time and place of the Sabbath.

The judges should also take the reputation of the accused into consideration. Thus, the judge's discretion remained very broad.[38]

In practice, however, a significant accumulation of denunciations resulted in formal accusations. The Trier courts initiated ex officio trials after twenty-eight denunciations had been made against Diederich Flade, twenty-five against Niclaus Fiedler, and nineteen against Hans Reuland, without witnesses having been questioned or any search having been made for material evidence. Fiedler even admitted during his own trial that the great number of denunciations must indeed seem to be very serious evidence against him.[39] This was apparently an expression of the dominant attitude on the highest court in the upper Electorate. Before he was himself accused, Fiedler had served as a juror on the Trier high court and had taken part in Flade's trial. This attitude evidently dictated Trier's 1603 legal opinion, as well. It is significant that the trial against Reuland in 1592, after the Witch Trial Ordinance came into effect, depended heavily on denunciations. This meant that the high court violated the spirit of the Witch Trial Ordinance, as did the prince elector and vicegerent, who both exerted personal influence on Reuland's trial.[40] Just as the 1603 report failed to mention the ordinance of Johann VII at all, so is there no evidence of a changed attitude toward denunciations or even of a decrease in the wave of trials. The territorial courts thus disregarded explicit territorial laws on a particularly sensitive point.

THE PRACTICE OF PERSECUTION:
STRUCTURES AND DEVELOPMENTS IN SWABIAN AUSTRIA

How did the persecution-minded populace proceed against individuals once primary causes, in eventual conjunction with corroborating factors, had given rise to witchcraft suspicions against them and when rumors and denunciations incriminated those individuals? Scholars have recently shown that it was committees of the common people who organized most of the witch hunts in the Saar-Moselle-Rhine area. No evidence can be found for similar organizations among the commoners of the Neckar-Danube-Lake Constance region. To describe each region strictly according to its own particular circumstances, we will need to discuss the two separately and only then undertake a comparative synopsis in a third section.

In just a few cases in Swabian Austria, rural communities collectively and forcibly banished supposed witches. In at least four cases, spontaneously formed groups from the populace delivered witchcraft suspects from their houses to the territorial lord's jail in tumultuous acts of violence without any official oversight. All four cases occurred in the persecution-intensive region of Hohenberg; three of the women concerned came from the local elite.[41]

The option of an accusatory trial procedure played hardly any role in Swabian Austrian witch trials. We find clear accusations from individual, private accusers in only the case of Anna Michlerin in Altdorf, in 1619, and in four Günzburg trials, two of which took place in 1582 and the others in 1627 and 1630, respectively.[42] Only in the 1619 case did the court convict the suspect because, as has been shown, the private accuser only officially acted alone in this case, but actually functioned as the speaker for a political group. In the other cases, the accusers had to pay for the trial costs. In one case, the accuser spent a day imprisoned in a tower; another accuser was exiled.

Apart from these exceptions, the witch trials in Swabian Austria were inquisitorial trials in which local officials reacted to rumors and complaints from the populace that had been expressed to officials or town councilors.[43] As the authorities took up witchcraft suspicions and initiated inquisitorial trials, private plaintiffs did not have to undergo the risks of litigation. There was now no need for them to file accusations in court. Territorial officials and town councilors learned of witchcraft suspicions unofficially, through rumor. The sheriffs functioned directly as the mouthpieces of the rural populace. In Wurmlingen, at least, the village sheriff arrested witches himself, although he was not authorized to do so. In some cases, the Rottenburg authorities refused to admit the people he had arrested to the territorial jail, but they never punished the sheriff. In addition, rural collectives formed as accusers. In Hirschau in 1601, the "common citizenry of the people" collectively brought charges against a suspect. Even in cases where a special speaker of the village communities appeared as accuser, there was no real parallel to the committees of the Moselle region.[44] The witch-hunting groups never developed any sustained activity. They simply documented the rumors that circulated in the villages. Moreover, the local witch-hunting advocates from the populace never performed any further investigations.

The proceedings against Agatha von Sontheim were a significant exception.[45] The peasants of the villages Obernau and Wendelsheim organized against the noblewoman, jointly collecting examples of suspect behavior and delivering them to the vicegerent in Rottenburg with a request for an official inquest. The villages presented themselves as collectives, perhaps consciously and for tactical reasons. This ad hoc measure did not, however, lead to the creation of specific institutions that functioned beyond that single case. Nevertheless, von Sontheim's case had serious repercussions for the relations between officials and villagers below the level of administrative norms and institutions. Vicegerent Wendler agreed to the noblewoman's arrest. Nonetheless, she was not arrested by the Rottenburg sheriff but by a group of armed peasants from Obernau and Wendelsheim. On the way to Nellingsheim, the peasants made their intentions public. Von Sontheim's arrest and her escort to the Rottenburg jail caused a sensation. Wendler probably allowed the peasants to play this role to maintain as much distance as possible between himself and the murky legal status of the case; there was contention, for example, over whether Nellingsheim fell under the jurisdiction of the Rottenburg high court. In the process, however, the vicegerent conceded a certain autonomy to the rural populace in proceeding against witches. The populace, both urban and rural, certainly interpreted Wendler's behavior as an indication that he was ready to meet local demands for witch hunts and to accept concrete actions taken against witches. The representative of the territorial lord had validated the organized actions of the subjects in a very prominent manner.

Town councils had considerable influence on the witch hunts in Swabian Austria—an influence that took different directions in the individual Habsburg territories. Midelfort has argued that the urban elite, from which the councils were drawn, kept their distance from the witch concept, although he was unable to prove this in the case of the seventeenth-century Catholic elite.[46] While Midelfort's argument does not fit Hohenberg, it does seem basically correct for the rest of Swabian Austria.

Between 1582 and 1585, the council of Günzburg had to deal with two married couples mutually accusing each other of witchcraft. When the local investigation balked, the quarreling parties turned to the territorial government in Innsbruck. In this way they circumvented the jurisdictional authority of the town. But even this step brought no resolution. The town obtained legal opinions stating that the evidence was insufficient to start a trial. The conflict reduced one of the couples to poverty, so that trial and imprisonment expenses reverted to the town. It was clear to the town council's members that if they had quickly and decisively rejected such witchcraft accusations, they might have saved time, expenses, and the intervention by Innsbruck into the town's judicial system. In addition, it may be that for the councilors, this conflict, dealing with charges of witchcraft that could not be proved, had brought all such trials into question, for they had produced the unedifying spectacle of one accusation of witchcraft merely provoking equally unprovable counter-charges of witchcraft. Thereafter, the town refused to assist the territorial lord in investigations against witches. In 1613, the councilors' attitude brought them into conflict with the newly appointed

Habsburg ruler of Burgau, Margrave Karl, who had established his residence at Günzburg. Answering recent popular demands for witch hunts, Karl developed a short-lived interest in witch trials. He attempted to establish his image as a sturdy opponent of the witches and took the initiative in a trial. To deny Karl just this chance for distinction, the council blocked the trial. The council hired jurists who advised against the trial and, breaking from their usual practice, conducted a search of the suspects' houses that quite naturally turned up nothing. In the end, the burgomasters appeared as defense witnesses testifying to the good reputation of the suspects. At that point, the case collapsed. Here of course the town councilors were defending their independence from the Habsburg Margrave and using very far-reaching means to do so. Their refusal to compete with Karl's witch-hunting zeal, however, demonstrates that they were not merely concerned with their jurisdictional rights. Their actions were an expression of genuine skepticism concerning the witch trials. The Günzburg council maintained this position. Beginning around 1630, specific accusations of harmful magic were punished as slander, and in at least once such case, the town council and the officials of the sovereign worked hand in hand again.[47]

The 1619 witch trial against Anna Michlerin in Altdorf had clear political implications, indeed. It may have been because of Michlerin's trial that the local town council, which had observed the events from a distance, began discouraging witch trials. In 1672, the council of Altdorf decided on a drastic measure against witch trials. The council effectively forbade all accusations of witchcraft, a prohibition that targeted not just witchcraft slander, which was already punishable, but also all formal witchcraft accusations before the criminal court. The cause for this prohibition was not rooted in events in Altdorf or in the Landvogtei. It may be that the Altdorf prohibition was a reaction to an outbreak of witch trials in 1671 in the sister territory of Hohenberg, when two people were executed. Thus, the council came to oppose witch trials in general. Despite their skepticism, however, the territorial authorities of Swabian Austria—unlike those of the Electorate of Trier—never took equally drastic measures against witch hunting. But when officials of the Landvogtei attempted in 1683 to subpoena a witness for a witch trial, the town council of Altdorf threatened military resistance.[48]

Prior to 1617, no records concerning witch trials are left from the town council of Stockach, the Nellenburg administrative center. After 1617, however, the council consistently punished witchcraft defamation as a form of insult, even when it was clearly not a case of slander but a genuine charge of witchcraft.[49] The territorial lord maintained fairly tight control over the territorial court in the Hegau and the influence of the town council on judicial matters there was more substantially limited than in the rest of Swabian Austria.

The town councils of the Landvogtei, Burgau, and Nellenburg had several reasons for opposing or suppressing witchcraft trials. First, councilors did not want to give the Habsburg territorial lord any opportunity to use criminal justice as a means or expression of his power. Unlike proceedings against other crimes, local courts could reject witchcraft trials, because they were evidentially extremely weak. With their restrictive policy toward witch hunts, the free imperial cities had already demonstrated that this was a real possibility. Herein lay the politically explosive potential of witch trials. Complying with popular demands for witch hunting could be a means for someone to gain or maintain power. The cities of the Landvogtei, Burgau, and Nellenburg already recognized this danger when the Habsburg officials displayed a readiness to take the rumors and persecutory desires of the populace seriously. A coalition of the territorial lord and the ordinary people loomed, which would have reduced the authority of the town councils. Swabian Austria thus participated in a development that one can observe throughout the Holy Roman Empire. Even if representatives of the territories or cities were not involved as accusers or accused, the epochal conflict between territorial states and cities or towns repeatedly provided reasons for supporting or rejecting witch trials.[50]

To do justice to the specific situation in Swabian Austria, however, we must recognize that the precautions imposed by the *Carolina* sharply limited the ability of the territorial lord to carry out witch hunts. Hence, the potential for conflict was mitigated from the start. This holds true for all of Swabian Austria. As was shown in chapter 1, the Innsbruck government had even enacted regional laws for Nellenburg and Burgau that were completely in accordance with the *Carolina*. Hence, in the parts of the territory where persecutions were relatively sparse, positively mild laws were in effect. Skepticism regarding the implementation of legal norms in judicial practice is nonetheless advisable.

As has been shown, because of the more favorable economic situation in Burgau, the Landvogtei, and Nellenburg, ordinary people there had no pronounced interest in witch hunts. Why did the town councils of these territories show even less interest in prosecution? Through their privileged access to information, councilors could place any reports on witch trials coming in from other territories into the political context of their own cities. This meant that while keeping a critical distance, they could learn from the experience of others. For the eastern and southern parts of Swabian Austria, in addition to absorbing lessons from the negative examples of the Fürstprobstei of Ellwangen and its sister territory of Hohenberg, they could learn from the positive examples of the imperial cities of Ulm, Constance, and Augsburg. The councils of Stockach, Altdorf, Burgau, and Günzburg each had only twelve members. They represented elites who had established their clear separation from the majority of the people. It lay in their political interests to pay attention to what was going on in their towns without becoming dependent on local demands. This was the situation in most southern German cities, which generally showed little inclination to hunt witches.[51]

In Hohenberg, by contrast, peasants, winegrowers, and the lower and middle social strata in the rural towns experienced no opposition from the urban councils in pursuing witch hunts. Unlike the rest of Swabian Austria, in Hohenberg there was no clear division between the poor, agrarian social strata and the members of the town councils. The councils of the Hohenberg towns were, moreover, unusually large. The figures mentioned above bear repeating here. Rather than 12, as in all other Swabian Austrian cities, the town council of Rottenburg had 48 members; the councils of Schömberg and Oberndorf each had 24 members; that of Horb had 60 members; and those of the small towns of Binsdorf and Fridingen, which were essentially villages with urban charters, each had 18. The size of these councils alone ensured that more than the economic elite was represented in them. People of middling wealth also sat on them. Although a 1615 census taken for military recruitment showed that the average wealth of a councilor in Horb and Rottenburg was only twice that of the average urban resident, in Horb the wealth of 8 percent of the population exceeded the average wealth of a councilor, and in Rottenburg fully 12 percent did so. Thus, the councils in Hohenberg represented the inhabitants better than those in any other territory of Swabian Austria. The size and social composition of these urban councils guaranteed a greater congruence of interests in Hohenberg between the council members and the general populace than existed in Nellenburg, the Landvogtei, or Burgau.[52]

Looking back, a Rottenburg citizen described how the town council had collaborated with urban and rural commoners at the peak of the trials in 1596: "At the urging of surrounding villages, the common citizenry . . . have requested of the burgomasters that the evil women be seized and executed. . . . [T]his the burgomasters told the officials." The Rottenburg town council argued for prosecuting those who had been denounced and reproached Vicegerent Wendler several times at the height of the Rottenburg witch hunt for not proceeding decisively enough against the witches. Testifying before a visitation commission in 1604, the councilors all clearly favored the witch hunts.[53]

In the town of Horb, the council was an even stronger proponent of witch hunting. Common people from the town and countryside supported the councilors in this role. As if it were only natural, they regarded their own councilors—not the territorial officials—as the proper initiators and organizers of trials. In 1607, testifying before an Austrian commission, a member of Horb's town council demanded new witch trials. The sources pertaining to the smaller Hohenberg towns are less rich, but they permit us to see that there, too, councils did not oppose the popular demand for witch trials.[54] Councilors accepted or even shared the popular demand for witch hunts. As the councils had obtained some criminal jurisdiction, they were capable of transforming this popular demand into concrete trials. As noted earlier, in ex officio proceedings in Hohenberg it was not the sheriff but the senior councilor who presided over trials. All of the Hohenberg witch trials were officially run inquisitorial trials, and that meant they were presided over not by the sheriff but by a town councilor. The town councils functioned as a pressure group to ensure that territorial officials would officially investigate rumors of witchcraft. In this way such officials gave up their right to preside, and the most influential positions in criminal justice went to the town council.

In the towns of Hohenberg, two councilors in each town served as investigators. In this role they largely determined the actual course of the trials. In Rottenburg, the incompetent Sheriff Hans Georg Hallmayer, who by the end of his long term in office (1569-1607) was senile, proved totally incapable of controlling the trials. He generally took no part in interrogating witches and even had town constables represent him at executions. Sheriff Johann Veser of Horb came into office in 1595 at the onset of the great wave of witchcraft trials there and was removed from office in 1606 as they ended. Earlier, Veser had been convicted of fraud, and he stood under suspicion of manslaughter. He owed his appointment largely to the support of a burgomaster with whom he shared a godfather, and he always represented council interests with only very superficial control by the bailiff. At least at times, Johann Veser left the criminal investigations to the town council and the town scribes. Binding the sheriff to the will of the council was part of the process by which the Horb town council managed to usurp the territorial lord's authority in administration and justice. In Horb, the directives of officials from Hohen-berg's administrative center, Rottenburg, were simply ignored.[55] The Horb council conducted confiscations in criminal trials under its own power and authority. The council had usurped the administration of justice to such a degree in 1605 that it independently punished adultery and violations of the peace and collected fines that were actually owed to the territorial lord. Thus, the town councils were effectively able to control the officials of the territo-rial lord in judicial affairs.

In summary, the significance of the Hohenberg town councils depended on the fact that they did not represent just a small, socially isolated elite, as did councils in other parts of Swabian Austria. Instead, they shared the problems and interests of the majority of the people, including their desire for witch trials. The councils had, however, also attained substantial practi-cal influence over criminal justice through conflict with the territorial lord's officials. The councils thus represented the interests of the people but were a part of the criminal justice system. The collaboration between the common people and the town councils in pursuing witch hunts was the necessary foundation for the actual trials that took place in Hohenberg.

When members of the elite fell under suspicion of witchcraft and tried to escape the resulting attacks, they only reinforced social distrust. Rotten-burg officials, especially the vicegerent and sheriff, accepted bribes. They favored members of the elite in trials or actively helped them to flee. They manipulated confessions. The sarcastic description of the Hohenberg trials, "the poor into ashes, the rich [reach] into the pocket," expressed the anger of the lower and middle classes. Ordinary people conflated genuine skepti-cism concerning witchcraft trials with the venality of Christoph Wendler and his fellow officials. Protests against the unfairness of the witch hunts were numerous: "The rich are let go, the poor are taken down; even the child in its mother's womb knows all about that."[56] These accusations were not entirely accurate. It was characteristic of Hohenberg that the consensus for witch hunting, shared by almost the entire society, was not restrained by group solidarity within any social class. In Rottenburg and Horb, councilors demanded witch trials against their own peers. The same was true for ter-ritorial officials. Cases of favoritism and corruption, however, meant that the desire to prosecute members of the elite came to be seen as a way to treat "poor" and "rich" defendants equally in the witch trials and thus only increased popular support for the trials. Proceeding harshly against witches, without regard for individual status, became veritable proof of official pro-bity. At their executions, convicted witches from the lower classes sometimes demanded harsher proceedings against members of the elite. They abandoned the simple form of denunciations against individuals in favor of a general accusation of the upper class as a whole.[57]

How did the representatives of the territorial lord use what limited powers they still had? Did they try to implement any of the skeptical or restrictive measures that were in place in Innsbruck? Hohenberg officials never made an attempt to apply the strict guidelines of the *Carolina* to local trials in order to limit trials. In combination with their fear of witchcraft, the eroding authority of the territorial officials was too weak to support a skeptical position. Even so, aside from Veser in Horb and one bailiff in Oberndorf during the late witch hunts, there is no evidence of any official actively advocating witch trials. Vicegerent Wendler was passive. In one case, he even criticized the witch hunts. In conversation with councilors he once said, "The witches cannot do anything; it is all mere delusion." In this he was repeating the position of Johann Brenz, about whom he had probably learned during his studies in Tübingen. Brenz had insisted that witches were actually powerless. All magic, he argued, was performed by the Devil, acting as the instrument of God's wrath. Witches simply lived under the delusion that they possessed magical powers.[58] So Wendler was familiar with one idea that could have mitigated the witch hunts, yet he never drew any practical conclusions from it.

Being a power player and political realist, Wendler did not wish to risk any conflict with the restless citizenry, who were already distrustful of him or even hostile. The vicegerent only threatened the local proponents of witch hunting when, over his objections and abandoning any remnant of orderly procedure, they wanted to start lynching suspects. People blamed Wendler's inaction for the fact that the witches had done so much harm.[59] Suspicions that Wendler was himself a witch were thus reinforced by criticisms of his failure to prosecute witches.

The Innsbruck government promoted the *Carolina* as a guideline, but this position could not be transplanted to the localities of Swabian Austria because of the weak administrative structure there. The strategies that the central government developed to counter these weaknesses, moreover, were mutually contradictory and were not consistently maintained, so that they were not only unsuccessful but, at times, even counterproductive. Aside from cases in which a sheer lack of personnel compelled the government to refuse to instruct local officials,[60] the Innsbruck government strove to obtain reliable information and to make as many decisions as it could by itself. The territorial lord attempted to use judicial administration as a tool to consolidate

its power in Swabian Austria. In witch trials, the Innsbruck government
heard appeals from local officials as well as from witch hunters and suspects.
Innsbruck did not insist that petitioners use official channels and instead
allowed them to approach the central government directly. These "central-
ist" tendencies of the Innsbruck government failed, however, because the
government did not have sufficient control over its own administration to
function actively or take the initiative. Crimes, including witchcraft, did not
fall under the jurisdiction of the high authorities and did not have to be reported to the central government. Such a duty to report and a strictly organized administration did characterize both the Palatinate and Württemberg,
which had far less witch hunting than did Swabian Austria.[61] To be effective,
Innsbruck's right to give guidance as legislator and to issue individual decrees
and directives was dependent on two specific factors: first, the obedience of
Swabian Austrian regional and local officials and their willingness to provide
reliable information; and second, the ability of those accused to contact Innsbruck. As a rule, both factors worked against the government. Hardly any
information flowed in from far-away Hohenberg. This explains how the peak
of the witch hunts in Rottenburg in 1596 could actually go unnoticed by the
government. This lack of information was even more serious in light of the
fact that, in 1596, an Innsbruck printer published a broadside about the witch
trials in Hohenberg that was well informed about events in Rottenburg.

Local officials and town councils regularly ignored directives obtained by
trial victims requiring changes in trial procedures. In most Swabian Austrian
witch trials, local courts clearly disregarded the guidelines of the *Carolina*,
even though Innsbruck had repeatedly insisted on them. In the 1590s, the
central government was well aware of that local officials and town councils
in Hohenberg were disobeying orders, yet they were unable to bring them
under control. Even when torture and executions were carried out against
the express will of the government, Innsbruck's reaction amounted to nothing more than a sharp letter of protest.[62]

One case with central significance for the course of the witch trials in
Hohenberg deserves closer examination: the trial of Christina Rauscher,
daughter of Horb Burgomaster Martin Gerber. With the help of the Innsbruck government, Gerber's family attempted to secure a leading position
in Horb, despite opposition from the old town council elite. In this, Gerber's
wife, Anna, and his daughter Christina, wife of the wealthy landlord Johann
Rauscher, had supported him wholeheartedly. Witchcraft suspicions against
Gerber's family surfaced in a chain of trials that began in 1597-99. Against
the council, which pushed for Christina's arrest, the family traveled to Inns-

bruck and obtained the appointment of a commission of clerics charged with the task of investigating. In addition, Innsbruck told the town council that it should request a legal opinion from the University of Freiburg. As usual, Innsbruck emphasized that everyone had a right to appeal to the archducal government. The clerical commission attested to Christina's innocence in 1600 and was promptly accused of bias by the council.[63] The council then threw Christina and her husband into a dungeon for several days, without any charges. A lengthy legal battle followed, between the town and the Rauschers, who demanded compensation for their imprisonment, and between Christina Rauscher and Sheriff Veser, for slander. It was rumored that Veser had attempted to extort denunciations against Christina.

In the course of this conflict, Christina Rauscher appealed repeatedly to Innsbruck for help. She was again arrested and held for several days. Asked for the reason, the burgomaster only stated that if she would "henceforth leave the government in Innsbruck alone, things will go well for her." Clearly, the town council wanted the Rauschers to submit to its authority. By contrast, Christina kept insisting: "She has no lords here, but in Innsbruck and Rottenburg." In the end, Innsbruck declared that the council had shown bias and that the government would settle all disputes itself. But then, on November 29, 1604, members of the town council raided Christina Rauscher's house and arrested her. She was charged with witchcraft and tortured, even though she was seven months pregnant, resulting in the loss of the child. There was no longer any question of observing the guidelines of the *Carolina* or heeding the Innsbruck government. The questions asked during torture only occasionally referred to the charge of witchcraft. Christina was also interrogated regarding her contacts with Innsbruck. The town council itself and the town scribe conducted these interrogations.[64] Although the councilors certainly seemed mainly interested in eliminating the Rauscher family as a political force, this does not mean that the questions about magical crimes, which they pursued with great persistence, were not genuine. The Gerber-Rauscher family had pushed their economic and political ambitions forcefully and in the process had evoked witchcraft suspicions. The council then naturally turned against both; they had come to be "evil people."

With the help of his Tübingen lawyer, Johann Rauscher began to petition the officials in Rottenburg, the count of Zollern as governor, the bishop of Constance, and the Innsbruck government for his wife's release. In accordance with the power structure in Hohenberg, although all of these external parties supported Rauscher and even though favorable legal opinions were provided, the Horb council was able to hold the suspect for nearly a year and continue torturing her. During her entire imprisonment, the accused woman could not be forced to confess. The council aborted the trial only after the Innsbruck government intervened by sending a commission to Hohenberg. I will discuss the activities of that commission in chapter 6.[65]

The Innsbruck government kept a far better grip on Nellenburg, Burgau, and the Swabian Landvogtei than on Hohenberg. These lands lay closer to the center and were easier to reach. In Hohenberg at the end of the sixteenth century, the territorial lords was dependent on the willingness of people and institutions in Hohenberg to provide information, and it was all too easy for the Hohenberg authorities to mislead the central government or leave it totally in the dark about the local situation. By contrast, the highly splintered territories of Burgau and the Landvogtei—and, to a lesser degree, Nellenburg—were so full of conflict that it was necessary for local officials to maintain close ties to the central government. The jurisdictional struggles with nearly all of the neighboring territories that confronted those parts of Swabian Austria throughout the sixteenth and seventeenth centuries could be settled only through direct contact with Innsbruck. The government repeatedly sent investigating commissions into eastern and southern Swabian Austria, one after the other. Between 1558 and 1654, eighteen such commissions went to the Landvogtei alone. Moreover, most of the secular and ecclesiastical territories that surrounded eastern and southern Swabian Austria belonged to clients of the Habsburgs.[66] For their part, they naturally turned to Innsbruck as a negotiator in conflicts with regional or local officials of Austria. In addition, there were conflicts between the Habsburg Court of Appeals in Swabia and the courts of Burgau and the Landvogtei. The government became the referee for these conflicts, too. The result was that a dense network of information and communication developed in the Habsburg-dominated Lech-Danube–Lake Constance region that converged in Innsbruck. Thus, reports on eastern and southern Swabian Austria not only flowed continuously, but they came in from various perspectives. No "monopoly of information" developed like that which had come into existence in Hohenberg. The unclear and conflict-laden circumstances in eastern and southern Swabian Austria made that region dependent on the central government. As in parts of Switzerland during the fifteenth century, competition among courts and unclear jurisdictional boundaries actually created legal stability.[67] There was no room for juridical discretion that might have allowed the legally questionable witch trials to become mass phenomena.

In contrast, however, during the 1580s and 1590s, Hohenberg did not experience any inspections. Its neighbors respected most of its boundaries, and

Hohenberg's position as a virtual enclave with its old opponent Württemberg had an insulating effect.

All together, the Hohenberg witch trials thus represent the failure of Habsburg central authority and the victory of local autonomy. Either the local officials were unable to prevail against popular demands for witch hunts, or else they allowed themselves to become tools of those demands.

We cannot understand the actual trial procedures without their political and administrative background. However, we must examine the trial procedures themselves most closely. Ultimately, the use of torture and the courts' decisions concerning the admissibility of evidence and witnesses determined the outcome of the trials.

One of the demands that the Innsbruck government repeatedly brought to bear on the local trials in Swabian Austria was that the courts had to obtain legal opinions from trained jurists. This demand was totally in accordance with the *Carolina.* At the beginning of the greatest wave of trials in Hohenberg, the Rottenburg court indeed acquired such a legal opinion. It was entitled "New Advice on Revealing Old Witches." An imperial councilor, the bailiff of Haigerloch, and the jurist Johannes Halbritter of the University of Tübingen had written it at the government's request in 1594. The opinion repeated the *Carolina's* recommendations regarding evidence. However, contrary to the *Carolina,* it stipulated a detailed catalog of leading questions, which essentially placed particular points in the mouth of the witness. The learned jurists did grant the accused the right to a defender, who, along with the accused, was to be allowed access to all of the trial records. Rumors and denunciations were not supposed to suffice for an arrest because, the consultants maintained (basing their opinion on the famous jurist Joost Damhouder), the Devil deceived witches by appearing as completely innocent people at the Sabbath. An important argument against accepting denunciations was thus already well known at the beginning of the greatest wave of trials, yet it had no effect on practice. The opinion went on to read, self-contradictorily, that investigations always vindicated accusations made by children. Prior to this legal opinion, Innsbruck had announced its willingness to accept the testimony of two girls—Maria Ulmerin and her sister—as relevant in court. In this respect, the legal opinion justified the government's orders. While this legal opinion, drawn up at the government's order and partly by Habsburg officials, remained at least formally based on the *Carolina,* an opinion written in 1598 for the zealous Horb town council took an entirely different approach. Unfortunately, we cannot tell who wrote that opinion. Explicitly contradicting the *Carolina,* the legal opinion followed

Bodin in recommending the unrestricted use of denunciations as sufficient indication for arrest and torture. In 1613, the Günzburg council had several foreign jurists draft legal opinions. If an opinion did not reflect the cautious approach of the council, the councilors simply ignored it and obtained a new one. It is clear that the authorities succeeded in acquiring legal opinions that agreed with their positions on the matter, from skepticism, through moderate willingness to persecute, and on to radical approval of witch hunting. Evidently, we can observe the formation of a modern market of competing experts. Scholarly jurists did not dictate to the courts, and instead the courts simply used jurists with whom they concurred.[68]

Very few records of witness interrogations from Swabian Austrian witch trials survive. During the main phase of the trials in Hohenberg, the courts avoided the examination of witnesses entirely. The authorities proceeded to arrest and torture simply on the basis of denunciations. After 1670 and 1680, foreign jurists and the Innsbruck government complained that witnesses were not being sworn in. As with witness testimony, usually the Hohenberg courts did not subject denunciations and confessions to any critical review. The authorities failed to search for material evidence such as ingredients for sorcery. This irresponsible handling of evidence and denunciations was reinforced by inattentiveness in taking confessions. For example, the absence of the pact went unnoticed in individual confessions. The court personnel simply accepted witches' confessions of specific instances of harmful magic even if the same confessions claimed that the pact had been sealed only years later.[69]

The frequency of the trials demonstrates that during the height of the witch hunts the courts were extremely careless in the examination of individual cases. The first arrest of the great wave of trials in Rottenburg in 1596 took place on April 19; another must have followed it on April 26. Confessions then followed in quick succession on May 3, 7, 8, 20, and 21; two are dated May 28; and one each are dated on May 30 and 31 and June 1. On June 5, two accused persons confessed; on June 6, three confessed. Then, on July 31, twelve other women were executed. The same two councilors presided over all of these trials. They were the youngest and least experienced members of the council. With only a town scribe as secretary, often even without so much as the assistance of the sheriff, they worked very quickly, indeed.[70]

As the charge of witchcraft was practically impossible to prove, the courts tended to accept auxiliary evidence specifically to put the witch hunts on a seemingly more stable foundation. However, in the territories under investigation here, such auxiliary evidence was only of marginal significance.

Only in a single case in Stockach in 1680 did the court cite the inability to shed tears as an incriminating element. The *stigma diaboli,* the Devil's mark, played a somewhat more important role in the trials. The Devil's mark was an insensitive and bloodless pigmentation with which the Devil supposedly branded his witches, like livestock. In Hohenberg, the *stigma diaboli* appeared during the trials of the 1620s and 1630s and for the last time in 1710; in Nellenburg, it appeared in 1663 and 1680. But in no case did this "evidence" have a decisive effect. In 1530, in Rottenburg, the court failed to force several to confess despite excessive torture. Then the suspects' body hair was shaved. As torture had already begun, the court was not presumably searching for a Devil's mark to incriminate the defendant but, rather, was seeking to find or eliminate whatever charm might have been hidden in the hair to guarantee silence. The author of the *Malleus Maleficarum* had expressly recommended this procedure and had used it himself. The Rottenburg executioner in 1530 was a certain Wolf Valch from Ravensburg, who may have known about Kramer's procedures during the earlier witch trials in that city. At around the same time, another executioner from Ravensburg was summoned to Nördlingen as an expert on torturing witches. Later, however, the court of Swabian Austria employed the practice of shaving witches only in isolated cases in 1650 and 1680.[71]

In Swabian Austrian witch trials, the customary torture was the so-called *Aufziehen* (*strappado*). If one could survive torture without confessing, the courts accepted this as exoneration; exceptions to this rule occurred in only a few cases during the height of the persecution waves. But the length and repetition of torture must have often exceeded the degree permitted by the *Carolina.* In the few late cases for which local officials submitted records for legal review, the Innsbruck government continued to criticize the improperly harsh application of torture. In 1660, the court for the territory of Gutenstein, which had fallen under Habsburg control, condemned the eleven-year-old Maria Paumannin to *"sectio venae"* (i.e., bleeding to death). In 1664, a nun from Urspring was sentenced to the same death, and in another case in Altdorf, in 1680, the judges considered this punishment again.[72] The condemned were to have their arteries cut in a hot bath so that they bled to death. The authorities considered this mode of punishment an act of mercy. The jails—usually some cellar room of the courthouse or an otherwise empty tower of the town wall—were in wretched condition. At least five women suspected of witchcraft died in Swabian Austrian jails, one of whom starved to death. In Horb and Rottenburg, two towers that were used as witches' jails still exist: the Schütte Tower of Rottenburg and the Luzifer Tower of Horb.

Alleged witches were imprisoned in the Luzifer Tower of Horb. The tower was named after the morning star, Lucifer, because it faces east.

In Rottenburg, some alleged witches were imprisoned in the Schütte Tower. Today, the Schütte Tower is part of the Rottenburg correctional facility.

The strange name of the second building is probably derived from the fact that it faces east, toward Lucifer, the morning star.[73]

When the courts found the evidence lacking, they made the defendants swear never to appeal the case and released them. Even that had drastic social repercussions. Generally, the judges combined release with banishment or house arrest.[74] For most of the trial victims, the immediate result must have been impoverishment.

The usually strained financial situation of the Habsburg archdukes might have driven them to confiscate the goods of all those convicted.[75] Because the Innsbruck government could not control the local officials in Hohenberg, the center of the witch hunting, however, the Innsbruck treasury never realized any income from confiscation or fines there. Instead, fines received only expanded the personal influence of local Habsburg officials. No opportunity to attain mentionable gain arose from the trials for the cities or for the individual councilors.

A legal opinion on court costs gives the earliest evidence of the expenses of witch trials. In 1580, a jurist familiar with Swabian Austria stated that confiscations were unusual. In response to specific inquiries from Burgau (1595) and Oberndorf in Hohenberg (1598), Innsbruck rejected the practice of confiscation. Also, Innsbruck claimed the right to decide on the level of the fine on a case-by-case basis, based on the seriousness of the crime and the economic situation of the family. There is, however, no evidence that each individual case was actually sent up the official channels. When in 1605 the heirs of Oberndorf trial victims complained to the government that their inheritance had not been turned over to them by the local officials, they got nowhere. This case suggests that local courts rarely or never consulted Innsbruck about fines. In response to an inquiry from Innsbruck in 1598 on how Nellenburg regulated witch-trial expenses, Stockach took two years to respond. As a rule only the trial expenses, 30 to 40 florins, were taken from the property of the condemned. The remainder went to the heirs. The local officials reserved the right, however, to demand additional fines according to the circumstances of each case. There is no evidence as to whether Innsbruck responded to this disclosure, which violated the directive it had issued in the Oberndorf case. By 1603, however, the government had "forgotten" the entire discussion, asking the local officials once again how the Swabian Austrian trials were financed. That this confusion even arose shows that the central government had no real interest in witch trials as a source of income.[76] One might call this a half-hearted centralism, which on the one hand unrealistically attempted to collect detailed information and to make as many decisions as possible, yet on the other did not implement any generally applicable rules and hence became dependent on the willingness of local authorities to cooperate. Cost controls, which might have inhibited trials, were thus relinquished. Effectively, local officials paid for trial costs and reimbursed themselves through fines with no reference to Innsbruck. Even so, there were no rumors that any particular official had enriched himself through witch trials.

Despite the relatively low expenses, the trials drove some poor families into financial distress. If the property of a trial victim was insufficient to cover the expenses, the territorial lord had to assume the rest of the bill. The cities did not share the costs. If the assumption of costs proved too great a burden for the local administration, the Innsbruck chamber was supposed to pay them.[77]

The Practice of Persecution: Structures and Developments in the Electorate of Trier

As has already been shown, autonomous committees formed by communities to resolve clearly defined issues constituted an important part of the local self-government of villages in the Saar-Moselle-Rhine region. Witch committees were simply a particular manifestation of these communal committees. Although we cannot prove that such committees existed in the Electorate of Trier, many reports of such bodies survive from the immediately surrounding territories. Such committees always originated in the village assemblies, but these German community assemblies were not like Massachusetts town meetings. The assemblies were usually spontaneous gatherings of community members, which gained strength from the immediacy and spontaneity of the occasion, and possibly also from their tumultuous character. Their effectiveness and attractiveness as self-governing bodies derived in part from the fact that they could react immediately to new situations. The village assembly formed a confederation and appointed a committee. In this way, the village assemblies, which only met briefly, were able to create lasting, if not permanent, structures and institutions. The villagers created their confederation by swearing collectively that they would adhere to the consensus of the community assembly. This aspect of the confederation seems to have been very important. The Witch Trial Ordinance of the Electorate considered a brief description necessary: "The community [has] come together, made their particular confederation and commitment to stand together as one man and to risk life and property together for the common cause."[78] This was the foundation of the communal witch hunts and their salient feature. We can follow the trend of such communal confederations through to the last known witch hunt in which the Electorate participated, in the domain of Wehrheim (under the shared control of Trier and Nassau). There, even at the end of the 1680s, the "allied subjects" backed up their witch committees. The parallels to sworn confederations in the formation of peasant troops during the Great Peasants' War of 1525 are evident. Indeed, the government of the Electorate of Trier saw these oath-bound collectives of subjects as a potential threat. The confederation concretely grounded the power of the committee, which was the proclaimed advocate of the will of the community, and thus acquired both external importance and internal legitimacy. Any villager who dared to criticize the committees' activities was also criticizing the village community itself. On the same principle, villages founded committees that were responsible for community groups larger than a single village. Regional committees sometimes served an entire high court district. For these, each village chose one or two individuals to form a shared committee with the delegates of neighboring communities.[79]

Evidently, it took more than a diffuse sense of crisis and merely general demands for witch hunts to produce witch trials. It took a political decision and administrative initiative to start a witch hunt. Accordingly, contemporaries always remembered the exact date that a local witch hunt began.[80] The trials thus had the character of campaigns that had been initiated through conscious decisions.

The manner in which village assemblies established a committee varied from place to place.[81] The oldest source on the founding of a witch committee reports that in 1564, in the territory of Elter in modern Luxembourg, a village created a committee at the initiative of a private individual. The peasants formed a confederation by grasping a staff that was planted in the earth. The confederation was not entirely voluntary; the communal authorities would fine anyone who refused to cooperate. One repeatedly encounters this means of forming a confederation—villagers in turn touching a staff or knife—with only small variations in the later sources. It appears to have been widespread; children even imitated it in their games. In 1587, in the village Benrather Hof of St. Maximin, the confederation formed when every resident swore with a handshake to assist the reeve. The reeve, who represented the community as a collective, thus became the guarantor of collective action. For the witch committee of the communities of Mallendar, where the Electorate of Trier shared rule with the County of Wittgenstein, a charter of establishment was drafted in 1631 and signed by every community member who could write.[82]

The committee could investigate witches, bring criminal charges, and even arrest suspects. There was no mention of the committee's responsibility to the community. Instead, the Mallendar charter unilaterally empowered the committee to act "in the name of the community."

The committees always had fewer than ten members. All committee members were elected, as a rule by acclamation.[83] In 1591, the Trier Witch Trial Ordinance attempted to make the founding of a committee dependent on government authorization, and in some cases (in shared domains) such formal authorization actually took place.[84] For the territory of the Electorate of Trier itself there is no similar evidence, and the government never seems to have rejected a committee member. The territorial lord (the prince-archbishop) simply accepted the witch committees, tacitly or explicitly. Thus, the territorial government accredited them as organs of self-government. A part of the "bait-and-switch" that determined the character of the committees becomes clear here: to usurp sovereign functions, the committees formally fulfilled the territorial lord's requests.

Committee members usually belonged to the upper and upper-middle social strata of the villages, but they were not generally members of the older village elite of jurors. That certainly does not mean that committee members were literate, or that they had specialized legal knowledge. In 1593, the abbot of Brauweiler saw the committee of the village Klotten as nothing more than a "bunch of boorish idiots." That committee attained great influence over the electoral administrative town of Cochem the following year. Admittedly, many of the territorial and community officials also had no legal training. Some of the members of witch committees in the Electorate of Trier rose to positions of social prominence. Annen Kasper, who had belonged to the Föhren committee in 1590, appeared in 1630 as a juror. In 1620, the sheriff, reeve, and one juror of a village in the district of Wittlich all noted that they had previously sat on a witch committee.[85]

The committees collected witchcraft accusations from inhabitants who brought forward both general demands for witch hunting and the names of specific suspects. Suspects repeatedly complained that committee members had intensified witchcraft suspicions through deliberate manipulations. In addition, it is possible that committee members expressed their own witchcraft suspicions against particular people even if they did not previously have such a reputation.[86] The committees would question witnesses, whose statements scribes and notaries wrote down, and would then reformulate the results as charges and present them to the officials of the Electorate. The questioning of witnesses was then simply repeated before the territorial court.

Then the witch committees appointed a time for a hearing, called witnesses, and invited local officials to the hearing. There is no evidence that the officials themselves called any witnesses. Of course, a committee only permitted witnesses for the prosecution, among whom their own committee members or relatives might be found.[87]

A significant part of the committees' activities consisted in finding out about and documenting denunciations of people from their villages. If denunciations were to be read aloud before local witches were executed, committee members attended the executions in the neighborhood and took notes. Usually, however, the committees contacted territorial officials and requested extracts from the confessions of executed witches. At least during the first great wave of trials during the late sixteenth century, territorial boundaries do not appear to have played any role. The courts of the Electorate willingly provided information concerning denunciations to committees both within the Electorate of Trier and beyond its borders. One episode illustrates the possibilities this presented for witch hunters. Sometime before 1600, a committee member from Schweich in the Electorate appeared at an interrogation under torture in the high court district of St. Maximin; he spoke with the notary who was recording the interrogation and gave him money. Later, the notary asked the accused if any of them had seen certain specific suspects from Schweich—whom he named—at the Sabbath. The active search for denunciations and frequent contact with jurists meant that the members of witch committees commonly undertook investigative journeys, in one case as far as Cologne. The villages remunerated committee members for their travels and, unsurprisingly, "official" and "private" trips were not always clearly distinguished.[88]

When officials of the territorial lord could ensure little or no jail guard, then members of the committee and villagers served as guards. Previous scholarship has drawn attention to the key role that jail personnel played in witch hunts. Regarding committees, the 1630 Witch Trial Ordinance of Prince Elector Philipp Christoph mentioned illegal methods of torture (*"inventiones torquendi"*) and found it necessary to emphasize that "only the authorities are permitted to conduct torture." In a legal opinion that he wrote for Philipp Christoph in 1629, the jurist and historian Melchior Goldast (1578-1635) spoke of "common, uneducated . . . peasant judges" who refused to accept voluntary confessions and instead insisted on torture. Goldast had visited Coblenz in 1629 and, in a book he wrote on witchcraft, provided a detailed description of a case from the district of Ehrenbreitstein. He was probably alluding to committees from the Electorate of Trier.[89]

The necessity of written charges and the legal language in which they had to be couched required witch committees to employ at least one scribe with legal experience, especially during waves of trials.[90] With a view to the requirements of the Witch Trial Ordinance, the committees often endeavored to justify their actions with legal opinions from professional jurists. For this reason, in the Electorate of Trier witch committees regularly hired university-educated, middle-class jurists, choosing from among the professional jurists in Trier and Coblenz. Some jurists developed into acknowledged experts and "juridical entrepreneurs" whom witch committees repeatedly hired over the years. Dr. Johann Moeden of Coblenz was known as *"malleus sagarum"* (i.e., the hammer of witches, echoing the title of the *Malleus Maleficarum*). Of course, genuine interest in eliminating witches did not preclude an interest in personal financial gain. It was in the financial interests of the urban jurists to accommodate the witch committees' wishes. In light of the competitive pressure among the lawyers, none of them could be critical of the witch hunts without suffering financially. Beyond individual honoraria, the urban jurists could effectively reach out to the rural regions through long-term involvement in the witch trials. Through the committees, they came into contact with the leaders of the villages, and in the same way they became acquainted with the territorial lord's local representatives. Thus, the witch trials offered career opportunities to the jurists involved. Alongside financial gain and career advancement, it was also possible for jurists to criminally abuse their access to denunciations. To set an example, the government impaled the head of a notary on a spike at the gallows of Coblenz in the mid-seventeenth century because he had inserted false denunciations into a written confession.[91]

Supported by judicial specialists and their own experience, witch committees often displayed extraordinary confidence when dealing with their territorial lords. They imitated the titles of territorial officials and, unlike their lords, they unconditionally claimed that they served the will of God. One committee had the nerve to quote sections of Roman law and the Vulgate to officials of the Electorate.[92]

In the cities of Trier and Coblenz, there were no committees at first. The cities did not participate in the committee phenomenon, which was an administrative structure of the villages. In Trier, however, an organization rooted in urban tradition did seize the initiative in the witch hunts: the guilds. At the beginning of February 1590, committees appeared, at first within individual guilds, who set them up to keep members of "witch families" out of their trade organizations. Delegates of such witch committees would then form an eight-member "committee of the committees." Strictly speaking, this was not a communal organization like the village committees but a guild organization. Loyal to the government of the Electorate, however, the city council refused to relay this committee's charges to the prince elector. Only after massive public pressure did the council yield in the summer of 1590. The activities of the witch committee of the Trier guilds ended in 1596 along with the first great witch hunt, and during the seventeenth century no committees reemerged in the city.[93]

In 1486, Heinrich Kramer had criticized the Coblenz court of the Electorate of Trier as the very model of a backward judiciary that had not yet acknowledged the threat of witches. The trial wave of 1492-94 in Boppard proves that the courts soon abandoned this cautious stance. Nonetheless, the chronicler of the Eberhardklausen monastery complained that during the witch hunts of the early sixteenth century, the officials of the Electorate still required what he considered excessive incriminating evidence.[94] The officials lost caution during the main phase of the witch hunts, but they never took the initiative. Court officials essentially shared the popular desire for witch hunting, readily cooperating with the committees and passively accepting the results of their investigations. If conflicts of interest arose between the central government and the rural communities, local and regional officials tended to side with the villages. When the district commissioner of Mayen had to enforce a trial moratorium ordered by the prince elector in 1600, he asked permission to show his orders to the village witch hunters. He apparently considered it necessary to show them that he acted under compulsion. If the committees felt insufficiently supported by their local officials—as, for example, when trial victims dared to defend themselves by complaining to the high courts—then the committees appealed directly to the territorial government.[95]

As district commissioner of Pfalzel and Grimburg and vicegerent of Trier from 1583 to 1600, Johann Zandt von Merl occupied an unusual position. Despite initial reticence, he became a proponent of witch trials after contact with the committees. He disregarded both the Trier Witch Trial Ordinance and the *Carolina*. After 1584, by order of the prince elector, Vicegerent Zandt conducted the trials of prominent men as the official prosecutor for the city of Trier. Those trials were due largely to denunciations collected by rural committees. Yet to the most determined witch hunters, Zandt still seemed too mild. Heinrich Bock, the Trier publisher who produced a German translation of Binsfeld's tract in 1590, dedicated that text to the vicegerent, sheriff, council, and jury of Trier. In his preface he warned undutiful judges that

they should fear the wrath of God if they neglected witchcraft. Although at
the end of the preface he distinguished the Trier authorities from such bad
judges in a few short sentences, his implicit criticism was clear. Bock's warnings accorded with popular complaints in the 1590s that territorial officials
and the council were too lax in hunting witches. This specific complaint and
the general resentment against people from among the prince elector's inner
circle ensured that in 1591/92, Zandt and his wife were also denounced.[96]

Legally, the witch committees acted as accusers in accusatory trials. They
had at their disposal, however, their own apparatus for investigations and a
local judicial infrastructure with their own legal advisers. The authorities
accepted their investigations just as they did those from investigators in ex
officio (inquisitorial) trials. Accordingly, the witch trials in the Electorate of
Trier were nothing like accusatory trials (a contest between equal adversar-
ies) described by the *Carolina*.[97] In this respect, even formal participation in
an accusatory trial procedure was a deceptive. Most rural communities had
lost their right to criminal jurisdiction in the early sixteenth century, but they
partially regained it in the witch trials.

These local coalitions of witch committees, officials, and jurists consolidated to protect themselves and preserve their autonomy. The Witch Trial
Ordinance of 1591 had criticized the committees for driving trial costs to ex-
orbitant heights through their "great disorderly banquets, eating, and drinking."[98] Traditionally, village committees had a social function, with shared
meals as one of their activities. The Lower Court Ordinance of 1537 and the
Officials' Ordinance of 1574 had already attempted in vain to limit expensive
banquets for jurors at the defendants' expense. With the witch hunts, these
"business dinners" accumulated, and the accused had to pay the bill. At such
shared meals, committee members met with jurists, territorial officials, and
members of the local elite who, as jurors or witnesses, also frequently joined
for the sake of socializing.[99] These free "working dinners" in the context of
the witch trials were of immense significance for the exchange of information
and for opportunities to forge business and social connections or to advance
one's social status. A network of mutually shared interests and information
developed, which the central government of the Electorate found very difficult to control or even to infiltrate.

How did the highest level of the judiciary of the Electorate and the prince
electors react to the witch trials?[100] There is no evidence of any direct call
to proceed against witches. Yet the witch-hunting excesses at the end of the
sixteenth century would have been impossible without at least the passive
approval of Prince Elector Johann VII. This elector exerted his direct per-

sonal influence only in the trial of Diederich Flade, the first trial against a prominent person in the city of Trier, and even in that trial one can hardly speak of Johann as a driving force. After long hesitation, he ordered Flade to be arrested only when Flade, after two failed attempts to flee the Electorate secretly, asked permission to join a monastery and then brazenly promised the archbishop the right to use his property in return. Only after two priests denounced Flade after confessing their own pact with the Devil did Johann allow his former liegeman to fall from office. Flade confessed a week later and was executed on September 18, 1589. In the trials of Niclaus Fiedler and Hans Reuland, Johann gave the official order for an inquest only after collecting numerous denunciations. Although Johann VII officially forbade autonomous committees in 1591, he actively accepted materials produced by them. Evidently, the trials in the city of Trier in the 1580s and 1590s did not follow the *Carolina* any more closely than did any other trials in the Electorate.[101]

According to the Witch Trial Ordinance of 1591, the high courts of Trier and Coblenz should have been informed about every witch trial in the Electorate through the submission of case files. Admittedly, even then they could only work with whatever material the committees collected and only with officials submissive to the committees. In the incomplete archival sources, a collection of fifteen decisions from the Coblenz high court survive from the years 1591-93 for the district of Mayen. These decisions testify to a significant eagerness to prosecute, although the actions of the high court suggest that the Witch Trial Ordinance was not completely disregarded. In addition, there are twenty-nine transcripts of information requested by the high court of Trier from the years 1610 to 1612. In three cases, the high court ordered further investigations because details of the case had not been sufficiently established. In ten cases, the suspects were to be arrested and interrogated, first without and then with torture according to the guidelines of the *Carolina*. In the remaining sixteen cases, the Trier jury decided to acquit. Unfortunately, we can no longer determine the grounds on which the high court made its decisions. In the witch hunts in the Electorate, the witch committees typically took up direct contact with the high courts, without the mediation of local officials. This clearly contradicted the intention of the Witch Trial Ordinance of 1591, which sought to strengthen the position of local officials. The fact that the territorial government allowed its own bureaucracy to be circumvented thus also revealed its weakness. Moreover, the witch committees did not always obey the dictates of the high courts. Three of the sixteen acquittals repeated previous decisions. As a rule, local officials accepted the legal opinions of the committees' jurists and did not contact the high courts. Indeed, the Witch

Trial Ordinance of 1630 still assumed that the witch committees operated outside the authorities' control.[102]

Nonetheless, those trial victims who could bring the necessary knowledge and means to bear could hope to avoid being found guilty by turning to the high courts or the territorial lord. An example bears mentioning. Through multiple petitions to the high court in Coblenz in 1602, the wealthy juror Simon Dietherich not only obtained his release after an initial round of torture, but he was also restored to his office as juror, and the committee was made to bear the trial expenses. When Dietherich returned from a pilgrimage, which the committee interpreted as an attempt at flight, the committee immediately arrested him again. After a new supplication, he was released on bail at the order of Prince Elector Lothar von Metternich and over the protests of the district commissioner.[103] Witchcraft suspects' petitions to the imperial appeals court of the Reichskammergericht essentially had the same function and effect as turning to the territorial high courts. Violations of the *Carolina* presented an opportunity to prove that rights had been disregarded or that a whole trial had been invalid.[104] Of course, local witch-hunting proponents experienced such appeals as instances of scandalous corruption and unequal treatment when certain well-heeled witchcraft suspects managed to draw the attention of territorial or imperial appeals courts and thus avoided a trial or at least a guilty verdict. In 1684, local witch hunters put this grievance in almost the same words as in Swabian Austria: "The poor into ashes, the rich into the pockets."[105]

A high point in the conflict between committees and territorial lord in the Electorate of Trier came during the witch hunts in Cochem in 1594/95. In 1592, the committee of the village Klotten had caused thirty people to be executed. These trials had also provided denunciations against numerous persons from the city of Cochem. The city council and the district commissioner ignored these charges. Then the leader of the old guard of Cochem allied himself with the Klotten committee. Together, they were able to compel the city council to accept the formation of a Cochem witch committee. Winegrowers and tradesmen—that is, people unqualified to sit on the city council—composed the new witch committee. In a process reminiscent of the struggle of the medieval guilds against the patriciate, this committee effectively established itself as a second government in the city. Large parts of the populace no longer respected the authority of the council, and to avoid conflict, the local officials of the prince elector gave the committee free rein. In addition, some committee members appear to have exploited the witch trials as a source of extra income by charging high rates for imprisonment.

Contact with the high court in Coblenz was effectively cut off. For months, the committee carried out a series of tumultuous arrests. In the dungeon of Cochem castle, committee members used torture without any restraint. The trials were frequently directed against social climbers and individuals who were politically favorable toward the territorial government. The central government suppressed the Cochem witch hunt at the end of 1594, when members of the elite finally succeeded in drawing the attention of the Coblenz high court and the prince elector to the serious miscarriages of justice perpetrated by the witch hunters. To maintain its own power, the central government of the Electorate now had to take action against the Cochem "coup," which had sought local autonomy. The Coblenz high court took the committee's trials under review and found them invalid. The committee itself was sentenced to repay the trial expenses.[106] Needless to say, after this scandal there were no more witches in Cochem.

The Witch Trial Ordinance of 1591 condemned the committees as "rebellious confederations."[107] As the example of Cochem vividly emphasizes, however, the territorial government faced not open rebellion but the threat of a semi-legal loss of power. The rural communities succeeded for a time in repelling the power of the territorial state, which had only just begun to establish itself in the rural areas in the Electorate of Trier. The witch trials became the means for and expression of this development. The effort to repel territorial lordship exploited the very means that the central government itself had forced on the agents of the community: advisory jurists, notaries, and, of course, the local officials of the territorial lord, whom the committees brought to heel. The committees availed themselves of these instruments quite effectively. They competed with the territorial government and, using the government's own tools, effectively excluded it from their communities and from the actual witch hunts.

After the excesses in Cochem, another scandal took place in Trier in 1596. A man accused of witchcraft began denouncing the Jesuits. Surprisingly, the Jesuits were vulnerable, for there had already been denunciations against members of the order.[108] Then, in addition, the accused man insisted that nearly every member of the secular high court was also a witch. Previously, individual members of the court had indeed been denounced, and some had even been condemned. Now the suspect denounced nearly all of them simultaneously. The explosion in the city was enormous: "Res erat plena publici tumultus (The matter was full of public uproar)." Given the precedents of Diederich Flade, Niclaus Fiedler, and the juror Kesten, as well as the clear hostility with which the local idea of witchcraft was used against elites, probably all of the high court jurors felt seriously threatened. The first step taken against Kesten and Fiedler had been their exclusion from participating in court sessions.[109] When it became known that every juror was to be replaced, the urban elite may well have felt the threat of immediate trials or even a development like that in Cochem, without any guarantee that the prince elector would intervene again. The denounced individuals actively attempted to prove their innocence and to show that "one should not trust such sayings concerning . . . diabolical witchcraft." What exactly the jurors did next is unknown. Certainly they had opinions written for them and submitted petitions to the prince elector. In the end, the Jesuits succeeded in persuading the denouncer to revoke all of his accusations. The high court then had him executed immediately, perhaps with the secondary objective of allowing him no chance to renew his denunciations.

After 1596, the number of witch trials in the Electorate fell off abruptly. Personal shock and dismay, as well as the efforts expended to prove that witchcraft accusations were unreliable, certainly deprived the witch hunts of their intellectual basis before the high courts and among leading officials. The parallel to the trial of Christina Plum in Cologne, which led to the end of the trials in that city, is obvious.[110] Nevertheless, as previous developments had shown, the central institutions of government lacked any real power to put a permanent end to the trials throughout the Electorate.

The structural conditions and major lines of conflict of the witch hunts in the Electorate therefore did not change after the end of the first major wave of trials. The disillusionment of 1596 evaporated. Local coalitions of witch committees and local officials, with the help of the urban jurists they employed, were able to continue ignoring or annulling the weak attempts at control by the prince elector's government, when events beyond the Electorate's control brought the second great wave of trials to an end. In 1631, the Electorate fell squarely into the destructive path of the Thirty Years' War. Prince Elector Philipp Christoph's continued support for France, despite the presence of Spanish troops, brought the Electorate into the center of the French–Habsburg conflict. The Electorate of Trier became a battlefield and marching ground for Spanish, French, Swedish, and imperial armies. Social and administrative chaos caused by military occupation and the flight of parts of the populace robbed the witch trials of their organizational basis.[111]

What do the sources tell us about the organization of the actual trials and trial procedures in the Electorate? The committees' investigations were limited to collecting witness testimony and denunciations. As a rule, the officials of the Electorate were satisfied to accept this evidence without expanding or reviewing it further. "Auxiliary evidence," however, did play a role in the Electorate. In the so-called cold-water test, the suspect was bound and thrown into a body of water. If she sank, her innocence was proved. Both Peter Binsfeld and Elector Johann VII sharply rejected such water tests, so they must have been important during the early persecutions. Binsfeld explicitly noted that the practice had crept in some years previously—that is, probably at the beginning of the massive witch hunts in 1586, and possibly as one of their vehicles. He also claimed that failing the water test was often viewed as sufficient incrimination to justify torture. Like the prince elector, he sternly rejected this "auxiliary evidence." The Devil's mark (*stigma diaboli*) was mentioned in only one trial. In the 1492-96 trials in Boppard, the executioner shaved the suspects after arrest to remove any charms that supposedly guaranteed silence. But after that, these precautions appeared in only two isolated cases, without any recognizable connection to Boppard or to each other: in 1582 in Trier and in 1630 in Pfalzel, each time after an initial round of torture had proved unproductive.[112]

The usual means of torture was the strappado. In the city of Trier, a most unusual jail for witches can still be seen. The prince electors built their Renaissance residence around the ruins of a huge Roman basilica, originally erected for Constantine the Great, and the prince electors used part of this basilica as a jail. Today, after substantial renovation, the basilica is used as a church. According to the *Carolina*, surviving torture without confession should exonerate the accused, and as a rule in the Electorate it actually did. But during the peaks of the witch hunts, the officers of the Electorate proved unwilling to accept this exoneration. Even in the city of Trier, where there was no local committee, any stalwart denial only resulted in the repetition of torture, even if no new evidence had emerged. The *Carolina* also permitted a defense—that is, a legal advocate who worked for acquittal—but usually this was only a member of the city council who immediately before the execution gave a ritual plea for a mild judgment. The courts considered any real defense expensive and pointless. Not only the officials and committees, but also the families of the accused, often expressly rejected defense attorneys.[113]

Flade's attempt at defense had an unusual quality. During his first interrogation, he had said, "Whether, however, the evil enemy . . . has found cause . . . to change himself into my person through transfiguration is, so help me God, unknown to me." Later, his statement read: "He believes that the evil enemy represented him at the places where, according to the denunciations, he was seen, but to his knowledge he never has appeared there himself in the flesh."[114] Here Flade was reviving the old debate regarding the reliability of

The Renaissance palace of the prince electors in Trier was built around a huge Roman basilica. Part of the building was used as a jail for witches.

denunciations. The Devil could appear at the Sabbath in the form of anyone he wished, and so all denunciations were unreliable. Clearly this was a problem with immense implications. Perhaps Flade was reproducing an argument that he had encountered during his days as a student. In Louvain and Orléans, he may also have become acquainted with the tradition of Andrea Alciati, who supported this critical position on denunciations by citing the *Canon Episcopi.* However, by the late sixteenth century the controversy was common property among demonologists, and Flade might also have learned of it even from Binsfeld.[115] Whether through fear or ignorance, however, Flade did not conduct his argument correctly. He stated "that the Devil had ensnared him through his own voluntary consent, and had *therefore* represented him in person and appeared to others in form and deed. . . . The evil enemy took his will for this purpose." Here Flade was repeating exactly the argument of the advocates of witch hunting, although we cannot sense any pressure from the interrogator.[116] This argument held that the Devil could indeed appear at the Sabbath in the forms of people, but only in the forms of those people who had either directly or implicitly given him their consent to do so. In practice, this meant that the Devil could only assume the shape of a witch. Consequently, any person seen at the Sabbath was guilty, whether he was present himself or only a demon in his form. Separated from the Sabbath concept, this idea became the basis of the "spectral evidence" in the witch trials at Salem Village, Massachusetts, in 1692/93. In the later Trier witch trials, the idea sporadically surfaced that witches allowed the Devil to appear in their guise, as in the cases of Niclaus Fiedler and Hans Reuland.[117]

A part of Diederich Flade's fame is based on the fact that demonological literature referred to him as a skeptic of the witch hunts. Delrio placed him alongside Weyer: "In our times with great effort and force Doctor Flade, one of the councilors of the Prince Elector of Trier, insisted on the same thing [as Johann Weyer], but Peter Binsfeld has opposed him with an erudite written refutation of his error, in a published *Disputation on the Confession of Witches....* Flade was arrested and he confessed to his crime and his deceit and was consumed in fierce flames."[118] In the trials in which Flade served as juror, there is no trace of any doubt concerning the reliability of denunciations. The jury of St. Maximin and the secular high court of Trier attested to Flade's zeal as a witch judge. Also, in his writings Elector Johann VII never reproached Flade for any reluctance in proceeding against witches. Although he discussed Flade's trial, Cornelius Loos said nothing to indicate that Flade had shown any doubts about trials for witchcraft.[119] Later in this chapter, I will discuss further the context of Delrio's comment, as well as its value as a source.

Witches in the Electorate were usually executed though strangulation, followed by burning, and the condemned were burned not at the stake but, rather, in a brushwood shack. In a few cases, the territorial lord pardoned witchcraft suspects. The prerequisite for a pardon may have been self-incrimination. In Reuland's declaration of repentance—the only such which remains—he expressly declared that he never committed harmful magic himself. One could thus have argued that in such cases witchcraft had not included any physical harm and that it therefore should be punished as heresy. That made it possible to pardon the repentant sinner and waive punishment.[120]

The government of the Electorate showed no interest in confiscations and never attempted to use witch trials as a source of income. Binsfeld actually mentions in passing that confiscations were forbidden.[121] As a matter of course, Diederich Flade asked the prince elector to guarantee that the provisions of his last will and testament were observed, according to which an estate worth more than 40,000 gulden was to be distributed. Johann deducted only a portion of what Flade owed to the Electorate, amounting to 1,000 gulden. The archbishop also assumed Flade's loan of more than 4,000 gulden to the city of Trier but specified that the city should pay the pensions for the parishes of the city from this. The city budget today still includes an item reading "payment obligation from Flade's bequest" that allocates about 350 euros in support to the churches of Trier. It appears that the treasury confiscated all of a person's property only in cases when a suspect fled or committed suicide.[122]

Expenses for witch committees' investigations, including pay for notaries, consultants, messengers, and guards, as well as expenses for the committee members, did consume considerable sums. As these trials were officially (i.e., formally) accusatory trials, the government did not need to concern itself with funding them. Yet the members of witch committees also assumed no financial risk. The victims or their families had pay all of the trial costs. If a family was incapable of doing so, the community had to pay, and this indeed became the rule. If several communities formed a shared committee, they bore the costs of the proceedings collectively. At the end of the 1620s, communities had to deposit money with the district commissioner as evidence of their ability to pay; otherwise, no witch committee would be allowed. Occasionally, committees would borrow money when no advance financing by the commune was possible. The rule that the accused and their relatives—or if their wealth was insufficient, the community—assumed the trial costs was just as valid even in cases of acquittal. After 1687, one committee attempted to implement the scandalous rule that all acquitted suspects had to pay a flat rate of 50 Reichstaler.[123]

Generally villages committed themselves voluntarily to repaying the costs of witch trials. We can explain this first by their general fear of witchcraft but also by the fact that, through employment as messengers or guards, everyone could profit from the prosecutions. In addition, any opposition to the financial conduct of the committees was taken as evidence of witchcraft. Villagers accepted the concept of the communal repayment of costs so unquestioningly that it became a constituent part of the fantasy of witchcraft near the end of the witch hunts, but with its meaning reversed: To prevent trials, the witches of Wehrheim supposedly also collected money in the mid-1680s. They were said to have come up with the impressive sum of 500 gulden and to have collectively bribed the officials of the Electorate, who then did not comply with the people's demand for a witch hunt.[124]

For the committees, managing their expenses in this way meant that their financial resources were only exhausted when the community could not stand any more. In the matter of expenses, therefore, trial victims had not only the committees against them, but the entire community. A trial commissioner of the Electorate stated in 1683 that the victims of witch trials, even if they escaped the death penalty, were "dead in both a civil and economic sense."[125] Johann Linden had already criticized the financial interests of the agents of persecution: "Sometimes notaries, scribes, and innkeepers grew rich. The executioner rests from his labor on a noble horse in the very image of a courtly nobleman, dressed in gold and silver, and his wife competes in her luxurious dress with noble ladies."[126] Loos, too, alluded to this element of the witch hunts in the Electorate when he described them as a new alchemy, which turned human blood into gold and silver. This is one of the few points where Loos agreed with his chief opponent. Binsfeld, the "idealistic" witch hunter, had noted that trial costs often ruined the families of witches. He was presumably alluding to charges imposed by committees.[127]

The prince electors themselves had no interest in this redistribution of property, which drove an ever growing portion of the populace to ruin. At the end of the 1620s, the situation had come to a head once again because of the agricultural crisis and growing war taxes. The government of the Electorate commissioned a legal opinion on the subject of confiscation in witch trials, written by Melchior Goldast in 1629. It grew into a short monograph dedicated to Prince Elector Philipp Christoph von Sötern. The text went to press posthumously in 1661 and attained much more widespread significance. Apart from a brief trial description, the book contained only general statements about the Electorate of Trier. Goldast showed himself to be a moderate advocate of witchcraft trials. Fundamentally, he argued, the property of an executed person could be confiscated in the Electorate, just as in Swabia and Tyrol. Only the criminal court judge should have the right to impose confiscation, however, not the witch committees, as some had argued. The innocent, moreover, should not suffer from the punishment of the guilty; this meant that the family of a trial victim should not lose their property, and courts had to keep trial costs as low as possible.[128] Goldast's legal opinion became the template and starting point for Elector Philipp Christoph's Witch Trial Ordinance of 1630, which attempted to establish a fixed system of charges.

A letter from Johann Wilhelm Hausmann von Namedy, cathedral provost in Trier, to the imperial confessor Wilhelm Lamormaini (1570-1648) completely contradicted the policy of the central government of the Electorate and the text of the Witch Trial Ordinance. According to the letter, the prince elector was fining witches rather than having them executed in order to meet the financial needs of the Electorate.[129] Most likely, this was a polemical and intentional misinterpretation. Hausmann was a zealous political opponent of Philipp Christoph. He also claimed that the archbishop had attempted to kill his political opponents with a "murder prayer."[130]

With their extensive investigations, witch committees had effectively taken over the work that usually fell to officials of the territorial lord. Based only on the practice of the reimbursement of expenses and without any regular income, this system could not be financed over the long term. Community payment could only take up the slack for a time. Those committee members and others who attempted to extract financial advantages from the witch trials each followed private interests. Nobody was ever willing or able to pull these interests together into a lasting financial plan. Villages stopped hunting witches when they could no longer cover the expenses, not even with confiscations. Uninterrupted waves of trials in any given village lasted no more than three years. In 1630, the community of Föhren reflected on why it had discontinued the witch hunt begun in 1588 after three years: "It is, however, true that the expenses accumulated until we could no longer pay, so that these trials and hunts had to be halted." A committee member explained that "on account of the committee we had suffered damage from the expense, and so we desisted and abandoned the witch trials."[131] Johann Linden, too, cited financial shortages as a reason for the end of the witch hunts: "When, however, this rabble [of witches] was not exterminated by the vigorous application of Vulcan [i.e., burning at the stake] and . . . when the commoners had been impoverished, laws were passed and put into effect with respect to the profits and expenses for inquisitions and their inquisitors and suddenly, just as in war, for which money is the nerve, the impetus for prosecuting [witches] ceased."[132] The economic distress of the rural populace was not only the cause of the witch hunts in the Electorate; it also set a limit to them.

Overview and Comparison

In both of the regions under investigation, territorial lords, obeying the demands of the *Carolina* but largely inactive, faced local officials who tolerated witch hunts and the rural and urban lower and middle social strata that actively demanded them. Local officials and groups of subjects thus succeeded in conducting witch trials largely without the approval, or even against the will, of the territorial lord. Local witch hunters disregarded specific directives from the central governments and more general principles of law. From this, a conflict arose between the lord and his subjects in which the latter succeeded—at least, at first. Jurists found themselves writing legal opinions just to satisfy the expectations of the person who commissioned them and that therefore lacked all potential for making a critical difference.

The witch committees of the Electorate of Trier and the town councils of Swabian Austria were collectives of subjects that decisively affected the development of the witch trials in their regions. Although these were fundamentally different institutions—groups of peasant delegates called into existence ad hoc to prosecute witches versus lasting urban administrative institutions without any specific mandate for witch hunting—we can find similarities. Town councils and committees were traditional self-governing bodies of commoners. To become active, they required no more than formal approval from the territorial lord. That does not mean that they always necessarily opposed the government of their territorial rulers or that these governments regarded them as insubordinate. Indeed, they derived part of their authority from communication and cooperation with the territorial lords.

Comparison reveals a further difference between the structures of persecution that is of central importance to understanding them: The witch committees of the Electorate of Trier and the town councils of Hohenberg clearly functioned as the driving force behind the witch trials, while the town councils in Nellenburg, Burgau, and the Landvogtei were just as clearly a restraint on prosecution. The cause has already been made clear. The town councils of southern and eastern Swabian Austria comprised small, consolidated elites who had largely distanced themselves from the majority of the rural populace. As the local elite and the prince elector dominated the city councils of the Electorate of Trier, they were hardly representative of the populace. In contrast to them, the witch committees of the Electorate and the town councils of Hohenberg were open to the majority of peasants and provincial townsfolk. The fact that the communal assemblies of the Electorate of Trier constituted and commissioned their own committees attests to the political desire of the village communities for a representative body. Because the town councils of Hohenberg filled vacancies by co-optation and not by elections, they cannot be described as "democratic" institutions. Nonetheless, the Hohenberg councils—and in Swabian Austria, *only* the Hohenberg councils—could almost be thought of as representative bodies. The differing composition of such councils was a consequence of these southwestern German towns' having different kinds of constitutions. It would take another comparative study to discover whether cities and towns with the same constitutional traditions always experienced similarly structured witch hunts.

A decisive precondition for intense witch hunting in the two regions under investigation was the existence of traditional bodies of self-government that represented the majority of the populace. In both regions, the popular demand for witch hunts found expression in these civic groups, and witch hunting thus fit into the regional institutions of self-government. But within the framework of the witch hunts, these traditional bodies also adapted to new kinds of authority. In so doing, they combined the characteristics of popular pressure groups with the official organs of justice. Thus, in the witch hunts they provided a nearly uninterrupted response to popular demands.

Conflict arose between the officials of the territorial state and the representatives of ordinary subjects because they had increasingly different desires for witch hunting and, consequently, increasing differences about how to think about the evidence for witchcraft. It has already been mentioned that the governments of Swabian Austria and the Electorate of Trier, emphasizing as they did the rules of the *Carolina*, tended to read the varied and diffuse grounds for suspicion as a reason not to prosecute at all, while the populace demanded that an unlimited variety of incriminating evidence be accepted as legally relevant. Both territorial governments avoided extremes; the Trier government never absorbed Binsfeld's harsh advice. With concern for the stability of law, both governments conservatively stressed conformity to imperial law. This alone was sufficient to set them firmly against the populace. In both regions, villagers and townspeople criticized local officials who did not distance themselves from their territorial lord and affiliate themselves with the commoners' demand for witch hunts. They even suspected such officials of witchcraft. Membership in the ruler's clientele became a source of distrust and a socially disruptive factor in itself: it became one of the primary sources of witchcraft suspicion. When members of the upper classes who were suspected of witchcraft succeeded in using their contacts with the territorial lord to their advantage, commoners in both regions saw this as corruption: "The poor into ashes, the rich [reach] into the pocket."[133] In almost verbatim agreement, prosecutors in the Electorate and in Swabian Austria demanded justice, not in the restricted sense of legal proceedings in accordance with the *Carolina*, but in the sense of equal treatment, without regard for personal status.

With the comparative approach, we can now critically evaluate Delrio's claim that Flade was an opponent of the witch trials. The many denunciations against Flade never included this charge; nor did it appear in the rumors that circulated about him in Trier. Precisely this last point is very significant. Note that Christoph Wendler, who remained indifferent to the witch hunts, was attacked for this, denounced as a witch, and defamed in rumors. Even a partially skeptical position regarding witch hunting on Flade's part would quite probably have provoked a similar reaction. Similarly, any Rottenburg officials who did not respond to popular demands for witch hunts fell under suspicion of witchcraft. They were treated with such hostility on this account that similar allegations run through the local sources like a red thread.

It therefore seems most unlikely that a case of skepticism in Trier would show up only in Delrio's account and not in the actual sources from Trier. We can only conclude that in reality, Flade never demonstrated the critical stance that Delrio attributed to him. For his part, Delrio was under immense pressure to explain Flade's well-known case. Previously, demonologists had always simply assured judges that witches could not harm them because they stood under God's special protection in their battle against the Devil's allies.[134] But here a prominent judge in a prominent city had been exposed as an ally of the Devil, a fact that demanded comment. Flade could not have been innocent; that would have meant conceding that a prominent man had suffered judicial murder. Thus, nothing remained for Delrio but to denounce Flade as a neglectful, false judge who had never stood on the side of justice but had always been on the side of the witches and their advocates, just as Johann Weyer had been. In this way, Flade's case was distorted into a barb against Weyer.[135] This comparison also reveals that Delrio and the residents of Rottenburg used the same argument, although in two different directions. Wendler, the official who never proceeded of his own will against witches, had to be guilty of witchcraft. Flade, the official who was clearly guilty of witchcraft, could never have proceeded against witches of his own free will. The logic was the same for each statement, and both were false.

But comparison reveals even more. The system-building comparison can become an analogical comparison according to Theodor Schieder's typology: We make statements about a known object that belongs to a wider system and then identify which of the statements are probable for other objects within this system. With generally similar contexts, it becomes possible to make inferences from one object to another and thus to leap over uncertainties in the sources in a credible manner. Friedrich Schiller was the first to explore this method of comparison, and Bernheim established it as a method of source criticism.[136] This comparative method cannot be strictly described as irrefutable proof—a rarity in historical scholarship, at any rate—but it does provide plausibility and more coherent results than other interpretations of the sources.

By aggressively moving against representatives of the territorial lord and by eagerly conducting witch trials against the lord's instructions, local agents enabled witch hunts to reach their full form as an expression of the conflict-ridden relations between subject and territorial state. In their organization, their agents, and their victims, the witch hunts in the Electorate of Trier and Swabian Austria were both means and expression of the quest for local autonomy. Following the work of Keith Thomas and

Alan Macfarlane, in an early attempt to approach the witch hunts from a psychological-historical perspective, Robert Muchembled and Thomas Schoenemann tried to see the witch hunts as part of the cultural transformation of modernization. Conservative attempts to resist this crisis-laden transformation led to the persecution of "scapegoats," who were held responsible for the negative causes as well as the results of the social transformation.[137] If we consider the establishment of the territorial state as a social and political transformation that many commoners opposed, however, we can show through comparative observation that the witch trials did not just vaguely assail exchangeable "innocents" but at least partially attacked the very agents of this transformation.

Schoenemann's suggestion comports well with Joseph Gusfield's concept of symbolic legislation. Proponents of witch hunting in both their motives and actions were similar to the "moral entrepreneurs" whom Gusfield and others have described.[138] "Moral entrepreneurs" are organized groups of people who, in defense of their dwindling social influence, exert immense pressure on legislatures to effect laws against other social groups, against whom they impute immoral conduct or behavior harmful to the community. Without its being mentioned or even consciously recognized, the people they attack are often actually the social competitors of these moral entrepreneurs. When such moral entrepreneurs press for legal reforms, it is less a matter of achieving practical sanctions than a matter of representing their social power. The corresponding laws therefore have a symbolic rather than strictly instrumental character. As important as it might be to re-examine witchcraft legislation and perhaps the entire attitude of the early modern state toward the crime of witchcraft in light of this concept, it would be of only limited benefit to the interpretation of events in the regions in question. But the concept of moral entrepreneurship and of symbolic legislation also needs to be modified; there were not only symbolic laws but also symbolic administrative activities and judicial practices. Because of the openly expressed willingness of local witch hunters to interpret any wrongdoing as an indication of witchcraft, however, there were no purely symbolic activities. Symbolic and practical goals always overlapped. Still, if we concentrate on the symbolic aspects of the judicial process, we find that witch trials always had a "conservative" orientation. In and by means of criminal justice, the old leadership engaged in an ongoing struggle with newer institutions. In this manner, they not only attained their goal of maintaining social and political power, but they could even increase their influence. The concept of symbolic law, which was de-

veloped for the consolidated state of the twentieth century with separation
of powers, quickly reaches its limits when we apply it to the witch trials. On
the one hand, through their cooperation with the central authorities of the
territorial lord, moral entrepreneurs could effectively call on the state to take
action against its own agents, ultimately against its own interests. On the
other hand, through the creation of a profoundly local system, it was less that
the communal witch hunters exercised pressure on the territorial state than
that they competed with it. While they did not form a state of their own, they
developed their own jurisdictional-administrative sphere.

The social transformation or, more accurately, social and political conflict behind the trials can also be set within the framework of the communalism concept. In his study of communalism, Peter Blickle has described
"politically constituted communities which were equipped with a basic array
of privileges in legislative, judicial, and punitive matters." These privileges
then had to find an "appropriate institutional expression" in which the "basic forms of representation" had to be cultivated.[139] The witch hunts conducted by the Hohenberg town councils and the witch committees of the
Electorate of Trier, traditional self-governance and representative bodies of
the ordinary people, can therefore be considered forms of communalism.
Part of Blickle's concept is that communities enjoyed rights of their own and
did not exercise an authority that had been delegated by the territorial lord.
The witch-hunting bodies of the two territories, with only formal authorization from the territorial rulers, were entirely dependent on and legitimized
by the legal traditions of the towns and communities. Moreover, they competed with the institutions of the territorial state for control of the courts.
This conflict was much more important than any of the conflicts that arose
between the representatives of the communities and the territorial lord at
the regional estates.[140] As Blickle has suggested, the means of consolidating
communal power was a newly developed demand for judicial or administrative action.[141] The judicial apparatus of the territorial state was too poorly
developed to satisfy the local demand for witch hunts, as it did not conduct the trials with the desired "efficacy" and pace. Thus, local communities
strove to establish control over the courts and began to form a judiciary of
their own.

As forms of communalism, the witch hunts in the two regions can be
ranked among other large movements, such as guild uprisings or the communal Reformation. As a key to understanding the specific histories of these
trials along with hunters and the hunted, communalism appears to have

more explanatory power than other major concepts, such as confessionalization, acculturation, or social disciplining, which have been linked to the
witch hunts.[142]

Communalism did not, however, mean isolationism or localism. The
committees of the Electorate of Trier cooperated among themselves, with
the committees of other territories, and with urban "service providers" such
as jurists. In this regard, the Hohenberg towns moved in narrower circles, as
they cooperated primarily with neighboring villages.

The development of the territorial state both in the Electorate of Trier and
in Swabian Austria, moreover, was already so far advanced that local powers
sought contact and made compromises with the territorial lord in practice.
The leaders of the commoners usually cooperated with the local officials. In
both territories, this succeeded to the general satisfaction of the populace.
In effect, communities established their own power either by including and
accommodating or by repressing the local officials of their lord. Because of
the physical proximity of the Trier government and its high courts, the witch
committees of the Electorate had to comply with the government's desire
for formally correct trial proceedings more than was true for the Hohenberg
towns. Because of this need, the Trier committees fended off their lord by
soliciting professional legal advice and by keeping close accounts of trial expenses. These practices became excellent instruments to ward off the regu-
latory efforts of the territorial sovereign. The town councils of Hohenberg
attained an even greater degree of autonomy because, unlike the councils in
other Habsburg territories, the central government scarcely controlled them.
Because of their independence, they were largely able to control the judiciary
and avoid the need to set up their own costly structures alongside the existing
bureaucracy. In this they had an advantage over the Trier committees. They
could avoid financial shortages, and long, continuous series of trials became
possible.

Despite this multifaceted complexity, therefore, we can identify two opponents whose conflict shaped the witch hunts in both the Electorate of Trier
and Swabian Austria: the communal representative bodies and the territorial
lord. The agents of the communal order struck at the agents of the territorial
state, which was constantly striving to re-mold the communes and to incor-
porate them into its larger state order.

5

"Let No One Accuse Us of Negligence"

*The Influence of the Witch Hunts in Swabian Austria
and the Electorate of Trier on Other Territories*

On May 17, 1596, Professor Martin Crusius of the University of Tübingen in Württemberg noted in his diary that witches had been burned in Rottenburg. He commented morosely, "In my lecture today on Thucydides I had only a few auditors for they had gone there to watch."[1] The students evidently knew perfectly well what was taking place in Württemberg's neighboring state of Hohenberg. They appear to have endorsed the execution of witches, for we hear nothing of student protests. The students thought of the execution as a sensational spectacle. Witnessing it was worth missing the lecture.

In the following discussion, I will examine how neighboring territories perceived the witch trials in the Electorate of Trier and Swabian Austria. First, I will observe the role of journalism and printed works of demonology in spreading reports of witch trials beyond the boundaries of the two territories. Then I will discuss the active collaboration of neighboring territories in the witch hunts themselves.

DEMONOLOGY AND JOURNALISM

Although the comparatively mild witch hunts throughout the rest of Swabian Austria aroused no general attention, the great number of witch trials in Hohenberg did cause excitement in other territories. Sensational broadsheets reported the Hohenberg mass trials. In some of these, the number of the executed was dramatically exaggerated. Already by the early 1580s, the public seems to have regarded high numbers of victims in Hohenberg as entirely credible. All the same, witch hunts in Hohenberg did not particularly stand out amid all of the trials then coming to notice. The public attentively followed all of the witch hunts that were unfolding at just that time in many southwestern German territories. Hohenberg seemed to be only an extreme case within a larger development.[2]

The witch hunts in the Trier region—contemporary authors did not clearly differentiate between the archbishopric, the Electorate, and the city of Trier—not only received much more publicity, but that publicity also had a different quality. The reason for this was the exceedingly high number of witch trials in the Electorate, starting in the late 1580s. The Electorate became a widely observed paradigm for the new type of witch hunt: the mass witch hunt, in which the victims no longer numbered in the dozens but in the hundreds. The tutor of the sons of the Duke of Bavaria reacted with horror after a visit in Trier: "What we hear of these vicious witches here borders on the unbelievable. Everywhere around here we see almost more stakes from burned witches than green trees. Like the heads of the hydra, more witches always grow back." Broadsheets spread word of the high victim count and exaggerated the number further.[3]

The Electorate was also important as an example of intense witch hunting because the government feared a loss of prestige if it distanced itself from the popular demand for witch hunts. The vicegerent was willing to bring charges against a member of the Trier elite only if incriminating rumors "rang out everywhere and in other provinces, so that it would not be said that we were not willing to do anything about it." Loss of prestige also loomed, however, if other territories reproached the Electorate and its capital city with the high number of witches as a symptom of failing religious conviction. In 1592, Petrus Cratepolius and Johannes Reckschenkel, theologians from Cologne, stated: "The Evil One seems to have set up camp among the people of Trier." It was apparent that the archbishop/prince elector had been unable to defend the Christian order. Some authors expressed more fundamental skepticism. The humanist Hermann Weinsberg of Cologne flatly concluded from the great number of witch trials in Trier that legal abuses must have taken place there. The second-largest wave of trials in Trier during the 1620s, however, went unnoticed by the journalism of that time because mass witch hunts had erupted in the Franconian Prince Bishoprics (e.g., Würzburg and Bamberg) that eclipsed those in the Electorate.[4]

The Electorate of Trier thus became a model of witch hunts that showed no regard for person or social standing, but it also became proof that society had been thoroughly infiltrated by witches. Diederich Flade became *the* example of the necessity of hunting witches without respect for personal status.

The Flade trial was featured in a Fugger news sheet in 1590 as well as in 1624 during a debate among low-level government officials over the treatment of upper-class witches in the Prince Bishopric of Augsburg. Simon Wagnereckh, the spokesman for witch hunting at the Bavarian court, cited Flade's case in 1602 as an "example known throughout the Empire" that proved the reliability of denunciations.[5]

The trials of prominent men in Trier had a huge journalistic impact. In 1593, Thomas Sigfridus of Leipzig wrote a short work in which he dealt with witchcraft generally.[6] In a second edition of this work in 1594, he prefixed a copper etching with a rhymed explanation that purported to depict sorcery and the Sabbath in the Electorate of Trier. Sigfridus had acquired the etching and the rhyme from another author who can no longer be identified. The mention of rich witches and a "witch king" may be an allusion to the trials of prominent men. Otherwise there are no strong parallels between Trier trial events and Sigfridus's description. His sensational account, which integrated horror and comedy, was intended more to entertain than to inform, and the witch scene was set in Trier only because it was widely known that many trials had taken place there.

Before the mid-1580s, more Protestant territories experienced witch trials than did Catholic ones. When the Electorate—a Catholic and, moreover, an ecclesiastical territory—descended into mass witch hunting, a confessional paradigm shift took place. Other Catholic territories might see the frontrunner role as a mark of superiority, but it also made Trier the object of harsh Protestant criticism. First of all, Protestants could condemn the massive witch hunts in Trier as an injustice, for which they held the Catholic Church and the papacy accountable. The Hessian superintendent Georg Nigrinus, for example, viewed the Trier trials of 1592 as just one more crime of the papacy. Even if Protestant authors favored witch hunting in general, they could still interpret the great number of the trials in a Catholic territory as evidence that "superstitious" Catholicism had made people susceptible to diabolic temptation. In 1605, the Protestant preacher David Meder cited the much exaggerated figure of 7,500 witch burnings in the Electorate of Trier, claiming that monks of the archdiocese of Trier even forgave the sin of witchcraft during confession.[7]

The witch hunts of Swabian Austria excited a similar confessional polemic, but to a lesser degree. The Württemberg Lutheran Crusius explained the fact that there were so many witches in neighboring Swabian Austria by invoking the supposed Catholic susceptibility to diabolic temptation. In 1664, the Innsbruck government even attempted to prevent word of a witch trial getting out to avoid inciting attacks of this sort from Lutheran neighbors. Generally, contemporaries were quite willing to interpret witch trials in territories of a differing confession as evidence of moral failings rather than as praiseworthy.[8]

In demonological and legal literature, the witch trials of Swabian Austria left scarcely a trace. Authors from other territories ignored provincial Swabian Austria, and it lacked an intellectual tradition of its own in the sixteenth century.[9] Only the imperial magistrate Adam Keller—district commissioner of Stockach and an imperial councilor—briefly mentioned the witch trials in two of his works. He followed the arguments of Delrio and—especially on the question of trial expenses—those of Binsfeld.[10] It has been shown that Binsfeld's critical stance toward trial expenses probably derived from his actual experience with the committees' expenditures in the Electorate of Trier. On this question, the Electorate thus influenced the scholarly debate concerning witch trials in Swabian Austria. Keller's stance may have affirmed the already moderate practice in Swabian Austria as regarded trial expenses. Martin Gerbert, prince abbot of St. Blasien and a "universal scholar," was a descendent of Martin Gerber of Horb. Although he did know his family history, he said nothing in a demonological work that he published in 1776 about the witchcraft accusations against Gerber's wife and his daughter Christina Rauscher. Despite his support for the controversial exorcist Gassner, moreover, Gerbert discussed witch beliefs with caution.[11]

The strongest external impact of the Trier witch trials came through demonological literature. In the bull "Summis desiderantes" (1484), Innocent VIII had already mentioned Trier in a list of territories particularly troubled by witches. Kramer had this bull printed together with his *Malleus Maleficarum,* and so the Electorate and region of Trier were authoritatively associated with witchcraft quite early on. In his *Malleus Maleficarum,* however, Kramer only touched on the Electorate briefly. Peter Binsfeld, one of the most important proponents of the witch doctrine, came from the Electorate of Trier. Even a modern reader can recognize that in his *Tractatus de confessionibus maleficorum et sagarum* (1589) Binsfeld pursued his argument logically and rigorously. His knowledge of the relevant literature was impressive, and he did not lose himself in gossipy anecdotes, as did Heinrich Kramer and Martin Delrio. Within three years, Binsfeld's intelligent book had been published in three separate German translations, and expanded Latin editions appeared in 1591, 1596, 1605, 1622, and 1623. Confessional boundaries scarcely played a role in the reception of Binsfeld's work.[12]

Although he repeatedly insisted that experience demonstrated the validity of his argument, Binsfeld included far fewer illustrative examples in his book than did Kramer and Delrio. Yet Binsfeld was well informed about witch trials throughout the Moselle region. He called on the juror Heinrich Hultzbach and Vicegerent Johann Zandt as informants. In the first edition of his work, he drew explicitly on the trials of the Electorate in only a few places. The last version of the *Tractatus* that Binsfeld himself edited provided a substantially expanded text with a few more examples from the Electorate. Nevertheless, Binsfeld's book directed further public attention to the massive witch hunts in the Electorate of Trier, which he saw as bolstering the validity of his witch doctrine. When the Electorate refused to conduct witch trials after 1652, the Reformed County of Nassau-Dillenburg was critical: Was the Electorate not clearly betraying its own traditions by dissociating itself from the universally respected expert, Binsfeld?[13]

Under Binsfeld's influence, the Catholic ecclesiastical authorities harshly punished a theological attempt to refute witch trials. The Catholic theologian Cornelius Loos, originally from the Dutch city Gouda, formulated a radical critique in his book *De vera et falsa magia*. The book was probably written in 1589 but never published. Loos saw the pact, sex with the Devil, the Sabbath, and the harmful magic of witches, particularly weather magic, as nothing more than dreams and illusions. He argued that because demons were pure spirits that could not take on physical form, it was impossible for them to have any effect on tangible reality. To him, the confessions of witches thus provided evidence only of delusions or of excessively harsh torture. Loos inveighed against Binsfeld's demonology, describing it as a misinterpretation of Exodus 22:17, which Loos interpreted as condemning not magicians but poisoners. He stated further that Binsfeld was denying the force of the *Canon Episcopi*. At first, Loos attempted to spread his ideas through letters and sermons, but he appears to have had no success in Trier. His argument, which was likely based on Weyer, was probably too radical to be acceptable. When Loos tried to have his book on magic published, Binsfeld intervened. In 1593, he had Loos arrested and compelled him to retract his work, an act that took place in the presence of Papal Nuncio Octavio Frangipani. Thus, although the highest clerical office did not force the recantation, it did indirectly condone it.[14] Binsfeld had come closer to obtaining the dogmatic force of papal recognition for the fully elaborated doctrine of witchcraft than anyone since the time of the 1484 papal bull. Here again, theoretical reflection and actual witch hunts were closely interrelated. Binsfeld claimed that the Trier witch trials proved that Loos was wrong. Loos's retraction read: "Given that the most worthy archbishop and elector of Trier not only has had witches and sorcerers in his Electorate appropriately punished, but has also passed laws regarding the organization and financing of witch trials, I was thoughtlessly rash thus tacitly to accuse the abovementioned archbishop of Trier of tyranny."[15] Delrio published Loos's recantation in full. In this way, following the first mass witch hunts with their socially inclusive list of victims, the Electorate of Trier became notorious in yet another important way.[16] Binsfeld's triumph over Loos effectively silenced all German Catholic opposition to the witch hunts. For an entire generation, until the time of Adam Tanner, throughout the European heartlands of the witch craze Catholic theologians and jurists did not dare to criticize Kramer, Bodin, or Binsfeld.

Because the middle classes of southwestern Germany came to accept the demonology emanating from Trier, we can say that the events and ideas of Trier had a distinct influence on the practice of witch hunting in Swabian Austria. In 1604, a tanner from Rottenburg's lower middle class attempted to convince visitation commissioners from Innsbruck of the necessity of witch hunting, using scholarly arguments: "The witness, who was otherwise rather a windbag, . . . also wished to present something from Peter Binsfeld and Jean Bodin."[17] The sources do not mention how the tanner had become acquainted with the works of Binsfeld and Bodin. It is possible that against the background of the already awakened fears of witchcraft, demand for the works of these authors had escalated. Partial copies may have been circulating. Later on, a Hohenberg village priest had access to the Spee's *Cautio Criminalis* in this form. We cannot find any similarly direct reference to Binsfeld in the incomplete source material from the local committees of the Electorate.

Three strands of information pertaining to the witch trials in the Electorate thus formed. The first, of course, consisted of local manuscript sources.[18] In addition, there were reflections of the witch hunts in the documentation of daily events in chronicles and pamphlets. Finally, and with the broadest and farthest-reaching effects, there was the learned demonological discussion, in which examples from the Electorate played an important role and within which Binsfeld, an author from the Electorate, played a crucial part. The witch hunts in the Electorate of Trier had super-regional importance because of this threefold tradition and because the Electorate was a forerunner in the transition to mass witch hunts conducted without regard for anyone's personal status. The mere fact that parts of Swabian Austria had hunted witches more intensely than neighboring territories was not sufficient to make any part of Swabian Austria as important as the Electorate

for the overall development of the great witch hunt. Swabian Austria merely participated in larger trends. There was no distinctly Swabian Austrian demonological tradition.

COOPERATION AND CONFRONTATION: WITCH TRIALS AND RELATIONS WITH NEIGHBORING TERRITORIES

Denunciations appearing in the courts of one territory against individuals in the jurisdiction of another functioned as a vehicle for the spread of witch trials. Swabian Austria was not nearly as active in this regard as the Electorate of Trier. There was no correspondence regarding denunciations in witch trials between the individual territories of Swabian Austria. The individual provinces were located far apart, so there was relatively little contact between residents of the sister territories. Thus, there could be no denunciations that linked the witch hunts in the individual territories of Swabian Austria with each other. In addition, as has been noted, these courts usually ascribed little importance to denunciations. If a person from Swabian Austria was denounced in another territory, the courts did not take this as a reason to open an investigation.[19]

The authorities of Swabian Austria, however, were always willing to provide information on denunciations on request from other territories. Swabian Austria provided such assistance to the imperial city of Rottweil and to the counties of Zollern, Fürstenberg, and Waldburg. Each time, Swabian Austria simply responded to a request from the other territory; Swabian Austria never drew other territories' attention to denunciations against its subjects on its own initiative. Witch hunts in Swabian Austria do not seem to have functioned as a role model for other territories. Hohenberg, the only province in which a mass of trials developed, was almost entirely surrounded by the Duchy of Württemberg. The well-organized central government of Württemberg controlled all witch trials so that inhabitants had hardly any chance to influence the trials. The government officials took a skeptical stance toward witch hunting. The Hohenberg trials therefore had only a muffled impact.[20]

The situation in the Electorate of Trier was entirely different. Through denunciations, witch hunts in neighboring territories had a direct influence on the Electorate. Until 1652, the judicial authorities of the Electorate automatically considered denunciations against their subjects from external jurisdictions to be legally potent. In return, the Electorate willingly provided the authorities as well as the local witch committees of other territories with

information regarding denunciations of their subjects.[21] The witch trials of
the Electorate were directly emulated. In 1634, the village of Dreis (north of
Trier) asked the abbot of Echternach, the ruler with local jurisdiction seated
about twenty miles to the southwest, to allow it to investigate witches. In
the trials of "our neighbors"—that is, the Electorate of Trier—"so many were
found and questioned that we cannot hope to be entirely pure and free [of
the crime of witchcraft] ourselves." Thus, even without a direct connection
between the Electorate and neighboring territories in the form of denunciations, the Trier persecutions served as a role model. They appeared to show
how great the menace of witchcraft really was. In 1599, the committee of
the villages Wadern and Dagstuhl (southeast of Trier) used the trials in the
Electorate to justify its desire to hunt witches: "Sorcery . . . has now become
rampant, and in the Electorate of Trier and thereabouts, a great number of
people have been executed for this sin." One could easily add more examples
of this sort.[22]

In both of the regions under investigation, ordinary people showed a
greater interest in denunciations and a better memory for them than did the
government. Commoners watched trials in other territories with an eye for
denunciations against their fellow subjects and village neighbors and did so
more intensively than their own officials. They pushed to have their court
register these denunciations officially.[23]

Lords from the lower nobility who lacked criminal jurisdiction passed
witch trials on to the criminal courts of Swabian Austria. Cooperation in
witch trials between these neighbors and local Habsburg officials was generally free of tension. Disagreements arose only in isolated cases concerning
trial expenses.[24] The lower nobility who had criminal cases tried at the high
courts of the Electorate of Trier behaved similarly. Only the imperial knights
of Kesselstatt bear mentioning here. From their village of Föhren (about ten
miles north of Trier), in the years 1568, 1586-91, and 1630-31, at least fifteen
cases were passed to Trier's district of Pfalzel. The driving force was clearly
the knight Kesselstatt and the local witch committee. Here we find the earliest evidence of a practical influence of the Electorate on neighboring territories. In 1568, Knight Georg von Kesselstatt transferred a witchcraft suspect
from Föhren to the officials in Pfalzel. The woman withstood torture without
confessing, so the court released her. Kesselstatt had her immediately rearrested and at least part of her property confiscated. Archbishop Jakob III
von Eltz then brusquely threatened Kesselstatt with sanctions.[25] To be sure,
the main concern of Jakob III was to defend the Electorate's criminal jurisdiction. But his intervention did have a mitigating effect on the trials.

Neighboring territories that were entirely independent of Swabian Austria and the Electorate, respectively, were able to turn conflicts over witch trials into very serious political problems. An admittedly problematic document from a very early trial in Nellenburg testifies to such political tensions. Prior to 1497, three witchcraft suspects were brought to the Austrian court in Stockach. They came from the territory of Bohlingen, to which Nellenburg laid claim against the counts of Sulz. Perhaps the Habsburg officials were more willing than those of Sulz to punish the "new" crime of witchcraft, but in effect they weakened Sulz's authority over Bohlingen.[26] A key trial, which shows the distribution of power and initiative within the context of territorial disputes, is the already frequently mentioned case of Agatha von Sontheim. She was the ruler of Nellingsheim, a small knightly territory bordering on Hohenberg that claimed imperial immediacy—that is, the lords of Nellingsheim claimed to be subject only to the emperor himself.[27] In the trial against von Sontheim, Christoph Wendler pursued his own goals. Nellingsheim did not belong to Hohenberg, which he directly administered. If he could take over a criminal case from that territory and even subject the lord of that territory to accusation before his court, this would have represented the implementation and acceptance of Hohenberg's political dominance over Nellingsheim. Wendler's sphere of influence would thus grow, providing another example of the way he used raw power politics for his own advantage. Christoph Wendler von Bregenroth also had a private quarrel with the lords of Ehingen, von Sontheim's closest relatives, who had attempted to oust him from the knightly canton of Neckar-Schwarzwald, which was the corporation of the lower aristocracy of the region. The lords of Ehingen did not consider Wendler von Bregenroth—a recently knighted upstart—to be their equal.

Directly after von Sontheim's arrest, a group of knightly nobles enjoying imperial immediacy vehemently demanded her release. Like von Sontheim, these nobles were Protestants, and some of them were related to her. Archduke Ferdinand ordered Rottenburg to prepare to defend itself in case of a military conflict with the nobles. The main argument of the knightly party was the imperial status that they ascribed to von Sontheim's estate of Nellingsheim. Citing Nellingsheim's imperial immediacy, the nobles succeeded in persuading Emperor Rudolf II to intervene. A month after the arrest, the emperor ordered the trial halted until the question of jurisdiction could be clarified. The Protestant-dominated knightly party had demanded—certainly not without ulterior motives—that the trial be transferred to the Duchy of Württemberg as a neutral party. This suggestion could have had disadvantageous consequences for small Hohenberg in its ever contentious relationship with this large Protestant neighbor. The emperor therefore ordered that the witch trial against von Sontheim be separated from the debate over Nellingsheim's imperial immediacy. Against the wishes of the knightly party, he transferred the witch trial to the council and burgomasters of the biconfessional imperial city of Augsburg in 1591.

A conflict then broke out between Christoph Wendler and the group of nobles over the amount of the imprisonment costs and the bail given for von Sontheim's release. The negotiations soon came to an impasse, in particular because von Sontheim's relatives refused to pay several hundred florins in imprisonment charges and to post bail of 10,000 florins. To once again win the flagging support of his archduke, Wendler presented an entirely new argument to Innsbruck: by condemning von Sontheim—or, at least, by sequestering Nellingsheim for the restitution of trial costs—it would be possible to reintroduce into Nellingsheim the Catholicism that von Sontheim had recently suppressed. All of these conflicts and von Sontheim's imprisonment had rested on Wendler's claim that Nellingsheim was indeed subordinate to Hohenberg's jurisdiction in criminal cases. In October 1593, however, the archducal government determined that there was no evidence in its archives that Nellingsheim was actually subordinate to Habsburg overlordship or to the Rottenburg high court. It had become clear that, through misrepresentations, Wendler had launched a long-lasting legal dispute in which he had used the authority of the archduke for his own personal gain. In response, Wendler repeated his "re-Catholicization" argument with greater insistence. He was clearly playing on the Counter-Reformation zeal of Archduke Ferdinand II here; it was not the heart of the conflict.

The case of Agatha von Sontheim took a bizarre turn, however, when the imprisoned women protested against her planned release. She feared, probably rightly, that her relatives wanted to have her declared insane to bring Nellingsheim under their control. She herself then offered Nellingsheim—possibly at Wendler's suggestion—to the Austrian archduke as security for being released without subjecting her to her family. Ferdinand accepted and in the end gave Wendler the task of re-Catholicizing Nellingsheim. Agatha von Sontheim was left in peace until she died two years later in the house of a Protestant minister. The case of Agatha von Sontheim shows clearly that even in conflicts with other states, the vicegerent could manipulate the Innsbruck central government almost at will. With his control over information, he could ensure the archduke's assistance and wage a direct conflict with the local knighthood over jurisdictional rights.

One encounters a similar primacy of the local, a communalism that interlinked local officials and peasant subjects, in the conflict surrounding the village of Neuhausen. The conflict over Neuhausen was complex. Neuhausen sat in one of the few areas where the exact boundaries of the Duchy of Württemberg were unclear. Both Württemberg and the Habsburg Landgraviate of Nellenburg laid claim to lordship over the village and its valuable forest. Since 1560, the officials of the landgraviate had been trying to dislodge the Protestant minister whom Württemberg had appointed in Neuhausen. The minister had already disrupted a Catholic procession in Nellenburg and had berated such rituals as "idolatrous and criminal." In May 1578, the archduke of Habsburg and the duke of Württemberg agreed on a shared commission to collaborate in settling the jurisdictional conflict over Neuhausen. In the summer of 1578, before the commission could meet, fifty men from Nellenburg raided the home of the infamous poacher Sebastian Mayr and his wife by night and took them both as accused witches to jail in the Nellenburg administrative center of Stockach. Raid-like arrests by the commoners were a feature of popular witch hunting in both of the regions under investigation, but the arrest of the Neuhausen suspects was carried out with the explicit endorsement of the local Habsburg officials. A few days after the arrest, moreover, the Habsburg forester and the Stockach officials had an Austrian mandate put up on the door of the church in Neuhausen, whereby they hoped to demonstrate that by all rights the town belonged to the Habsburgs. Only when Duke Ludwig of Württemberg lodged an official protest with the Innsbruck government did the Swabian Austrian territorial government become aware of the events. Even before the government reacted, Sebastian Mayr—who had apparently not been investigated further for witchcraft—confessed to poaching, and his wife was burned as a witch along with four others. The government denounced the local officials' raid, as did the Austrian archduke Ferdinand II. The raid was clearly seen as a disruption of the negotiations with Württemberg. The archduke and his government were not prepared to give up the compromise that the joint commission sought by engaging in a risky attempt to create a fait accompli.[28] They were apparently unwilling to conduct the confessional controversy with Württemberg through the medium of witch trials or even to cater in a populist manner to the wishes of their subjects. The trial of Anna Michlerin was similarly complex. The Altdorf court was entirely prepared to discriminate against the Habsburgs' political opponents in the witchcraft trial. But the driving force was unequivocally the village political clientele of the district, not the central government in Innsbruck. The latter apparently did not even know about the incident.[29]

In one of the last witch trials in Swabian Austria, the court of Stockach investigated a woman from Ramsen in 1680/81. Swabian Austria and the Swiss Confederation had disputed the rights over Ramsen continuously since the 1540s. Ramsen was Calvinist, and so the conflict also had a confessional aspect. In this case, the Stockach officials acted purely reactively. The desire for a witch trial clearly came from the populace of Ramsen, who actively asked the Nellenburg officials to initiate proceedings. The Habsburg officials did not follow the wishes of the villagers and start a witch hunt. Bypassing the accusations of the village populace, the Nellenburg officials inquired extensively into such problems as the pact, relations with the Devil, and the Sabbath. In the end, the Innsbruck government declared the entire trial invalid because of procedural errors. This time, neither the central authorities nor the local officials attempted to use the witch trial to gain ground in the jurisdictional conflict or to draw the populace of the contested region to their side through populist appeals.[30]

Self-incriminations sometimes did force the Habsburg government to take action even in precarious political situations. In 1658, eleven-year-old Barbara Gibsin accused herself of witchcraft in Calw, Württemberg. She claimed to have been taken to the Sabbath by her grandmother, who did have a foul reputation. The grandmother, however, lived in Horb in Swabian Austria. The Württemberg sheriff had the child and her parents banished without further ado, and Barbara Gibsin moved to Horb, where she again accused herself of being a witch. This time, however, she claimed that her former employer in Calw had seduced her into witchcraft. Württemberg officials chose to believe that the grandmother in Horb was the young witch's teacher, whereas Swabian Austria insisted that Barbara's former employer in Calw had taught her witchcraft. Swabian Austria and Württemberg each informed the other that the actual guilty party resided on the other side of the border and that the primary investigation should therefore focus on that person. By this late date, both territories had succeeded in distancing themselves from witchcraft trials and were attempting to "offload" the trial onto others. In the process, they each avoided acting so energetically as to burden their relationship with the other. The Horb authorities finally expelled Barbara Gibsin in 1660, apparently without ever passing a formal verdict in her case.[31] Swabian Austria as well as Württemberg thus abstained from investigations and punishments. Similarly in 1670, officials from the territory Sigmaringen-Hohenzollern refused to try a seven-year-old girl who—

probably because of self-incrimination—was rumored to be a witch. The bailiff of the neighboring Habsburg territory Gutenstein informed Innsbruck of this procedural failure. Only when Sigmaringen ignored the Innsbruck government's demands for an investigation did the government commission the bailiff to initiate a trial of the girl and thus violate the jurisdiction of a neighboring territory.[32] The Habsburgs wished to maintain the stability of imperial law in accordance with the *Carolina*.

Even though the witch hunts in the Electorate of Trier and the witch committees themselves influenced neighboring territories, the central government of the Electorate never attempted of its own initiative to "export" witch hunts into other territories or to impose its witch-trial legislation on neighboring states. In 1597, a conflict arose between the Electorate of Trier and the Electorate of Cologne. A certain Lucia Teimens supposedly had used witchcraft to spread the plague. After her arrest and a first round of torture, she was able to flee from Kell in the Electorate of Trier to nearby Kray in the Electorate of Cologne. The Trier authorities ordered her arrest should she return to their jurisdiction but did not seek extradition. Thereafter, peasants from Kell ambushed the suspect in the territory of Cologne and lynched her. Officials of the Electorate of Cologne in Andernach raised a strong protest and went as far as to dispatch troops to the borderlands. Nonetheless, the two states agreed to negotiate a solution. They confirmed the demarcation of the border and had new boundary stones placed in the area around Kell and Kray. As in other cases, here it was clearly not the territorial governments but their subjects who were responsible for violating the border.[33]

Only at the beginning of the mass witch hunts did the Electorate of Trier actively encourage a neighbor to prosecute witches. In Alken, rule over which the Electorate of Trier shared with the Electorate of Cologne, a Trier sheriff arrested a woman suspected of witchcraft and condemned her to death, probably in the mid-1580s. On the intervention of an official of Cologne, which at the time did not yet share the persecutory zeal of neighboring Trier, the court released the suspect. Under the protection of the Electorate of Cologne, the woman was even able to remain in Alken.[34] The Electorate of Trier apparently did not wish the situation to give rise to conflict with its powerful co-ruler, so the Trier witch hunters implicitly accepted the fact that there could be mistakes and miscarriages of justice in witch trials. This example of obviously faulty proceedings in a witch trial attracted attention even in the city of Cologne.

After 1592, the Electorate of Trier exported witch trials into the "tri-ruled" land, where the Electorate shared power with the lordship of Winneburg and the County of Sponheim.[35] Once again, the driving force was not the government of the Electorate but the populace. Intensive witch trials in the Electorate of Trier had provoked fears of witchcraft that drove ordinary people to demand that their rulers undertake trials out of an acute sense of threat. In addition, certain individuals from the shared domain had been denounced during trials within the Electorate. At that time, this was reason enough for the Electorate to support trials in the shared domain. While the government of Sponheim consistently attempted to prevent or delay trials, a coalition of witch hunters developed among representatives of the populace and officials of Winneburg and the Electorate. The district commissioner from the Electorate, Karl von Kesselstatt, and his colleague from Winneburg conducted a witch hunt without or against the express will of Sponheim's District Commissioner Franz Römer. They scheduled interrogations on days when they were certain Römer could not be present. And whereas Trier and Winneburg wanted to impose the trial costs on the accused, Sponheim wished this burden on the accuser. From this, of course, conflict arose over the reimbursement of expenses, a conflict that contributed to ending the wave of trials. Although clearly against the trials, the government of Sponheim could not radically refuse to participate; pressure from the populace was too great for that. In addition, there was also the danger that proponents of witch hunting might accuse Sponheim of lacking religious zeal. Simply boycotting the trials might have done Sponheim more harm than good. Such a denial of justice could have provided sufficient cause for the Electorate of Trier to take over the conduct of proceedings single-handedly.

This situation changed only in the 1620s. The Sponheim government, which under the influence of the Palatinate had previously been so critical of witchcraft trials, now fundamentally changed its position. Spanish troops had occupied part of Sponheim. Following the Edict of Restitution in 1629, the Electorate of Trier openly aimed at the re-Catholicization of the territory. Seeking to present as little vulnerability as possible, Sponheim officials conducted witch trials according to the wishes of the populace. At the end of the 1620s, just as in the 1590s, the populace of the "tri-ruled" territory became "infected" by the witch hunts of the Electorate of Trier. The years 1640 and 1652 witnessed the same constellation. Whenever the Sponheim authorities wavered, the rural populace sought to force their hand by hinting at the possibility of turning to the Electorate of Trier. They contended with an accusatory undertone that, "in all the neighboring villages, the rulers of the Electorate of Trier have commanded their subjects to proceed with the

extermination of sorcery, in which they are diligent, but because we lie between them, they tread heavily on us, thinking that we . . . do not wish to have
the weeds destroyed."[36] There is no evidence that the rulers of the Electorate
really "commanded" these villagers to hunt witches. No such command was
needed. Rather, the Trier authorities were more willing than the Sponheim
officials to cooperate with the local witch-hunting committees. In general,
the Electorate showed neither more nor less persecutory zeal for witch trials
in its shared domains than for trials within the Electorate itself.

Unlike the cases we have seen in Swabia, the Electorate never attempted
to use witch trials as a means to consolidate or expand its sphere of influence.[37] This certainly does not mean that the Electorate would not defend
its jurisdictional rights. In 1591, Count Palatine Karl von Birkenfeld, co-ruler
with the elector of Trier in the Kröv territory (on the Moselle, downriver
from Trier), had two women arrested for witchcraft and then released them
without consulting the Electorate. The officials of the Electorate rearrested
both and investigated them. Although the officials of the Electorate came
to no different conclusion in the case than did their Palatine colleagues, the
Electorate did not wish to leave the decision in this case solely to Birkenfeld's
discretion.[38]

Territories often collaborated effectively in prosecuting alleged magicians when they mutually extradited fleeing witchcraft suspects. One such
far-reaching cooperation developed between the territories of Habsburg and
Waldburg.[39] Waldburg's ruling princes, the lord stewards (*Truchsessen*), were
the initiators and driving force here. They began by requesting information
about any of their subjects who might have been denounced in Hohenberg.
In 1626, Innsbruck permitted Waldburg for one year to transport such witchcraft suspects through Habsburg territory to a Waldburg high court. In 1627,
the Habsburg government extended the privilege for another year and expanded it to cover criminals of all sorts. In the fall of 1625, Wilhelm Heinrich Lord Steward of Waldburg had had an investigation for witchcraft and
embezzlement launched against Paul Alber, one of his bondsman who had
become a wealthy officeholder. The lord steward confiscated Alber's possessions. After the court had released Alber from imprisonment after an appeal
from his friends, he fled to Swabian Austria and asked the Innsbruck government for assistance against Waldburg. When local officials then hesitated
to comply with the lord steward's repeated requests for extradition—which
he promised not to regard as a precedent if any quarrels about the jurisdiction in the region should arise—the Innsbruck government finally relented
in May 1626.[40]

In 1628, Kaspar Klaiber from Kallenberg brought a complaint in Innsbruck about the high expenses that Wilhelm Heinrich Lord Steward of Waldburg was demanding for the trial and execution of Klaiber's wife, who had been condemned as a witch. Presumably a supporter of the noble Erzbergs, whom Wilhelm Heinrich had only ejected from Kallenberg in 1626 with Innsbruck's assistance, Klaiber had already turned to Innsbruck several times because of Waldburg's unfairness. Even after Klaiber had personally visited Innsbruck, however, the government turned him down; no investigating commission was formed. Once Waldburg promised to proceed mercifully, Klaiber was sent back to Kallenberg, where the lord steward immediately had him arrested.[41]

With Klaiber, as with Alber, the Innsbruck government turned down individuals from territories that had fallen from their direct control into the hands of lesser nobles. These were men who explicitly sought access to the Habsburg government as a protective overlord against the power of the regional nobility, but Innsbruck ignored possibilities for intervention. This is all the more remarkable given that, at least in Alber's case, Innsbruck had a strong position because of the ongoing conflict between Waldburg and Erzberg. If Innsbruck hoped to improve its long-term relationship with Waldburg in this way, however, its policy failed.[42]

The Electorate was also always willing to extradite witchcraft suspects to neighboring territories. Trier officials handed over several fleeing witches to St. Maximin, and in 1592 Johann VII threatened Sponheim with violence when he was refused the extradition of two women.[43]

To sum up: obviously, no witch was worth a war. In conflicts with external territories, the goal of both the Habsburgs and the prince electors of Trier was not expansion of their rights or territory, as a rule, but the confirmation and protection of existing power relations. These governments avoided risks as much as possible. Government officials did not use witch trials as instruments for territorial expansion in jurisdictionally contested border regions, and in any event, witch hunts would scarcely have been effective. The archducal and electoral governments had very clear notions of their real strength. For them, the formation of their state territories proceeded through consolidation, not expansion or realignment of boundaries.[44] In conflict-ridden relations with Waldburg and Württemberg in the Swabian case, and with Sponheim and the Electorate of Cologne in the Rhineland, witch trials were potentially disruptive factors that could destabilize a precarious equilibrium. Accordingly, both of the territories under investigation strove to deal with trials quickly and to avoid any escalation. For the governments, witch trials were never consciously deployed or manipulated to accomplish political goals vis-à-vis other territories. Rather, they were irritations.

In conjunction with local officials, however, commoners were the driving force behind witch trials that sometimes led to conflict between the territories under investigation and other states. Local supporters of witch hunts did not respect the boundaries of territorial states in their investigations or in their trials. Witch committees and city councils, as *communal* representative bodies, ultimately remained bound to the local commune. Organizational steps beyond the local level always aimed only at satisfying the needs of the witch hunter's particular community. Thus, the witch hunts challenged the fundamental principle of sovereignty, the territorial state. Part of the danger of the communalism of witch hunting lay in its general disregard for territorial boundaries, which were, of course, essential for any territorial sovereign. To that extent, the witch hunts could push princes into highly dangerous situations. They triggered conflicts with other states that involved nothing less than the question of sovereignty itself. The princes of Swabian Austria and the Electorate of Trier proved unwilling to gamble at such high stakes.

6

"A Slippery and Obscure Business"

The End of the Witch Hunts

GRADUAL DWINDLING IN SWABIAN AUSTRIA

The witch trials depended on popular demand for witch hunts, strong organizations of commoners, local authorities friendly or indifferent to persecutions, and very weak control by the central institutions of the state. In Hohenberg, the scandalous case of Christina Rauscher destroyed this system, and the case thus has significance for the end of the witch hunts generally in the Habsburg territories of Swabian Austria. The repeated complaints of the Gerber–Rauscher family, the clear insubordination of the Horb town council, and complaints concerning Christoph Wendler's corruption led the Innsbruck government to plan a visitation of Hohenberg. As soon as the new territorial lord, Archduke Maximilian III, had taken office, the first visitation was dispatched. That first visitation of Rottenburg took place from January 10 to November 17, 1604.[1] Maria Ulmerin, who as a child had triggered the worst of the Rottenburg witch hunts with her denunciations, had returned to Hohenberg by then. Arrested in Rottenburg, she resumed her denunciations, which immediately resulted in more arrests and executions. At first, the visitation commissioners took no notice of this testimony. They gathered information regarding the irregularities of the vicegerent's conduct in office and regarding the witchcraft suspicions against him. All together, fifty-three people were questioned. Questions about the management of witch trials occupied much of their time. The commission had become aware of problems through Wendler's prejudicial behavior in Horb. The demand for witch hunts, however, had not been broken; the people of Rottenburg were merely complaining of the unequal treatment of witchcraft suspects.

They denounced suspects to the commissioner, thirty-three living persons all together, including at least eighteen from the elite. But several people did raise complaints that the investigators had proceeded to torture too quickly, without searching for incriminating evidence, and that Sheriff Hans Georg Hallmayer left interrogation and torture to two town councilors.[2]

The Rottenburg councilors recognized the threat that the commission posed to their local autonomy. They even threatened town residents with penalties for cooperating with the commissioners.[3] Shortly after the commission's departure, denunciations from a witch trial were publicly read out against the wife of the landlord with whom the commission had resided. Nonetheless, at first the visitation commission only collected information, without taking any concrete measures. On February 25, 1605, six more women were burned in Rottenburg.[4] Yet this was to be the last group execution of witches in the town.

Accused by Maria Ulmerin of sexual abuse, Hallmayer was arrested and confessed in early 1605. He died in jail. Christoph Wendler was summoned to Innsbruck and arrested under suspicion of corruption. Although the Innsbruck authorities remained cautious regarding the accusation of witchcraft, they reserved the right to initiate a trial at some later date. Wendler died in 1608 immediately following his return to Swabian Austria. The government's suddenly harsh actions had a clear impact in Horb. After nearly a year of fruitless protests against her arrest, Christina Rauscher was released in the summer of 1605. Then the Rauschers lodged complaints against the council and Sheriff Veser. In letters, Rauscher's Tübingen lawyers not only demonstrated that her trial had not followed the *Carolina,* but they also fundamentally disputed the use of denunciations as sufficient evidence for torture and dismissed the Sabbath as pure illusion. In this, the learned jurists relied on Johann Weyer and the *Canon Episcopi.*[5]

Around the end of 1605 and the beginning of 1606, another archducal visitation took place in Hohenberg, collecting testimony for a corruption trial against the vicegerent. In addition, the visitation commissioners gathered complaints from the Rottenburg populace. Individual families lodged renewed complaints of miscarriages of justice and biased trial management. Not in direct connection with the visitation, but as a reaction to the numerous complaints of the Rauscher family, the government launched an investigation of Sheriff Veser and the entire Horb council.[6] The Innsbruck government summoned Veser and the Horb town scribe and threw them temporarily into jail. The questions formulated for the interrogation of the Horb sheriff departed from concrete, individual cases and criticized the witch trials more generally in light of the *Carolina*. Veser and the town scribe were suspended from office, and the government placed the burgomaster of Horb under temporary house arrest. It ordered all current trials halted immediately.

In early 1607, another archducal visitation, headed by Imperial Councilor Christoph Franz von Wolkenstein of Rottweil and District Commissioner Adam Keller of Stockach, traveled to Rottenburg and, for the first time, to Horb. One of the official tasks of this visitation commission was to investigate irregularities in the trials of Christina Rauscher and a certain Anna Haug, who had starved to death in jail. Decisive measures were now taken in both Horb and Rottenburg, where the commissioners replaced the judges and portions of the council with individuals selected by the commissioners themselves. The commissioners based their extreme measure expressly on miscarriages of justice and corruption in the witch trials. This demonstration of the central government's power punished the institutions responsible for the witch trials in both towns. In addition, Rottenburg was required in the future to submit all witchcraft cases to Innsbruck for a decision. This was effectively the end of local autonomy in trials of magic. A direct result of the visitations was the Hohenberg Police Mandates (*Policeyordnung*), which became binding for the entire county in 1607-9. In the sections that covered the organization of criminal trials, the Hohenberg Police Mandates repeated verbatim "some new ordinances and points from the lord commissioners' instruction for Rottenburg," which the visitation commission had released at the beginning of 1607. Denunciations were still to be recorded, but the Police Mandates forbade publicly reading them at executions. The Police Mandates also generally required greater caution in the use of torture. The fact that the Hohenberg authorities actually followed the Police Mandates, whereas before they had openly ignored decrees from Innsbruck, was due to the rapid growth of the central government's local power in the form of visitations. No subsequent violations of the Police Mandates can be found from Horb or Rottenburg. In Oberndorf (to the south of Horb), however, where the commissioners never went, numerous trials took place in the 1630s (see later in this chapter), although a Police Mandate with the same content was at least officially in effect there.[7]

Christina Rauscher was the driving force behind the reform of the Hohenberg courts. In 1607-9, she traveled many times to Innsbruck and spoke personally with Archduke Maximilian III. She received official orders from the government to return to Horb accompanied by a new archducal commission and thereafter to report back to Innsbruck—an extraordinary recognition of her accomplishment. Rauscher and her husband resided in Innsbruck almost uninterruptedly from 1610 until her death in 1618, but the sum of around 10,000 florins that she demanded from Horb as final compensation for damages and reimbursement of trial costs was never paid.[8]

After the forceful Innsbruck intervention, the thrust of the Hohenberg witch trials shifted to marginal groups.[9] Then a conflict arose in Rottenburg between the Hohenberg villages, which demanded continued witch trials, and the Margrave Karl von Burgau (1580-1618), son of Archduke Ferdinand of Tyrol. In the summer of 1614, the residents of several villages lodged complaints against the sheriff of Rottenburg, because he did not crack down on witches with "proper seriousness." The background of this complaint was that the Rottenburg officials had finally obtained a judicial consultation concerning seven witches, as required by the Innsbruck directives. The law professor Johann Halbritter of Tübingen composed this consultation, but he recommended torture in only one case. His opinion thus fell far short of the expectations of the local witch hunters. Margrave Karl ordered a report and then decided that Halbritter's legal opinion should be binding.[10] Apparently, Karl did not have any confessional prejudices against the law professor of Lutheran Tübingen.

In 1615, Karl introduced a comprehensive administrative reform with his "Information Points for Hohenberg Officials." The sheriff was no longer to conduct criminal investigations alone but had to seek the help of the marshal and court scribe. Trials were now also to take place one at a time. The hasty and mass witch trials of the late sixteenth century were not to be repeated. Presumably, the marshal and court scribe replaced the town councilors who had previously conducted criminal trials together with the sheriff; here we can see the process of "patrimonialization" and professionalization of the legal system, which the Innsbruck regime used to marginalize the urban middle-class authorities and to negate the influence of ordinary people. Karl became an exponent of this administrative and political development, the proto-absolutism of the early seventeenth century. For the witchcraft trials, it was far more important that Karl's "Information Points" forcefully reformed the administration of trial finances for the first time. A son's or daughter's legal portion of inheritance from an executed person could be confiscated to cover the entire expenses, but only up to a third of the estate. We should regard this as quite a moderate rule.[11]

Given the poor state of the sources, however, it hard to tell whether this directive was actually effective, but we have not found any case for Horb, upper Hohenberg, or Rottenburg in which Karl's order was directly defied. There is, however, also only one surviving case, from Rottenburg in 1650, in which the rule was applied for certain.[12] Karl's directive was issued only for Hohenberg; he did not issue any similar directives for the rest of Swabian Austria, which lay as a whole under his authority. The Innsbruck government itself, however, deviated several times from Karl's regulation. In 1620, the officials in Burgau, Nellenburg, and Hohenberg were instructed that trial expenses should be paid from the property of witches, and all remaining possessions should be confiscated. Two months later, apparently in response to complaints from the provinces, the government inquired of the local officials regarding who normally bore the trial costs. Unfortunately, their letters in response have been lost. In 1630, Innsbruck ordered the treasury of Burgau to advance payment for witch-trial expenses from the funds of the margraviate but to require families of the trial victims to repay the costs as far as possible. In 1641 and 1650, however, Innsbruck confirmed to Hohenberg that Margrave Karl's regulation was still generally valid.[13] In the matter of trial expenses, confusion—not confiscation—was the rule in Swabian Austrian witch hunts.

The new attitude toward witch trials that the visitations had created found clear expression in Hohenberg in the 1620s. At the turn of the century, inquisitorial trials had been triggered by witchcraft suspicions or rumors of witchcraft, which were accepted without question and expressed in public. Such suspicions or rumors were brought to the attention of officials without any privately lodged formal accusations. By the 1620s, officials had become far more critical of such suspicions. The success of complaints to the visitation commissions and Christina Rauscher's partial success, moreover, had demonstrated to potential trial victims that one could effectively defend oneself against witchcraft defamation. In Hohenberg as well as in its Swabian Austrian sister territories, witchcraft accusations were increasingly punished as slander, and convicted slanderers had to pay heavy fines. In one case in which a slanderer had called for the lynching of a witchcraft suspect, he was even banished. Only self-incriminations could break through this new skepticism toward witchcraft rumors and accusations, and even they no longer always constituted full proof. In 1621, a small girl from Horb denounced herself as a witch. The clergy of Horb decided that the child suffered from delusions. Whereas in previous cases they had simply counseled child-rearing measures instead of criminal justice, they had now come to doubt that the child was in fact a witch. The first such dismissal of a witchcraft suspicion by the Hohenberg clergy had been in the case of Christina Rauscher. The later course of that case had validated the opinion, and Innsbruck had accepted the counsel of these clerics.[14]

Witch fears and the belief in witchcraft, however, had not declined among the inhabitants of Swabian Austria. Indeed, in Swabian Austria, witchcraft accusations increased in the 1620s as part of a wave of massive trials that swept over broad stretches of central Europe. However, it was no longer possible to transform these local accusations into trials.[15] Nellenburg, the Landvogtei, and Burgau still evidenced a climate generally unfavorable to trials, a climate that had already protected those territories from the great trial wave at the end of the sixteenth century. In Hohenberg, the archducal visitations had chastened local officials and permanently banished witch hunters from the town councils. For the time being, no one from these two groups was willing to organize witch trials or serve as a spokesman for witch-hunting groups from the populace. Here it becomes clear that there was no simple causal connection between socioeconomic crisis and witch trials. With harvest failures, an outbreak of the plague, and the increasing burdens of war, Hohenberg came under terrible pressure in the 1620s and 1630s, as did large stretches of central Europe. This crisis was far more severe than that at the end of the sixteenth century.[16] But catastrophic witch hunts like those from around 1600 did not occur in Swabian Austria because of the changed structures of political and administrative power.

Severe witch hunts did take place in the Hohenberg bailiwick of Oberndorf. Between 1609 and 1626, twenty-seven women and seven men were burned there. At least one of the women was a member of a family represented in the council.[17] As in Rottenburg and Horb at the end of the sixteenth century, these trials were directed by largely autonomous local authorities. Innsbruck was clearly not informed. The names of supposed accomplices continued to be read publicly. Bailiff Brenneisen, under whose tenure in office most of the witches were executed, was known for his arbitrary decisions.[18] The moderate regulations of Margrave Karl's Police Mandates and the commissions' massive impact just to the north were apparently insufficient to connect Oberndorf with the central government in Innsbruck and to prompt greater caution in these witch trials. In addition, the territory of Oberndorf had only come under Habsburg control in 1594, and it was thus by far the newest part of Swabian Austria. The local sense of independence may well have been more pronounced there than in the rest of Swabian Austria. Brenneisen's dismissal in 1626 achieved the same calming effect in Oberndorf as the change of personnel had in Horb and Rottenburg in 1607. For ten years, there were no further witch trials.

Witch hunting in Swabian Austria took a new direction with a cluster of witchcraft accusations in Burgau in 1630/31. All of the administrative difficulties that had curbed the witch hunts in southern and eastern Swabian Austria were in force there. Sheriff Johann Widman complained that his fellow officials considered it beneath their station to participate in witch trials. The town councilors showed no interest whatsoever in witch trials, possibly in reaction to the shocking example of recent intensive witch hunts in surrounding territories.[19] A certain Michael Lechlmayer, whom Widman had arrested under suspicion of witchcraft, denounced residents of the town as well as subjects of neighboring territories. Both the town and these bordering states completely refused to cooperate with Innsbruck and forbade the Habsburg officials of Burgau to usurp their jurisdictional rights. Lechlmayer later repeatedly recanted his testimony, however, and the officials were soon confronted with "a denunciation, a revocation of the denunciation, and then a revocation of the revocation." These problems delayed the trial considerably, and expenses began to mount, so that by September 1640 the treasury of the Margraviate of Burgau found itself in financial difficulties. Still, the Innsbruck government insisted on proceeding strictly according to the *Carolina*. In November 1631, following a personal consultation with Archduke Leopold, the government decided to permanently employ a jurist whose sole responsibility would be to oversee the management of the Burgau witch hunt. Dr. Leonhard Neusesser was hired as the witch commissioner. Neusesser claimed to have experience with witch trials from his experience as a lawyer in Offenburg and an official in Eichstätt.[20] In the Prince Bishopric of Eichstätt, witches had been prosecuted continuously since 1617, and in the imperial city of Offenburg, there had been a catastrophic mass witch hunt in 1627–29. After the ruling class in Offenburg had raised protests, the council had suddenly halted the trials at the beginning of 1630. Although it is not clear what role Neusesser may have played in Eichstätt and Offenburg, this experience clearly formed his background when he applied for the position in Burgau: mass witch hunts with profound social consequences, which, in retrospect, had been recognized as unjust or at least doubtful. Neusesser received a fixed salary of 500 florins, so he had no financial interest in initiating trials. Indeed, he oversaw only two trials in Burgau, and their outcome is unknown. Only in 1649 did the Burgau authorities again conduct investigations into witchcraft. In 1635, Neusesser left to become district commissioner of Ortenau,[21] after closing down those trials still pending and rejecting at an early stage of investigation any other accusations that had surfaced, judging them not legally relevant according to the *Carolina*. Innsbruck had not hired Neusesser to push witch trials forward but to oversee their legality, and Neusesser must have been well aware that it would not serve his career to ignore the stipulations of the *Carolina*. This was the fundamental difference between Neusesser and other professional witch-trial commissioners such as those of the Franconian Prince Bishoprics and the Electorate of Cologne, as well as District Commissioner Musiel from the territory of St. Maximin on the border of the Electorate of Trier.[22]

The "Instruction and Conclusions, Concerning Circumstances under Which Persons Can Be Proven Witches" (Innsbruck, 1637) has already been discussed in the first chapter.[23] The "Instruction" came too late to have much impact on Swabian Austrian trial practices. In 1641, however, Hohenberg once again reacted to a child's denunciation of several women. The Innsbruck government was informed that trials had begun, and the government ordered that legal opinions be obtained from jurists and the judgment be submitted to Innsbruck before any sentence was carried out. Rottenburg officials and the town council ignored this order and had at least four women executed, informing Innsbruck only after the fact. The Innsbruck government under Archduchess Claudia punished this disobedience and forced the town to pay the entire trial costs, the substantial sum of 350 florins. This was the first time that the government used trial expenses successfully to moderate the witch-hunting zeal of local authorities. Rottenburg halted all pending trials immediately. In 1645, the people of Rottenburg demanded, vehemently but in vain, that the Innsbruck government return control of their courts to them.[24]

The witch hunts in Oberndorf, the last fiercely persecutory region of Swabian Austria, collapsed not from outside pressure but because of internal difficulties. In 1636, a woman and a certain Lorenz Schwarz were arrested for witchcraft in Oberndorf. In addition to witchcraft, Schwarz confessed to numerous murders and burglaries, hundreds of crimes all together, but later repeatedly recanted his confession. Schwarz's confessor was the Oberndorf priest Dr. Justus Haussmann, who had studied in Freiburg. In 1617, he had become a priest, and in 1631, he had become a dean. When Schwarz escaped from jail, Haussmann held a sermon on December 10, 1636, in which he "revoked and recanted the confessed crimes" in the fleeing suspect's place. Unfortunately, the exact text of this sermon is not extant. Certainly, Haussmann did not simply make himself the mouthpiece of the escaped male witch. After he had been rearrested, Schwarz showed surprise over Haussmann's words and proceeded to confess that he had never expressed himself in the manner represented in the sermon. It may be that Haussmann composed the recantation himself, independent of the actual intentions of the accused, but whatever the origin, Haussmann's sermon provoked a very strong reaction from officials and the populace. They saw it as a "remarkable affront" to the authorities. Among the people, it triggered "confusion," which led to "not insignificant difficulties in this particular criminal trial and also to dangerous obstruction of justice." Because the authorities feared "difficulties" with future witch trials, Haussmann's sermon had probably offered fundamental criticism of witch trials. Nobody had ever before questioned trial procedures so openly in Swabian Austria.[25]

Some of Haussmann's private writings do survive in which he discusses criminal trials, the duties of a confessor for criminals, and the value of denunciations, following the cautious provisions of the *Carolina*. He resolved the problems of whether torture could be repeated if an earlier confession were revoked and whether torture could be used on holy days, explicitly following the recommendations of Peter Binsfeld, whom he quoted directly. Nonetheless, he rejected the practice of summary justice and the use of particularly harsh judicial procedures in handling the *crimen exceptum* of witchcraft. He admitted that scholarly opinion on this question was divided but stated clearly in the end, "See the most recently published book, *Cautio Criminalis* [by Friedrich Spee], Question no. 43."[26] Haussmann thus dealt extensively with particular questions regarding the treatment of witch trial victims, demonstrating a grasp of the expert literature and of fundamental problems with witchcraft trials that the local lay judges could not read about because such works were in Latin. We can assume that Haussmann had become acquainted with the *Cautio Criminalis* and had composed his work on criminal procedure prior to Schwarz's trial. This conclusion is supported by the description of the *Cautio Criminalis* as "most recently published." Haussmann must therefore have read Spee between 1631 and 1636. Accordingly, we may consider Justus Haussmann as one of the first to take Spee seriously. Haussmann's work on the subject also includes a multi-page transcription of selections from the *Cautio* in an unknown hand.[27] The transcription closes with "This *Cautio Criminalis* should not be given to anyone." Whether Haussmann knew the entire text or only these selections remains unclear; we cannot find any copy of the *Cautio* in his estate or in the library of the Augustinians, the nearest large clerical library. Local officials did report Haussmann's sermon to the Innsbruck authorities, who then complained about him to the bishop of Constance. The bishop, however, apparently ignored these complaints, probably because Haussmann's brother was one of his closest associates. Justus Haussmann died on April 28, 1656, in Oberndorf.[28]

Despite Haussmann's sharp critique, Schwarz was executed in February 1638. It is noteworthy that, even after his final confession, the council and bailiff hesitated for four full months before they ordered the sentence carried out. When one last chain of witch trials took place ten years later, the locality once again experienced a massive and public disruption of its trial procedures, when a condemned man revoked his confession during the sensitive ritual of the execution, calling down God's wrath on the judges. The charge of being in league with the Devil could not have been more effectively refuted.[29]

After 1636, then, problems and crises erupted within the trial procedures of Oberndorf. On an administrative level, the vigorous objections of trial victims disrupted the previously frictionless course of the trials. On the cognitive level, if we ask how these late trials were understood, such denials may have sparked doubts about the fairness of the trials. Haussmann's criticism supported both of these obstructions and so helped push Oberndorf closer to conditions in the rest of Swabian Austria.

Spee's work also had a direct effect on the Swabian Austrian witch hunts through a written legal opinion that the Tübingen law faculty composed for Rottenburg. In response to specific inquires from a prosecutor, a suspect in Rottenburg had confessed to participating in the Sabbath. Yet the suspect insisted that she had seen only the Devil at the dancing place. Probably the accused woman knew that she would be asked for denunciations and was trying to avoid having to name accomplices. The Rottenburg authorities recognized this confession as atypical and inquired of Tübingen whether the woman, who had already confessed to all of the other components of the crime of witchcraft, could be tortured again to make her identify accomplices. Tübingen decided no. The faculty cited question 44 of the *Cautio Criminalis* as an authority without distancing themselves from it in any way. Most likely, the faculty accepted it as a simple fact when the anonymous author identified himself as Catholic. Clearly, the Tübingen jurists felt as little inhibition in citing a Catholic author as the Rottenburg officials did in asking a Protestant university for advice. For the first time in a Swabian Austrian witch trial, denunciations were viewed not only with caution but as fundamentally worthless. Local officials and the government accepted the legal opinion, thus implicitly relinquishing one of the foundations of mass witch hunting.[30]

During the second half of the seventeenth century, Swabian Austria witnessed two major new developments that finally brought the witch hunts to an end. The Innsbruck government initiated a most significant trial reform and simultaneously took note of a new theological concept of witchcraft.

In 1666, the central government dismissed out of hand a witch trial that Rottenburg had presented to it for judgment. The government objected that in this case, as was usual in Hohenberg generally, the accused had only been given a town councilor as a pro forma advocate. Following successful conviction and immediately prior to the execution, this pro forma advocate was supposed to plead for a mild sentence in a ritual exchange of question and answer before the court. Innsbruck stated that this did not suffice as a "defense." "It is our command to you herewith, that henceforth you should *hear* such criminal persons' statements *with their defenders* and draw judgment *accordingly.*" At the beginning of the century, Innsbruck had been perfectly willing to accept the usual local procedure, but now the government rejected it as unsatisfactory and legally questionable. Henceforth, local authorities had to provide a genuine legal defense in each trial. Around the same time, a suspect came before the court in Stockach. On explicit orders from Innsbruck, she was also provided a defense. The government also ordered the court always to follow this procedure in the future before it reached a verdict.[31] In 1679, the Innsbruck government again required this new practice in a directive to the bailiff of the mediated Habsburg territory of Gutenstein, which bordered on Hohenberg. There a witchcraft case had to be retried because the accused had received no defense. The local officials should "order a defense for this person ex officio" and provide the defender with all the prior trial records. Thus, the court now had to appoint an official defender. Whether this also meant that the state would have to bear the expense for the defense remained unclear. In 1680/81, Innsbruck also explicitly demanded that suspects be assigned a defender in three Altdorf trials. In 1680 in Stockach, it was stated quite clearly that at the trial's beginning a jurist was to be made available to the accused as her defender. This defender should receive full access to the trial record, and no verdict could be reached without his vote. Yet in trials in 1671 and 1711 in Rottenburg, Innsbruck made no mention of such a defense.[32] Although caution is required in judging the practical impact of the new regulation—in only one Rottenburg case is it clear that the sentence was not death but exile—it still seems clear that a true reform of the witch-trial administration was under way. It was no longer a matter of passively allowing a defense but of actively establishing a legal right to defense, a public defender, in witch trials. Even if only in rare cases, and certainly more in theory than in practice, the Habsburg government was taking a very advanced stance on criminal defense.[33] The Innsbruck government had introduced yet another criterion for orderly trial proceedings, by imposing a new element on the Swabian Austrian trials that delayed and complicated the proceedings. Because a defender, by definition, had to fight for the cause of the accused, he had to be entirely different from a mere legal consultant. The pressure on witch hunters increased.

Alongside this trial reform, a new theological concept arose. In a trial in Rottenburg in 1666, the Innsbruck government insisted that direct questions regarding apostasy and heresy be asked. Because the offender appeared repentant, she was shown mercy and banished. At Innsbruck's behest, she was allowed to leave jail after performing a religious penance. In another case, in Altdorf in 1681, the sisters Maria and Katharina Wilhelmin were tried for witchcraft.[34] Although they were presumably charged with the same crimes, at Innsbruck's instigation the court reached different verdicts. Because Katharina showed no repentance, she was executed. Her sister, however, was released on the condition that she take religious instruction. The court based its punishments exclusively on the offender's readiness to repent and convert. That Katharina pleaded for forgiveness and called on God immediately before her execution was insufficient to change the verdict. It was thus clearly not a matter of the criminal's almost ritualistic public prayer and confession of sins before the execution and its supposedly deterrent effect on the audience. In their verdict, the Innsbruck officials now actually evaluated the offenders' readiness for internal "conversion."

The archducal government did not describe its decision as an unusual act of mercy. No one had submitted special appeals in favor of the suspects. In the Electorate of Trier, the remission of a sentence sometimes occurred when there were no charges of harmful magic, but this happened only in a very few, exceptional cases. By contrast, Innsbruck was developing a new policy on witch trials. This "pastoral" transformation of witch hunting, marked by greater interest in conversions then in convictions, was not consistently present in Innsbruck's decisions. Nonetheless, pastoral treatment and the simultaneous demand for a full defense contributed to the fact that it was becoming notably more difficult to obtain a guilty verdict in witch trials. We can only guess the basis on which the interest in conversion rather than punishment rested. The government did not specifically justify its directives. Possibly it was the influence of the *Malleus Judicum* (The Hammer of Judges [ca. 1628]) by the Protestant doctor Cornelius Pleier, who in turn was redeploying the arguments of the Calvinist theologians Hermann Witekind and Anton Praetorius. Both belonged to a school of Calvinist thought prevalent in the Palatinate where, as early as the second half of the sixteenth century, the conversion of a witch was granted more importance than worldly punishment.[35] The Innsbruck Witch Trial Ordinance of 1637, influenced by Tanner, breathed not a word about pardoning repentant witches. Nonetheless, the influence of the prominent Innsbruck Jesuit Tanner, who had published shortly before Pleier, probably prompted the new development. Tanner described witchcraft as an essentially religious crime, a surprisingly "conservative" conceptualization of witchcraft that embraced the traditions of popular Catholicism and had helped to deter witch hunts in some parts of Swabian Austria.[36] Tanner strongly recommended prayer, fasting, and good works, as well as the use of church magic as defenses against witchcraft. He considered loose sexual mores to be a gateway to witchcraft and believed that by simply destroying immorality, witchcraft could be largely eliminated.[37] Here witchcraft lost its character as a serious crime to be combated by any means possible. Tanner clearly sought to push witchcraft out of the sphere of secular law and back into the religious sphere whence it had come. His intentions were thus diametrically opposed to those of Heinrich Kramer and Peter Binsfeld, who had discredited church magic as a weapon and effectively advocated criminal proceedings as the only possible defense against witchcraft. As seen in the Innsbruck Witch Trial Ordinance, Tanner erected relatively high obstacles to a guilty verdict before a criminal court. He also greatly strengthened the religious and ministerial weapons against witchcraft. "Thus truly as regards spiritual methods, it is certain that they are of much greater importance for exterminating this vice than any . . . human methods." Tanner concluded his argument brilliantly by quoting the slightly arrogant words of St. Paul that made clear that fighting the Devil's human minions should be below a Christian's dignity: "Put on the whole armour of God that you may be able to stand against the wiles of the Devil. For we wrestle not against flesh and blood, but against principalities, against powers, against the rulers of the darkness of this world, against spiritual wickedness in high places" (Ephesians 6:11-12). Tanner drew another conclusion from his pastoral transformation of the witchcraft concept. He demanded that witches who confessed *extra iudicium* (i.e., outside a legal procedure) and repented should not be punished. In this way, supported by the citation of Paul and the Inquisitorial practice of giving a one-time pardon to repentant heretics, Tanner was able to separate the battle against the Devil from the struggle against the witches. "Verily I do not doubt that with this humiliation [the pardon of repentant witches] the Devil will be more confounded and restrained than with a thousand executions."[38] Tanner did not criticize the interweaving of immorality and sin with witchcraft, as described in chapter 3 with the "avarice" motif, but he eliminated its relevance to criminal law.

The correspondence between Innsbruck's directive and Tanner's argumentation is clear. Witchcraft was in the process of changing back into heresy. In one case, the government explicitly identified witchcraft as "haeresis."[39] To be sure, even if the witch were mainly a heretic, she had to face punishment. The concentration on witchcraft as a religious crime implied that self-denunciation was the only valid means of proof. At the same time, however, self-denunciation was the prerequisite for avoiding secular punishment. The government of Swabian Austria was prepared not to punish the witch if the offender showed signs of a conversion. In this way, not only was a guilty verdict made more difficult to obtain, but the witch trial also no longer made much sense as a criminal trial.

On January 12, 1631, Duke Maximilian of Bavaria released a mandate that reflected the increasingly cautious practice in Innsbruck. The influence of Tanner, who had long taught in Bavarian Ingolstadt, may be suspected here, as well.[40] Readers may recall that during the witch hunt in Salem Village in 1692/93, it became the rule that confessed and repentant witches were not executed. The Massachusetts authorities never provided a theologically based reason for forgoing punishment. However, in this rule—and in the scenes of reconciliation that played out between repentant witches and their supposed victims—we can see a variant of the pastoral transformation of witchcraft.[41] The fact that nineteen persons preferred to die in Salem rather than accept the dishonor associated with confession, however, warns against speaking of pastoral treatment of witchcraft simply as an improvement.

Part of the reform program of Empress Maria Theresa (1717-1780) was a vigorous campaign against witch trials. First, she gave official instructions that witchcraft trials be submitted to her personally for decision, effectively complicating and extending official channels so much as to virtually exclude the possibility of a verdict. Then, in 1766, she promulgated a new law that characterized most cases of supposed witchcraft as delusion or fraud. The 1766 law did not fundamentally reject witchcraft as impossible, but it required "genuine signs of a truly magical" effect. Maria Theresa understood the old weakness of witch trials to be the fact that magic could not be proved with actual evidence. This had been the heart of the judicial treatment of witchcraft. But recognizing this spelled the end of the trials—and, indeed, she intended nothing less.[42] However, this new law had no real consequences for Swabian Austria, where the last witch trial had ended fifty-five years earlier.

Indeed, Rottenburg authorities conducted the last witchcraft investigation in 1710/11, when renewed failures of the wine harvest triggered pressure from the populace for witch hunts. In this atmosphere of new witch fears, suspicions against Anna Wollensäckhin of Weiler coalesced into the last Swabian Austrian witch trial. A Tübingen legal consultation suggested that a trial be opened, reflecting Tübingen's new interest in witch trials in the early eighteenth century. Although the ensuing investigations produced no results, in the face of massive pressure from the populace, local officials hesitated to release the accused. When the central government in Innsbruck received word of this, it ordered the immediate cessation of the proceedings. This order had to be repeated three times before the last witch trial of Swabian Austria was finally brought to an end.[43]

The End of Witch Trials in the Electorate of Trier

In the domain of Mensfelden (east of Coblenz), the Electorate of Trier shared rule with Nassau-Saarbrücken and the knight Waldecker von Kaimt (on the Moselle). In 1631, the rulers agreed to rotate the administration of criminal justice among the three of them every six months. In the 1640s, the Electorate of Trier cooperated with the Mensfelden witch committee.[44] Christ Preusser was a Protestant and vassal of the counts of Nassau-Saarbrücken but also the under-sheriff for the Electorate in Mensfelden. The witch committee of Mensfelden first began collecting witness testimony against Preusser in 1648. When District Commissioner Johann Wilhelm Walrabstein held the high court jurisdiction for Waldecker in 1652, the committee again presented records from its investigations of Preusser on June 12, 1652. Preusser then sent a supplication to the Electorate of Trier in which he asked for assistance, arguing that the proper high court over Mensfelden was Coblenz, a city in the possession of the Electorate of Trier. Clearly, Preusser wished to bring the Electorate over to his side by asserting the sovereignty of the Electorate over Mensfelden. In addition, he commissioned legal consultations on his own case from the law faculties in Giessen and Mainz. Knight Waldecker then had Preusser arrested without informing his co-rulers, and the Electorate of Trier insisted that all three lords be included in the trial. The Electorate effected Preusser's release. Preusser then brought in the Reichskammergericht (Imperial Chamber Court). As the highest court of appeals in the empire, the Reichskammergericht in turn declared Waldecker disqualified because of a conflict of interest and ordered in September 1652 that Saarbrücken and Trier should conduct the trial without him. The Electorate then seized the initiative definitively: It insisted on reversing the confiscation of Preusser's property that Waldecker had ordered and threatened the Mensfelden witch hunters' committee with a 100 florin fine if it proceeded against Preusser on its own authority. All complaints were to be submitted to the high court in Coblenz for processing. The people of Mensfelden mocked the messenger of Trier who delivered these decisions, and they even insulted the archbishop. While the Electorate of Trier had serious difficulties establishing its local authority, Waldecker enjoyed considerable respect in Mensfelden. Because he was willing to satisfy the popular demand for witch hunts, unlike the Electorate and Nassau-Saarbrücken, he won support among the populace, support that the other two co-rulers lost. Of course, Waldecker did not possess a high court with educated jurists, as the Electorate did. Just as during the earlier and more massive witch hunts, then, commoners, their representatives and a local ruler rallied against the territorial state on behalf of a communalistic order.[45]

In early March 1653, Waldecker arbitrarily had Preusser arrested. The Electorate saw this as a dangerous intrusion on its jurisdictional rights to its "detriment" and terminated cooperation with Waldecker in all matters of criminal justice. The further actions of the Electorate in the trial against Christ Preusser were unparalleled in the witch trials of either the Electorate or Swabian Austria. On March 17, 1653, officials of the Electorate from Mensfelden and Camberg, including the Limburg district commissioner, a lawyer, and two armed soldiers, went to Kirberg, to the residence of the Nassau-Saarbrücken sheriff responsible for Mensfelden. Before the entire community, the Trier officials announced that they intended to free Christ Preusser but that this move did not violate the rights of Nassau-Saarbrücken. All the same, they did not inform the government in Saarbrücken. The deputies from the Electorate then proceed to Mensfelden and demanded the key to the jail. When they were refused, the Trier officials commanded that the jail door be broken open. The Trier district commissioner justified himself saying that Preusser's liberation had to be quickly accomplished, as he "had received an order from Regensburg [where the prince elector as attending the coronation of Ferdinand IV], which he was obliged to obey. What he . . . did, his lord the prince elector would [later] justify to his lordship the high count of Saarbrücken." Thus, the authorities of the Electorate of Trier violently freed a supposed witch from jail. They levied a fine of 150 florins against the inhabitants of Mensfeld for insubordination and ordered them to pay the fine within ten days or one hundred soldiers from the fortress Ehrenbreitstein would occupy the village.[46]

We should not suppose that the Limburg district commissioner was acting on his own authority in liberating Preusser. Such a risky, legally questionable, and politically explosive measure would have exceeded his authority and discredited him with his own government, as would his claim to have the military in the fortress Ehrenbreitstein at his disposal. Waldecker protested, and Saarbrücken reacted irritably, claiming that the Electorate had injured its rights in Mensfelden.[47] Certainly, the Trier district commissioner did in fact act on the direct command of the archbishop, as he claimed, even though no record remains of any written order. This is not surprising, as the prince elector later ordered that witch-trial records should be destroyed.[48] Was the Electorate simply halting as quickly as possible a trial that was being conducted against its mandate? Did it wish to regain its influence in the shared territory through fines and threats of military action, directed not at Waldecker but at the people of Mensfelden? The means that were employed seem too excessive and counterproductive for this, especially as the affair resulted in a cooling of relations between the Electorate and the relatively powerful County of Nassau-Saarbrücken. It seems instead that the Electorate of Trier was essentially in the process of terminating witch trials as a whole. Preusser had to be freed from jail before his jailers could force him to confess that he was a witch, a confession that would have justified the actions of local proponents of witch hunts. Moreover, the village and its committee, the motor of the persecution, had to be compelled to withdraw from the trial.

Unlike Waldecker, the Electorate strove to maintain a precarious balance of power in Mensfelden. Once again, the witch hunts functioned as a disruptive factor in the foreign policy of the Electorate, not as a means to expand its power. In May, the co-rulers finally agreed to have the case settled jointly by a commissioner from each.[49] Nonetheless, a protracted legal battle developed over the personnel and venue of the commission. The Electorate's willingness to collaborate with the other co-rulers in deciding this case was not authentic, and it did not produce any actual results beyond merely delaying the trial. Fighting the witch trial, Preusser appeared again before the Reichskammergericht, charging his accusers of bias and invalid procedure. He continued to enjoy the strong support of officials of the Electorate. They guaranteed Preusser's freedom and offered him advice; the Electorate's sheriff in Mensfelden testified that he would vouch for Preusser with "his life and limb." An investigatory report presented by two jurists of the University of Giessen, on whom the co-rulers had been able to agree after years of negotiation, stated in effect only that it was practically impossible to find unbiased jurors in the area. Preusser distrusted everyone, "Very like a man who can find no tree in the forest from which he wishes to hang." In November 1659, Johann Gottfried Kolb of Nassau-Saarbrücken was appointed commissioner in the Preusser case. He indicated to the Electorate for the first time after seven years of negotiations that the Saarbrücken government might be willing to end the trial without any final verdict. Financially exhausted, Waldecker gave up. Preusser appears for the last time in sources from mid-1662; he was still the under-sheriff in Mensfelden.⁵⁰

As late as 1648 and 1651, the Trier district commissioner for Limburg (Lahn) had essentially permitted witchcraft trials, so the break that came in 1652 was sharp.⁵¹ The spectacular rescue mission in the summer of that year and the subsequent work of Trier officials on Preusser's behalf strongly suggest that this shift depended on an explicit order from the territorial lord, the prince archbishop. A new elector took office on March 12, 1652: Prince Elector and Archbishop Karl Kaspar von der Leyen. In a secret letter written seven years later, Karl Kaspar admitted that he had forbidden witch trials throughout the Electorate. He stated, "Because [witchcraft] is a secret crime, its oft-attempted extirpation prior to and at the time of our taking electoral and princely office had resulted in all sorts of judicial excesses, fraud, wastefulness, and injustice, so that we were urgently compelled to prohibit and forbid completely such trials and inquisitions in our Electorate; since then we have prospered, God be praised." Karl Kaspar was well aware of the difficulties his ban had caused in the shared domains: "In our own possessions we did not fail to provide this offense with an authorized remedy of some other sort," but in the multi-ruler territories, he urged the use of all legal means to end the individual trials or, at the very least, to make them follow the provisions of the *Carolina*.⁵²

Karl Kaspar's prohibition of witch trials was not proclaimed publicly but functioned instead as a secret directive for the courts and officials of the Electorate. According to the prince elector's letter in 1659, witch trials were not gradually stifled but, rather, forbidden in a single, positive act. When exactly Karl Kaspar enacted the prohibition has been unclear until now. In 1659, the prince elector was looking back on his prohibition from some distance. The archivist Walter Rummel has dated Karl Kaspar's secret mandate against witch trials to the beginning of July 1653, when the prince elector forbade any further trials in the shared domain of Beltheim until he should return from a journey. He gave the impression that he wished to view any case records himself. Reserving judgment in witch trials to the personal decision of the sovereign was an oft-used administrative trick to end them circumspectly. Prussia's Friedrich Wilhelm I and Maria Theresa acted similarly.⁵³ In light of the trial against Preusser, however, in which the officials of the Electorate all consistently advocated and acted on the suspect's behalf, we can date the prince elector's prohibition a full year earlier than Rummel supposed. It was probably already in effect when Christ Preusser turned to the prince elector with his first supplication, or else it was issued during the first struggle over his trial. Accordingly, the prohibition against witch trials most likely occurred in spring or early summer of 1652 and was thus one of the first official acts of Karl Kaspar von der Leyen.

It is no longer possible to say to whom Karl Kaspar's 1659 letter was addressed. It was obviously an official of the prince elector, probably someone who had just arrived in Mensfelden immediately before the end of Preusser's trial. Johann Gottfried Kolb, who collaborated on Preusser's case as Nassau-Saarbrücken's commissioner, made the existing copy of Karl Kaspar's letter. Perhaps the letter's addressee had shown him the archbishop's missive after Kolb decided to help end the trial in late November 1659. Kolb was aware of the significance of the letter; although "not secret," it was still a "confidential state paper." Kolb subsequently adopted the prince elector's radically restrictive position on witch trials as his own. In 1680, when the count of Nassau-Saarbrücken was undecided on how he should respond to popular demands for witch trials, Kolb sent him a copy of Elector Karl Kaspar's letter.[54] At least indirectly, then, Trier's ban on witch hunting did have some foreign impact.

Because we can see no change in the prince elector's stance over the course of the trial against Preusser, we can assume that this trial was only the occasion or first opportunity for putting a previously composed, fundamental decision against witch trials into effect. Karl Kaspar had been the administrator of the cathedral chapter that had lost confidence in Archbishop Philipp Christoph von Sötern (1567-1652). With the passive support of the city of Trier, Karl Kaspar was able to break Philipp Christoph von Sötern's resistance through the threat of military force and was appointed in 1650 as Philipp Christoph's co-adjutant. Karl Kaspar's starting position as Philipp Christoph's successor was thus quite advantageous. Following his appointment as prince elector, his most important task was to recoup the losses from the Thirty Years' War, and he decided on several specific structural changes. In 1668, Karl Kaspar issued a new civil law code for Trier, the first legal reform in almost a century. The new prince elector systematically consolidated power as territorial sovereign. The prohibition against witch trials was part of this comprehensive reform program. The prohibition did not mean a rejection of the previous practice of Trier electors, but was instead the radical consequence of that practice. The prince electors before Karl Kaspar had sought to combat the abuses that accompanied witch trials as if they were only errors. From their failure, the new archbishop concluded not that it was a question of avoidable abuses but, rather, that high trial costs, insubordination among the common people, and violations of trial procedure and evidentiary law were integral to the witch trials. It must have been clear to Karl Kaspar that the witch trials had to be stopped to enable his program of development and centralization. The prince elector succeeded in extending the impact of his policy when, in consultation with the cathedral chapter, he named his nephew Johann Hugo von Orsbeck as his co-adjutant; indeed, Johann Hugo became his successor in 1672.[55]

The prohibition of witch trials in the ecclesiastical territory of the Electorate appears to have been as little influenced by theological arguments as was earlier legislation on magic. Whether the prince elector/archbishop was theologically unable or unwilling to escape Binsfeld's shadow remains an open question, but it is insignificant. That Karl Kaspar turned away from the witch trials for pragmatic reasons implies that he had distanced himself from the whole demonological discussion. Friedrich Spee, the great opponent of the witch hunts, spent the last years of his life in Trier, died in 1635, and was buried in the crypt of the Jesuits' church. Did Spee have any influence on the end of the witch trials in the Electorate? Beginning in late 1652, Spee's *Cautio Criminalis* appeared among the defense texts of Coblenz advocates for witch trial victims in Sponheim. The Coblenz lawyers obviously valued Spee's work and knew its author by name, although at that time only anonymous editions of the *Cautio* had appeared.[56] Due to a lack of sources, however, we do not know whether this influenced any of the prince elector's councilors.

The immediate cause of Karl Kaspar's reforms was also the condition of their success. The Thirty Years' War had brought substantial population loss and migration to the Electorate of Trier, through flight and other effects of war and through limited immigration after the war's end. The communalistic society of the townsmen and villagers, whose internal tensions had spawned suspicions of witchcraft, had organized the witch trials communally. With concern for local autonomy, these communes had defended themselves against the intervention of the territorial lord. But the war had severely shaken this society, and in some areas it had even collapsed. The social network, the structures of self-government, and the village milieu had been destroyed in many places. Communalism had lost its foundation. Rural society recovered more slowly from the social chaos of war than did the structures of the state, to which it could no longer offer resistance.[57]

Although the surviving sources shed clear light on the measures taken to end the witch trials in the shared domains of the Electorate, there is no corresponding evidence from the Electorate itself. Regarding "how" witch trials actually came to an end, our only information comes from a neighboring territory, when it chose to criticize the Electorate's judicial authorities. In 1659, a court scribe from the County of Leiningen-Westerburg, who had requested from the Electorate excerpts of confessions containing denunciations, declared himself dissatisfied. "In previous trials many persons were . . . executed, some of whose files are still to be found in the chancellery, but those confessions in curia [i.e., the high court of Coblenz] have been lost and misplaced—let me not say through malice and fraud." Trial records submitted to the high courts were processed no further and never sent back. If local courts observed the requirement to submit case files to the high courts, this meant the end of their witch trials. We should notice, however, that Karl Kaspar not only instructed his high courts but also gave directives to the local criminal courts not to accept any more accusations. Violations of the elector's prohibition can scarcely be found; the end of the witch hunts came abruptly in the Electorate of Trier. Two death sentences were carried out in Boppard in 1653, and two other trials with unknown results took place in 1657 in the remote enclave of St. Wendel. The last investigation began there in 1660. The territorial lord was presumably not in sufficient control of the enclave. Montabaur witnessed its last investigations in 1659/60; their outcome is unknown.[58] Against the background of the weakened structures of the villages and rural towns, it apparently sufficed to direct the officials of the central government no longer to cooperate with local committees and to accept no further accusations. That broke the power of the communal witch-hunting associations and ultimately caused their disappearance.

Karl Kaspar systematically eliminated the witch-trial records of the Electorate so that, should his successors prove willing to hunt witches, the records could not be examined for denunciations.[59] The criticism from Leiningen-Westerburg cited earlier bears witness to this. What the source describes as "lost" meant nothing less than intentionally destroyed. The fact that the witch-trial sources of the Electorate are much more poorly preserved than those of neighboring territories argues for a fairly thorough destruction of records. As we have seen, Karl Kaspar attempted to keep his prohibition of witch trials secret. He probably believed that he could not confront the people of the Electorate with such a radical step without encountering massive opposition. In addition to that, if the prohibition were proclaimed, he could anticipate a negative reaction from outside, from other territories. Although the height of the witch trials was long past by the beginning of the 1650s, it was not possible for a self-defined Christian and godly government officially to terminate the battle against the purported allies of the Devil.[60]

In addition, Karl Kaspar could not publicly seem to condemn his predecessors in office, men who had borne the political responsibility for so many witch trials.

Because the Electorate did not officially or publicly reject witchcraft trials, a dilemma arose in the shared domains. To be able to slow or stop the witch hunts, one had to take part in them from the start, but this meant indirectly legitimating witchcraft trials as such. The hard and enduring fight of the prince electors' officials against trials in the shared domains of the Electorate was the last and the most positive chapter of the long and dismal story of the Trier witch hunts.

In Wehrheim we find the problems of witch-hunting communalism brought to a burning focus as though by a concave mirror. The officials of Nassau-Dillenburg played the roles there that the rulers of the Electorate of Trier and their local officials had played during the two great waves of witchcraft trials. But from 1652 on, officials of the Electorate were able to function quite differently, following the elector's prohibition and his consolidation of government in Trier. They now took active steps against the communalism of the trials. In the territory of Wehrheim (between Limburg and Frankfurt), where lordship was shared between the Electorate and Nassau-Dillenburg, control over trials shifted every six months between the two rulers, similarly to Mensfelden. In a witch hunt in Wehrheim in 1651/52, the Electorate initially assumed management of the trials in its turn and, in this privileged position, actively lent support to the prosecution. The high court in Coblenz readily allowed the examination of old denunciations and wrote orders for torture and execution. One last trial, which had opened before Karl Kaspar von der Leyen took office, ended with an execution on May 8, 1652, during the first days of his tenure. In the following year, however, despite Nassau-Dillenburg's objections, Trier ended the witch hunt. For thirty years, the authorities did not pursue existing denunciations any further.[61] The dramatic reversal of the Electorate's witch-trial policy comes into clear view in the shared domain of Wehrheim.

After a generation, however, massive popular demand for witch hunting broke out again in Wehrheim, in 1682, after three fires extensively destroyed the village in February and April. Ordinary people explained these conflagrations as attacks of magical arson. From April 1682 onward, the Nassau-Dillenburg district commissioner in Wehrheim, Johann Michael Eulner, proved himself a zealous promoter of witch trials in collaboration with the local witch committee. The Electorate's sheriff in Wehrheim, Hans Georg Vest, exerted himself just as consistently to stop or slow the witch hunt. At the request of the Dillenburg government, the Trier elector, Johann Hugo von Orsbeck, agreed to shared proceedings. In fact, however, the Electorate delayed the trials through a series of procedural tricks. In the end, the Coblenz juror Stephan Dölthsch conducted the trials on the Electorate's behalf, with the notary Johann Schwalb serving for Dillenburg, but from the very beginning Dölthsch refused to cooperate effectively.[62]

Contrary even to the wishes of the accused, the Electorate of Trier insisted on a legal defense. The sheriff of a neighboring village had had experience with many witch trials, but the Electorate rejected him as advocate for the defense—to Dillenburg's complete surprise—ostensibly on the grounds of insufficient legal experience. The Electorate then undertook a step that made its intentions clear: Dölthsch, the Electorate's commissioner, personally took over the office of defender. First, after one of the suspects had died in jail, he drew attention to the poor jail conditions, because "jail should not be used as a punishment." There was actual evidence, he argued, for neither arson nor witchcraft. Dölthsch argued that the Dillenburg official had interrogated the suspects without proper preparation and had tortured them without sufficient cause for suspicion. Witnesses had been questioned with even less respect for legal procedure than in a civil case. The most serious point of Dölthsch's argument was that the entire community had "decided upon the complete elimination and destruction" of the suspects. Accordingly, every single member of the community could be considered a mortal enemy of the accused and thus disqualified as witnesses. Trier's commissioner characterized the alliance of the entire community (embodied in the committee) as a criminal conspiracy against a specific group of people. Each person who participated in the "conspiracy" automatically lost his credibility as a witness. In its response, the committee rightly recognized that communally initiated witch hunts were being thrown into general question. If none of the sworn judicial confederates could appear as witnesses any longer, then no more trials could be conducted. Dölthsch accordingly demanded that all of the suspects be released. The committee should pay all of the expenses and provide compensation for accusation and imprisonment.[63]

With that, the period of cooperation between Dillenburg and the Electorate of Trier came to an abrupt end. Dölthsch and his successor as commissioner and defense attorney, Johann Andreas Ziehler, continued to delay the trials and escalated expenses to make the trials as unattractive as possible. They were able to bring one trial to an end. Despite Trier's strongest protests, however, Nassau-Dillenburg succeeded in having two persons executed after hasty trials in early 1683. Locally, the witch committee boycotted the court dates set by Ziehler, and the inhabitants turned to violent confrontation. The local official of Nassau-Dillenburg, together with the populace, challenged the Electorate's right to rule. Opposition to the witch trials had so thoroughly undermined the power of the Electorate's local administration that the people of Wehrheim actively chose a different ruler, opting for one whose officials were willing to satisfy the popular desire for witch hunts. That did not mean that the government in Dillenburg was merely exploiting the local conflict to improve its claim of sovereignty or even that it condoned this civil unrest. Dillenburg, too, was worried about the rebellious behavior of the Wehrheim peasants.[64]

The judicial abuses that had been all too common during the massive trials in the Electorate of Trier were repeated in an alarming manner in Wehrheim under District Commissioner Eulner. The Dillenburg government tolerated these excesses because it believed it would otherwise lose so much support among the populace that its right to rule would be weakened. By early 1682, the community of Wehrheim had already openly threatened the Nassau-Dillenburg government with refusal to pay taxes and with emigration should it not take action against the witches. Eulner rattled his government further by claiming that the "prince elector parson" (an insulting term for the archbishop of Trier) wanted to use the witch trials to bring Wehrheim entirely under his control and re-catholicize it. Meanwhile, in Nassau-Dillenburg itself, the courts tried witches with restraint, according to the rules of the *Carolina*. The influence of the Netherlands and concerns over the economic effects of the trials had made the government cautious.[65]

In the end, the commissioners of the Electorate of Trier and Nassau-Dillenburg refused each other access to their court records. Ziehler accused Eulner of serving the local witch committee more than his own government. Ziehler's task was clearly not to allow the people to lead the trials in collaboration with the authorities but to make them a party that ultimately could itself be accused of conspiracy. The government of the Electorate supported him, explicitly referring to the orders of the prince elector himself. In the end, Ziehler publicly stated that he wished to free all of the suspects. He criticized the committee for its persecutory zeal, saying sarcastically that "the heads of men do not grow back like a willow tree." Dillenburg's officials, Schwalb and Eulner, were able to secure support among the populace by vociferously and publicly distancing themselves from the Trier officials' resistance to witch hunting, throwing insults and even threatening violence. Eulner clearly understood the strategy of the Electorate: it would protract the trials until the expenses of continuing became too great for Wehrheim.

Part of this strategy was that officials of the Electorate purposely ran up great expenses and attempted to delay as long as possible the remuneration of the agents of Nassau-Dillenburg and of the local committee. The Electorate of Trier consistently refused any assistance in covering any trial expenses. As part of this "strategic impoverishment" policy, in the summer of 1684 the Electorate insisted on the payment of the imperial tax for the Turkish war, even though the community of Wehrheim had been economically devastated following the fires of 1682. Admittedly, the Electorate lost further support among the populace because of this. But the Electorate consciously refused to improve its popular standing by complying with local demands for trials.[66] The trials thus soon encountered massive financial difficulties. In the end, Eulner attempted to push through a rule that everyone who was released from jail should have to pay about 50 Reichstaler. The Electorate fought this measure as well as property seizures. The conflict over trial finances lasted well into 1688.[67] The trials themselves finally came to an end. The strategy of the Electorate—to delay the trials and make them more difficult through ever increasing expenses—had succeeded.

Only when the Electorate renounced witch hunting did the witch hunts become a significant source of conflict in its relationships with other territories. Witch trials became a cause and object of debate among states. The conflict over political power among territories was thus a part of the debate over witchcraft, while it seems clear that witchcraft trials were not really a tool of state building.

Overview and Comparison

The end of the witch hunts came "from above" in both of the regions under investigation. The witchcraft trials did not decline or peter out; they were actively terminated. Just as the earlier economic crisis did not simply and necessarily lead to witch hunts, neither did a slackening of this crisis bring about the end of the witch hunts. Legal consultants and commissioners in both territories were always mere tools and mouthpieces of their employers. In Swabian Austria, the territorial government in Innsbruck became aware of scandalous abuses in connection with the witch hunts in Hohenberg, and it brought those trials to an end through a series of massive interventions in local practice. Through visitations and new expense regulations, and above all by replacing local officials, communalism was at least partially brought under control. It was initially necessary to bring the power of the territorial sovereign into effect locally; new legal norms did not bring about this transformation, but the appearance of the lord's representatives at the actual trials did. Government officials appointed new people to the Hohenberg town councils, the traditional representative bodies of the subjects that previously had managed the witch hunts. In this regard, they became similar to the city councils of the Electorate of Trier. These interventions between 1604 and 1615 spelled the end of mass witch hunting in Swabian Austria. Under these difficult administrative circumstances, however, witch trials continued to occur there in exceptional cases for about a century. In the Electorate of Trier, the territorial lord forbade witch trials in a single positive act of legislation to eliminate troubles that could disrupt governmental order and the subjects' economic life. The physical proximity of the seat of government to the courts and the generally superior administrative and judicial structure of the Electorate meant that visitations like those in Swabia were unnecessary. The existing administration of the Electorate of Trier enforced the elector's prohibition. A prerequisite for this, however, was the partial collapse of the political and social system of village communities in the wake of the Thirty Years' War. Witch trials in the Electorate came to a complete end within a few years. Only in the shared domains, where the officials of the Electorate could not manage the trials alone, and where the conflict of two or more rulers strengthened the communities' power, did the witch trials continue for over thirty years longer. In the Electorate, just as in Swabian Austria, the end of the witch hunts was a function and an instrument of the consolidation of territorial rule.

Of course, ordinary people in Swabian Austria and the Electorate of Trier still lived in fear of witches. We cannot even show that the political leaders of the Electorate or the Habsburg states no longer "believed" in witches. The spiritual or pastoral transformation of the witch concept gradually pushed the battle against witchcraft out of the realm of criminal justice. The Innsbruck government's new concern for the conversion of witches even proves that the authorities had absolutely no doubt about the reality of contact between humans and demons. The end of witch hunting ensued from pragmatic causes, to ensure the stability of law and internal peace, and was implemented through pragmatic means—those of court reorganization. The battle against witch trials did not proceed from any "enlightened" battle against the belief in magic. Neither did it proceed from any careful new theological position, as we can see most clearly in the Electorate of Trier. Intellectual or religious changes certainly could help to mitigate the witch hunts, as we can see in the secular territory of Swabian Austria, but such changes were not a prerequisite for bringing these trials to an end. At the end of the Middle

Ages, in both territories, the authorities, legislatures, administrations, and courts had offered witch trials to the populace as an option for action. This option remained only one of many, and it was affected to varying degrees by regionally and chronologically varied developments. The end of the trials did not come when the ordinary people no longer demanded the option of witch trials. It came, instead, when the authorities either completely withdrew the offer, as in the Electorate of Trier, or when they complicated the offer with so many prerequisites and restrictions that it became practically impossible to act on it, as in Swabian Austria.

Conclusion

In conclusion, we will review the most important results from Swabian Austria and the Electorate of Trier. At the same time, we will examine the results from our comparisons to see what conclusions can be drawn for witchcraft trials more generally, in line with the goal of looking for systematic generalities.

In Swabian Austria, at least 531 individuals were executed in witchcraft trials; in the Electorate of Trier, at least 792 were executed. Because both regions connected harmful magic and women, only about 9 percent of the trials in Swabian Austria and 12 percent of the trials in the Electorate targeted men.

The idea of witchcraft expressed in the trials of Swabian Austria and the Electorate of Trier resembled that of learned demonology. In both territories, however, ordinary people as well as the authorities had no real concept of witches as a diabolic sect. The rulers of the ecclesiastical Electorate of Trier were no more interested in theological notions of witchcraft than were the rulers of secular Swabian Austria. Local agrarian pressures focused on harmful magic, and especially weather magic, as the very heart of witchcraft. Stories about witchcraft also incorporated motifs from folk legends. Hence, the fantasies of witchcraft proved able to pull together all sorts of material, including popular stories. Demons and witches took the place of traditional fairies and ghosts. Learned demonology and traditional spirit beliefs distorted each other and combined into a regional popular demonology. This distortion of demonology resulted not in a weakening but in an intensification of witch fears. Witchcraft attained greater "presence," as witches gained new power and occupied greater space within the popular imagination. The figure of the witch "conquered new territories," growing in the popular mind, becoming more important, and being used more widely to explain certain kinds of phenomena. Materials from folk legends, reformulated to fit ideas of witchcraft, became evidence in criminal trials. The trend in Hungary and Silesia that Gabor Klaniczay and Karen Lambrecht have examined was diametrically different; following a strand of folk beliefs in those regions, the authorities began attacking "*magia posthuma*"—that is, the magic of harmful ghosts and vampires. In this way, a kind of symbolic criminal justice seems to have created (perhaps even consciously) an outlet that deflected popular suspicions away from the "evil people" in their midst whom one might blame for harm.[1]

In both regions under study, the sources do not point to any behavior patterns common to all witchcraft suspects. The common suspicions of women and the poor, suggested by learned demonology, were overcome in both regions, most clearly in the trials of Diederich Flade and Christoph Wendler. This variability was not simply a consequence of the fact that witchcraft was an imaginary crime. The explosive potential within notions of witchcraft consisted precisely in the fact that any negatively experienced behavior could be interpreted as "evidence" of witchcraft. The range of behavior that could foster witchcraft suspicions was entirely open. Witchcraft trials usually embraced this unlimited diffusion of causes for suspicion, and thus these trials were not so much an exception within the practice of criminal justice as its structural opposite. This is especially true if we understand criminalization as a variable process of labeling that depended heavily on context. It was not that authorities declared various modes of behavior to be criminal but, rather, that the authorities and the populace were willing to accept an unlimited multitude of generally non-criminal actions as evidence for one and the same capital crime. This interpretation does not mean that we have been defeated by the complex processes underlying the genesis of suspicion or that we have paid too little attention to the social positions of the trial victims; we have examined both of these thoroughly. We might expect that one region or the other would come to narrow the range of suspicion and concentrate on just one or a few types of suspects. A strong predominance of a particular, clearly definable group among the trial victims or subtle differences might have become common. But we have found no general pattern of narrowed suspicions in the Electorate of Trier and Swabian Austria, and this proves that witchcraft suspicions remained generally open and variable. If we try to build a system based on the comparisons undertaken here, we can conclude that there was what we can term an "evil people principle"—that is, that any conflict at all could generate the suspicion that one's adversary was actually in league with the Devil. The systemic comparisons here go far to show that this "evil people principle" was a basic precondition for witch hunting.

The witch hunts in both regions were also characterized by a fundamental tension between the ordinary people (who demanded and organized witch trials) and the territorial lord (who often hesitated). Territorial legislation and, over broad stretches, the practice of the territorial rulers of Swabian Austria and the Electorate of Trier continued to emphasize the rules of the *Carolina*. Binsfeld's apocalyptic rigorism had no effect on the laws of the Electorate. It seems clear enough that major agrarian crises and the basic sense of crisis shaped the popular demand for witchcraft trials, but the actual decision to initiate trials always depended on an active political process. Who made that decision and who applied it depended on who was able to control the judiciary. As is clear in the case of Hohenberg, once the government became critical of the witch hunts and was able to enforce its decision-making authority, even a drastic worsening of agrarian conditions could no longer trigger a wave of trials. No part of Swabian Austria was touched by the massive witch hunts that swept the empire at the end of the 1620s.

Initially, however, the local institutions of the territorial state in both territories were so weak that decision making and real power lay with self-governance bodies of the populace. Accordingly, the traditional, local representatives of ordinary people held the decisive leverage in the great witch hunts. The fact that in each case a different local group held levers of power explains why the witch hunts in the Electorate of Trier and Hohenberg were so different from those in the rest of Swabian Austria. The witch committees of the Electorate and the town councils of Hohenberg were representative bodies that shared and represented the fears of the majority of the people. In contrast, the town councils of Nellenburg, the Landvogtei, and Burgau were small, self-contained bodies of local elites who were never as severely affected by economic crises. They were not prepared to tolerate witch hunting, because they feared the social and political unrest that often accompanied it, but also because they did not wish to give the officials of the territorial lord a chance to curry favor with ordinary citizens by exercising their right to try all capital cases.

The communalism that characterized the witch trials in both territories took aggressive forms. Simple systems of criminal justice appeared on the local level that quickly transformed the demand for witch hunts into trial clusters. Needless to say, these trials violated fundamental rules of legal due process. This development succeeded, however, because the group that dominated the trial management was partial to or a spokesman for popular demands for witch hunts. The town councils and witch committees of our two regions held a dual position as holders of official or quasi-official positions in court and as members of an extrajudicial pressure group. As a form of communalism, this system strove for the greatest autonomy possible. In addition to that, witch hunters understood that any outside influence would disable their system. When they allowed outside influence, the very existence of their system was jeopardized. The legal opinions solicited by committees in the Electorate were nothing more than window dressing on a very simple system, because actual trial management remained in the hands of the communal witch-hunting committees. They ignored all laws and regulations that subjected this system to external control. Moreover, this communalistic system found itself legitimated with every condemnation. The financial difficulties into which the committees of the Electorate fell due to the various economic interests of their members resulted in repeated local breakdowns of individual witch hunting campaigns but not in the collapse of the committee phenomenon itself.

The witch trials developed immense social and political significance because suspicions emerged from an open process. Once we see that witchcraft suspicions developed from a host of different social situations, we can investigate individual groups of witchcraft suspects. In both of the regions under investigation, contemporaries suspected social climbers of witchcraft, assuming that, as agents of the developing territorial state, they pursued their own political and economic interests against the locally established elite. Here was a vicious circle. Striving for independence, the communal institutions that organized local witch trials accepted as legally compelling the same multitude of causes for suspicion that played a role in witchcraft rumors and accusations among the populace. But their communal struggle for autonomy in itself also pushed them into conflict with the territorial lord and with any individuals whose political or economic loyalties clashed with the communalistic concentration on the local. When representatives of the community then interpreted as "avarice" any political or economic connections that went beyond or even against the traditional local order, these connections became a cause for witchcraft suspicions. Not only did communalism determine the administrative form of the witch hunts, it also helped the witch hunters to identify the witches. The communal system thus legitimized itself and isolated itself from criticism.

If we take a look at other German regions, we find similar developments even in officially organized witch hunts. The ecclesiastical princes of Franconia and parts of the Rhineland created small special administrations that were isolated from the rest of the judiciary and had witch hunting as their sole purpose. These special tribunals behaved very like the small communal organizations of witch hunters in the Electorate of Trier and Hohenberg. They also came under massive pressure as soon as a foreign court, such as the Reichskammergericht, began to disrupt the local organization. Here, too, witch hunters were ready to suspect people as witches who stood outside the princely system that legitimated the witch hunters.[2] Of course, witchcraft accusations could also be used as weapons to damage (political) opponents. In the sources examined in this study, however, I could not find a single clear-cut case of this. It seems that those who supported witchcraft trials were profoundly naive about their own motivations and attitudes. Representatives of any organizations or concepts different from their own easily came to seem like "evil people." In saying this, however, we are not reviving the rationalistic concept of the "witch craze," because we must take seriously the fact that, for contemporaries, witches were part of reality, including social and political reality.

Against this background, actually denying that witches posed a threat, as Johann Weyer or Cornelius Loos had done, could not make much headway. Skepticism concerning the validity of denunciations, although always present, never escalated into doubt concerning the danger of witchcraft. The connection between the ordinary and the fantastic was too close for such an exclusive interpretation of "reality"; it was a connection too useful on too many levels. The witches were, so to speak, integrated into the social construction of reality. Denying witches would have implied denying the reality of everyday life. Nonetheless, the magical state of communalism was susceptible to attack.

The advocates of witch trials associated harm and misbehavior with witchcraft. In consequence, they conducted criminal trials that accepted rumors of witchcraft without adequate judicial caution and almost without any critical reflection. This system was simple but comprehensive. Indeed, the mutual interpenetration of witch beliefs and magic, on the one hand, and politics, economics, and justice, on the other, was totally characteristic of the witch hunts. Both realms could stimulate the witch hunts, but both could also curtail them. As soon as alternative ways of thinking and acting emerged in any of these realms—that is, as soon as they became more complicated—the simple system of witch hunting broke down.

Believing in witchcraft offered ways to interpret misfortune and concrete religious-magical ways to do something about it. Ordinary people mainly wanted protection from the witches, while the authorities mainly sought the punishment of the Devil's allies. If an extensive array of church magic satisfied the needs of the populace, then contemporaries were far less likely to look for witches if they suffered personal or social crises. If such powerful church magic did not exist, witch hunts were certainly not inevitable, but they became more likely in times of crisis. Thus, we should always view the intensity of witch hunting in a region against the background of what religious interpretations of suffering existed in the region, both among individuals and in society. We also need to consider the specific religious-magical remedies available to address concrete problems, such as healing prayers against illness or cults of saints and blessings against weather damage. Even if witch trials and protective magic might rise and fall together, they nonetheless competed with each other. Thus, the complex systems of protective magic and popular religiosity were not simply a context that supported witch beliefs. Folk magic and popular Catholicism, cunning folk and unorthodox priests, catered to the popular demand for magical aid and protection and in doing so provided a real alternative to witch hunts. This holds true even though, as we have seen, the witch fantasy absorbed many popular beliefs that had originally belonged to entirely different contexts, and even though folk magicians occasionally worked as "witch finders."

When the Jesuit Adam Tanner provided a new theological understanding of witchcraft and the Devil, suggesting that one could rob demons of their human tools not by executing them but by converting them, he contributed to weakening the drive for witch hunting in the archducal Swabian government. To be sure, that drive had never been strong. Unlike in Swabian Austria, however, a theological reorientation following Tanner or Spee did not take place in the ecclesiastical territory of the Electorate of Trier, perhaps because the figure of Peter Binsfeld loomed too large.

The church influenced the witch hunts mainly by granting (or refusing) alternative ways to interpret misfortune or fend off witchcraft. I must, of course, note that the present work has concentrated only on Catholic territories. The Württemberg reformer Johannes Brenz moralized the concept of God's permission of suffering and demanded that parishioners repent rather than lay the blame on witches. Generally speaking, the rise of confessionalism and denominational strife reduced the options for dealing with the crime of witchcraft, but they did not necessarily lead to an intensification of witch hunting.

It is clear that changes in the administrative and jurisdictional sphere had immediate effects on the witch trials. Political intervention offered the best chance to curtail the witch hunts effectively, because the driving forces behind the most massive witch hunts were the popular organs of self-governance, without or even in opposition to the territorial governments. As soon as the territorial lord could avoid being misled by biased information from local agents and summoned the power to subjugate the judicial structure to its control and thus "de-localize" it, the witch-hunting system collapsed. Each new level of review, each new supervisory level—such as defense attorneys, high courts, commissions from the sovereign, and the government itself—disrupted the simple, autonomous system that was based on the proximity of witch-hunting demands to jurisdiction. Because witch trials were always based on highly questionable evidence, once the government subjected them to juridical discussion, the trials stopped. The central governments' reforms functioned in this way in Swabian Austria as well as in the Electorate of Trier, along with its shared domains. Prince Elector Karl Kaspar von der Leyen's radical renunciation of witch trials in 1652 naturally accelerated this process, but he used the same means as others did elsewhere and did not produce any significantly different course of events.

If the communal organization of witch hunts depended on limiting the territorial lord, the termination of trials represented an important (if partial) victory for the territorial state. Differently put, the territorial state's larger principle of spatial order conquered the communal concentration on local space. The witch hunts, as serious abuses of the judiciary, provoked a reaction from the territorial sovereign. The trials became obvious and convenient targets for criticism. Thus, in contrast to what some historians have alleged, the witch hunts themselves did not serve as a vehicle for a policy of acculturation or indoctrination on the part of the religious and secular authorities. Rather, the apparatus of central government gained significant ground by controlling, limiting, and finally ending the witch hunts. This does not mean that the territorial authorities merely exploited the fight against witch trials as a pretext to get a foothold in local structures of power. In Swabian Austria as well as the Electorate of Trier, the scandalous state of criminal justice was without doubt a genuine matter of concern. All the same, in light of the dominance of local officials in the practice of witch hunting, it was not possible to control that practice without proceeding against the simple communal system. So the struggle against witch trials consolidated the territorial state by means of a "double negative": the authoritarian negation of the communal negation of the territorial state apparatus. But this development was possible only if the territorial government had first succeeded in gathering the information and resources necessary to overpower the forces of communalism.

If we wish to pose the question of the function of the trials—which in light of the judicial murders could be denounced as cynical[3]—it seems clear that as an expression and means of communalism, the witch hunts had a short-term functionality, at most. They provoked the consolidating territorial state to get tougher, and because they claimed a very high number of trial victims, the counter-measures of the state authorities were obviously justified. The state of the ancien régime thus transformed peasants and townsfolk into subjects with the help of the witch hunts, not by favoring them, but by controlling and ending them. This was why the Enlightenment could ridicule witch beliefs as the "superstition" of the lower class and the backward rural populace. At the same time, the trials themselves began to appear in an entirely different light. It was no longer the witches but the witch hunters who were the "evil people."

Appendix

Chronology and Quantitative Analysis of the Persecutions

I have counted all court proceedings against the crime of witchcraft in Swabian Austria and the Electorate of Trier that went at least as far as interviewing witnesses. I did not include medieval sorcery proceedings and trials of treasure hunters.[1] Where the sources are unclear, I always chose the lowest possible victim count. The chronology permitting, I have merged victims known by name but for whom an exact execution date is not know with summary lists. These statistics thus represent a minimum count. In accordance with the entire approach of this work, witch trials that were carried out in mediated or shared territories have been left out altogether.[2]

TABLE 1 WITCH HUNTS IN SWABIAN AUSTRIA

Year	Death		Other trial outcome		Outcome unknown		Sources[a]
	Female	*Male*	*Female*	*Male*	*Female*	*Male*	
1493				1			StAA, VÖ Lit, 631, fols. 90r–v
Before 1497	2		1				Zimmermann, "Hochstift Konstanz," 367
1521			1				GLAK, 8/1259
1528	1						Dillinger, "Grafschaft Hohenberg," 20
1530	6	4	2	1			Dillinger, "Grafschaft Hohenberg," 20; GLAK, 67/734, fol. 370r; StA Günzburg, 5.115
1531							Dillinger, "Grafschaft Hohenberg," 21
1554			2				HStASt, B 19, Bd. 3, fol. 193r–v
1558	9						Dillinger, *Hexenprozesse in Horb*, 13, 45
1559	3						Dillinger, *Hexenprozesse in Horb*, 13, 45
1560			1				Dillinger, *Hexenprozesse in Horb*, 13, 45
1564	2		2				Dillinger, *Hexenprozesse in Horb*, 45
1565			1				Dillinger, *Hexenprozesse in Horb*, 14, 45
1567			1				Behringer, Bavaria, 434
1571			1				Midelfort, *Witch Hunting*, 203

TABLE 1 WITCH HUNTS IN SWABIAN AUSTRIA (*continued*)

Year	Death Female	Death Male	Other trial outcome Female	Other trial outcome Male	Outcome unknown Female	Outcome unknown Male	Sources[a]
1572	1						HStASt, B 17, Bd. 21, fol. 233v
1575	2						TLA, Pestarchiv, VI 12, XXVIII 142
1578	24		1	1			TLA, Hofrat, Auslauf, Karton 67, Kopial bücher: An die fürstlich Durchlaucht, 1578, fol. 835r; Dillinger, "Grafschaft Hohenberg," 40
1580	9						Dillinger, "Grafschaft Hohenberg," 40
1581	3						Dillinger, "Grafschaft Hohenberg," 41
1582	5+b						Dillinger, "Grafschaft Hohenberg," 42
1583	32			1			Dillinger, "Grafschaft Hohenberg," 41-42
1584	.				2+		TLA, Kopialbücher: An die fürstliche Durchlaucht, 1584, fols. 481v–482r
1585	9		3	1			StAA, VÖ Lit, 649, fol. 480r–v; Dillinger, "Grafschaft Hohenberg," 42
1587	14		1				Dillinger, "Grafschaft Hohenberg," 42-43
1588	2						Dilllinger, "Grafschaft Hohenberg," 43
1589	8	1					Dillinger, "Grafschaft Hohenberg," 43, 46, 69
1590	24		1				Dillinger, "Grafschaft Hohenberg," 45-47
1594	2+		6	1			Dillinger, "Grafschaft Hohenberg," 43, 50-51
1595	12+		2				StAA, VÖ Lit 650, fol. 486r, 513v; Dillinger, "Grafschaft Hohenberg," 51
1596	42		1				Dillinger, "Grafschaft Hohenberg," 56-59
1597	1		1				Rückert, 35; Dillinger, *Hexenprozesse in Horb*, 47
1598	15		2	1			Dillinger, "Grafschaft Hohenberg," 59, 62, 100
1599	21	1	3	2			StAA, VÖ Lit, 651, fol. 471r, 474v; Dillinger, "Grafschaft Hohenberg," 59; idem, *Hexenprozesse in Horb*, 47-48
1600	23	2					StA Günzburg, 5.232; Dillinger, "Grafschaft Hohenberg," 60-61, 95
1601	15		3				Dillinger, "Grafschaft Hohenberg," 61, 89
1603	6	1	1				TLA, Geheimer Rat, Auslauf, Karton 639; Dillinger, "Grafschaft Hohenberg," 62; Zingeler, 149
1604	4		2	2			TLA, Geheimer Rat, Einlauf, Karton 6;8, Hs. 1390, fol. 81; Dillinger, *Hexenprozesse in Horb*, 48
1605	22		4	1			TLA, Geheimer Rat, Einlauf, Karton 4; Dillinger, "Grafschaft Hohenberg," 104, 106
1606			2				Midelfort, *Witch Hunting*, 211
1607		1					Dillinger, "Grafschaft Hohenberg," 108
1608	1						Dillinger, "Grafschaft Hohenberg," 108
1609	11	3					Dillinger, "Grafschaft Hohenberg," 112, 122-23
1610		1				1	StA Günzburg, 5.267 ; Dillinger, "Grafschaft Hohenberg," 74
1613	1		8				StA Günzburg, 5.267; Dillinger, "Grafschaft Hohenberg," 112-14; idem, *Hexenprozesse in Horb*, 48
1615	4	3	1				HStASt, B 40, Bü 543; Dillinger, "Grafschaft Hohenberg," 123-24
1616	5	1					Dillinger, "Grafschaft Hohenberg," 124
1617			3				StA Stockach, C.VIII, 1, fol. 122r; Dillinger, *Hexenprozesse in Horb*, 48

Year	Death Female	Death Male	Other trial outcome Female	Other trial outcome Male	Outcome unknown Female	Outcome unknown Male	Sources[a]
1618			2	1			StA Stockach, C.VIII, 1, fols. 15r, 24v, 26r
1619	1						Zürn, "Abseits," 72
1620	3		1				HStASt, B 17, Bd. 28, fols. 3v, 112v, 140r; StA Stockach, C.VIII, 1, fol. 20r
1621	7		2	6			StA Stockach, C.VIII, 1, fol. 111r; Dillinger, "Grafschaft Hohenberg," 117, 124
1623				1			Behringer, Bavaria, 449
1625	6	3	2	1			StAA, VÖ Lit, 654, fol. 236v; Dillinger, "Grafschaft Hohenberg," 118-19, 125
1627			3	1			Völk, no. 9; Dillinger, *Hexenprozesse in Horb*, 49
1628			4	1			StAA, VÖ Lit, 655, fol. 83v; Völk, no. 9; Dillinger, "Grafschaft Hohenberg," 124
1629				1			StA Stockach, C.VIII, 2, sine folio
1630					1		StAA, VÖ Lit 655, fol. 251v
1631	2	1					StAA, VÖ Lit 655, fol. 251v, 349v, 423r–v
1636			2				StA Oberndorf, A 128; Dillinger, "Nemini," 279
1637		1					StA Oberndorf, A 128
1638	5	1					Dillinger, "Nemini," 184
1639		1					Dillinger, "Grafschaft Hohenberg," 129
1641	3+						TLA, Pestarchiv, XXXVIII 498; Dillinger, "Grafschaft Hohenberg," 121
1643			1				Dillinger, "Grafschaft Hohenberg," 122
1648	1	1					Dillinger, "Grafschaft Hohenberg," 129
1649	1	1					StAA, VÖ Lit, 656, fol. 131v; Dillinger, "Grafschaft Hohenberg," 129
1650	1	1	1				Dillinger, "Grafschaft Hohenberg," 133; idem, *Hexenprozesse in Horb*, 49
1652			1				Dillinger, "Grafschaft Hohenberg," 134
1657			1				StA Burgau, Ratsprotokoll, fol. 438r
1658			3				Dillinger, "Grafschaft Hohenberg," 135-36
1660			1				Dillinger, "Grafschaft Hohenberg," 138
1663	1		1		2		HStASt, B 17, Bd. 10, fol. 140v; StA Stockach, C.VIII, 2, sine folio
1664			1				HStASt, B 17, Bd. 34, fol. 335r–v
1665			1		1		HStASt, B 17, Bd. 10, fol. 206r; StA Stockach, C.VIII, 2, sine folio
1666	1						HStASt, B 17, Bd. 35, fol. 198r
1667			1				Dillinger, "Grafschaft Hohenberg," 139
1671	1	1	1				Dillinger, "Grafschaft Hohenberg," 139-41
1680	1		2				HStASt, B 17, Bd. 44, fols. 540r, 754r–v
1681	1						Barth, 162
1683			1				TLA, Hs. 5923, fol. 483v
1695			1				HStASt, B 17, Bd. 54, fol. 470r
1710				1			Dillinger, "Grafschaft Hohenberg," 145
1711			1				Dillinger, "Grafschaft Hohenberg," 147

Note: Date listed is the year of the trial.

[a]Authors for whom only one title is included in the bibliography will be listed here only by name. Citation of supporting documentation is limited to a single source in each case.

[b]Plus sign (+) indicates that given number was exceeded by an unknown amount.

TABLE 2 GENDER DISTRIBUTION OF THE CONDEMNED IN SWABIAN AUSTRIA

	Trials	Men	Women
Total	529	50	479
As % of total	100	9.5	90.5
Death sentences	406	25	381
Death sentences as % of total	76.7	50	79.5

Geographically, the witch trials in Swabian Austria were distributed unevenly. About 80 percent of the trials for which evidence exists took place in Lower Hohenberg, at the courts of Rottenburg, Horb, and Oberndorf. The records of the Innsbruck government mention certainly not all but some of the witch trials in Swabian Austria. This evidence suggests that the extremely uneven distribution of witch hunts is not merely due to a loss of records in Upper Hohenberg, Nellenburg, Burgau, and the Landvogtei. In contrast to Hohenberg, in the rest of Swabian Austria there were in fact no chain trials that extended beyond five cases. When compared with Vorarlberg, another territory of the Habsburg west under the direct control of the Innsbruck government, the impression that Hohenberg experienced extraordinarily intense persecutions is confirmed. In the course of two hundred years, there were more than 400 witch trials in Hohenberg; in Vorarlberg, there were only 165 trials in about one hundred fifty years, although the population of Vorarlberg was probably two and half times larger. In Hohenberg, death was the verdict in about 85 percent of trials, while in Vorarlberg, a death sentence was pronounced in only about 58 percent of cases.[3]

We can identify several persecution waves of varying intensities in Swabian Austria. The witch hunts began gradually at the end of the Middle Ages. An early concentration of trials developed in Swabian Austria, as in the entire German southwest, around 1530/31. The subsequent pause and the return to harsher proceedings against witches at the end of the 1570s also conform entirely to regional trends.[4] The number of trials in the following years through 1605 fluctuated considerably, yet they formed distinct peaks in 1583, 1596, and 1599. Apart from the gap in 1590–93, there were no longer any periods of more than a single year without trials. After 1609, single trials were the most common, apart from a comparatively weak cluster at the beginning of the 1620s.

Viewed in relation to the total population, witch trials were more common in Swabian Austria than in the Electorate of Trier. All the same, one cannot simply conclude that the intensity of persecution was greater in Habsburg territories, as the chances of escaping the death sentence were considerably slimmer in the Electorate of Trier. The proportion of trials that ended in executions, however, was roughly as high in the persecution-intensive region of Hohenberg as in the Electorate of Trier (around 85 percent compared with about 89 percent).

In addition to the witch trials of the Electorate of Tier listed below, there were proceedings against persons of unknown gender, of whom 49 were executed during the first wave of persecution between 1585 and 1596 in Müstermaifeld and Coblenz.[5] I have been unable to find further information on reports of trials against twelve women from Blieskastel and three people of unknown gender from the Electorate of Trier's southern exclaves, Blieskastel and St. Wendel.[6]

TABLE 3 Witch hunts in the Electorate of Trier

Year	Death Female	Death Male	Death Unknown	Other trial outcome Female	Other trial outcome Male	Outcome unknown Female	Outcome unknown Male	Outcome unknown Unknown	Sources[a]
Before 1486				1					Kramer, book 2, chap. 2, sec. 1, 529
1490/91						2			Weisenstein, 479-80
1492				1					Hoffman and Dohms, no. 123, 79
1492-94	30+[c]								Rummel, "Phasen," 258
1495/96	1					1			Weisenstein, 480
1497		*[d]							Hoffman and Dohms, no. 151, 95
1501/02	1								Weisenstein, 480
1508		*							Hoffman and Dohms, no. 214, 133
1516	4								Hoffman and Dohms, no. 260, 528
1517/18	2								Weisenstein, 480
1525		*							Hoffman and Dohms, no. 686, 323
1527						2			Weisenstein, 481
1528/29	3					2			Weisenstein, 481
1538/39						2			Weisenstein, 481
1541/42	*	*		1		1			Weisenstein, 481; Lauer, *Hexenverfolgung*, 23
1560						2			Hoppstädter, 263
1568				1					LHAKO, 1 C 37, 115
1570	2								Krämer, *Kurtrierische Hexenprozesse*, 80-82
1571						1	1		Hoppstädter, 263
1572						1			LHAKO, 1 C 103
1577/78	3								Weisenstein, 481
1580	2								Kettel, "Hexenprozesse in der Grafschaft Gerolstein," 364-65
1582	2					1			StB Trier, 1534/166, 13, 21; Weisenstein, 482
1584				2					StB Trier, 1533/170, fol. 252r
1585	2+				1				LHAKO, 211/3036; *Annuae*, 275-76
1586				1					Voltmer and Weisenstein, 17
1587	133	6							LHAKO, 211/2979; *Annuae*, 254-55; Voltmer and Weisenstein, 29, 43, 49; Rummel, "Phasen," 260, 265, 269; Mohr, 7-8
1588	17+	1		2	2				LHAKO, 1 C 14125; StA Trier, DK, 54 K 657, 237, 250, 340, 403; StB Trier, H1533a/171, fols. 5v, 76v; Voltmer and Weisenstein, 6, 27, 48-49; Gerteis, "Die kurfürstliche Zeit," 58-61; Weisenstein, 483
1585-89			57						StB Trier, H1533a/171, fols. 55v–56r
1589	11+	4		2					LHAKO, 211/2206; 2233; LAS, 38/558; Voltmer and Weisenstein, 77, 87, 204; Weisenstein, 483, Voltmer, "Zwischen Herrschaftskrise," 91-92
1590	10	3							LHAKO, 56/419, fol. 97r; StA Trier, DK, 54K657, 67, 99; StB Trier, Hs. 1533/170, fols. 11r–12v; Voltmer, "Zwischen Herrschaftskrise," 91, Weisenstein, 483

TABLE 3　Witch hunts in the Electorate of Trier (*continued*)

Year	Death			Other trial outcome		Outcome unknown			Sources[a]
	Female	*Male*	*Unknown*	*Female*	*Male*	*Female*	*Male*	*Unknown*	
1590/91		2		3	1				*Annuae*, 341
1591	9	3	4		1				LHAKO, 1 C 37, 108; LAS, 38/136; StA Trier, DK, 54 K 657, 17, 37, 75, 103; StB Trier, 1533/171, fols. 3v, 53v; Voltmer, "Zwischen Herr-schaftskrise," 92, Gerteis, "Die kur-fürstliche Zeit," 64; Niessen, 74
1592	2+	5							StB Trier, 2180a/45a, 12, 32; Voltmer and Weisenstein, 184, 257; Rummel, "Phasen," 268
1591–93	15								LHAKO, 1 C 4324
1593	39+	3							LHAKO, 627/113, fols. 37r, 40r; *Annuae*, 234; Rummel, "Soziale Dynamik," 37; idem, "Phasen," 272; Labouvie, "Rekonstruktion," 56; Baumgarten, 254
1593/94		1							Voltmer and Weisenstein, 267
1594	10+	5		1	1				LHAKO, 1 C 9193; StB Trier, 1534/166, fol. 29v; StA Trier, DK, 54 K 239; FÖAH[b], 1, 9, 12; Voltmer and Weisenstein, 56; 143, Junk, 137; Rummel, "Soziale Dynamik," 38-39; idem, "Phasen," 270
1594/95	2+								*Annuae*, 521; Voltmer and Weisen-stein, 48; Junk, 137
1595	1		1			1			LHAKO, 211/3028, 16, 1 C 9191
1595–96	1								LHAKO, 56/419, fol. 93v
1596	5	2				1			LHAKO, 56/419, 69v; *Annuae*, 232, 283; Lauer, *Hexenverfolgung*, 69; Fisenne, 5
1596/97			*						LHAKO, 33/8182, fol. 7r–v
1597		1	*						LHAKO, 1 C 41, 1413-14; Fisenne, 5
1598	1			1		1	1		LAS, vdL 2752; 2777; *Annuae*, 346
1597–99				1	1				LHAKO, 56/419, fol. 12r
1599	1			1		2			*Annuae*, 414; Heisterkamp, 69-70; Kettel, "Hexenprozesse in der Graf-schaft Gerolstein," 365
1580–1601	2		5+						*Annuae*, 401; Kettel, "Hexenprozesse in der Grafschaft Gerolstein," 367
1601	1			1	1				LHAKO, 1 C 45, 159; *Annuae*, 570, 608-9
1602		1			1	3	2		LHAKO, 1 C 7944; *Annuae, 534; Ket-tel, "Hexenprozesse in der Grafschaft Gerolstein," 363*
1606	1+								Bundesarchiv, ASt. Frankfurt, FSg, 2/1, film 23, 1524; Schmidt, *Heimat-chronik*, 255
1607		1					1		*Annuae*, 687-88
1610		1		5	1				StB Trier, 1534/166, fols. 56r–70v

Year	Death Female	Death Male	Death Unknown	Other trial outcome Female	Other trial outcome Male	Outcome unknown Female	Outcome unknown Male	Outcome unknown Unknown	Sources[a]
1611				2					StB Trier, 1534/166, fols. 61r, 62v
1613	1								Gappenach, "Münstermaifelder Kriminaljustiz," 56-57
1617				1					StB Trier, 1534/166, fol. 69r
1618				1		1			StB Trier, 1534/166, fol. 69v
1624	1					1			Michel, 413; Oster, 120
1625		1							LHAKO, 33/12344, fol. 44r
1626	1								Wyttenbach, "Abermaliger Beytrag," 116
1627	1								Lauer, *Hexenverfolgung,* 31
1628	5+								Rummel, "Phasen," 276
1629	16+	3	22	1					HHStAW, 339/433, 339/138; LHAKO, 1 C 18827, 33/8853, fol. 34r, 56/1922, fol. 1449v–1451v, 211/2997, fol. 28v; Bellinghausen, 176; Gappenach, "Münstermaifelder Kriminaljustiz," 56-57; Heisterkamp, 69-70; Kettel, "Hexenprozesse in der Grafschaft Gerolstein," 371; Krämer, *Kurtrierische Hexenprozesse,* 13; Rummel, "Phasen," 276
1629/30	2	2		1					Krämer, *Kurtrierische Hexenprozesse, 10, 19, 44*
1630	12	9		3	1	2			Bundesarchiv, ASt. Frankfurt, FSg, 2/1, film 21, 1206; 23, 1524; LHAKO, 33/8859; 211/3027; BAT, Abt. 5.2, no. 43, 10; StA Trier, DK, 54 K 239, 54 K 657, 163; StB Trier, Hs. 1534/166, fol. 94r–95r; Kettel, "Hexenprozesse in der Grafschaft Gerolstein," 364, 371; Krämer, *Kurtrierische Hexenprozesse,* 17; Rummel, "Phasen," 276-77, 317
1628–31			81						Rummel, "Phasen," 277
1631	4					2			LHAKO, 211/3013, fol. 11v; StA Trier, DK, 54 K 657, 404, 442; Rummel, "Phasen," 276-77
1639				1					Rummel, "Phasen," 279
1642	1+			1					Rummel, "Phasen," 280, Voltmer, "Zwischen Herrschaftskrise," 104
1643	*								Rummel, "Phasen," 280
1645	1								HHStAW, 339/146
1645/46	1	1							Krämer, *Kurtrierische Hexenprozesse,* 45
1648	2	1							Krämer, *Kurtrierische Hexenprozesse,* 45
1651	2	1			1				HHStAW, 339/148, fol. 9r, 369/446; Michel, 413
1652	2	1							Krämer, *Kurtrierische Hexenprozesse,* 19, 29, 45
1626–52	6	1							Gappenach, *Münstermaifeld,* 140

TABLE 3   WITCH HUNTS IN THE ELECTORATE OF TRIER (*continued*)

Year	Death			Other trial outcome		Outcome unknown			Sources[a]
	Female	Male	Unknown	Female	Male	Female	Male	Unknown	
1652						2			Rummel, "Phasen," 281
1653	1								Rummel, "Phasen," 282
1655								*	Lauer, *Hexenverfolgung,* 27; Bettingen, 544
1657						1	1		Lauer, *Hexenverfolgung,* 27
1660								*	Rummel, "Phasen," 282

Note: Date listed is the year of the trial.

[a]Authors for whom only one title is included in the bibliography will be listed here only by name. Citation of supporting documentation is limited to a single source in each case.

[b]My thanks to Dittmar Lauer, who gave me photocopies of sources from the Archiv der Fürsten Öttingen-Wallerstein in Harburg (FÖAH).

[c]Plus sign (+) indicates that given number was exceeded by an unknown amount.

[d]Asterisk (*) indicates that data were not quantifiable.

TABLE 4   GENDER DISTRIBUTION OF THE CONDEMNED IN THE ELECTORATE OF TRIER

	Trials	Men	Women	Unknown
Total	792	94	457	242
As % of total	100	11.9	57.7	30.5
Death sentences	703	66	395	242
Death sentences as % of total	88.8	70.2	86.4	100

In the Electorate of Trier, after the first intense persecutions at the end of the fifteenth century, two waves of witch trials developed: the years from 1587 to 1596 and then from 1629 to 1631. The first large wave did not build up gradually but began with an explosion of trials. Unfortunately, only a single chronicle report survives regarding the execution of 120 persons in the district of Pfalzel. Due to the substantial loss of sources in the Electorate caused by the intentional destruction of records, the absence of parallel sources means that we cannot evaluate the chronicler's assertions. Even so, while the dating to 1586 or 1587 may be uncertain, the victim count should be accepted, as the chronicler is generally reliable, and there is no evidence that contradicts him.[7] The trials ended many years after the enactment of the Witch Trial Ordinance of Johann VII. The case of the Electorate of Trier thus stands as a warning against simply explaining the course and intensity of the witch hunts as the result of implementing the *Carolina* in territorial law. The incursion of the Thirty Years' War into the Electorate, which extensively hindered the work of the courts, explains the abrupt end of the second wave of persecution after only two years. We must note that Swabian Austria did not participate in the second great wave of trials that gripped the Electorate of Trier and many other parts of central Europe around 1630.[8]

The discovery that the high point of the witch hunts coincided with the climatic distress known as the Little Ice Age has been of great significance for recent witchcraft research.[9] In the Electorate, the peaks in the agricultural crisis were largely identical to those of the waves of witch trials.[10] Although the worsening climate must also have affected Swabian Austria, however, and although there was indeed a wave of trials there around 1590, the second wave of trials around 1630 never materialized. It becomes clear that we cannot simply trace the origin of the witch trials back to the Little Ice Age. As we have seen, numerous other circumstances separated the developments in the Habsburg territories from those in the Electorate of Trier and the general trend of the witch hunts in the first half of the seventeenth century. Nonetheless, the influence of the weather should not be underestimated. Individual weather events such as storms, frosts, and floods provoked witch panics in both of the territories under investigation.[11]

The poor condition of the sources makes any statistical evaluation of the trial data quite difficult. The reader should understand all evaluations as statements of trends in the manner of a sample. For the Electorate of Trier, even an assessment of the gender distribution among the accused is problematic, because so many trials are mentioned

TABLE 5   FAMILY STATUS OF TRIAL VICTIMS IN SWABIAN AUSTRIA

	Widowed	Married	Single	Child	Unknown
Men as % of total	0.19	2.1	0.19	0.39	6.56
Women as % of total	8.77	17.17	1.72	2.29	60.62
Proportion of death sentences for men as % of respective group	100	45.45	0	50	53.45
Proportion of death sentences for women as % of respective group	78.26	66.67	66.67	25	87.54

TABLE 6   FAMILY STATUS OF TRIAL VICTIMS IN THE ELECTORATE OF TRIER

	Widowed	Married	Single	Child	Unknown
Men as % of total	0.55	1.83	1.1	1.28	7.14
Women as % of total	2.75	13.37	0.73	2.28	38.75
Proportion of death sentences for men as % of respective group	66.67	50	50	42.86	84.6
Proportion of death sentences for women as % of respective group	80	87.67	75	0	92.03

only summarily. Nevertheless, the number of men among the victims of the witch trials lay below the European average in the territories under comparison and was clearly even lower in Swabian Austrian than in the Electorate of Trier.[12] The proportion of death sentences in trials against women was significantly higher in both territories than in trials against men.

Based on these data on family status, we can make a general estimate for the ages of the affected individuals. As married or widowed women, most trial victims must have been over twenty-five years of age.

In the 1580s, a Habsburg officer who knew Swabian Austria well stated categorically that witches were "usually poor."[13] There are no detailed reports from contemporary observers. Here we can only roughly divide the accused into the lower, middle, and upper social strata, taking into account not only possessions but also prestige or infamy.[14] The attempt to find trial victims on tax or census records only rarely succeeds. I have counted as upper class any individuals who possessed monetary wealth that exceeded the local average by 50 percent. I also considered the possession of horses sufficient for inclusion in this group, as was marriage to or kinship with officeholders such as priests, jurors, city councilors, or sheriffs, or higher administrative positions. I have defined

TABLE 7 SOCIAL STATUS OF TRIAL VICTIMS IN SWABIAN AUSTRIA

	Upper class	Middle class	Lower class	Unknown
Men as % of total	2.67	0.76	1.91	4.09
Women as % of total	7.06	6.1	8.77	68.64
Proportion of death sentences for men as % of respective group	42.86	25	60	74.21
Proportion of death sentences for women as % of respective group	64.86	65.62	65.23	84.85

TABLE 8 SOCIAL STATUS OF TRIAL VICTIMS IN THE ELECTORATE OF TRIER

	Upper class	Middle class	Lower class	Unknown
Men as % of total	5.61	0.18	1.28	4.83
Women as % of total	5.86	1.46	1.28	49.1
Proportion of death sentences for men as % of respective group	48.26	100	57.14	85
Proportion of death sentences for women as % of respective group	78.12	75	85.71	88.03

membership in the lower class here by a record of begging, lack of a fixed residence, dependent occupations such as maid or servant, membership in a dishonorable profession, or pronounced difficulties in maintaining basic subsistence.

Clearly, members of the upper class were not capable of preventing investigations against them. The persecution of men in the Electorate was higher than in Swabian Austria. This was, however, particularly pronounced among men from the social elite, although—as should be expected—in both territories such men enjoyed relatively good chances of not being found guilty. Women from the ruling class, however, did not succeed in escaping the death sentence significantly more frequently than women of other classes. We should not disregard, however, the reservation that proceedings against members of the social elite would be more likely to leave traces in the source material than those against members of the lower class.

Glossary

Every territory of the Holy Roman Empire had its own hierarchy of offices and courts. An office that was of crucial importance in one territory might be entirely lacking in another territory.

Ammann   mayor; head of the administration of a town. The mayor was answerable to the prince even though the town authorities participated in the selection of the mayor. Also known as *Stadtammann.*

Amt   district; a territorial unit used for taxation, policing, and military defense.

Amtmann   district commissioner; high official of the elector of Trier, roughly equivalent to the Swabian sheriffs, responsible for an *Amt.*

Dorfschultheiss   the village sheriff, the official representative of the prince without criminal jurisdiction, roughly the equivalent of an English village constable, who nonetheless could be responsible for the collection of taxes.

Kurfürst   prince elector; a prince who enjoyed the exclusive right to elect the German king. Originally, there were seven prince electors.

Kurfürstentum   electorate; territory governed by a prince elector.

Landammann   bailiff; an official who formally presided over a criminal court. Also known as *Obervogt.*

Obervogt   bailiff; an official who formally presided over a criminal court. Also known as *Landammann.*

Obervogtei   bailiwick; district of a criminal court under a bailiff's authority.

Reichskammergericht   Imperial Chamber Court, appeals court of the German empire, highest court in the empire.

Schöffengericht   high court.

Schultheiss   sheriff; official of the prince, head of the law enforcement agency, responsible for a town or a district. Officially subordinate to a district commissioner or bailiff. However, a sheriff could substitute permanently for his superior. The sheriff often served as the president of the criminal court.

Stadtammann   mayor; head of the administration of a town. The mayor was answerable to the prince even though the town authorities participated in the selection of the mayor. Also known as *Ammann.*

Truchsess   lord steward, the hereditary ruler of Waldburg, near Swabian Austria.

Unterschultheiss   an under-sheriff, who had powers equivalent to a village sheriff.

Vogt   sheriff; official of the prince, head of the law enforcement agency, responsible for a town or a district. Officially subordinate to a district commissioner or bailiff. However, a sheriff could substitute permanently for his superior. The sheriff often served as the president of the criminal court.

Zender   Reeve.

Notes

ABBREVIATIONS

BAT	Bistumsarchiv Trier
BayHStA	Bayerisches Hauptstaatsarchiv München
GLAKG	enerallandesarchiv Karlsruhe
HHStAW	Hessisches Hauptstaatsarchiv Wiesbaden
HStASt	Hauptstaatsarchiv Stuttgart
LHAKO	Landeshauptarchiv Koblenz
StAA	Staatsarchiv Augsburg
StAS	Staatsarchiv Sigmaringen
StA Burgau	Stadtarchiv Burgau
StA Günzburg	Stadtarchiv Günzburg
StA Horb	Stadtarchiv Horb
StA Konstanz	Stadtarchiv Konstanz
StA Oberndorf	Stadtarchiv Oberndorf
StA Reutlingen	Stadtarchiv Reutlingen
StA Rottenburg	Stadtarchiv Rottenburg
StA Rottweil	Stadtarchiv Rottweil
StA Stockach	Stadtarchiv Stockach
StA Trier	Stadtarchiv Trier
StB Trier	Stadtbibliothek Trier
TLA	Tiroler Landesarchiv Innsbruck
UAT	Universitätsarchiv Tübingen

INTRODUCTION

1. Neugebauer-Wölk, "Wege aus dem Dschungel," 316–29; Lambrecht, *Hexenverfolgungen und Zaubereiprozesse*, 402–3; Gaskill, "The Devil in the Shape of a Man," 168–71; Behringer, *Witches*; Irsigler, "Hexenverfolgungen," 15–22.

2. Broedel, *The Malleus Maleficarum*; Ostorero, *L'Imaginaire*.

3. *Die Peinliche Gerichtsordnung Kaiser Karls* V (hereafter, *Carolina*), Art. 21, 40–41, Art. 44, 52, Art. 52, 55–56, Art. 109, 78.

4. Midelfort, *Witch Hunting*, Schnabel-Schüle, *Überwachen*, 21; Evans-Pritchard, *Witchcraft*. In an earlier work, Evans-Pritchard was already decisively working comparatively: Evans-Pritchard, "The Morphology and Function of Magic." Caro Baroja, *Las Brujas;* Behringer, "Hexenforschung," 557; Midelfort, "Recent Witch Hunting Research"; Thomas, *Religion;* idem, "History and Anthropology"; Behringer, "Geschichte der Hexenforschung," 123–24. Rainer Walz has pursued ethnological questions in historical witch research: see Walz, *Hexenglaube.* On comparisons between contemporary witch hunts and early modern European witch hunts, see Behringer, *Witches;* idem, *Hexen,* 12–31.

5. New details on the total number and distribution of trials are in Behringer, *Witches and Witch-Hunts,* 150; Dillinger, *Hexen und Magie,* 88–92. The comparative approach to demonological literature (as opposed to witch trials) is not included here. On this, see, e.g., Eerden, "Der Teufelspakt"; Franz, "Der Malleus Judicum . . . im Vergleich"; Labouvie, "Hexenforschung"; Scheffler et al., "Umrisse," 15; Behringer, *Witchcraft Persecutions in Bavaria;* Midelfort, *Witch Hunting;* Füssel, *Hexenverfolgungen;* Lambrecht, *Hexenverfolgungen und Zaubereiprozesse,* 402–15. Achim Baumgarten, who with the Naheraum selected a natural geographical definition for his region of investigation, worked through the various political territories of this region, but the comparative perspective is almost entirely absent: Baumgarten, *Hexenwahn.* An exception to the general absence of comparison is found in the research overview of Lorenz, "Einführung und Forschungsstand"; for the general trend, see Degn et al., *Hexenprozesse;* Isenberg and Mölich, *Hexenverfolgung;* Franz et al., *Hexenprozesse.* Schwillus, *Kleriker;* Schulte, *Hexenmeister.*

6. Monter, *Witchcraft in France and Switzerland.* Robert Rowland's essay provides a contrasting narrative rather than an analytical comparison: Rowland, "Fantasticall and Devilishe Persons."

7. Burke, "The Comparative Approach"; Ankarloo, "Witch Trials."

8. Bloch, "Pour une histoire comparée."

9. Schieder, "Möglichkeiten," 189–90.

10. Haupt and Kocka, "Historischer Vergleich," 11–15. There is an English translation of that article: cf. Haupt and Kocka, "Comparative History." However, because this translation is much abriged, working with the original text is recommended. For older approaches, see the survey in Puhle, "Theorien"; cf. also the multifaceted overview of Cohen and O'Connor, *Comparison.*

11. Schieder, "Möglichkeiten," 191–201; Tilly, *Big Structures,* 61–64, 81; Braembussche, "Historical Explanation," 13–17. Heinz-Gerhard Haupt and Jürgen Kocka limit themselves to the description of a single variation, without attempting to develop an encompassing typology of comparison: Haupt and Kocka, "Historischer Vergleich," 26–39.

12. Durkheim, *The Rules,* 147–58; Lorenz, *Konstruktion der Vergangenheit,* 231–39, 270.

13. Welskopp, "Stolpersteine," 348–49.

14. Espagne, "Sur les limites." For criticism of Espange, see Daum et al., "Fallobst," 10–11. For an overview of cultural transfer, see Middell, "Forschungen."

15. Cohen and O'Connor, "Introduction"; Middell, "Kulturtransfer"; Kaelble and Schriewer, *Vergleich*. Haupt has demonstrated the problems and possibilities of a decisively comparative European history: Haupt, "Die Geschichte Europas."

16. Daum et al., "Fallobst," 9–14; Haupt and Kocka, "Historischer Vergleich," 26–29. Nonetheless, a discussion of comparison at the macro-level can be avoided here, as the present work is intended as a regional study. See Skocpol and Somers, "The Uses of Comparative History." Comparative works on National Socialism belong here, as well. See, e.g., Waldmann, "Gewaltsamer Separatismus," or for system comparison in overview, see Jäckel, "Die zweifache Vergangenheit."

17. Bloch, "Pour une histoire comparée," 15–16; Haupt and Kocka, "Historischer Vergleich," 9; Espagne, "Sur les limites," 112–16. On avoiding typologies, see Schieder, "Möglichkeiten," 195–202. Braembussche, "Historical Explanation," 14.

18. Bloch, "Pour une histoire comparée," 15–16; Welskopp, "Stolpersteine," 435; Haupt and Kocka, "Historischer Vergleich," 11.

19. Sönke Lorenz coined the term "Midelfortian school" in 1997 in Hohenheim during a talk celebrating the twenty-fifth aniversary of Midelfort's book: see Lorenz, "Einführung und Forschungsstand," 195–96.

20. Fabricius, *Die Karte von 1789*, 107–219.

21. Herberhold, "Die österreichischen Donaustädte," 713–16, 723–27; cf. Gönner and Miller, "Die Landvogtei Schwaben," 688–96. On witch hunts in these regions, see Barczyk, "Stadt Waldsee," Hämmerle, "Die Saulgauer Hexenprozesse."

22. Sharp distinctions are in Haupt and Kocka, "Historischer Vergleich," 10–11; more pragmatic is Daum et al., "Fallobst," 20–21.

23. Birlinger, *Volksthümliches*, 1:142–57; Rückert, "Der Hexenwahn"; Sauter, *Zur Hexenbulle*, 49; Völk, "Ein Günzburger Hexenprozeß"; Willburger, "Hexenverfolgung," 138–39; Giefel, "Zur Geschichte der Hexenprozesse"; idem, "Zur Geschichte der Reformation Reformation," 412–14. Soldan, Heppe, and Bauer, *Geschichte*, 1:512–13. In the 1986 edition of this work, the entire passage is missing: Soldan, Heppe, and Ries, *Geschichte*. Janssen, *Culturzustände*, 8:618, 668–69.

24. Midelfort, *Witch Hunting*, 90–94; for statistics, see 201–29; Kempf, "Die Hexenverfolgung im Raum Rottenburg"; idem, "Hexenverfolgung in Rottenburg"; idem, *Die Chronik*, 354–81.

25. Behringer, *Witchcraft Persecutions in Bavaria*, 19, 79, 94, 133, 163, 172, 202; Zürn, "Abseits," 61–66. Greater detail is in idem, *Ir aigen libertet*, 486–503.

26. Dillinger, *Hexenverfolgungen in der Grafschaft*; idem, *Böse Leute*. These are among the sections deleted for this abridged translation.

27. Crusius, *Diarium*. This Tübingen edition, dated 1927–1961, was only a partial edition. The original manuscript is in the Universitätsbibliothek Tübingen (Mh 466). Crusius, "Annales suevici," is translated in *Schwäbische Chronick*, ed. Johann Jakob Moser (hereafter, Crusius, *Chronick*). Tschamser, *Annales*.

28. Binsfeld, *Tractatus* (1589). The same in German is idem, *Tractat* (1590). This edition is reproduced almost exactly, including page numbers and almost without editing, in idem, *Tractat* (2004). I will quote the substantially enlarged 1596 edition only if it provides crucial new information: idem, *Tractatus* (1596). On the life and work of Binsfeld, see Dillinger, "Binsfeld."

29. See the bibliography on witch trials in the Trier region in Voltmer and Weisenstein, *Das Hexenregister*, 91*–104*; Wyttenbach and Müller, *Gesta Trevirorum*, 53–55; Brower and Masen, *Antiquitatum*, 2:422–23, 425; Soldan, Heppe, and Bauer, *Geschichte*, 1:228, 471–75, 514–15, 2:1; Janssen, *Culturzustände*, 8:500, 582–85, 604–5, 633–43; Duhr, *Die Stellung*, 29–35.

30. See, e.g., Wyttenbach, "Noch ein höchst merkwürdiger Hexen-Proceß"; Burr, "The Fate"; Laufner, "Dr. Dietrich Flade"; idem, "Das Inventar"; Zenz, "Dr. Dietrich Flade"; Hammes, *Hexenwahn*, 168–92; Liel, "Die Verfolgung," 48–80; Niessen, "Hexenprozesse." Reactionary nonsense is in Laven, "Die Hexenprozesse."

31. Krämer, *Kurtrierische Hexenprozesse*. On early mentionings of the committees, see Voltmer, "Monopole," 12. Rummel, *Bauern;* idem, "Exorbitantien und Ungerechtigten"; idem, "Phasen." On witch committees beyond the borders of Trier, see Koppenhöfer, *Die mitleidlose Gesellschaft*, 242–44; Labouvie, *Zauberei*, 82–95. On the Rhine region, see Bátori, "Schultheiß"; Becker, "Hexenverfolgung," 124–25; Fuge, "Le Roi."

32. Labouvie, *Zauberei;* idem, *Verbotene Künste*.

33. Voltmer, "Monopole"; idem, "Gott."

34. Brommer, *Kurtrier*, 883. I thank Dr. Klaus Graf for pointing out the relevant passage in Brommer's book to me.

35. Weisenstein, "Zaubereiprozesse"; Rummel, "Phasen," 264–82.

36. "Annales Novesienses," 4, 520–738; Mechtel, *Die Limburger Chronik;* cf. Rummel, "Phasen," 260, 269, 272, 328; Lorenz et al., *Himmler*.

1. "Authority and Liberties for the Country and the People"

The quote that serves as the title of this chapter is from TLA, Kopialbücher: An die fürstliche Durchlaucht, 1569, fol. 276r.

1. Stolz, *Geschichtliche Beschreibung*, 4:17–23. On the term "Swabian Austria," see ibid., 42. The following is drawn from Quarthal, *Landstände*, 13, 17–25, 57–65. For details of Swabian Austria itself, see map 2 on p. 18.

2. Hirn, *Erzherzog Ferdinand*, 1:463–64.

3. Quarthal and Wieland, *Die Behördenorganisation*, 44–45.

4. The following is drawn from Quarthal, *Landstände*, 22–24, idem, "Die Verfassungsänderungen," 124.

5. The following is drawn from Quarthal, *Landstände*, 57–58.

6. Giefel, "Zur Geschichte der Verfassung," 375–76; Stemmler, "Die Grafschaft Hohenberg," 584; Theil, *Rottenburg*, 12–15; Müller, "Horb," 22–23; idem, "Geschichte der Stadt Oberndorf," 254.

7. Müller, "Horb," 24; idem, "Geschichte der Stadt Oberndorf," 258; Giefel, "Zur Geschichte der Verfassung," 378.

8. Theil, *Rottenburg*, 16. The composition of the Horb council is from TLA, Allgemeines Leopoldinum, Karton B, no. 133. On earlier developments, see Theil, *Rottenburg*, 15–16; Müller, "Horb," 24. idem, "Geschichte der Stadt Oberndorf," 158. On the 1607 ordinance, see HStASt, B 41, Bd. 9, Binsdorfer Policeyordnung, 6–7, Schömberger Policeyordnung, 6, Fridinger Policeyordnung, 6. Theil, *Rottenburg*, 16; Müller, "Horb,"

24; idem, "Geschichte der Stadt Oberndorf," 158; TLA, Allgemeines Leopoldinum, Karton B, no. 133.

9. More extensively, see Dillinger, *Böse Leute,* 45–47.

10. TLA, Hs. 2402, 419; HStASt, B 41, Bd. 9, Rottenburger Policeyordnung, fol. 8r.

11. GLAK, 67/739, fol. 314v–315v; Wagner, *Aus Stockachs Vergangenheit,* 40–44; Tumbült, "Die Landgrafschaft Nellenburg," 13–16; Berner, "Die Landgrafschaft Nellenburg," 613–18; Bohl, *Die Stadt Stockach,* 72–78.

12. Berner, "Die Landgrafschaft Nellenburg," 41–44; Kramer, "Die Landgrafschaft Nellenburg," 361–64; Bohl, *Die Stadt Stockach,* 78–100; GLAK, 67/735, fol. 66r.

13. GLAK, 61/8238–240, 118/166; Barth, *Geschichte,* 68–72; Berner, "Die Landgrafschaft Nellenburg," 618–19; Kramer, "Die Landgrafschaft Nellenburg," 362–63; Jänichen, "Zur Geschichte," 8–15.

14. On the reform of 1562, see StAA, VÖ Akten, 1387, 34; Barth, *Geschichte,* 72–73. Wagner, *Aus Stockachs Vergangenheit,* 10–11; Barth, *Geschichte,* 73–74; Berner, "Die Landgrafschaft Nellenburg und die Reichsritterschaft des Kantons Hegau-Bodensee," 77; Kramer, "Die Landgrafschaft Nellenburg," 362; Bohl, *Die Stadt Stockach,* 80, 93–96. The lists of jurors are from GLAK, 61/8238, 61/8239, 61/8240. See Berner, "Die Landgrafschaft Nellenburg und die Reichsritterschaft des Kantons Hegau-Bodensee," 78; Kramer, "Die Landgrafschaft Nellenburg," 362–63.

15. GLAK, 118/20, 118/176, 118/385, 123/228, 18/3, 118/5, 67/738, fols. 24r–32v, 37v–38r. See Kramer, "Die Landgrafschaft Nellenburg," 363; Berner, "Die Landgrafschaft Nellenburg," 622–24; Roth von Schreckenstein, "Der sogenannte Hegauer Vertrag."

16. Wüst, *Günzburg,* 26–45, 83–87, 93–95; idem, "Ius superioritatis territorialis," 212–16. A list of mortgages is in Krebs, "Die Verfassung," 134–36. Nowosadtko, "Meister," 464–83; Schmid, "Die Biberacher Scharfrichter," 411–15.

17. Auer, *Geschichte,* 34–35; Krebs, "Die Verfassung," 133, 138–48; Wüst, "Historische Einleitung," 16–19, 47–49.

18. StAA, VÖ Akten, 371, 706, 786, 789, VÖ Lit, 631–38, 643, fol. 223r–240v; Behringer, *Witchcraft Persecutions in Bavaria,* 21; Wüst, *Günzburg,* 45–49, 105–59.

19. Gönner and Miller, "Die Landvogtei Schwaben," 683.

20. The quote is from Hofacker, "Die Landvogtei Schwaben," 61. Gönner and Miller, "Die Landvogtei Schwaben," 683–84; Hofacker, *Die schwäbischen Reichslandvogteien;* idem, "Die Landvogtei Schwaben," 64–69; Quarthal, *Landstände,* 38–51; Wieland, "Das leitende Personal," 341–64; Reißenauer, *Münzstätte,* 10–12. The Habsburgs were especially interested in the Landvogtei because the ruler of that territory could legally claim the title of "Prince in Swabia," which was regarded as a crucial part of the heritage of the Hohenstaufen emperors and thus as the basis for a renewal of the ancient dukedom of Swabia: Stolz, *Geschichtliche Beschreibung,* 29–30.

21. Nagel, "Altdorf-Weingarten," 60–65, 75; Gönner and Miller, "Die Landvogtei Schwaben," 689–91, 701; Eitel, "Ravensburg," 266–70; Schneider, "Das Koster Weingarten," 421–37.

22. StAA, VÖ Akten, 203, 371; HStASt, B 60, Bü 212–13; see Gönner and Miller, "Die Landvogtei Schwaben," 690; Hofacker, "Die Landvogtei Schwaben," 59–61; Eitel, "Ravensburg."

23. Fischer, "Das kaiserliche Landgericht," 239–41; "Deß freyen kayserlichen Land-

Gerichts in Obern und Nidern Schwaben Ordnung 1618," in Burgermeister, *Teutsches Corpus,* 2:696–97.

24. StAA, VÖ Lit, 652, fol. 519v–520r, 653, fols. 70v, 202v, 437r–v, 440r, 456v; HStASt, B 60, Bü 152, 212, 156–56b; Fischer, "Das kaiserliche Landgericht," 270–73.

25. Dienst, "Magische Vorstellungen," 73; Rapp, *Die Hexenprozesse,* 13–14; *Carolina,* Art. 21, Art, 44, Art. 109, 40–41, 52, 78. See Lorenz, "Der Hexenprozeß," 133–40.

26. Barth, *Geschichte,* 26; StAA, VÖ Lit, 634, fols. 245r, 260r–v, 326r, 365v.

27. On the Instruction, with a partial copy, see Tschaikner, "Die Zauberer- und Hexenverfolgung in Tirol," 81–112. On Tanner, see Dillinger, "Adam Tanner."

28. HStASt, B 40, Bü 314, vols. 1–4; Müller, "Die Musterregister," 146–50, 161–63; Müller, "Geschichte der Stadt Oberndorf," 481; Müller, "Die Musterregister," 135–36, 141.

29. Stolz, *Geschichtliche Beschreibung,* Beilage no. 2, 164–65.

30. Schuster, *Agrarverfassung,* 34; Bohl, *Die Stadt Stockach,* 44–46; Stolz, *Geschichtliche Beschreibung,* Beilage no. 2, 165; Schuster, "Das Musterregister."

31. Nagel, "Altdorf-Weingarten," 84–85; Stolz, *Geschichtliche Beschreibung,* Beilage no. 2, 165.

32. StAA, Vorderösterreich und Burgau, MüB no. 27, fol. 84r; Auer, *Geschichte,* 65–66; Stolz, *Geschichtliche Beschreibung,* Beilage no. 2, 165.

33. Quarthal, "Die Verfassungsänderungen," 128–29; idem, "Zur Wirtschaftsgeschichte," 395; Kolleffel, *Geographische und topographische Beschreibung,* 7; Auer, *Geschichte,* 60; Hacker, *Auswanderung,* 37, 42; Stolz, *Geschichtliche Beschreibung,* 82–83.

34. Stolz, *Geschichtliche Beschreibung,* no. 2, 167; Schuster, "Fridingen"; Quarthal, "Zur Wirtschaftsgeschichte," 409–16; Müller, "Die Musterregister," 150, 172–73.

35. Schuster, *Agrarverfassung,* 86–92, 121, 217; Stolz, *Geschichtliche Beschreibung,* Beilage no. 1, 148–49, 151–52; Spahr, "Geschichte," 191–99; Kolleffel, *Geographische und topographische Beschreibung,* 18–19; Auer, *Geschichte,* 36.

36. Marx, *Geschichte,* 1:214, 245–46, 295–98, 324–25; Aubin, "Das Reich," 2:32; Haxel, "Verfassung," 53, 61, 66–69, 74, 84.

37. Kerber, *Herrschaftsmittelpunkte,* 207–32, 248–57, 269–72; Haxel, "Verfassung," 67, 75–77; Marx, *Geschichte,* 1:213.

38. For the geography of the Electorate and its major towns, see map 3 on p. 32. Janssen, *Kurtrier,* 606–10; Lott, *Die Todesstrafen,* 37–41; Scotti, *Sammlung,* 1(113):494–500; generally, see ibid., 3:1694; Haxel, "Verfassung," 75. The official title "*Vogt*" was used as a synonym for "*Amtmann*" in the Electorate of Trier: ibid., 42–43.

39. Janssen, *Kurtrier,* 370; Scotti, *Sammlung,* 1(113):495, 497–99.

40. Janssen, *Kurtrier,* 53; Hollmann, "Die Städte," 51, 58–61.

41. Haxel, "Verfassung," 73; Janssen, *Kurtrier,* 598; Kentenich, "Beiträge zur Gechichte des Landkreises," 44–45, 134–35.

42. Cf. the overview in Janssen, *Kurtrier,* 598–99; see esp. ibid., 77, 101, 356–58, 545.

43. Ibid., 52; Lott, *Die Todesstrafen,* 43–44, 70–71; Schmitt, *Bernkastel,* 190.

44. Laufner, "Triers"; Marx, *Geschichte,* 1:225. For more exact geographical descriptions of the provinces, see ibid., 1:198–200; Haxel, "Verfassung," 74–79; Irsigler, "Wirtschaftsgeschichte," 145–46; Kerber, *Herrschaftsmittelpunkte,* 297–300; Schmidt, *Heimatchronik der Stadt und des Landkreises Koblenz,* 72–73, 78; Schnelling, *Die Archive,* 9–12.

45. *Undergerichtsordnung des Ertzstiffts Trier,* fol. XXVVIIr–v. Scotti did not publish the lengthy text. See *Carolina,* Art. 219, 130–31. See Lott, *Die Todesstrafen,* 103–7.

46. Scotti, *Sammlung,* 1(99):367–80, esp. 373–74. Schmidt, *Heimatchronik der Stadt und des Landkreises Koblenz,* 63, 88–90; Bellinghausen, *2000 Jahre Koblenz,* 146–47, are misleading.

47. Laufner, "Triers," 162–63; idem, "Politische Geschichte," 3–5, 7; Scotti, *Sammlung,* 1(123):510–12, 515–18; Lott, *Die Todesstrafen,* 43; Haxel, "Verfassung," 75; Zenz, "Die weltliche Kriminalgerichtsbarkeit," 188.

48. Nikolay-Panter, *Entstehung,* 79, 83, 91–92, 107–9.

49. Ibid., 79–89, 102–7; Janssen, *Kurtrier,* 501, 547, 601–2.

50. For many examples, see Nikolay-Panter, *Entstehung,* 39–55.

51. Ibid., 50–58; Schmidt, *Heimatchronik der Stadt und des Landkreises Koblenz,* 94–95; Lott, *Die Todesstrafen,* 44–45.

52. Nikolay-Panter, *Entstehung,* 76–78, 110–13; *Undergerichtsordnung des Ertzstiffts Trier,* fols. Vv–VIIr; Scotti, *Sammlung,* 1(113):498.

53. Nikolay-Panter, *Entstehung,* 69–78; Hollmann, "Die Städte," 56.

54. Scotti, *Sammlung,* 1(152):554–61; Trusen, "Rechtliche Grundlagen," 208, 216–17. Lott, *Die Todesstrafen,* 120–22, is not always entirely correct.

55. About Württemberg, see Schnabel-Schüle, *Überwachen,* 55, 123; Raith, "Herzogtum Württemberg," 225–36; about Kurpfalz, see Schmidt, Die *Kurpfalz*; idem, *Glaube,*.

56. Scotti, *Sammlung,* 1(152):559; see *Carolina,* Art. 109, 78. Binsfeld, *Tractatus* (1589), fols. 20r–33r, 53v–57r, 122r–124v.

57. Rudolph, *Quellen,* no. 297, 544–45.

58. Scotti, *Sammlung,* 1(194):612–15.

59. Ibid., 1(142):535–41, 537–38.

60. Blattau, *Statuta,* 3(1):2.

61. Fabricius, *Die Karte von 1789,* 2:146–58; Lott, *Die Todesstrafen,* 20–21; Hausmann, "Die Städte," 65; Irsigler, "Wirtschaftsgeschichte," 101.

62. Antoni, *Studien*; Irsigler, "Wirtschaftsgeschichte," 101–2, 145–46.

63. Irsigler, "Wirtschaftsgeschichte," 101, 162–63; Schmitt, *Bernkastel,* 302–3; Hausmann, "Die Städte," 68–69.

64. Antoni, *Studien,* 5–6, 12–13, 22–34; Feld, *Das Städtewesen,* 15–20; Lott, *Die Todesstrafen,* 21–25; Antoni, *Studien,* 22–34; Kentenich, "Beiträge zur Geschichte des Landkreises Trier," 134; Janssen, *Kurtrier,* 180, 185, 196–97, 279, 282–84, 315–17, 365, 367, 369, 380, 384, 508–9, 540, 543–44, 558.

65. Franz, "Die Hexenprozesse in der Stadt Trier," 348; Mechtel, *Die Limburger Chronik,* 158–94; Irsigler, "Wirtschaftsgeschichte," 146, 200; Kyll, "Reben," ; Laufner, "Wein," 53–58; Irsigler, "Wirtschaftsgeschichte," 102, 146, 198–201; Janssen, *Kurtrier,* 508–9.

2. Golden Goblets and Cows' Hooves

1. Labouvie, *Verbotene Künste,* 76–85.

2. The following is according to ibid., 19–22, 76–85 (verbatim quotes are on 20, 81).

3. Schmidt, *Volksglaube,* 275–85; Zender, "Glaube," 148–57; Behringer, "Geschichte der Hexenforschung," 604.

4. Kieckheffer, *European Witch Trials*, 5–8.

5. StAA, VÖ Lit, 631, fols. 90r–v, 140v.

6. Kramer, *Der Hexenhammer*, book 2, chap. 1, secs. 7 and 14, 420, 487. See also André Schnyder's reprint of the 1486 edition: Schnyder, *Malleus Maleficarum*. I will quote Schnyder's commentary only: ibid., 2:379. More details are in Müller, "Heinrich Institoris," 409–12; see also Laer, "Die spätmittelalterlichen Hexenprozesse," 23, 25.

7. StA Günzburg, 5.115; Giefel, "Zur Geschichte der Reformation," 412–13; Midelfort, *Witch Hunting*, 91.

8. The following is drawn from Rummel, "Die Anfänge," 122–24, 129; idem, "Gutenberg," 95–96. Kramer's activities in the Trier region will be discussed later.

9. Kramer, *Der Hexenhammer*, book 3, chap. 2, sec. 8, 651–52; Binsfeld, *Tractatus* (1589), fol. 30v; Behringer, *Hexen und Hexenprozesse*, no. 65, 109–10; Müller, "Heinrich Institoris," 407.

10. Hoffman and Dohms, *Die Mirakelbücher*, no. 151, 95.

11. Rummel, "Gutenberg," 95–113.

12. HStASt, I 13, Bü 3; Krämer, *Kurtrierische Hexenprozesse*, 80–83.

13. Thompson, *Motif-Index of Folk-Literature*, F 342, F 342.1, F 348.5. The essence of a folk legend in contrast to a fairy tale is precisely that it is told and understood as real: see Röhrich, *Sage*, 44–45.

14. Birlinger, *Volksthümliches*, 1:127–28. More details are in Tantsch, "Deutsche Teufels- und Hexennamen"; StA Rottenburg, A 9.1/2, Aussage Michael Pusper; "Grässle," in Fischer, *Schwäbisches Wörterbuch*, 3:801; cf. ibid., "Gras," 794–97. There is no connection with "*grässlich* (ugly, horrible)." Thompson, *Motif-Index of Folk-Literature*, F 233.1, F 482.2.1; see also Mengis, "Art. Grau," 1123; idem, "Art. Grün," 1181.

15. Krämer, *Kurtrierische Hexenprozesse*, 32; Lauer, *Hexenverfolgung*, 48.

16. StB Trier, Hs. 2180a/45a, 27; Franz, "Ein 'dämonologischer Gang,'" 511.

17. StB Trier, Hs. 1533/171, fol. 58r, Hs. 2180a/45a, 27; LHAKO, 1 C 9191, 8.

18. On Flade, see StB Trier, Hs. 1533a/171, fol. 119v. On others, see StA Trier, DK, 54 K 657, 405–7; Binsfeld, *Tractatus* (1589), fol. 28v.

19. TLA, Sammelakten, Reihe B, Abt. 16, Lage 4, no. 6, Urgicht Maria Ulmerin; StA Rottenburg, A 9.1/2.

20. Barth, *Geschichte*, 156–57.

21. HHStAW, 369/447.

22. StB Trier, Hs. 1533a/171, fol. 100v.

23. On negative transformation, see Thompson, *Motif-Index of Folk-Literature*, D 457.2.3., G 303.21.I. On positive transformation, see ibid., F 451.5.1.4, F 342.1; StB Trier, Hs. 1533/171, fol. 22v, Hs. 2180a/45a, 82.

24. HStASt, A 209, Bü 851a; StA Horb, A 313; StA Rottenburg, A 9.1/2; StB Trier, Hs. 1534/166, 9, 13; LHAKO, 1 C 18827, 1 C 2664, 7r–8v, 56/419, fol. 83r; HHStAW, 369/372; see Kramer, *Der Hexenhammer*, book 2, question 1, chap. 1, 364–71; Schnyder, *Malleus Maleficarum*, 2:372.

25. StA Oberndorf, A 132, Urgicht Lorenz Schwarz; StA Rottweil, Criminalia II/I/V/1/12b. See also Birlinger, *Volksthümliches*, 1:156; StA Horb, A 318; StA Rottenburg, A 9.1/2, Urgicht Barbara Wild, Agnesa Widtmayer; on the Electorate of Trier, see LHAKO, 1 C 9191, 17, 29, 89, 211/3036, 9; StB Trier, Hs. 1534/166, 21.

26. On personal threats, see, e.g., StB Trier, Hs. 2180a/45a, 50, 52, 74–75; LHAKO, 1 C 9191, 29, 36–37, 40, 1 C 9193; see also Franz, "Geistes- und Kulturgeschichte," 336. On witches' plans to attack cities and forests, see LHAKO, 1 C 9191, 35; StB Trier, Hs. 1533a/171, fol. 63r.

27. StA Günzburg, 5.115, 5.267; StA Rottenburg, A 9.1/2; HStASt, B 40, Bü 544.

28. Krämer, *Kurtrierische Hexenprozesse*, 21–35; Dillinger, "Die Hexenverfolgung in der Landvogtei Schwaben," 142–43; HHStAW, 369/456, fols. 192v, 209r, 171 Z 3832, fol. 108r; HStASt, B 61, III, Bd. 142. On transformation into sheep, see StA Rottweil, Criminalia II/I/V/1/12b; see Thompson, *Motif-Index of Folk-Literature*, D 135. On transformation into cats, see StB Trier, Hs. 1534/166, 18; Thompson, *Motif-Index of Folk-Literature*, G 211.1.7.

29. On Swabian Austria, see, e.g., StA Horb, A 317; UAT, 84/24, fols. 478r–481v; on the Electorate of Trier, see LHAKO, 1 C 9191, 18, 33/12334, fols. 125r, 128v, 56/419, fols. 39v–40r.

30. On Swabian Austria, see, e.g., StA Rottenburg, A 9.1/2; StA Horb, A 315; on the Electorate of Trier, see StB Trier, Hs. 1534/166, 17; LHAKO, 1 C 9191, 13.

31. On Swabian Austria, see, e.g., Dillinger, "Die letzte Hexe," 152–53; on the Electorate of Trier, see StB Trier, Hs. 1534/166, 17.

32. StA Horb, A 317; StB Trier, Hs. 1534/166, 19–20.

33. HStASt, B 37a, Bü 118; StA Rottenburg, A 9.1/2; StB Trier, Hs. 1534/166, 6, 12.

34. LHAKO, 1 C 9191, 35, 33/8609, fol. 4v; StB Trier, Hs. 1533a/171, fol. 12v; Fisenne, "Lucia Teimens," 5.

35. TLA, Hs. 2402, 256. For further documentation, see pp. 98–102.

36. See, e.g., TLA, Pestarchiv, XXVIII; on this, see Thompson, *Motif-Index of Folk-Literature*, D 1782, D 2143.1.1. A reference to Revelations 16 is unlikely; in weather or witch sermons, allusions to this passage are not found: see Moser-Rath, *Dem Kirchenvolk*.

37. HStASt, B 37a, Bü 118, Urgicht Dorothea Zürnin; StA Rottenburg, A 9.1/2, Aussage Agnesa Volmar.

38. LHAKO, 1 C 14125; StB Trier, Hs. 1533a/171, fol. 26r, 62r–v, 108r, Hs. 1534/166, fol. 96v, Hs. 1533a/171, fols. 101r, 110r, Hs. 2180a/45a, 93, 95. Weather sorcery was already described quite similarly in the Lucerne witch trials around 1450: see Behringer, *Hexen und Hexenprozesse*, no. 52, 83–84.

39. See Duerr, *Dreamtime*, 1–11.

40. HStASt, B 37a, Bü 15, B 371, Bü 147, B 41, Bd. 9, Religionsordnungen.

41. Binsfeld, *Tractatus* (1589), fol. 75r–v; idem, *Tractatus* (1596), 258–64; Barth, *Geschichte*, 158.

42. HHStAW, 369/453, fol. 7v.

43. Regarding desecration of the host in Swabian Austria, see, e.g., StAA, VÖ Lit, 651, fols. 474v–477r, 490r–491r; StA Horb, A 317; Birlinger, *Volksthümliches*, 1:137–39; in the Electorate of Trier, see e.g., LHAKO, 1 C 9191, 41; StB Trier, Hs. 1533/171, fols. 52v, 108v. For details on the consecrated host ring, see Dillinger, *Böse Leute*, 151–56. On the Devil undermining faith, see Birlinger, *Volksthümliches*, 1:146; Midelfort, *Witch Hunting*, 92. On Mary called a whore, see StB Trier, Hs. 1533/171, fol. 23v. The term actually used for "whore" was "*breitt.*" That word was derived from the Latin "*praeda*," for "prey." In the language of mercenaries, the term was an insult and a menace. Not only prostitutes

but all women could be called "prey," as rape was often considered the prerogative of the victorious mercenary. Once more, the demons were linked with the semi-vagrant, semi-criminal bands of mercenaries, see LHAKO, 1 C 9191, 15. For Flade on faith, see StB Trier, Hs. 1533a/171, fol. 96v (verbatim quote on 97v).

44. As attempted by Rowland, "Fantasticall and Devilishe Persons," 167–69, 184–88. On the Sabbath as a condensation of older traditions, see Ginzburg, *Ecstasies*, 15–28; as a religious assembly, see Dülmen, "Imaginationen," 100–127.

45. See generally Bahrdt, *Schüsselbegriffe*, 182–87; Schäfers, "Gesellschaft," 95–101.

46. On witch pipers, see, e.g., HHStAW, 171 Z 3832, fol. 108r, 369/453, fol. 7v, 369/456, fol. 194r; LHAKO, 211/3013, fol. 12r, 211/3027; StA Trier, V 22, 6; StB Trier, Hs. 1533a/171, fol. 61v; LHAKO 33/8853, fol. 34r. See Biesel, "Die Pfeifer," 299–301. On corpses, see StB Trier, Hs. 1533/171, fol. 52r, Hs. 1533a/171, fols. 62r–64r, 111r, Hs. 1534/166, 20. See Roper, *Oedipus*. The world turned upside down is in Delrio, *Disquisitionum*, book 2, chap. 26, 189–92. Maxwell-Stuart's edition of Delrio's book is not quoted because it shortens the original text substantially. On reversal motifs, see, e.g., StA Rottenburg, A 9.1/2; StB Trier, Hs. 1533/171, fol. 5r; cf. Schild, "Die Dimensionen," 45–40.

47. StA Rottweil, Criminalia II/I/V/8/63.

48. On trappings of wealth, see, e.g., StA Rottenburg, A 9.1/2; StA Horb, A 317, A 318; StB Trier, Hs. 1533a/171, fol. 55r, Hs. 2180a/45a, 39; LHAKO, 211/2246, 20. On the rich witches' arriving in style, see StB Trier, Hs. 1533a/171, fol. 52r–53v, 54v, 55r, 58v, Hs. 1533/171, fols. 6v, 9v; HHStAW, 369/456, fol. 193r; TLA, Hs. 2402, 388, 542, Hs. 1390, fol. 253v–254r. On tableware in Swabian Austria, see, e.g., TLA, Hs. 1390, fol. 142v; in the Electorate of Trier, see Krämer, *Kurtrierische Hexenprozesse*, 16; StB Trier, Hs. 1533/171, fol. 36r; LHAKO, 33/8609, fol. 4r–v. Enthroned, see TLA, Hs. 2402, 110–11; StB Trier, Hs. 1533a/171, fol. 77v.

49. The entirely incorrect description in Le Roy Ladurie, *Peasants*, 203–10, is clearly indebted to Michelet's speculation. On this, see the summary in Behringer, "Geschichte der Hexenforschung," 518–19.

50. StB Trier, Hs. 2180a/45a, 53, 1533a/171, fols. 55r, 68r; HStASt, B 37a, Bü 118, Urgicht Dorothea Zürnin. See Dillinger, *Hexenprozesse in Horb*, 18–19.

51. See, e.g., on Swabian Austria, Birlinger, *Volksthümliches*, 1:133; HStASt, B 37a, Bü 118; StA Rottenburg, A 9.1/2; StA Horb, A 318; Lauer, *Hexenverfolgung*, 71; LHAKO, 1 C 9191, 13. Dillinger, "Grafschaft Hohenberg," 30–32, Lauer, *Hexenverfolgung*, 71; StB Trier, Hs. 1533a/171, fols. 76v, 77r–86v, Hs. 2180a/45a, 22; LHAKO, 211/3013, fol. 13r. A suspect even claimed that only the rich witches from the city of Trier were capable of committing weather sorcery: LHAKO, 211/2282, 29.

52. Irsigler, "Wirtschaftsgeschichte," 102–4, 201.

53. LHAKO, 211/2246, 12, 211/2280, 12.

54. Bender-Wittmann, "Hexenglaube," 123–24.

55. LHAKO, 211/2263, 27; StB Trier, Hs. 1533a/171, fol. 13r.

56. Dillinger, *Böse Leute*, 129–31.

57. See, e.g., StA Rottenburg, A 9.1/2, Prozeß Michael Pusper; StA Horb, A 318; StB Trier, Hs. 1533a/171, fol. 74r–v, 61v, 85v–86v.

58. HStASt, I 13, Bü 3; StA Horb, A 318; StB Trier, Hs. 1533a/171, fols. 61v, 74r–v, 85v–86v, 101r, 110r, Hs. 2180a/45a, 93.

59. Labouvie, "Männer"; Schwerhoff, "Hexerei."

60. On Swabian Austria, see TLA, Hs. 2402, 444, 665, 835; UAT, 84/24, fol. 479v; StA Rottenburg, A 9.1/2; Birlinger, *Volksthümliches*, 1:156–57; on the Electorate of Trier, see StA Trier, DK, 54 K 657, 388; LHAKO, 56/419, fol. 14r, 211/2985, 22. As a rule, treasure hunters used magic. They were almost exclusively male: cf. Dillinger and Feld, "Treasure-Hunting."

61. See, e.g., for Swabian Austria, TLA, Pestarchiv, XXVIII 142, Hs. 2402, 543; Birlinger, *Volksthümliches*, 1:140, 142; for the Electorate of Trier, StB Trier, Hs. 1533a/171, fol. 51v–52r. See Müller-Bergström, "Art. Zwerge," 1064–66; Steller, "Art. Pferd," 1638.

62. On the *Alp*, see, e.g., for Swabian Austria, Völk, "Ein Günzburger Hexenprozeß," no. 9; for the Electorate of Trier, StB Trier, Hs. 1534/166, 22. Ranke, "Art. Alp," 287–95; idem, "Art. Trude," 1173–74; Olbrich, "Art. Trudenstein," 1174–76; Delumeau, *Angst*, 1:131–32.

63. The Walter case is in Völk, "Ein Günzburger Hexenprozeß," no. 9. For other *Truden* cases, see StA Trier, DK, 54 K 657, 125–26, 247, 352–53; LHAKO, 1 C 14126. Binsfeld briefly mentioned "night pressers," which he identified with "Silvani and Fauni." By this he meant sexual demons, not witches: Binsfeld, *Tractatus* (1589), fol. 51v.

64. StA Horb, A 320; Völk, "Ein Günzburger Hexenprozeß," no. 9; StB Trier, Hs. 1534/166, 22. On the dangers of seeing spirits, see, e.g., LHAKO, 1 C 7944, fols. 22r–23r, 1 C 18827; HHStAW, 369/455, fols. 83r, 209r; TLA, Hs. 2402, 950–51; HStASt, B 17, Bd. 35, fol. 119r–v.

65. TLA, Hs. 2402, 59, 277, 386, 396–97, 497, 793–94, 860–61, 950–51; see Thompson, *Motif-Index of Folk-Literature*, F 236.1.3, F 361.3.2, F 331.1.; see also Mengis, "Art. Geistertanz," 556–57. In nineteenth-century collections of legends, the Spitzberg hill is described as the dwelling place of white women—that is, fairies and ghosts—who mislead travelers: Meier, *Deutsche Sagen*, 90–91; Birlinger, *Volksthümliches*, 1:61.

66. StB Trier, Hs. 2180a/45a, 26–27, 81–82, 90–91; see Mengis, "Art. Geist," 488–91; Thompson, *Motif-Index of Folk-Literature*, N 815.

67. TLA, Hs. 2402, 542, Hs. 1390, fols. 253v–254r.

68. Crusius, *Chronick*, 2:419.

69. LHAKO, 211/1647, 24, 211/2977, 17, 211/2983, 10, 29 B 196, 107–8; see also Kettel, "Hexenprozesse in der Grafschaft Gerolstein," 362–67. Contemporaries considered it a great misfortune and a divine punishment to have to "walk" as a ghost, trapped between the visible world and the hereafter.

70. On this, see Behringer, "Geschichte der Hexenforschung," 521–24, 604–8.

71. See, e.g., HHStAW, 339/148, fols. 46r–48v. More details are in Horsley, "Who Were the Witches?" 689–715. On determining cause of illnesses, see LHAKO, 33/12334, fol. 127v; STA Trier, DK, 54 K 657, 388, 459; TLA, Sammelakten, Reihe A, Abt. 16, Lage 2, no. 4; StA Rottenburg, A 9.1/2.

72. See HStASt, B 40, Bü 543; Völk, "Ein Günzburger Hexenprozeß," no. 9. For comparison beyond Europe, see the research overview in Beattie, *Other Cultures*, 207–9. Binsfeld, *Tractatus* (1589), fols. 122r–124v; see *Carolina*, Art. 21, 40–41.

73. Selig, "Ein Hexenprozeß," 39–42.

74. HStASt, B 40, Bü 544; UAT 84/24, fols. 478r–487v; StA Rottenburg, A 9.1/2; Birlinger, *Volksthümliches*, 1:137; LHAKO, 211/2979, 211/3034, 1 C 14125.

75. LHAKO, 211/2985, 22.

76. See Labouvie, *Verbotene Künste*, 164–68, for discussion of the state of research.

77. On the Wittlich Jew, see LHAKO, 1 C 18827. On executioners, see STA Trier, DK, 54 K 657, 246; Dillinger, *Hexenprozesse in Horb*, 39–40. Most illuminating is Schmid, "Die Biberacher Scharfrichter," 413–14; Behringer, *Hexen und Hexenprozesse*, no. 65, 109–10; Binsfeld, *Tractatus* (1589), fol. 32r; StAA, Hochstift Augsburg, Neuburger Abgabe Akten 1221, fol. 335r. See Nowosadtko, "Meister,"; Behringer, *Shaman of Oberstdorf*, 113–17, 130; Behringer, *Witchcraft Persecutions in Bavaria*, 124–28, 162–63.

78. TLA, Hs. 2402, 835, 851; StA Trier, DK, 54 K 657, 51, 53, 90, 115, 119, 173, 212, 328, 332–33; LHAKO, 1 C 9191, 32–34; Kettel, *Von Hexen und Unholden*, 30.

79. Binsfeld, *Tractatus* (1589), fols. 19v–23r, 27r–28r; cf. BAT, Abt. 20, no. 21, 875.

80. The following is drawn from Quarthal, "Die 'Fridingische Unruhe,'" 42; Dillinger, "Ein Fridinger Hexenprozeß," 134. On Valentin Marquart's good reputation among the populace, see HStASt, B 17, Bd. 40, fols. 74r–v, 620v.

81. On Michelet and his followers, see Behringer, "Geschichte der Hexenforschung," 518–19; Ehrenreich and English, *Witches*.

82. TLA, Pestarchiv, XXVIII 142; StA Trier, DK, 54 K 657, 164–65, 239–41.

83. Dillinger, *Hexenprozesse in Horb*, 22–23; UAT 84/24, fols. 478r–487v; StA Trier, DK, 54 K 657, 405–25.

84. On this, see Beattie, *Other Cultures*, 208–10; cf. Walz, *Hexenglaube*, 37–39.

85. LHAKO, 1 C 11249, fol. 3; HStASt, B 17, Bü 670. On God's name, see Thompson, *Motif-Index of Folk-Literature*, G 303.16.8, G 303.16.2.3. On church bells, see, e.g., Hoffmann and Dohms, *Die Mirakelbücher*, no. 151, 95; LHAKO, 211/3036, 8; StB Trier, Hs. 1533/171, fols. 51v, 52v, Hs. 1536/166, fol. 96r–v; HStASt, B 17, Bü 670; see Kramer, *Der Hexenhammer*, book 2, chap. 2, sec. 7, 590; Thompson, *Motif-Index of Folk-Literature*, G 303.16.12, D 789.10; Labouvie, "Hexenspuk," 85–86. Perkmann, "Art. Läuten," 938–49; Labouvie, *Verbotene Künste*, 144–45. Modest Mussorgsky used the motif of the bells driving away the witches in his composition "A Night on the Bare Mountain." Binsfeld, *Tractatus* (1589), fol. 136v–139v.

86. See, e.g., on Swabian Austria, TLA, Sammelakten, Reihe B, Abt. 16, Lage 2, no. 4, Pestarchiv, XXVIII 142; StA Horb, A 320; UAT, 84/62, 613; on the Electorate of Trier, LHAKO, 1 C 9191, 92; StB Trier, Hs. 1534/166, 18; StA Trier, DK, 54 K 657, 352; see Labouvie, *Verbotene Künste*, 143–44.

87. *Annuae 1586/1587*, 255–56.

88. TLA, Sammelakten, Reihe B, Abt. 16, Lage 4, no. 6; StA Rottenburg, A 9.1/2; StA Oberndorf, A 132; LHAKO, 1 C 911, 1 C 18827; StB Trier, Hs. 1533/171, fol. 21v; StA Trier, DK, 54 K 657, 126. On preventative blessing, see Kramer, *Der Hexenhammer*, book 2, chap. 2, sec. 6, 565–70. On unorthodox blessing, see Labouvie, *Verbotene Künste*, 79.

89. Feßler, *Wunderwürckender*, 1, 12, 165; Spahr, *Kreuz*, 32–34, 118–20; Rudolf, "Die Geschichte des Blutritts," 703, 707–8; idem, "Heilig Blut," 554–59; Nagel, "Das Heilige Blut," 202, 210; Rudolf, "Heilig Blut," 204–12, 554, 560.

90. Feßler, *Wunderwürckender*, 2, 7, 84–114; Hölz, "Abt Johann Christoph Raittner," 142; Rudolf, "Heilig Blut," 554–60; Nagel, "Das Heilige Blut," 206, 212. More details are in Stegemann, "Art. Hagel, Hagelzauber," 1313–18.

91. On this, see Wrede, "Art. Benedikt," 1031–35, 1034–35; Jakoby, "Art. Benedik-

tussegen," 1035–36; Franz and Hennen, "Hauskreuze," 120–23; Hoffmann-Krayer, "Art. Zachariassegen."

92. Feßler, *Wunderwürckender,* 2, 7, 107–9.

93. Hölz, "Abt Johann Christoph Raittner," 142.

94. Here, see generally Jakoby, "Art. Benediktussegen," 1035–36; regarding Weingarten specifically, see Spahr, *Kreuz,* 105, 113.

95. Feßler, *Wunderwürckender,* 2, 8, 114–19; Rudolf, "Heilig Blut," 554.

96. On the bat as a symbol for the fear of light in general and specific senses, see Biedermann, *Knaurs Lexikon,* 145. Such an interpretation is close to the depiction itself. To interpret the bat here as an animal with intrinsically magical properties seems too far-fetched. In the regional traditions, there is no corresponding motif. Similarly, bat's blood is not mentioned as an ingredient for the witches' salve.

97. Nagel, "Das Heilige Blut," 208–9.

98. Stolz, *Die Urbansbruderschaft,* 19–22; cf. the overview in Geary, "Humiliation," 123–40, examples 135–37; see also Binsfeld, *Tractatus* (1589), fol. 30v; Goldast, *Rechtliches Bedencken,* 65.

99. Stolz, *Die Urbansbruderschaft,* 20.

100. Dillinger, *Hexenprozesse in Horb,* 32; Stolz, *Die Urbansbruderschaft,* 21–22; on Tübingen, see Crusius, *Chronick,* 2:355.

101. For the following, see Kyll, "Hagel," 159–68; Wolpert, "Fünfhundert Jahre Kreuzweg," 18–29.

102. Kramer's letter used the female form of *"maleficae"* decisively three times: ibid., 26–27.

103. For the following, see Kramer, *Der Hexenhammer,* book 2, chap. 2, secs. 1–8, 510–96, chap. 3, 601–796.

104. For the following, see Rummel, "Gutenberg," 95–113.

105. Hoffmann and Dohms, *Die Mirakelbücher,* no. 120, 76–77, no. 214, 133.

106. Ibid., no. 112, 71–72, no. 120, 77, no. 123, 79–80, no. 219, 137, no. 247, 150, no. 526, 259.

107. Ibid., no. 88, 57, no. 171, 105–6. The reference to Paul's miraculous deliverance is clear: see Acts 12, 1–12. On this, see Rummel, "Die Anfänge," 122, 128.

108. On this argument, see Behringer, "Zur Haltung Adam Tanners," 172, 174–77; Dillinger, "Adam Tanner," 43–45.

109. Blattau, *Statuta,* 2(88):380–81; Mechtel, *Die Limburger Chronik,* 160–61; Kyll, "Die Hagelfeier," 114–23.

110. Franz and Hennen, "Hauskreuze," 108; Kyll, "Die Hagelfeier," 123–40.

111. Binsfeld, *Tractatus* (1589), fols. 25v–35r.

112. See Zimmermann, "Hochstift Konstanz," 317–24.

113. Here see Eerden, "Der Teufelspakt," 52–54, 70–71.

114. See, e.g., *Annuae 1583,* 129–30; *Annuae 1588,* 163; *Annuae 1590/1591,* 340, 343–44, 394; *Annuae 1594/1595;* 521–22. *Annuae 1652,* 238 and *Annuae 1653,* 277, 289, are almost identical. Father Lukas Ellentz excelled as a confessor of witches: see Franz, "Ein 'dämonologischer Gang,'" 501–2. Ellentz supposedly brought witches to recant their denunciations at Flade's request: StB Trier, Hs. 1533a/171, fols. 11v–12r.

115. Duhr, *Die Stellung,* 32–33, 35. Behringer based his judgment on insufficient source material: Behringer, "Das 'reichskhündig Exempel,'" 445

116. Voltmer, "Zwischen Herrschaftskrise." Vestiges of the old fear of all-powerful Jesuits, rekindled by Nazi propaganda, still prevail in German culture.

117. Thomas, *Religion,* 593–98.

118. Beattie, *Other Cultures,* 202–41, esp. 202–5, 215–17. In contradiction to the main argument of his discussion of magic, Beattie admitted the possibility of selection based on efficacy in his discussion of religion: Beattie, *Other Cultures,* 233. See Labouvie, *Verbotene Künste,* 43.

119. Schnabel-Schüle, *Überwachen,* 202–10, 328–32.

120. Ibid., 122; see Binsfeld, *Tractatus* (1589), fols. 102r–103r. The witch hunters here found themselves in an ever-growing system of guilt and punishment. That God had ever permitted the Devil to cause harm by means of the witches was already an expression of his wrath: ibid., fol. 4r–v. Demonologists gave the merciful God of Christianity demonic aspects.

121. Midelfort, *Witch Hunting,* 34–45; Raith, "Herzogtum Württemberg," 229–31.

122. Rummel, *Bauern,* 157–58; TLA, Hs. 1390, fol. 87r–v, 109r; see also pp. 98–102.

123. According to the definition on pp. 41–42, this is true: The witch-trial phenomenon was generally scarcely controlled by the church or the state. It attempted to affect the imagined, extra-societal sphere to serve an internal purpose.

3. "If She Is Not a Witch Yet, She Will Certainly Become One"

The quote that serves as the title of this chapter is from TLA, Hs. 2402, 152.

1. HStASt, B 37a, Bü 118.

2. A divergent pattern is found in Walz, *Hexenglaube,* 269–305 (verbatim quote on 269).

3. *Carolina,* Art. 44, 52.

4. StB Trier, Hs. 1534/166, 15–16; StA Trier, DK, 54 K 657, 59, 90, 165, 328, 452, 454; StA Günzburg, 5.276; HStASt, B 41, Bd. 3, fols. 330v–332r; StA Stockach, C.VIII, 1, 1618, fol. 15r; Völk, "Ein Günzburger Hexenprozeß," no. 9; HStASt, A 209, Bü 679, B 41, Bd. 3, fols. 330v–332r. Ahrendt-Schulte, *Zauberinnen,* 60–63. A similiar finding is in Walz, *Hexenglaube,* 280.

5. HHStAW, 369/455, fols. 81r–85r.

6. Dillinger, "Hexen und Hexenverfolger in Obernau," 35, 40; HStASt, A 209, Bü 679; LHAKO, 33/12334, fol. 123r; StA Trier, DK, 54 K 657, 90, 180, 328, 337; StB Trier, Hs. 1534/166, 11–12, 16.

7. StA Horb, A 320; StA Trier, DK, 54 K 657, 81; LHAKO, 211/3012.

8. Binsfeld, Tractatus (1589), fols. 19v–23r (verbatim quote on fol. 18v); Blattau, *Statuta,* 2(44):320–24, 2(73):317–20. See *Annuae 1590/91,* 339.

9. StA Stockach, C.VIII, 1, 1620, fol. 20r.

10. See Köhler, "Zeiten," 96–104. The claim that the witch hunts were instrumentalized in the Trier region to eliminate secret heretics can be traced to Heppe's polemical "editing," as part of the Kulturkampf, in the second edition of Soldan: see Soldan and Heppe, *Geschichte,* 2:33–37. Burr had already drawn attention to the fact that this theory is not supported by the sources: Burr, "The Fate," 52–53. The centrist Johannes

Janssen aired his criticism in a half-page footnote: Janssen, *Culturzustände*, 8:640. In Bauer's 1911 edition of Soldan, the passage is not found. On the editing of Soldan's text, see Behringer, "Geschichte der Hexenforschung," 522–23, 528–29.

11. Giefel, "Zur Geschichte der Reformation," 413; Midelfort, *Witch Hunting*, 91–92; LHAKO, 1 C 13871; StB Trier, Hs. 1533a/171, fols. 96v, 97v; HHStAW, 339/138; HStASt, B 61, III, Bd. 128, 111; StAA, VÖ Lit, 651, fols. 474v–477r, 490r–491r; cf. HStASt, B 37a, Bü 121.

12. On Inich, see LHAKO, 56/419, fols. 21v–22r, 76v–77v. Inich's story combined various narrative materials. First the motif of Venus Mountain is combined with that of the sleeping army in a cave. One might see in the mention of the emperor and Naples the influence of the Hohenstaufen legend about the magical emperor who awaits his time to return and rescue Germany from great danger. This legend originally referred to Frederick II, who founded the University of Naples. A confusion of the similarly named Vesuvius for the Venus Mountain may also have played a role: see Jakoby, "Art. Hochschulen," 144. On threatening speculations, see HStASt, B 37a, Bü 118; LHAKO, 1 C 18827; HHStAW, 369/455, fols. 82r, 140r. Without an explicit threat, the *Carolina* (Art. 44, 52) could not be cited.

13. Dillinger, *Hexen und Hexenprozesse in Fridingen*, 41–42; LHAKO, 1 C 18827.

14. HHStAW, 369/456, fol. 205r; LHAKO, 1 C 18827; cf. Walz, *Hexenglaube*, 60–61.

15. Habermas, *Theorie*, 1:136–38, 440–51; cf. Taylor, *Mutual Misunderstanding*, 136–38, 188–84; Jütte, "Sprachliches Handeln," 159–63.

16. StA Oberndorf, A 128; StA Rottenburg, A 9.1/2; LHAKO, 1 C 14125; HHStAW, 171 Z 3832, fol. 108v; StB Trier, Hs. 1533a/171, fols. 16v–17r. On Mensfelden, see HHStAW, 339/148.

17. E.g., StA Rottenburg, A 22, no. 1, 802–3; StA Horb, B 83, 445–47, 468–69; LHAKO, 1 C 141251, 1 C 14126.

18. StA Trier, DK, 54 K 657, 391; HStASt, B 37a, Bü 118.

19. Dillinger, "Richter," 139; Walz, *Hexenglaube*, 336–40, 518–20.

20. Walz, *Hexenglaube*, 16–65, 218.

21. LHAKO, 1 C 14125. On pugnacious defendants, see TLA, Hs. 2402, 152; HStASt, B 37a, Bü 118; UAT, 84/24, fols. 495v–501r; StA Oberndorf, A 128. On inquisitions, see HStAW, 369/455, fol. 265v; cf. Walz, *Hexenglaube*, 282–84.

22. StA Stockach, C.VIII, 1, 1617, fol. 122r, 1618, fols. 24v–25r; StA Günzburg, 5.276; StB Trier, Hs. 1534/166, 19.

23. Cf. BAT, Abt. 5.2, no. 43, 10, about the Dillinger family; LHAKO, 56/419, fol. 81v, 1 C 2668, fol. 42v, 1 C 14125; HStASt, A 209, Bü 679; StA Stockach, C.VIII, 1, 1618, fol. 26; StA Horb, A 285, A 312; StA Oberndorf, A 128; Kempf, *Die Chronik*, 380–81; Voltmer and Weisenstein, *Das Hexenregister*, Stammtafeln, I–XV.3.

24. LHAKO, 56/419, fol. 90r, 1 C 7944, fol. 21r.

25. In a single case from the Electorate, a man threatened to beat his wife if she continued to visit a witchcraft suspect: LHAKO, 33/12334, fol. 131r; cf. UAT, 84/24, fols. 480v–481r; StA Horb, A 311; StB Trier, Hs. 1533a/171, fols. 16v–17r.

26. E.g., HHStAW, 369/453, fol. 8r; LHAKO, 56/419, fol. 14v, 1 C 911, 861, 1 C 14125, 1 C 2664, fol. 9r, 1 C 18827; StB Trier, Hs. 1534/166, 2; HStASt, B 17, Bd. 21, fol. 233v;

StA Stockach, C.VIII, 1, 1618, fol. 26; StA Horb, A 315; StA Oberndorf, A 132; Birlinger, *Volkstümliches*, 1:156–57; see Raith, "Herzogtum Württemberg," 228; Schleichert, "Vorderösterreich," 262; Fritz, "Reichsstadt," 419, 421; Dillinger, "Terrorists," 176.

27. See, e.g., Junk, "Aus der Hexenzeit," 137; Fisenne, "Lucia Teimens," 5; HHStAW, 369/447; StB Trier, Hs. 1534/166, 11–12; LHAKO, 1 C 7944, fol. 1v, 1 C 9191, 6; TLA, Sammelakten, Reihe A, Abt. 16, Lage 2, no. 4; HStASt, B 37a, Bü 118, B 19, Bd. 5, fol. 447v; StA Oberndorf, A 128, A 132.

28. HStASt, B 40, Bü 543; StA Horb, A 309, A 316; StA Rottenburg, A 9.1/2. In his overview, Klaits saw beggar women as "classic" suspects: Klaits, *Servants*, 86–103.

29. Thomas, *Religion*, 659–67; Macfarlane, *Witchcraft*, 172–76, 195–99; idem, *The Origins of Individualism*, 1–2, 59. See Schindler, "Die Entstehung," 306–11; Burke, "The Comparative Approach," 438.

30. LHAKO, 1 C 9191, 74; StA Trier, DK, 54 K 657, 119–22, 127, 132; StB Trier, Hs. 1534/166, 10–11, 16–17; HStASt, B 40, Bü 544; UAT, 84/24, fols. 478r–487v; StA Horb, A 309; StA Rottenburg, A 9.1/2.

31. TLA, Pestarchiv, XXXVIII 498; HStASt, I 13, Bü 4; StAS, Ho 177, Bd. 2, no. 128; StA Horb, A 299; StA Oberndorf, A 128; StA Rottenburg, A 22, no. 1, 802; StA Trier, DK, 54 K 657, 379, 452; LHAKO, 56/419, fol. 29v; Birlinger, *Volksthümliches*, 1:156–57; Dillinger, "Die letzte Hexe," 152–53; Krämer, *Kurtrierische Hexenprozesse*, 10, 13–15, 21–35.

32. Cf. Labouvie, *Zauberei*, 204–5; Walz, *Hexenglaube*, 64, 295–98.

33. LHAKO, 211/3013, fols. 12v–13r; HHStAW, 369/456, fol. 202v; StB Trier, Hs. 1533a/171, fol. 58v. See Dülmen, *Hexenwelten*, 352–53.

34. Sannwald, *Spitäler*, 301; Gerteis, "Sozialgeschichte," 83; Mündnich, *Das Hospital*, 12–59. On hospital witch dances, see TLA, Allgemeines Leopoldinum, Karton B, no. 133, Hs. 1390, fol. 118r–v, Hs. 2402, 490, 934–38; StA Horb, A 318; HStASt, B 19, Bd. 5, fols. 542v–544r; Sannwald, *Spitäler*, 23–34, 242–55. On hospitals and urban witchcraft, see Dillinger, "Hexenverfolgungen in Städten," 144–45.

35. HHStAW, 369/456, fol. 205r; StB Trier, Hs. 1533a/171, fol. 61v, Hs. 1534/166, 8, Hs. 2180a/45a, 79; LHAKO, 56/419, fol. 30v, 1 C 9191, 19. See Walz, *Hexenglaube*, 296.

36. E.g., TLA, Hs. 2402, 10–11, 16, 152, 162; HStASt, B 37a, Bü 10, 202; StA Horb, A 285.

37. HStASt, B 37a, Bü 11.

38. Krezdorn, "Wendler," 50–57.

39. HStASt, B 37a, Bü 202; TLA, Allgemeines Leopoldinum, Karton B, no. 133. Another case is in LHAKO, 56/149, fol. 30v.

40. See Walz, *Hexenglaube*, 296–98; Bender-Wittmann, "Gender," 124; Rummel, *Bauern*, 306–8; Voges, "Reichsstadt," 365–66.

41. StA Günzburg, 5.115; Dillinger, *Hexenprozesse in Horb*, 13–14.

42. Midelfort, *Witch Hunting*, 190–94.

43. StB Trier, Hs. 1533a/171, fol. 61v; Voltmer and Weisenstein, *Das Hexenregister*, 19–21.

44. Dillinger, *Hexenprozesse in Horb*, 26; StA Günzburg, 5.115; see Wüst, "Historische Einleitung," 17.

45. Kempf, *Die Chronik*, 380–81; Schön, "Geschlechter," 45, 47, 50–51, 55; Dillinger, *Hexen und Hexenprozesse in Fridingen*, 50.

46. StB Trier, 1409/2097, fols. 347v, 348v–349v, 352v–356v; Kerber, *Herrschaftsmittelpunkte*, 231–32; Zenz, "Dr. Dietrich Flade," 42–45; Laufner, "Dr. Dietrich Flade," 43–44, 48–49; Laufer, *Die Sozialstruktur*, 285, 319–20; Dillinger, "Richter," 129–30; Weisenstein, "Zaubereiprozesse," 476–78; Kempf, *Die Chronik*, 209–15.

47. Dillinger, "Hexenverfolgungen in Städten," 154–60.

48. StB Trier, Hs. 1533/171, fol. 17r.

49. See Dillinger, *Böse Leute*, 217.

50. StB Trier, Hs. 1534/166, fols. 29r–40r; Gemmel, *Chronik*, 71–72; Mohr, "Hexen," 1–9, 32–35, 41–44, 61–67.

51. The following is drawn from Selig, "Ein Hexenprozeß," 39–42; Zürn, "Abseits," 56–72.

52. StA Trier, Ms. 1393/103c, fols. 14v–16r; StB Trier, Hs. 1533a/171, fol. 53r; "Brief Johanns VII. an die theologische Fakultät, 14.1.1589," in Neller, *Conatus*, 34; Brower and Masen, *Antiquitatum*, 2:425; Zenz, "Dr. Dietrich Flade," 66–67.

53. TLA, Allgemeines Leopoldinum, Karton B, no. 133, Hs. 1390, Hs. 2402, 119, 157. In the same collection, there are numerous other statements made before Austrian investigatory commissions of a tenor similiar to those of the Rottenburg residents, cf. Krezdorn, "Wendler," 54–57; StAA, VÖ Lit, 655, fols. 394r–v, 442v–443v (verbatim quote on fol. 443r); LHAKO, 1 C 2664, fols. 74v–75v.

54. LHAKO, 56/726, 1 C 2664, 1 C 2671, fol. 56v, 1 C 2673, 44v, 49r–v, 56/726; cf. Rummel, "Soziale Dynamik," 34–40; Voltmer and Weisenstein, *Das Hexenregister*, 63*–71*.

55. StA Oberndorf, A 128; cf. Walz, *Hexenglaube*, 46–47.

56. TLA, Hs. 2402, 152, author's emphasis; letter of Johann VII, cited in Neller, *Conatus*, 34–35; HHStAW, 369/456, fol. 211r.

57. Binsfeld, *Tractatus* (1589) fols. 18v–45r (verbatim quotes on fols. 18v, 35v).

58. Demonology should not be understood here as the basis from which the recognizable witch image derived in practice. Rather, the theory and practice of the witch hunts, "elite culture," and "popular culture" need to be interpreted reciprocally as two sides of the same coin, with Flade simply as an example to illuminate the abstract observation of the Devil's power over wealth: Delrio, *Disquisitionum*, book 2, chap. 11, 164.

59. StB Trier, Hs. 1900/1479, fol. 33r; see Eerden, "Der Teufelspakt", 60.

60. See HStASt, B 37a, Bü 118; LHAKO, 211/2280, 13.

61. TLA, Hs. 1390, fol. 43v; StB Trier, Hs. 1533a/171, fol. 62v. On profit and disaster, see Krezdorn, "Wendler," 51–53; Kempf, *Die Chronik*, 380–81; StB Trier, Hs. 2180a/45a, 51, 65; Gerteis, "Sozialgeschichte," 86–88; cf. Binsfeld, *Tractatus* (1596), 143–46.

62. See, e.g., pictorial descriptions from popular and scholarly witch literature of the sixteenth and seventeenth centuries in Dülmen, *Hexenwelten*, app., 352, 364.

63. Kramer, *Der Hexenhammer*, book 1, chap. 18, 342–43; Bodin, *De la démonomanie*, book 3, chap. 3, 163–67; Binsfeld, *Tractatus* (1589), fols. 84v–85v, 104r–105r.

64. Delrio, *Disquisitionum*, book 2, chap. 11, 164–66.

65. TLA, Allgemeines Leopoldinum, Karton B, no. 133, Hs. 2402, 10–11, 16, 152, 162; HStASt, B 37a, Bü 10; StA Horb, A 285; LHAKO, 1 C 9191, 19, 38, 56/419, fol. 14r; cf. Janssen, *Culturzustände*, 8:638; Voltmer and Weisenstein, *Das Hexenregister*, 78, 81, 240.

66. Walz, *Hexenglaube*, 291.

67. Hence, the witchcraft accusation was more than a "multifunctional tool": Schwerhoff, "Hexerei," 345.

68. See Foster, "Peasant Society," 316–19; Dillinger, "Das Ewige Leben," 272–77; Dillinger and Feld, "Treasure-Hunting," 178–83.

69. See, e.g., Becker, "Hexenverfolgung," 119–20; Walz, *Hexenglaube,* 290.

70. See the overview in Beattie, *Other Cultures,* 209–13.

71. See, e.g., UAT, 84/24, fol. 484v; StAA, Hochstift Augsburg, Neuburger Abgabe Akten 1221, fol. 335r; HHStAW, 369/444.

72. Walz, *Hexenglaube,* 304; Schwerhoff, "Hexerei," 344; Briggs, *Witches,* 22–24. Gaskill makes this apparently negative finding into a major criticism of interpretations of witch trials that proceed from the succinct observation that they were shaped by law, belief, and conflict: Gaskill, "The Devil in the Shape of a Man," 170–71.

73. Schnabel-Schüle, *Überwachen,* 122.

4. "There Goes the Werewolf. We Thought He Had Been Caught Already"

1. TLA, Hs. 2402, 446, 490, 502. On lower classes as the driving force, see TLA, Allgemeines Leopoldinum, Karton B, no. 133; HStASt, B 40, Bü 544; UAT, 84/24, fols. 478r–487v; StA Horb, A 320. On lynching threats, see TLA, Hs. 2402, 502. On driving away suspects, see HStASt, B 40, Bü 543. On pressuring officials, see TLA, Hs. 2402, 396.

2. TLA, Allgemeines Leopoldinum, Karton B, no. 133; HStASt, B 40, Bü 544, A 209, Bü 851; UAT, 84/24, fols. 478r–487v; StA Horb, A 320. On Barbara Lutz, see TLA, Hs. 2402, 350. On the witch-hunting winegrower, see TLA, Hs. 2402, 105–6, Hs. 1390, fol. 135r; HStASt, B 37a, Bü 10, fol. 14r.

3. See, e.g, TLA, Hs. 5923, fol. 483v; StAA, VÖ Lit, 651, fols. 474v–477r; HStASt, B 61, III, Bd. 142; GLAK, 67/738, fols. 201v–202r; Dillinger, *Böse Leute,* 235, 250. On explosive persecutions, see details in Dillinger, "Grafschaft Hohenberg," 42, 60–62, 69–71, 82–83, 123–24, 141. Monter, *Witchcraft in France and Switzerland,* 100–102.

4. Crusius, *Chronick,* 2:222–24, 229; Midelfort, *Witch Hunting,* 201.

5. TLA, Hs. 1390, fol. 131r, author's emphasis.

6. Ibid., Hs. 2402, 403. On viticultural decline and inflation, see ibid., Hs. 1390, fols. 43r, 46r, 109r, 120v; HStASt, B 37a, Bü 118, 202; Crusius, *Chronick,* 2:357–58, 361, 370–71, 378; Birlinger, *Volksthümliches,* 1:139–40; Sannwald, *Spitäler,* 90; Quarthal, "Zur Wirtschaftsgeschichte," 409–16. That damaging weather constituted witchcraft was very clearly the view of contemporaries: TLA, Hs. 1390, fols. 43r, 46r, 109r, 120v.

7. See the overview in Midelfort, *Witch Hunting,* 201–30. On the Lake Constance climate, see Spahr, "Geschichte," 191–92, 194–201, 223–26.

8. "Annales Novesienses," 717; Wyttenbach and Müller, *Gesta Trevirorum,* 3:53.

9. Rummel, "Phasen," 329–30.

10. See ibid., 329; Irsigler, "Wirtschaftsgeschichte," 199–201. On Johann Linden, see Irsigler, "Wirtschaftsgeschichte," 198–201; Franz, "Geistes- und Kulturgeschichte," 333. On competition, see Rummel, "Hexenprozesse im Raum," 90.

11. Rummel, *Phasen,* 294, 319–20 (verbatim quote on 294).

12. Mährle, "Fürstpropstei," 327–31; Behringer, "Hochstift Augsburg," 357, 361–62; Midelfort, *Witch Hunting*, 96–98.

13. Wyttenbach and Müller, *Gesta Trevirorum*, 3:53, author's emphasis.

14. StB Trier, Hs. 1533/171, fol. 2r, Hs. 2180a/45a, 4. On the regional pattern of witch hunting, see Schormann, *Hexenprozesse in Deutschland*, 58; Rummel, *Bauern*, 316–21; Irsigler, "Hexenverfolgungen," 18–21; Dillinger, *Böse Leute*, 242.

15. StB Trier, Hs. 1533/171, fol. 2v, Hs. 2180a/45a, 3.

16. Ibid., Hs. 1533/171, fol. 17r.

17. TLA, Hs. 2402, 533, 569, author's emphasis.

18. Duhr, *Die Stellung*, 32–34. On the Rottenburg cleric in 1594, see HStASt, B 41, Bd. 3, fol. 333r–v. On denouncing Fiedler, see StB Trier, Hs. 1533/171, fol. 17r.

19. On accusations "in the face," see Walz, *Hexenglaube*, 320–30; examples from Swabian Austria are in TLA, Pestarchiv, XXVIII 142; HStASt, B 61, III, Bd. 142; LHAKO, 56/419, fol. 14r, 1 C 14125; StB Trier, Hs. 1534/166, 8. On the werewolf of Limburg, see HHStAW, 171 Z 3832, fol. 108r; see also Walz, *Hexenglaube*, 328–30, 431. On Flade, see StB Trier, Hs. 1533a/171, fols. 11v, 21v, 33r. On Wendler, see TLA, Hs. 1390, fol. 152r; HStASt, B 19, Bd. 5, fol. 410r–v. On shame notes, see Dinges, *Der Maurermeister*, 275–76.

20. See Müller, "Mobilität," 242–43. On damage to honor, see also Nowosadtko, "Betrachtungen," 230–48. For extensive discussion with parallels beyond the witch trials, see Dinges, *Der Maurermeister*, 293–302.

21. See, e.g., Birlinger, *Volksthümliches*, 1:153; UAT, 84/24, fols. 479v–480r; LHAKO, 56/419, fol. 46v, 33/12334, fols. 128v–129r; StA Trier, DK, 54 K 657, 352, 392.

22. LHAKO, 211/3027, 1 C 9191, 1–2, 74; Goldast, *Rechtliches Bedencken*, 117; *Annuae 1601*, 608–9.

23. StA Rottenburg, A 9.1/2.

24. Behringer, "Kinderhexenprozesse," 43–45; Weber, *Kinderhexenprozesse*.

25. StAA, VÖ Lit, 650, fols. 486r, 513r–514r, 567r–v.

26. See Dillinger, "Nichtseßhafte Frauen," 145–50. On early trials inspired by Ulmerin, see HStASt, B 19, Bd. 5, fols. 401v–402v. On denouncing powerful people, see Hs. 2402, 490–93, 971, Hs. 1390, fols. 87r, 118r–v. On Ulmerin in Constance, see TLA, Sammelakten, Reihe B, Abt. 16, Lage 4, no. 6; GLAK, 79/3387, Breisgau Generalia, fols. 40r–43r; HStASt, B 19, Bd. 5, fol. 448r; StA Konstanz, B I 80, fol. 68r, B II, Missiven, 1595; TLA, Sammelakten, Reihe B, Abt. 16, Lage 4, no. 7. See Roecken and Brauckmann, *Margaretha Jedefrau*, 227.

27. *Annuae 1588*, 164; StB Trier, Hs. 1533a/171, fols. 17v, 64r–v, 78r–v. On exorcism as proof of faith, see Midelfort, *Exorcism*. On possessed children, see *Annuae 1585*, 275–76. On Jeckel, see *Annuae 1586/87*, 255–56.

28. Binsfeld, *Tractatus* (1589), fol. 111r. On continuing denunciation, see Dillinger, *Böse Leute*, 254–55. On Diez in 1590, see Mechtel, *Die Limburger Chronik*, 160.

29. Behringer, *Hexen*, 203, is misleading in this regard.

30. On general disregard of the *Carolina* in practice, see Lorenz, "Der Hexenprozeß," 75–76; Trusen, "Rechtliche Grundlagen," 208. On single denunciations suffice: GLAK, 67/734, fols. 370r–371r, 377r–v, 384v–385v; HStASt, B 19, Bd. 1, fol. 140r–v. On the Rottenburg reprimand in 1554, see HStASt, B 19, Bd. 3, fol. 193r–v.

31. TLA, Hs. 2402, 425–35; Birlinger, *Volksthümliches*, 1:135, 142, 145, 150. See Mährle, "Fürstpropstei," 329; Behringer, "Erhob," 145–47, 160, 164–65; Gehm, *Die Hexenverfolgung*, 231–45.

32. Barth, *Geschichte*, 159; StAA, VÖ Lit, 655, fols. 394r–v, 379r–380v, 423r–424r, 436v–437r, 453r, 461v–462r.

33. Tanner, *Universa*, book 3, chap. 4, sec. 5, subsec. 2, para. 45, vol. 3, 959. See Schurer, *Die selige gute Betha*.

34. Barth, *Geschichte*, 159, 161; Krebs, "Die Verfassung," 149–50; TLA, Hs. 1390, fol. 201v, Hs. 2402, 434, Allgemeines Leopoldinum, Karton B, no. 133; GLAK, 65/728; StA Horb, A 311; StAA, VÖ Lit, 655, fols. 365r–366r, 369v.

35. LHAKO, 56/419, fols. 93v–94r; Scotti, *Sammlung*, 1(152):558; Voltmer and Weisenstein, *Das Hexenregister*; Rummel, "Soziale Dynamik," 47; idem, "Phasen," 258, 260.

36. Binsfeld, *Tractatus* (1589), fols. 79r–81r, 112v–114v (verbatim quote on 79v–80r); see Behringer, *Hexen*, 181; Rummel, *Bauern*, 206.

37. The text of the trial critic Loos, who was at some unknown time a member of the faculty of theology, was certainly not the (or even an) answer to Johann's request. The text could not have been written before 1592: see Franz, "Geistes- und Kulturgeschichte," 336. Kümper's questionable "edition" of Binsfeld's text has nothing more to add on this question than an unacknowledged paraphrase of my argument: Dillinger, *Böse Leute*, 260–62; see Binsfeld, *Tractat* (2004), ix. On the 1589 request, see StB Trier, Hs. 1533a/171, fols. 31v, 42r–v, 46v–47v, 81r, 87r–89r; Neller, *Conatus*, 34.

38. Rummel, "Phasen," 274, interprets the legal opinion as testimony, reflecting the practice under Prince Bishop Lothar. The opinion, however, did no so much give information on the contemporary witch hunt as it reported on the first wave prior to 1596. The formulation suggests that the new prince elector saw witch trials as a thing of the past. On the Bavarian debate, see BayHStA, Hexenakten, no. 4, Prod. 26, 35, 37. On the influence of Binsfeld and the legal opinion in Bavaria, see Behringer, *Witchcraft Persecutions in Bavaria*, 24, 220–23, 240, 260; idem, "Das 'reichskhündig Exempel,'" 442–44. There is no indication of Rémy's vote in Biesel, *Hexenjustiz*.

39. StB Trier, Hs. 1533a/171, fols. 54v–55v, 58v–64r, 68r–v, 74r–80v, 83r–87r, Hs. 1533/171, fol. 5v–11v, 35v–36v, Hs. 2180a/45a, 8–12, 19–24. This was not compatible with the provisos from the *Carolina*, Arts. 30, 31, 45–46.

40. StB Trier, Hs. 2180a/45a, 1, 5.

41. Birlinger, *Voksthümliches*, 1:153; HStASt, B 37a, Bü 118, B 19, Bd. 5, fols. 551v, 618v–619r; StA Horb, A 311. On rural communities banishing witches, see HStASt, B 40, Bü 543, A 209, Bü 851; Dillinger, "Die letzte Hexe," 152–53.

42. StAA, VÖ Lit, 649, fols. 39r–44r, 655, fols. 251v–252r; Völk, "Ein Günzburger Hexenprozeß," no. 9. On Michlerin, see Selig, "Ein Hexenprozeß," 41.

43. *Translator's note:* These inquisitorial trials were not conducted by the Roman Catholic Inquisition, but were brought on charges from the secular authorities as opposed to private accusers.

44. HStASt, B 40, Bü 544; UAT, 84/24, fols. 478r–481v; see also Dillinger, *Hexen und Hexenprozesse in Fridingen*, 31–33. On the Wurmlingen sheriff, see TLA, Hs. 1390, fols. 131r, 139r. On Hirschau in 1601, see HStASt, B 40, Bü 543.

45. The following is drawn from HStASt, B 37a, Bü 118.

46. Midelfort, *Witch Hunting,* 58–64, 190–94.

47. StAA, VÖ Lit, 655, fols. 251v–252r; Völk, "Ein Günzburger Hexenprozeß," no. 9. A similar trial took place in Burgau in 1657: StA Burgau, Ratsprotokoll 1657, 438. On the 1582–85 case, see StAA, VÖ Lit, 649, fols. 38r, 39r–44r, 53v–54r, 480r–v. On Günzburg refusing to assist in the witch trial, see TLA, Geheimer Rat (Hofregistratur), Aktenserie, 1604, carton 6. On Margrave Karl, see StA Günzburg, 5.276; Völk, "Ein Günzburger Hexenprozeß," no. 8–9. Attempts by the Habsburg government to interfere in Günzburg's criminal jurisdiction occurred repeatedly. A direct cause for Karl's measures cannot be found. The correspondence between Günzburg and the Innsbruck government at the beginning of the second decade of the seventeenth century, however, was noticeably sparse.

48. Dillinger, "Die Hexenverfolgung in der Landvogtei Schwaben," 134–35, 142–43.

49. StA Stockach, C.VIII, 1, 1617, fol. 122r, 1618, fols. 15r, 24v–25r, 26r, 1621, fol. 111v, Ratsprotokolle from 6/7/1629, 11/23/1663, 11/19/1665.

50. See also Dillinger, "Hexenverfolgungen in Städten," 156–60.

51. Midelfort, *Witch Hunting,* 78, 150, 162–63, 190–94, 205; Behringer, *Witchcraft Persecutions in Bavaria,* 39–43, 163–64, 327–28. On Ulm, see Schlaier, "Reichsstadt Ulm," 461–62. On Ellwangen, see Mährle, "Fürstpropstei"; Dillinger, "Hexenverfolgungen in Städten," 133–35, 156–59, 162, 165.

52. By contrast, Midelfort, *Witch Hunting,* 290–92. On the 1615 census, see HStASt, B 40, Bü 314, Bd. 1–4.

53. TLA, Hs. 1390, fols. 87r–87v, 115v, Hs. 2402, 502, 723–24, 793, 816, 835, 851, 882–86, 904–5, 912–15, 926–27, 932, 948, 950–52, 963.

54. Ibid., Kopialbücher: An die fürstliche Durchlaucht, Bd. 61, fol. 242v, Allgemeines Leopoldinum, Karton B, no. 133; HStASt, I 13, Bü 4, B 37a, Bü 118, B 19, Bd. 8, fols. 306r–v, 313v, A 209, Bü 851; StA Horb, A 310; StA Oberndorf, A 128.

55. HStASt, B 37a, Bü 25. Regarding Hallmayer, see TLA, Hs. 2402, 368, 422, 435, 905, 913, 952, Allgemeines Leopoldinum, Karton B, no. 133; Kempf, "Die Hexenverfolgung im Raum Rottenburg," 35. On Veser's godfather connection, see TLA, Allgemeines Leopoldinum, Karton B, no. 133; HStASt, B 19, Bd. 5, fol. 413v.

56. See, e.g., TLA, Hs. 2402, 368, 533, 569, 727. See Kempf, *Die Chronik,* 360–64. On manipulated confessions, see TLA, Allgemeines Leopoldinum, Karton B, no. 133, Hs. 2402, 490, 533–34, 664, 913; StA Horb, A 316.

57. TLA, Hs. 2402, 5–7, 51, 427, 429, 490, 580, 664, Hs. 1390, fols. 140v, 194v; HStASt, B 37a, Bü 118; StA Oberndorf, A 128.

58. Midelfort, *Witch Hunting,* 34–45; Raith, "Herzogtum Württemberg," 229–31. On Wendler's comment, see TLA, Hs. 1390, fol. 87r–v.

59. TLA, Hs. 1390, fol. 42v; further quotes in Kempf, *Die Chronik,* 361–64. On resisting demands for lynching, see TLA, Hs. 2402, 502; cf. Dillinger, "Richter," 129–32.

60. HStASt, B 17, Bd. 21, fol. 233v, Bd. 22, fol. 51v, Bd. 44, fol. 540r, B 19, Bd. 5, fol. 365r, Bd. 8, fols. 212v–213r; GLAK, 67/734, fols. 370r–371r.

61. Midelfort, *Witch Hunting,* 57, 79–80; Raith, "Herzogtum Württemberg," 231–35; Schmidt, "Die Kurpfalz," 210–12. On no duty to report, see HStASt, B 19, Bd. 5, fols. 518v, 551v, 612r, 616v, Bd. 6, 66v–67r, 503r, Bd. 8, fols. 212v–213r.

62. Dillinger, "Grafschaft Hohenberg," 89–92; see, e.g., HStASt, B 19, Bd. 5, fols.

448r, 518r–v, 539r, 549v, 633r–634r, Bd. 6, fols. 56v–57v, 66r–67r, B 37a, Bü 273; StA Horb, A 312.

63. The following is drawn from StA Horb, A 312, fols. 3r–6v, 10r–11r, B 83, 302–3, 341–43, 345–49, 357–59, 370–72. On the suspicious surface, see HStASt, B 19, Bd. 5, fols. 542v–544r, 547r–548r; StA Horb, A 309. On the trip to Innsbruck, see StA Horb, A 312, fol. 2v. The following is drawn from StA Horb, A 316; HStASt, B 19, Bd. 5, fols. 565r–566v, 576r–577v, 628r–629r.

64. TLA, Allgemeines Leopoldinum, Karton B, no. 133; StA Horb, A 311. See *Carolina*, Arts. 44, 58, 59, 52, 58.

65. The following is drawn from StA Horb, A 312, fol. 13r–19r; HStASt, B 19, Bd. 1, fols. 298v–299r, 370r–v; TLA, Allgemeines Leopoldinum, Karton B, no. 133.

66. Quarthal, *Landstände*, 38–47, 50–57; Dillinger, *Böse Leute*, 290–93.

67. Blauert, *Frühe Hexenverfolgungen*, 109, 116–17.

68. See Dillinger, "Hexenverfolgungen in Städten," 136–37. On Innsbruck accepting Ulmerin testimony, see HStASt, B 41, Bd. 3, fols. 328v–333r. On Günzburg consultations, see StA Horb, A 309; see Bodin, *De la démonomanie*, book 4, chap. 2, 214–15; StA Günzburg, 5.276.

69. TLA, Hs. 2402, 425–35; StA Rottenburg, A 9.1/2; Birlinger, *Volksthümliches*, 1:147, 175. Regarding few surviving witness interrogations, see Barth, *Geschichte*, 153–54; Selig, "Ein Hexenprozeß," 41–42; StA Günzburg, 5.276; UAT, 84/24, fols. 478r–481v, 84/62, 611–16. On witnesses not sworn in, see UAT, 84/24, fols. 484r–487v; HStASt, B 17, Bd. 44, fol. 65r; TLA, Hs. 2402, 425–35; StA Horb, A 312.

70. Dillinger, "Grafschaft Hohenberg," 38–43, 56–63.

71. StA Rottenburg, A 9.1/2; Barth, *Geschichte*, 157. *Stigma diaboli*, HStASt, B 17, Bd. 10, 136v, 140v; Barth, *Geschichte*, 152, 158; Dillinger, "Grafschaft Hohenberg," 146–47. On the Ravensburg executionerm, see Kramer, *Der Hexenhammer*, book 3, chap. 15, 492–95; Behringer, *Witchcraft Persecutions in Bavaria*, 79. Kramer's practice may also have been transmitted locally in oral tradition. A dynasty of executioners in Ravensburg cannot be proved.

72. While the nun was able to escape execution through flight (HStASt, B 17, Bd. 34, fols. 332r, 343v), Maria Paumannin was actually killed in this manner. At the execution, a scene played out of which the government's response to the report of the Obervogt in charge provides an impression: "We have received your report of and apology for . . . the evil course of the execution . . . with displeasure. Although the matter did take place in excess and against our careful ordinances, we must, however leave it at that." That both the central and local officials responsible for the killing later attempted to distance themselves from it is without parallel in the witch trials of Swabian Austria: HStASt, B 17, Bd. 33, fols. 288v, 300r–v. On Altdorf, see HStASt, B 17, Bd. 44, fol. 638r. On torture and exoneration, see, e.g., GLAK, 67/738, fols. 320v–321v; HStASt, I 13, Bü 3, B 40, Bü 543, B 37a, Bü 10; to the contrary, see HStASt, B 37a, Bü 121; StA Horb, A 312. On Innsbruck criticism of harsh torture, see HStASt, B 17, Bd. 10, fol. 136v, Bd. 45, fol. 66v.

73. Crusius, *Diarium*, 1:135; TLA, Hs. 1390, fols. 184v, 205r, 253r, Allgemeines Leopoldinum, Karton B, no. 133; HStASt, B 37a, Bü 118, B 17, Bd. 28, fol. 112v.

74. Riezler, *Geschichte*, 207; HStASt, B 37a, Bü 10, 237, B 40, Bü 543, I 13, Bü 3.

75. The almost complete loss of financial records from the cities and territories, especially in persecution-intensive Hohenberg, presents a significant source problem for the question of trial finances in Swabian Austria. The expenses for witch executions in Burgau cited by Schuhmann without any usable source reference have not been taken into consideration: Schuhmann, *Der Scharfrichter,* 81. Birlinger, *Volksthümliches,* 1:155, cites two Hohenberg executioners' expense records. The expenses for each ran to just under 15 gulden.

76. Manfred Tschaikner arrived at the same conclusion for Vorarlberg: Tschaikner, *Damit das Böse,* 164–65, 168. Confiscations unusual: TLA, Pestarchiv, XXVIII 142. Innsbruck on confiscations: StAA, VÖ Lit, 650, fols. 513r–514r. On the practice in neighboring territories, see ibid., 567r–v; HStASt, B 19, Bd. 5, fol. 539r. On Oberndorf in 1605, see HStASt, B 19, Bd. 6, fol. 328v. Stockach officials on managing trial expenses: HStASt, B 51, Bü 64c. 1603 inquiry into trial finances: TLA, Von der fürstlichen Durchlaucht, Bd. 7, fol. 518r–v.

77. HStASt, B 19, Bd. 5, fol. 594v, Bd. 7, fol. 140r, Bd. 8, fols. 212v–213r, B 37a, Bü 10, 11.

78. Scotti, *Sammlung,* 1(152).

79. Gerteis, "Die kurfürstliche Zeit," 59–60; Rummel, *Bauern,* 26–38. On Wehrheim witch committees, see HHStAW, 369/453, fol. 57v. On the potential threat of peasant confederations, see Blickle, Die Revolution, 147–50, 226–42. Arno Lott, however, cited *Carolina,* Art. 11, in connection with the committees, suggesting that they were grounded in the imperial law: Lott, *Die Todesstrafen,* 120; see *Carolina,* Art. 11, 35. To the contrary, it can be maintained that the witch committees were only traditional communal institutions, without any basis in written law or any law from beyond the region.

80. See, e.g., LHAKO, 56/419, fol. 89v; HHStAW, 369/456, fols. 191v, 207r. On the end of the preceeding trial chain, see ibid., fol. 200r; StA Trier, DK, 54 K 657, 165.

81. The witch ordinances of the Electorate explicitly said of the establishment of committees that the subjects had "many traditions in the conditions thereof": Scotti, *Sammlung,* 1:555.

82. LHAKO, 56/1922, 1446–49. The uncommon form of a sealed charter was probably chosen to provide a sound legal basis for the committee in the jurisdictionally sensitive context of the shared domain. On Benrather Hof in 1587, see Voltmer and Weisenstein, *Das Hexenregister,* 15*, 43*–45*; Rummel, *Bauern,* 38. Local-history groups believe they have discovered even older committees, but the sources are questionable: Voltmer, "Monopole," 23–35. In the County of Wertheim in the Main-Tauber region, in 1602, the residents of several villages allied themselves for the extermination of the witches by each cutting notches in a staff. The staff was carried through the villages in a procession. The government as well as residents of localities that were not yet included viewed the growing number of notches as evidence of the subjects' resolve to hunt witches: Weiß, "Grafschaft," 329. More significant than the superficial similarities is the nature of a martial demonstration, which the rituals had in common in Wertheim and the region of Trier.

83. Rummel, *Bauern,* 36–38; Voltmer and Weisenstein, *Das Hexenregister,* 42*.

84. HHStAW, 115/Villmar 12, fols. 73r, 76r, 107r–v; LHAKO, 56/1922, 1446; Scotti, *Sammlung,* 1(152):556; Rummel, *Bauern,* 41–42.

85. StA Trier, DK, 54 K 657, 184, 458; see Rummel, *Bauern,* 278–84. On the social status of committee members, see StA Trier, DK, 54 K 657, 39, 75, 103, 137, 140, 163, 203; Rummel, "Phasen," 277–84. On committee members' lack of legal knowledge, see LHAKO, 56/363, 72; Scotti, *Sammlung,* 1(152):555; Rummel, *Bauern,* 280–81.

86. See, e.g., LHAKO, 56/419, fols. 38r, 51r, 92v; HHStAW, 369/455, fol. 78r; StA Trier, DK, 54 K 657, 458.

87. StA Trier, DK, 54 K 657; LHAKO, 56/419, fol. 89v; HHStAW, 369/430, fol. 4r, 369/455, fols. 241r–248r.

88. StA Trier, DK, 54 K 657, 378–80; Krämer, *Kurtrierische Hexenprozesse,* 33–36. Details are in Dillinger, *Böse Leute,* 312. On the Schweich committee members' investigations, see StA Trier, DK, 54 K 657, 366, 380; StB Trier, Hs. 1534/166, fols. 38r–39r; Rummel, *Bauern,* 70–74.

89. Goldast, *Rechtliches Bedencken,* 105, 117. On his stay in Coblenz, see also Lea, *Materials,* 2:804. On the role of jail personnel, see HHStAW, 369/455, fols. 282v, 287r; Rummel, *Bauern,* 98–99; Midelfort, *Witch Hunting,* 107–8. The 1630 Witch Trial Ordinance is in Scotti, *Sammlung,* 1(194):613. On Cochem, see Rummel, "Soziale Dynamik," 42.

90. Rummel, *Bauern,* 74–75, 161–72; Voltmer and Weisenstein, *Das Hexenregister,* 61*–62*.

91. Rummel, "Friedrich Spee," 115. On the committees' use of legal opinions, see StA Trier, DK, 54 K 657, 366–80; Scotti, *Sammlung,* 1(152):556. On juridical entrepreneurs and Johann Moeden, see Krämer, *Kurtrierische Hexenprozesse,* 35; Kettel, "Hexenprozesse in der Grafschaft Gerolstein," 361, 368–70, 372; Rummel, *Bauern,* 164–68. The most important legal experts on witchcraft were Peter Omsdorf and Heinrich Hultzbach: Voltmer and Weisenstein, *Das Hexenregister,* 61*–68*. On career opportunities for jurists, see Rummel, *Bauern,* 56–67, 161–72. On the legal aid provided by urban lawyers for clients from the countryside, see Dillinger, "Hexenverfolgungen in Städten," 135–37.

92. HHStAW, 369/453, fols. 56r, 369, 455, fols. 61v, 78r–v, 201r–v; StB Trier, Hs. 1534/166, fol. 37r; Rummel, *Bauern,* 130.

93. StA Trier, Ta 100/2, fols. 102v, 104r–v, 107v–108r; Voltmer, "Zwischen Herrschaftskrise," 87–89, 104.

94. Kramer, *Der Hexenhammer,* book 2, chap. 2, sec. 1, 529–30. On Ediger, see pp. 67–68; Hoffmann and Dohms, *Die Mirakelbücher,* no. 151, 95, no. 350, 196–97.

95. LHAKO, 1 C 7944, fols. 22r–23r, 56/419, fol. 60r; StB Trier, Hs. 1534/166, fol. 35r–v; HHStAW, 369/456, fol. 2v, 23v; Rummel, "Die Anfänge," 127–32.

96. StA Trier, DK, 54 K 657, 275–77; StB Trier, Hs. 1533/171, fols. 1r–2v, 34r, Hs. 2180a/45a, 4; Binsfeld, *Tractatus* (1589), fols. 2r–5r; idem, *Tractatus* (1596), 387; Voltmer and Weisenstein, *Das Hexenregister,* 196, 252.

97. Rummel, *Bauern,* 140; see Kleinheyer, *Rechtsgestalt,* 17.

98. Scotti, *Sammlung,* 1(152):556, 560.

99. See, e.g., HHStAW, 369/455, fol. 63r; in general terms, Gerteis, "Die kurfürstliche Zeit," 61; Rummel, *Bauern,* 183–92; Nikolay-Panter, *Entstehung,* 71–72.

100. Franz Joseph Bodmann claimed that the three Rhineland archbishops met in Coblenz in 1487, received there an indult from Maximilian I for witch inquisitions, and discussed a common course of action against the allies of the Devil: Bodmann, *Rhein-*

gauische Alterhümer, 1:424. Which source he drew on for this remains unclear. As there is no parallel source, this is certainly a false report.

101. Rummel, "Exorbitantien und Ungerechtigten," 45; Lott, *Die Todesstrafen*, 111, are misleading. On inquest orders in Fiedler and Reuland trials, see StB Trier, Hs. 1533/171, fol. 2v, Hs. 2180a/45a, 4, Hs. 1533a/171, fols. 1r–4v, 38r–41r, 89v, 96r–99r, 109r, 112v, 114v; Dillinger, "Richter," 145–47.

102. Scotti, *Sammlung*, 1(194):613. See, e.g., HHStAW, 339/149. On Coblenz decisions in 1591–93, see LHAKO, 1 C 4324; Rummel, "Phasen," 269–70. For Trier transcripts in 1610–12, see StB Trier, Hs. 1534/166, fols. 55r–71r. On acquittals repeating previous decision, see ibid. fols. 57v, 60r, 66v.

103. LHAKO, 1 C 7944. Further examples are in Dillinger, *Böse Leute*, 328–29.

104. Oestmann, *Hexenprozesse*, 97, 552–53.

105. HHStAW, 369/455, fol. 318r; see Koppenhöfer, *Die mitleidlose Gesellschaft*, 238. In German, these sayings rhyme: "die Armen in die Asch, die Reichen in die Tasch."

106. LHAKO, 56/725, 56/1589; Rummel, "Soziale Dynamik,".

107. Scotti, *Sammlung*, 1(152):555–56. Rummel uncritically accepts the viewpoint of the territorial lord. Thus, he over-emphasizes the point that the witch hunts resembled insurrections: Rummel, "Phasen," 283.

108. The following is drawn from *Annuae 1596*, 233–34; Duhr, *Die Stellung*, 35; Reiffenberg, *Historia societatis*, 1:350. Voltmer ignored the Cochem context: Voltmer, "Zwischen Herrschaftskrise," 103.

109. See StB Trier, Hs. 1533/171, fol. 1r, Hs. 2180a/45a, 2.

110. See Irsigler, "Zauberei- und Hexenprozesse in Köln," 178–79; Dillinger, "Hexenverfolgungen in Städten," 158–59.

111. Rummel, "Phasen," 278–79, 318; Laufner, "Politische Geschichte," 17–21; Abmeier, *Der Trierer Kurfürst*, 4–18.

112. StB Trier, Hs. 1534/166, 13; StA Trier, DK, 54 K 657, 195; HHStAW, 369/447; Scotti, *Sammlung*, 1(152):559; Binsfeld, *Tractatus* (1589), fols. 115r–122r; see Lott, *Die Todesstrafen*, 94–95; Behringer, *Hexen*, no. 65, 109; Hammes, *Hexenwahn*, 170.

113. See, e.g., LHAKO, 655, 14, no. 65; HHStAW, 369/432, fol. 32r, 369/433, fol. 16r, 349/455, fol. 206v, 349/456, fol. 204r. On denial resulting in repetition of torture, see LHAKO, 1 C 37, 115–16, 56/726; StA Trier, DK, 54 K 657, 202, 431; StB Trier, Hs. 1534/166, 10, 13, 14, 20; Rummel, *Bauern*, 93–97.

114. StB Trier, Hs. 1533a/171, fols. 19v–20r, 96v.

115. Binsfeld, *Tractatus* (1589), fols. 141r–152r. I am grateful to Peter Heuser for the reference to Alciati. On Alciati, see Lea, *Materials*, 1:374–76; on the *Canon Episcopi*, see the text and explanation in Steinruck, "Zauberei," 13–18.

116. The quote is from StB Trier, Hs. 1533a/171, fols. 96v–97r, author's emphasis. For witch hunters' argument, see, e.g., Kramer, *Der Hexenhammer*, book 2, chap. 1, sec. 11, 459–60; Binsfeld, *Tractat* (1590), 144–52.

117. LHAKO, 33/8188, 255–56; HHStAW, 369/446, 369/447; StA Trier, DK, 54 K 657, 346, 354. On spectral evidence, see Drechsler, "The Use of Spectral Evidence," 185–208.

118. Delrio, *Disquisitionum*, book 5, chap. 5, 741; further mention of Flade is on book 2, chap. 11, 164, book 5, chap. 16, 838. Binsfeld never explicitly discussed Flade. Delrio's

description of Flade also influenced the Tyrol witch-trial critic Tanner: see Tanner, *Universa*, book 3, chap. 4, sec. 5, subsec. 4, para. 92, 1009. The evaluation of Flade as a skeptic was accepted by, among others, Soldan, Heppe, and Bauer, *Geschichte*, 1:473–74, and Behringer, "Hexenverfolgungen," 360.

119. StB Trier, Hs. 1900/1479, fols. 24r, 32v–33r; see also Eerden, "Der Teufelspakt," 59–60. Some witch trials in which Flade served as a juror did end with the death sentence. As the concept of the witches' Sabbath played a central role in these trials, Flade certainly did not criticize that concept: see LHAKO, 211/2275, 10, 17, 20–21, 27–28, 211/2276, 5, 16–17, 21, 24; StA Trier, T 174, Allgemeines Verwaltung Missif-Buch, 1586–90, fols. 210v–213v; Schmitt, *Die Kirche*, 228.

120. Dillinger, *Böse Leute*, 339–41.

121. Rummel, *Bauern*, 47, assumes that the Electorate of Trier differed from the Electorates of Cologne and Mainz in the renunciation of confiscation, but the official practice in each may have been similar: Pohl, "Hexenverfolgungen," 234–35. Schormann, "Die Hexenprozesse im Kurfürstentum Köln," 184. Binsfeld, *Tractatus* (1589), fol. 18r.

122. LHAKO, 1 C 37, 943–45, 1 C 41, 92. On Flade's bequest, see Laufner, "Die Gefangennahme," 67–68, 70–71; Franz, "Geistes- und Kulturgeschichte," 335.

123. HHStAW, 369/455, fols. l8r, 322v–323r; StA Trier, DK, 54 K 657, 382; LHAKO, 33/8187a, fols. 2v–3r, 56/1922, 1448; Rummel, *Bauern*, 50–51. On shared committees and shared costs, see StB Trier, Hs. 1534/166, fol. 35r–v; LHAKO, 627/113, fols. 23r, 26v, 37v; BAT, Abt. 5.3, no. 38a, 49–50, 53–54, 104; Mechtel, *Die Limburger Chronik*, 161; Rummel, *Bauern*, 46–49; Gerteis, "Die kurfürstliche Zeit," 60–61. On borrowing to cover costs, see StA Trier, DK, 54 K 657, 375, 380; HHStAW, 369/430, fol. 2r–v, 369/432, fol. 7v; see Rummel, *Bauern*, 33.

124. HHStAW, 369/453, fol. 16v, 369/455, fol. 66v. On opposition taken as a sign of witchcraft, see, e.g., HHStAW, 369/455, fol. 69r; StA Trier, DK, 54 K 657, 382.

125. HHStAW, 369/453, fol. 31r.

126. Wyttenbach and Müller, *Gesta Trevirorum*, 3:54.

127. Binsfeld, *Tractatus* (1589), fol. 18r–v. On Loos, see Behringer, *Hexen*, no. 218, 361.

128. Goldast, *Rechtliches Bedencken*, esp. 117, 131, 172–78; on Goldast, see Lea, *Materials*, 2:804–11.

129. Bauer, *Philipp von Sötern*, 1:415.

130. According to Hausmann, Philipp Christoph gave prayers for the dead for living persons to kill them. Purportedly he had killed two Habsburgs in this way; the emperor himself was to be his next victim, a prospect that he, like Rumpelstilsken, had supposedly celebrated in advance by exulting, "The emperor is dead, there is no more emperor, the house of Austria is entirely finished": quoted from Lauer, "Philipp," 38. Concerning the murder prayer, see Daxelmüller, *Aberglaube*, 156–60.

131. HHStAW, 369/456; LHAKO, 1 C 4324; StA Trier, DK, 54 K 657; StB Trier, Hs. 1534/166, fols. 58v, 63v–64r, 66v–67r; Mechtel, *Die Limburger Chronik*, 158, 160; Rummel, "Phasen," 268–69; Koppenhöfer, *Die mitleidlose Gesellschaft*, 230–40.

132. Wyttenbach and Müller, *Gesta Trevirorum*, 3:54.

133. HHStAW, 369/455, fol. 318r; TLA, Hs. 2402, 368.

134. See, e.g., Kramer, *Der Hexenhammer*, book 2, chap. 1, 348–55.

135. That Delrio suggested that Binsfeld wrote his tract in response to Flade's supposed criticism corresponds with this: Delrio, *Disquisitionum*, book 5, chap. 4, 741. Binsfeld, *Tractat* (2004), ix, is uncritical. Delrio's suggestion cannot be confirmed through the wording of Binsfeld's text or through any other source from the Electorate of Trier.

136. Schieder, "Möglichkeiten," 190–92.

137. Muchembled, *Popular Culture*; Schoenemann, "The Witch Hunt."

138. Gusfield, "Moral Passage," 175–88; Steinert, "Über symbolisches und instrumentelles Strafrecht," 101–16.

139. Blickle, "Die Reformation," 16. See idem, "Kommunalismus," 2:349–83.

140. Dillinger, Die politische Repräsentation.

141. Blickle, "Kommunalismus," 529–56, 537–51, 556; idem, "Die Reformation," 17.

142. On confessionalization see, e.g., the sophisticated discussion in Midelfort, *Witch Hunting*, 58–66. On the acculturation thesis, see Muchembled, "L'autre côté," 298–99; cf. the critical discussion in Biesel, *Hexenjustiz*, 29–32.

5. "Let No One Accuse Us of Negligence"

1. Crusius, *Diarium*, 1:89. Four years earlier, Crusius had had no qualms about permitting his own nephew to go to Rottenburg to see witches burn: ibid., 3:173.

2. Midelfort, *Witch Hunting*, 86–87, 121. For reports of Hohenberg trials see *Wahrhafftige und ein erschröckliche*; Janssen, *Culturzustände*, 8:618; Dillinger, *Hexenprozesse in Horb*, 15; *Zwo Newe Zeittungen*, quoted from Behringer, *Hexen*, no. 102, 158–60; *Wahrhafftig geschicht und eigentliche*, partially reprinted in Behringer, *Hexen*, no. 144, 228–29; the entire text is in Kempf, "Die Hexenverfolgung im Raum Rottenburg," 49–52; *Wahrhaffte und glaubwirdige Zeytung*, see Dillinger, "Grafschaft Hohenberg," 65.

3. Behringer, *Hexen*, no. 124, 204; see Behringer, "Das 'reichskhündig Exempel,'" 435–39.

4. StB Trier, Hs. 2180a/45a, 43; Heinz, "Bei den Trierern," 453–54; Irsigler, "Zauberei- und Hexenprozesse in Köln," 169–71, Behringer, "Das 'reichskhündig Exempel,'" 438.

5. Quoted from Behringer, "Das 'reichskhündig Exempel,'" 444.

6. Franz, "Die Hexenverfolgung im Kurfürstentum Trier," 68–73.

7. Meder, *Acht Hexenpredigten*, 35, 46. Rummel took David Meder's denominational polemics at face value and accepted his figures as largely reliable: Rummel, "Soziale Dynamik," 30; idem, "Phasen," 263–64. Behringer, "Das 'reichskhündig Exempel,'" 437; idem, *Witchcraft Persecutions in Bavaria*, 266–67.

8. Crusius, *Diarium*, 3:114, 132, 615; HStASt, B 17, Bd. 34, fols. 321v–323v, 327v–329r, 334v–335v, 343r–v. See Dillinger, "Hexenverfolgungen in Städten," 137–38.

9. See Schindling, "Die katholische Bildungsreform " 137–75, cf. the overview in ibid., 137–39.

10. Keller, *De officiis*, 532; see Binsfeld, *Tractatus* (1589), fols. 2r–3v; Keller, *De jure*, 275; see Binsfeld, *Tractatus* (1589), fol. 18r.

11. Gerbert, *Daemonurgia*, esp. book 1, chap. 64, 132–36.

12. Mather, *Magnalia*, 329. Innocent VIII, "Summis desiderantes affectibus," cited

in Kramer, *Der Hexenhammer,* 101–7. For Kramer on the Electorate, see ibid., 2, 2,1, 529–30.

13. Binsfeld, *Tractatus* (1589), fols. 111r, 122v; idem, *Tractatus* (1596), 37–41, 69, 235–36, 256, 264–65, 386–87, 672; HHStAW, 369/453, fol. 46v. Behringer sees Binsfeld as the guiding spirit of the witch hunts in the Electorate of Trier, as if he had so influenced trial practice there from the outset that it could be presented as the proof for his theoretical statements: Behringer, "Das 'reichskhündig Exempel,'" 440–42. But Behringer overestimates the likelihood that Vicar-General Binsfeld could influence trials before secular courts or affect the workings of the local committees that were so important in the Electorate of Trier. Also, the fact that Binsfeld only occasionally interspersed exemplars in his text argues against Behringer's assumption.

14. Zenz, "Cornelius Loos," 146–53; Eerden, "Der Teufelspakt." In fact, the Trier witch trials—in particular, Flade's case—were endorsed by Rome following Frangipani's report: see Roberg, *Geheime Nuntiaturberichte,* no. 441, 395, no. 419, 403.

15. Roberg, *Geheime Nuntiaturberichte,* no. 218, 361.

16. Behringer, "Das 'reichskhündig Exempel,'" 444–45. Loos's recantation is in Delrio, *Disquisitionum,* 5, app., 858–60.

17. TLA, Hs. 1390, fol. 109r.

18. Similarly, Behringer, "Das 'reichskhündig Exempel,'" 446–47.

19. StAA, VÖ Lit, 655, fols. 423v–424r; StAS, Ho 177, Bd. 4, no. 159.

20. StA Rottweil, Criminalia, II/I/V/1/12b, II/I/V/8/63; StAS, Ho 177, Bd. 2, no. 128, Bd. 4, no. 169; GLAK, 65/728, fol. 136r; HStASt, B 17, Bd. 29, fol. 126v; cf. Raith, "Herzogtum Württemberg," 202–4.

21. Rummel, "Phasen," 294–96, 300–303, 308–9; Dillinger, *Böse Leute,* 370–72.

22. HHStAW, 171 Z 4128; LHAKO, 33/8188, 56/2201, 340/1876; Rummel, "Phasen," 308.

23. HHStAW, 339/149; StA Reutlingen, K 7744. See also Fritz, "Hexenverfolgungen," 217; StA Oberndorf, A 130; GLAK, 65/728; Rummel, "Phasen," 287–88.

24. See Dillinger, "Grafschaft Hohenberg," 112; idem, *Böse Leute,* 372.

25. StA Trier, DK, 54 K 657; LHAKO, 1 C 37, 115–16.

26. Zimmermann, "Hochstift Konstanz," 367.

27. The following is drawn from HStASt, B 37a, Bü 118; cf. Krezdorn, "Wendler," 51–55.

28. GLAK, 67/738, fols. 24r–38r; TLA, Kopialbücher: An die fürstliche Durchlaucht, 1578, fols. 831r–837r.

29. Selig, "Ein Hexenprozeß," 39–42.

30. HStASt, B 17, Bd. 45, fols. 64v–67r; GLAK, 67/734, fols. 263r–v, 79/1606, 118/384–87, 118/389; see Berner, "Die Landgrafschaft Nellenburg," 621; Barth, *Geschichte,* 152–62.

31. Dillinger, "Grafschaft Hohenberg," 134–39. For a more detailed account of the child witch trials at Calw, cf. Weber, *Kinderhexenprozesse,* 289–91.

32. HStASt, B 17, Bd. 38, fols. 238r, 265v–267v. See also Kuhn-Rehfus, "Mit dem greulichen Laster," 430.

33. Fisenne, "Lucia Teimens," 5.

34. Irsigler, "Zauberei- und Hexenprozesse in Köln," 169–71.

35. The following is drawn from Rummel, "Phasen," 291–322.

36. LHAKO, 33/8182, fol. 27.

37. See Dillinger, *Böse Leute,* 380–83.

38. See Rummel, "Phasen," 290.

39. In 1589, a conflict arose over the extradition of a witch. Habsburg and Waldburg, however, quickly resolved the conflict: HStASt, B 17, Bd. 22, fols. 195r–196v, 200r–201r, 211v–212r.

40. HStASt, B 17, Bd. 29, fols. 87v–88v, 94v–95r, 151v–152v, 126v, 159v–160v, 195v, 196v, 309v.

41. Ibid., fols. 60r–v, 73v–74r, 81v–82v, 102r–103r, 127v, 202v–203v, 209r–210v, 280r–v, 330v–331r, 336r–v, 363v–364v, 372r, 377v–378v, 393v–395v; TLA, Kopialbücher: An die fürstliche Durchlaucht, 1625–26, fols. 460v–462v, Kopialbücher: Von der fürstlichen Durchlaucht, 1624–26, fols. 610v–611v. See also StAA, VÖ Lit, 654, fols. 236v–237r.

42. HStASt, B 17, Bd. 29, fols. 377v–378r.

43. LHAKO, 210/2227, 211/2241; StA Trier, DK, 54 K 239.

44. See Quarthal, *Landstände,* 395–400; Laufner, "Politische Geschichte," 12, 15–18, 25–28.

6. "A Slippery and Obscure Business"

1. Everything regarding the visitation commission that follows is drawn from the visitation protocol: TLA, Hs. 2402, Kopialbücher: Von der fürstlichen Durchlaucht, Bd. 7, fols. 660v–661r; HStASt, B 19, Bd. 5, fols. 633v–634r; Hirn, *Erzherzog Maximilian,* 2:11–14.

2. TLA, Sammelakten, Reihe B, Abt. 16, Lage 4, no. 6, Hs. 1390, fols. 81r, 142v, Hs. 2402, esp. 425–35, 523, 603; HStASt, B 19, Bd. 5, fol. 410r–v; Kempf, "Die Hexenverfolgung im Raum Rottenburg," 40–42.

3. The following is drawn from TLA Hs. 2402, 494, Allgemeines Leopoldinum, Karton B, no. 133.

4. HStASt, B 37a, Bü 10, B 40, Bü 543; Crusius, *Diarium,* 3:769.

5. TLA, Allgemeines Leopoldinum, Karton B, no. 133, Interrogatoria; StA Horb, A 311; Steinruck, "Zauberei," 13–16; Weyer, *De praestigiis daemonum,* 3, 17, 225–28. On Wendler's corruption charges, see TLA, Sammelakten, Reihe B, Abt. 16, Lage 4, no. 7, Hs. 2402, 368, 422, 435; Crusius, *Diarium,* 3:781; Krezdorn, "Wendler," 54–58; Hirn, *Erzherzog Maximilian,* 2:18.

6. The following is drawn from HStASt, B 19, Bd. 6, fols. 469r–470v, 489r–v, 512r–513r; TLA, Allgemeines Leopoldinum, Karton B, no. 133, Interrogatoria.

7. TLA, Allgemeines Leopoldinum, Karton B, no. 133, Littera C, no. 101; HStASt, B 19, Bd. 6, fols. 318r–319r, B 41, Bd. 9, Rottenburger Policeyordnung, fols. 27v–28r, Horber Policeyordnung, 31–32, Oberndorfer Policeyordnung, 26, Schömberger Policeyordnung, 13, Binsdorfer Policeyordnung, 16, Fridinger Policeyordnung, 14; StA Horb, A 319; StA Oberndorf, A 132.

8. HStASt, B 19, Bd. 7, fols. 62r, 120r–121v, 214v–215v; StA Horb, A 312.

9. StA Rottenburg, A 9.1/2, frag. 22.6.1610, Rechnungen; Birlinger, *Volksthümliches,* 1:152–57.

10. HStASt, B 37a, Bü 121, B 40, Bü 314; cf. Midelfort, *Witch Hunting,* 94, 212.

11. HStASt, B 37a, Bü 2; see Henning, *Handbuch,* 1:555–62, 750–56. At around the same time, Bocer in Tübingen endorsed total confiscation: Bocer, *Tractatus,* book 3, chaps. 44–47, 113–15.

12. HStASt, B 19, Bd. 8, fols. 452v–453r; cf. ibid., B 19, Bd. 8, fol. 169v; StA Oberndorf, A 132, which suggest that Karl's order was not always followed.

13. TLA, Pestarchiv, XXXVIII 498, Kopialbücher: Causa Domini, Bd. 22, fols. 146v–147r; StAA, VÖ Lit, 655, fols. 276v–277r; HStASt, B 19, Bd. 7, fol. 140r, Bd. 8, fols. 238r, 452v; GLAK, 67/740, fols. 294v–295r.

14. StA Konstanz, B II, Bd. 75, fols. 127v–128v, K II Fasz. 36; StA Horb, A 128; HStASt, B 19, Bd. 7, fols. 171r, 218r–219r 223r–v, I 13, Bü 4.

15. See Dillinger, "Grafschaft Hohenberg," 116–19; Völk, "Ein Günzburger Hexenprozeß," no. 9; HStASt, B 17, Bd. 29, fols. 87v–88r; StAA, VÖ Lit, 654, fol. 237r, 655, fol. 83v; GLAK, 65/728, fol. 136r; StAS, Ho 177, Bd. 4, no. 159; StA Stockach, C.VIII, 1.

16. See Sannwald, *Spitäler,* 99–183.

17. StA Rottweil, Criminalia II/I/V/1/12b, II/I/V/8/63; StA Oberndorf, A 121, A 128, A 130, B 17, Ratsprotokolle; Müller, "Geschichte der Stadt Oberndorf," 471.

18. TLA, Allgemeines Leopoldinum, Karton C, no. 161; Müller, "Geschichte der Stadt Oberndorf," 254–55.

19. Behringer, *Witchcraft Persecutions in Bavaria,* map 3; Midelfort, *Witch Hunting,* 217–18. On Burgau in 1630/31, see StAA, VÖ Lit, 655, fols. 251v–252r, 276r–v.

20. StAA, VÖ Lit, 655, fols. 277v–278v, 289v–291v, 321r–v, 336v, 337v–339v, 343r, 344r–v, 345v–346v, 348v–351v, 354r–355rv, 357v–358r, 362r, 365r–366r, 367r–368r, 369v, 369v–370r, 379r–380r, 385v–386r, 436v–437r, 454v–455r; TLA, Kopialbücher: Von der fürstlichen Durchlaucht, 1629–31, fols. 708v–709r, Kopialbücher: An die fürstliche Durchlaucht, 1631, fols. 111r–v, 508r–509v, Sammelakten, Riehe B, Abt. 7, Lage 1, no. 5; StAA, VÖ Lit, 655.

21. TLA, Kopialbücher: Von der fürstlichen Durchlaucht, 1632–36, fol. 51v; StAA, VÖ Lit, 655, fols. 461v–462r; cf. Behringer, *Witchcraft Persecutions in Bavaria,* 224–29, 314–16; Midelfort, *Witch Hunting,* 125–32.

22. As yet, no evidence has been found that comparable offices were created in other parts of Swabian Austria or in the surrounding areas: cf. Behringer, *Witchcraft Persecutions in Bavaria,* 224–29; Schormann, "Die Hexenprozesse im Kurfürstentum Köln," 186–89, 191; Lorenz, "Der Hexenprozeß," 75–76; Trusen, "Rechtliche Grundlagen," 208, Voltmer and Weisenstein, *Das Hexenregister,* 63*–71*.

23. TLA, Kopialbücher: Causa Domini, Bd. 27, fols. 120v–125v; see also p. 28.

24. HStASt, B 19, Bd. 8, fols. 212v–213r, 222v–223r, 237r–238r, 241v, 242v–243r, 265v, 273r–v, 306r–v, 313v; TLA, Allgemeines Leopoldinum, Littera C, no. 101, Kopialbücher: Causa domini, Bd. 27, fols. 381v–382v, 398r.

25. StA Oberndorf, A 132, B 17, Ratsprotokolle from 8/31/1637; TLA, Kopialbücher: An die fürstliche Durchlaucht, Bd. 61, fols. 242v–243r; HStASt, B 19, Bd. 8, fols. 120r–121v, 125r–v. For a more detailed account, see Dillinger, "Nemini".

26. StA Oberndorf, A 129. This work is not signed by Haussmann. Other manuscripts that he did sign, however, show the same hand: StA Oberndorf, A 752; cf. *Carolina,*

Arts. 31, 45–46. On the following, see ibid., Arts. 57, 58; Binsfeld, *Tractatus* (1596), 698–703, 716–17.

27. StA Oberndorf, A 129; see Spee, "Cautio criminalis," 3:25, 5–6:26, 43, 7:app., 89–91, 92–95, 151, 196–98. On Spee's reception, see also Lorenz, "Die Rezeption der Cautio Criminalis," 133–36.

28. StA Oberndorf, A 760; HStASt, B 19, Bd. 8, fol. 125r–v, Bd. 9, fols. 2r–v, 157r, 230v–231r, B 41, Bd. 190; cf. Dillinger, "Nemini," 283–84.

29. HStASt, B 19, Bd. 8, fols. 120r–v, 138r; StA Oberndorf, A 128, A 132.

30. HStASt, B 17, Bd. 38, fol. 534r–v. On the Rottenburg consultation, see UAT, 84/24, fols. 478r–481v, 484r–496v. See also Dillinger, "Grafschaft Hohenberg," 142–44; Spee, "Cautio criminalis," 44, 152–60.

31. HStASt, B 17, Bd. 35, fols. 263v–265v, 289v–290r, author's emphasis.

32. Ibid., B 17, Bd. 38, fol. 534r–v, Bd. 44, fol. 86r, Bd. 45, fols. 66v–67r, 150r, Bd. 68, fols. 709v–710v.

33. Sellert and Rüping, *Studien,* 1:211, 269–70, 464–65; Hettinger, *Das Fragerecht.*

34. HStASt, B 17, Bd. 45, fols. 149v–150v. On the Rottenburg case of 1666, see ibid., Bd. 35, fols. 256r–257v, 289v–290v, 390v.

35. Pleier, *Malleus judicum,* 85–96; cf. Schmidt, "Die Kurpfalz," 242–47.

36. Tanner, *Universa,* book 3, chap. 4, sec. 5, subsec. 127, Bd. 3, col. 1019; Behringer, *Witchcraft Persecutions in Bavaria,* 322–24, 355–57. Behringer saw Tanner's significance as limited to his criticism of torture and evidentiary law in the witch trials. The fuller signficance of Tanner's work largely escaped him: Behringer, "Zur Haltung Adam Tanners," 172–82. See Dillinger, "Adam Tanner."

37. Tanner, *Universa,* book 3, chap. 4, sec. 5, subsec. 5, paras. 114–22, vol. 3, 1016–19.

38. Ibid., paras. 132–34, vol. 3, 1020–22.

39. HStASt, B 17, Bd. 35, fol. 256r.

40. Behringer, *Witchcraft Persecutions in Bavaria,* 323–24. Here Behringer follows the old erroneous interpretation in Riezler, *Geschichte,* 266–67.

41. Cf. Boyer and Nissenbaum, *Salem,* 214–16.

42. Behringer, *Hexen,* no. 276, 406, 450–51.

43. StA Rottenburg, A 22, no. 1, 773, 796, 802–3, 809, 815; HStASt, B 17, Bd. 68, fols. 709v–710v, 867r–v, Bd. 69, fols. 97v–98r, 251v–252r; UAT, 84/62, 611–18. On Tübingen's stance, see Lorenz, "Die Rechtsauskunftstätigkeit der Tübinger Juristenfakultät".

44. HHStAW, 339/149, 369/455, 369/456, fols. 2v, 23v.

45. Ibid., 369/456, fols. 36r–v, 445–446r, 105r–107r, 165r–168v, 184r–v, 186r, 195r–196r, 211r–v, 219r–v, 288r–v, 295v, 302r–v. Oestmann, *Hexenprozesse,* 167–68, 240, 376, 447–48, is based on insufficient source materials; Rummel, *Bauern,* 249, is misleading.

46. HHStAW, 369/456, fols. 252r–254v, 290r–v.

47. Ibid., fol. 272r.

48. Ibid., fols. 90v–97r, 265r.

49. Ibid., fols. 73r–76r, 84v–85r, 100r, 235r, 298r–v.

50. Ibid., fols. 31v–32r, 60r–v, 73r–76v, 112r–v, 118r–v, 128r, 133r–v, 157v, 231v–236v, 330r–335v.

51. Ibid., fols. 195r–v, 234v.

52. Ibid., fol. 31v; cf. Rummel, "Phasen," 287–88.

53. Rummel, *Bauern*, 248–49. In "Phasen," 287, by contrast, Rummel speculates that the date fell in 1653 or 1654, without closer documentation. On Austria and Prussia, see Behringer, *Hexen*, no. 272, 448–49, no. 276, 450–51.

54. HHStAW, 369/456, fol. 30r–v.

55. Laufner, "Politische Geschichte," 24, 27–28; Ellerhorst, "Karl Kaspar," 44–46; Dirks, *Das Landrecht*, 16–23.

56. Rummel, "Friedrich Spee."

57. The development in the Saar region is entirely parallel: see Labouvie, *Zauberei*, 250–59.

58. HHStAW, 339/149, fol. 20r; see Rummel, "Phasen," 282; Lauer, *Hexenverfolgung*, 27. The report of 1660 is questionable: Müller, *Die Geschichte der Stadt St. Wendel*, 608–9.

59. Rummel, "Phasen," 287–88.

60. Idem, *Bauern*, 252; Roeck, "Christlicher Idealstaat," 379–405.

61. Koppenhöfer, *Die mitleidlose Gesellschaft*, 9, 222–40. Koppenhöfer's work is damaged throughout by the speculation, unsubstantiated by the sources, that the victims of the witch hunt in Wehrheim were crypto-Catholics.

62. HHStAW, 369/455, fols. 131r–136v, 203r, 207v, 217v, 219r, 242r.

63. Ibid., fol. 241r–248r, 252r–263r.

64. Ibid., 369/453, fols. 43r–v, 279v, 282r–v, 369/455, fols. 2r–3v, 290r–293v.

65. Ibid., 369/453, fols. 6r–v, 12v, 33r, 46r; see Koppenhöfer, *Die mitleidlose Gesellschaft*, 212–17.

66. HHStAW, 369/453, fols. 26r–35r, 42r–v, 46r, 52r, 59r, 68v, 295r, 369/455, fols. 63r–66r, 68r–75v.

67. Ibid., 369/453, fols. 5v–8r, 47r–51r, 59r–v, 369/455, fols. 18r, 21r–24v, 322v–323r.

CONCLUSION

1. Klaniczay, *Heilige*, 91, 93–96; Lambrecht, *Hexenverfolgungen und Zaubereiprozesse*, 383–401; cf. Kreuter, *Der Vampirglaube*, 105–7.

2. See Becker, "Hexenverfolgung," 118–21; Irsigler, "Zauberei- und Hexenprozesse in Köln," 175–77; Renczes, *Wie löscht man eine Familie aus?* 46–120.

3. Cf., e.g., Walz's sophisiticated examination of non-European approaches to magic with Midelfort's position. Midelfort dismissed considerations of functionality regarding the central European witch trials because of their devastating results: Midelfort, *Witch Hunting*, 154; Walz, *Hexenglaube*, 37–39.

APPENDIX

1. On this account, the count here deviates from Behringer, *Witchcraft Persecutions in Bavaria*, 435; Midelfort, *Witch Hunting*, 205; Weisenstein, "Zaubereiprozesse," 479.

2. In 1580, six executions took place in a neighboring territory of Burgau, not in Bur-

gau itself, as Behringer and Midelfort believed: Behringer, *Witchcraft Persecutions in Bavaria*, 100; Midelfort, *Witch Hunting*, 205; see also StAA, Herrschaft Haunsheim, 674.

3. Tschaikner, *Damit das Böse*, 68, 130–31, 212.

4. Midelfort, *Witch Hunting*, 86–87, 121, 201.

5. Heisterkamp, "Hexen"; Rummel, "Phasen," 271.

6. See Labouvie, "Rekonstruktion," 56.

7. "Annales Novesienses," 717; Voltmer and Weisenstein, *Das Hexenregister*, 23*. Rummel, "Phasen," 260, is in favor of accepting the figure; Voltmer, "Zwischen Herrschaftskrise," 71, is opposed.

8. See Behringer, "Erhob," 141–42.

9. Lamb, *Climate*, 232–66.

10. Rummel, "Phasen," 328–29; Irsigler, "Wirtschaftsgeschichte," 146, 200; idem, "Hexenverfolgungen," 15–16.

11. Dillinger, *Hexenprozesse in Horb*, 15–17; Kempf, "Die Hexenverfolgung im Raum Rottenburg," 50; Rummel, "Phasen," 260.

12. On this point, strong regional differences do emerge. However, all together about 20 percent of the victims of the witch hunts may have been men: Irsigler, "Hexenverfolgungen," 11. See also Labouvie, *Zauberei*, 33–34. On the gender issue in overview, see Bender-Wittmann, "Gender."

13. TLA, Pestarchiv, XXVIII 142.

14. Nowosadtko, "Betrachtungen," 234–41.

Bibliography

UNPUBLISHED PRIMARY SOURCES

Archives de l'État à Luxembourg (AÉL)
Le fonds van Werveke, Sorcellerie I

Bayerisches Hauptstaatsarchiv München (BayHStA)
Hexenakten, no. 4, Prod. 26, 35, 37

Bibliothek des Priesterseminars Trier
Hs. 30

Bistumsarchiv Trier (BAT)
Abt. 5.2, no. 43
Abt. 5.3, no. 38a
Abt. 5.5, no. 37–42
Abt. 20, no. 21

Bundesarchiv, Aussenstelle Frankfurt am Main (Bundesarchiv, ASt. Frankfurt)
FSg. 2/1-F, Film 7, 267
FSg. 2/1-F, film 8, 349
FSg. 2/1-F, film 11, 535
FSg. 2/1-F, film 13, 662
FSg. 2/1-F, film 21, 1206, 1261
FSg. 2/1-F, film 23, 1435, 1524
FSg. 2/1-F, film 26, 1763
FSg. 2/1-F, film 28, 1840
FSg. 2/1-F, film 29, 1879
FSg. 2/1-F, film 32, 2124, 2178
FSg. 2/1-F, film 35, 2389
FSg. 2/1-F, film 40, 2749

FSg. 2/1-F, film 42, 2933
FSg. 2/1-F, film 43, 3017

Generallandesarchiv Karlsruhe (GLAK)
B 82a / B 2, B 4, B 5
8 / 337, 358, 735−736, 1019, 1101, 1259−1260, 1533, 1557,
61 / 8238−8240
65 / 728
67 / 529, 730, 734−741
79 / 1606, 3387−3392
82a / 304
118 / 3, 5, 19−20, 166, 175−176, 185, 385, 473
123 / 228

Hauptstaatsarchiv Stuttgart (HStASt)
A 209, Bü 230, 466a−b, 679, 851, 851a
B 17, Bd. 1−2, 7−8, 10, 15−70, 98−99, 107
B 17, Bü 7, 10a−b, 670, 683
B 19, Bd. 1−9
B 19, U 110
B 29, Bü 24
B 37a, Bü 2, 6, 9−11, 15, 25, 118, 121, 197, 202, 231, 237, 247
B 40, Bü 120, 314, Bd. 1−4, 543−544
B 41, Bd. 3−4, 9, 11, 14, 16, 190
B 50, Bü 24
B 51, Bü 64c
B 57, Bü 2
B 58, Bü 137
B 60, Bü 140, 150a, 152, 155, 156, 156b, 212−213
B 61, III, Bd. 119, 128, 142, 145
H 14, Bd. 190
I 1, Bü 96b−c
I 13, Bü 3−4
I 30, Bü 4

Hessisches Hauptstaatsarchiv Wiesbaden (HHStAW)
115 / Villmar 12
171 Z 3832, Z 4218
339 / 138, 148, 149
340 / 1876
369 / 148, 372, 430, 432−434, 443−444, 446−448, 450, 453, 455−456

Landesarchiv Saarbrücken (LAS)
vdL 2752, 2757, 2777
22 / 4680
38 / 558, 769

Landeshauptarchiv Koblenz (LHAKO)
29 B 190
1 C 37, 41, 45, 103, 911, 2664, 2667–2668, 2671, 2673, 4323, 4324, 7744–7745, 7944, 8193,
    8401, 9191–9193, 12987, 13407, 13871, 14125–14126, 18827
51/52 / 66
33 / 8182, 8188, 8609, 8618, 8621, 8853, 8859, 8863, 12334
56 / 363, 419, 726, 1922, 2142, 2201
210 / 1646–1647, 2227
211 / 303, 2206, 2217, 2219, 2223–2229, 2231–2234, 2241–2246, 2263, 2275–2278, 2280–
    2294, 2975–2982, 2985, 3009, 3012–3013, 3026–3027, 3029, 3036
507 / 165
627 / 113
655 / 79
701 / 559

Pfarrarchiv Horb
Holl Regesten, 3 vols.
Taufbücher, 1610–41, 1641–1671

Spitalarchiv Horb
Rechnungen, 1607–1608

Staatsarchiv Augsburg (StAA)
VÖ Akten, 203, 309a, 371, 706, 786, 799, 819, 955, 972, 1127, 1387
VÖ Lit, 631–656, 740, 1386a
Vorderösterreich und Burgau, MüB, nos. 20, 20a, 27, 30, 36.1/2, 47, 99
Herrschaft Haunsheim, 674
Hochstift Augsburg, Neuburger Abgabe Akten 1221
Württembergische Extradition 1914, no. 674, 694
Schloßarchiv Rauhenzell, Ka VI A 1–2
Schloßarchiv Neuburg an der Kammel, G 2, F 13.1/2

Staatsarchiv Sigmaringen (StAS)
Ho 177, Bd. 1, no. 176
Ho 177, Bd. 2, no. 128
Ho 177, Bd. 4, nos. 159, 169

Stadtarchiv Burgau (StA Burgau)
Ratsprotokolle 1657

Stadtarchiv Günzburg (StA Günzburg)
5. 115, 154, 158, 175, 232, 237, 254, 260, 262, 267, 273, 276, 366–367a, 391, 426, 433,
    544, 553,
Ratsprotokolle, 1519–1627

Stadtarchiv Horb (StA Horb)
A 128, 285, 299, 308–320
B 1–3, 83, 202

Stadtarchiv Konstanz (StA Konstanz)
B I 80
B II, Bd. 75
B II, Missiven
K Fasz. 36

Stadtarchiv Oberndorf (StA Oberndorf)
A 128–132, 752, 754, 760
B 17–18

Stadtarchiv Reutlingen (StA Reutlingen)
K 7742–7745

Stadtarchiv Rottenburg (StA Rottenburg)
A 9.1/2
A 22, no. 1
A 25 R I
Film no. 21
Spitalarchivalien B 030–237, 030–238

Stadtarchiv Rottweil (StA Rottweil)
Criminalia II/I/V/1/12b, II/I/V/8/63

Stadtarchiv Stockach
C.VIII, 1–2

Stadtarchiv Trier (StA Trier)
2180b/124
DK, 54 K 657
Ms. 1393/103c
Nachlaß Milz, no. 18
SAM 60/1–18
T 174
Ta 100/2
V 22

Stadtbibliothek Trier (StB Trier)
Hs. 1409/2097
Hs. 1522/170
Hs. 1533/171
Hs. 1533a/171
Hs. 1534/166
Hs. 1900/1479
Hs. 2180a/45a

Tiroler Landesarchiv Innsbruck (TLA)
Allgemeines Leopoldinum, Kasten B, no. 133
Allgemeines Leopoldinum, Kasten C, no. 161
Allgemeines Leopoldinum, Littera C, no. 101

Alphabet. Leopoldinum, I/431, I/1034
Geheimer Rat (Hofregistratur), Aktenserie, Auslauf Regimentssachen, Kartons 639, 652
Geheimer Rat (Hofregistratur), Aktenserie, Einlauf Regimentssachen, Kartons 3–9, 118–122
Hofrat (Hofregistratur), Aktenserie, Auslauf Regimentssachen, Kartons 63, 67
Hs. 1390
Hs. 2402
Hs. 3984
Hs. 5923
Kopialbücher: An die fürstliche Durchlaucht, Causa Domini, Hofregistratur/Hofrat: Journale und Protokolle, Von der fürstlichen Durchlaucht
Kunstsachen, II 322, 389, 468, 488, 505
Pestarchiv, VI 12, XXVI 338, XXVIII 142, XXXVIII 498
Sammelakten, Reihe A, Abt. 6, Lage 3, no. 48
Sammelakten, Reihe A, Abt. 9, Lage 2, no. 48
Sammelakten, Reihe B, Abt. 6, Lage 3, no. 8,
Sammelakten, Reihe B, Abt. 6, Lage 3, nos. 25, 27, 29, 53
Sammelakten, Reihe B, Abt. 7, Lage 1, no. 5
Sammelakten, Reihe B, Abt. 7, Lage 3, no. 2
Sammelakten, Reihe B, Abt. 9, Lage 7, no. 3a
Sammelakten, Reihe B, Abt. 16, Lage 2, no. 4
Sammelakten, Reihe B, Abt. 16, Lage 4, no. 6–7
Select Ferdinandea, Karton 24

Universitätsarchiv Freiburg (UAF)
A 12 VI, VII
A 46/1, pars I–III
B 36/18

Universitätsarchiv Tübingen (UAT)
84/1, 84/24, 84/62
Findbuch 574/338

Universitätsbibliothek Tübingen
Mh 466 (Martin Crusius, *Diarium 1573–1604*, 9 Bd., ms.)

PRINTED SOURCES

"Annales Novesienses." In *Veterum scriptorum et monumentorum historicum dogmaticorum, moralium amplissima collectio,* ed. Edmund Martène and Ursinus Durand, 4:520–738 (Paris, 1729), repr. ed. New York, 1968.
Annuae litterae societatis Jesu anni 1581. Rome, 1583.
Annuae litterae societatis Jesu anni 1582. Rome, 1584.
Annuae litterae societatis Jesu anni 1583. Rome, 1585.
Annuae litterae societatis Jesu anni 1584. Rome, 1586.
Annuae litterae societatis Jesu anni 1585. Rome, 1584.

Annuae litterae societatis Jesu annorum 1586/1587. Rome 1589.

Annuae litterae societatis Jesu anni 1588. Rome, 1590

Annuae litterae societatis Jesu anni 1589. Rome, 1601.

Annuae litterae societatis Jesu annorum 1590/1591. Rome, 1604.

Annuae litterae societatis Jesu anni 1592. Rome, 1600.

Annuae litterae societatis Jesu anni 1593. Florence, 1601.

Annuae litterae societatis Jesu annorum 1594/1595. Naples, 1604.

Annuae litterae societatis Jesu anni 1596. Naples, 1605.

Annuae litterae societatis Jesu anni 1597. Naples: 1607.

Annuae litterae societatis Jesu anni 1598. Lyons, 1607.

Annuae litterae societatis Jesu anni 1599. Lyons, 1607.

Annuae litterae societatis Jesu anni 1600. Antwerp, 1618.

Annuae litterae societatis Jesu anni 1601. Antwerp, 1618.

Annuae litterae societatis Jesu anni 1602. Antwerp, 1618.

Annuae litterae societatis Jesu anni 1603. Douai, 1618.

Annuae litterae societatis Jesu anni 1604. Douai, 1618.

Annuae litterae societatis Jesu anni 1605. Douai, 1618.

Annuae litterae societatis Jesu anni 1606. Mainz, 1618.

Annuae litterae societatis Jesu anni 1607. Mainz, 1613.

Annuae litterae societatis Jesu anni 1608. Mainz, 1613.

Annuae litterae societatis Jesu anni 1609. Dillingen, n.d.

Annuae litterae societatis Jesu anni 1610. Dillingen, n.d.

Annuae litterae societatis Jesu anni 1611. Dillingen, n.d.

Annuae litterae societatis Jesu anni 1612. Lyons, 1618.

Annuae litterae societatis Jesu annorum 1613–1614. Lyons, 1619.

Annuae litterae societatis Jesu anni 1651. Dillingen, 1658.

Annuae litterae societatis Jesu anni 1652. Prague, n.d.

Annuae litterae societatis Jesu anni 1653. Prague, n.d.

Binsfeld, Peter. *Tractatus de confessionibus maleficorum et sagarum.* Trier, 1589.

———. *Tractat von Bekantnuß der Zauberer vnnd Hexen.* Trier, 1590.

———. *Tractatus de confessionibus maleficorum et sagarum,* 3rd ed. Trier, 1596.

———. *Tractat von Bekanntnuß der Zauberer und Hexen* (Trier, 1590), ed. Hiram Kümper. Vienna, 2004.

Blattau, Johann Jakob, ed. *Statuta synodalia, ordinationes et mandata archidioecesis trevirensis,* 9 vols. Trier, 1844–59.

Bocer, Henricus. *Disputationes de universo quo utimur iure,* (Tübingen 1607), ed. Johann Jakob Frisch. Strasbourg, 1634.

———. *Tractatus compendiosus de crimine majestatis.* Tübingen, 1608.

Bodin, Jean. *De la démonomanie des sorciers aveque la réfutation des opinion de Jean Wier* (Paris 1580), trans. Johann Fischart as *Vom außgelasnen wütigen Teuffelsheer* (Strasbourg, 1591), repr. ed. Graz, 1973.

Brower, Christoph, and Jacob Masen. *Antiquitatum et annalium Trevirensium libiri XXV (Anitquitates),* 2 vols. Louvain, 1670.

Bürckhle, Joseph Anton. *Des Freyen kayserlichen Land-Gerichts in Ober und Niedern*

Schwaben, auf Leykircher-Hayd und in der Gepürß Gerichtlicher Process, 2 vols. Frankfurt, 1742.

Burgermeister, Johann Stephan. *Teutsches corpus iuris publici et privati oder Codex diplomaticus*, 2 vols. Ulm, 1717.

Carpzov, Benedict. *Practicae novae imperialis Saxonicae rerum criminalium* (Wittenberg 1635), ed. J. Böhmer. Frankfurt am Main, 1758.

Clarus, Julius. *Sententiarum libri quinque sive practica criminalis* (Venice, 1568). Frankfurt, 1627.

Corpus iuris canonci (Leipzig, 1879), 2nd ed., 2 vols., ed. Emil Friedberg, repr. ed. Graz, 1959.

Cratepolius, Petrus. *De Germaniae episcopis et orthodoxis doctoribus.* Cologne, 1592.

Crusius, Martin. "Annales suevici," 2 vols. (Frankfurt am Main, 1595–96). In *Schwäbische Chronick*, 2 vols., ed. Johann Jakob Moser. Frankfurt am Main, 1733.

———. *Diarium*, 4 vols., ed. Wilhelm Göz et al. Tübingen, 1927–61.

Damhouder, Joost de. *Praxis rerum criminalium* (Antwerpen 1556; Antwerp, 1601), repr, ed. Aalen, 1978.

Delrio, Martin. *Disquisitionum magicarum libri sex* (Löwen 1599). Cologne, 1720.

———. *Investigations into Magic*, ed. and trans. P. G. Maxwell-Stuart. Manchester, 2000.

Die Chronik der Grafen von Zimmern, 3 vols., ed. Hansmartin Decker-Hauff and Rudolf Seigel. Darmstadt, 1964–72.

Die Peinliche Gerichtsordnung Kaiser Karls V. (Carolina) (Mainz 1533), 6th ed., ed. Arthur Kaufmann and Gustav Radbruch. Stuttgart, 1991.

Ein erschröckliche Geschicht vom Teufel und einer Unhulden, beschechen zu Schilta bey Rotweil in der Karwoche. 1533. Jar (n.p., 1533). Zentralbibliothek Zürich, PAS II 12/18.

Ein wunderbarlich erschrockenlich handelung, so sich auff den Grün Dornstag dis iars ynn dem Stedlein Schiltach mit einer bösen brunst durch den bösen geist gestifft begeben hat (n.p, 1533). Staatsbibliothek Berlin, Historische Flugschriften, 1533, no. 3.

Erasmus von Rotterdam: Opus epistolarum, 12 vols., ed. Percy Allen. Oxford, 1906–58.

Erbärmliche und Erschröckliche Zeittung von dem großen Wasserguß so in der Stadt Horb an dem Necker gelegen den 23. Juli dieses jetz laufenden 1584 Jahrs augenblicklich uberhandgenommen (n.p., 1584). Württembergische Landesbibliothek Stuttgart, HBF 2470.

Farinaci, Prospero. *Praxis et theoricae criminalis amplissimae libri duo* (Frankfurt am Main, 1597). Frankfurt am Main, 1728.

Feßler, Longinus. *Wunderwürckender auf dem Heil. Calvari-Berg entsprungener Gnadenbrunnen. Das ist Gründlicher Bericht und außführliche Beschreibung deß Hochheiligen und Wunderthätigen Hertz- und Seitenbluts Christi Jesu.* Altdorf, 1735.

Gaisser, Georg. "Tagbücher (1621–1655)." In *Quellensammlung der badischen Landesgeschichte*, 4 vols., ed. Franz Josef Mone, 2:159–528. Karlsruhe, 1848–67.

Gerbert, Martin. *Daemonurgia theologice expensa.* St. Blasien, 1776.

———. *Historia nigrae silvae ordinis S. Benedicti coloniae*, 3 vols. St. Blasien, 1783–88.

Goedelmann, Johann Georg. *Tractatus de magis* (Nürnberg 1584). Trans. as *Von Zäuberen, Hexen und Unholden.* Frankfurt am Main, 1592.

Goldast, Melchior. *Rechtliches Bedencken von Confiscation der Zauberer und Hexen-Güther.* Bremen, 1661.

Hoffmann, Paul, and Peter Dohms, eds. *Die Mirakelbücher des Klosters Eberhardsklausen.* Publikationen der Gesellschaft für rheinische Geschichtskunde, vol. 64. Düsseldorf, 1988.

Kramer, Heinrich (Institoris, Henricus). *Der Hexenhammer, Malleus Maleficarum (Straßburg 1486),* ed., trans., and comp. Wolfgang Behringer, Günter Jerouschek, and Werner Tschacher. Munich, 2000.

Keller, Adam. *De jure succendi ab intestato, das ist von Erbfalls Recht tractatus brevis.* Frankfurt, 1618.

———. *De officiis juridico-politicis chiragogici libri tres.* Constance, 1607.

Kolleffel, Johann Lambert. *Geographische und topographische Beschreibung der Markgrafschaft Burgau 1749–1753.* Photographic reprint of Hans Frei, ed., *Schwäbische Städte und Dörfer um 1750.* Weißenhorn, 1974.

Marsigli, Ippolito. *Practica criminalis, (Lyon 1542).* Cologne, 1581.

Mather, Cotton. *Magnalia Christi Americana* (London 1702), ed. Kenneth Murdock. Cambridge, Mass., 1977.

Mechtel, Johannes. *Die Limburger Chronik.* Wiesbaden, 1909.

Meder, David. *Acht Hexenpredigten.* Leipzig, 1605.

Neller, Georg Christoph. *Conatus exegeticus.* Trier, 1779.

Pleier, Cornelius. *Malleus judicum, Das ist: Gesetzhammer der unbarmherztigen Hexenrichter.* N.p., n.d. (presumably Nuremberg, 1628).

Reiffenberg, Friedrich. *Historia societatis Jesu ad Rhenum inferiorem.* Cologne, 1764.

Roberg, Burkhard, ed. *Geheime Nuntiaturberichte aus Deutschland: Kölner Nuntiatur, II/3, Nuntius Ottavio Frangipani.* Munich, 1971.

Rudolph, Friedrich, ed. *Quellen zur Rechts- und Wirtschaftsgeschichte der rheinischen Städte. Kurtrierische Städte. Volume 1: Trier.* Publikationen der Gesellschaft für rheinische Geschichtskunde, vol. 29. Bonn, 1915.

Scotti, Johann Jakob, ed. *Sammlung der Gesetze und Verordnungen welche in dem vormaligen Churfürstenthum Trier über Gegenstände der Landeshoheit, Verfassung, Verwaltung und Rechtspflege ergangen sind,* 3 vols. Düsseldorf, 1832.

Scheffer, Andreas Franz Xaver. *Ausführlicher Bericht der berühmten in der Reichsgefürsteten Marggrafschaft Burgau auf der kayserlichen Land-Strassen nächst dem Dorf Lempach in Schwaben gelegenen Königlichen-Lothringischen und großhertzoglich thoscanischen Wallfahrt Königin-Bild.* Augsburg, 1740.

Schnyder, André, ed. *Malleus Maleficarum. Faksimile der Ausgabe Straßburg 1486* (Heinrich Kramer), 2 vols. Göppingen, 1991, 1993.

Spee, Friedrich. "Cautio criminalis (Rinteln 1631)." In *Friedrich Spee. Sämtliche Schriften,* vol. 3, ed. Theo G. M. van Oorschot. Tübingen, 1992.

Tanner, Adam. *Universa theologia scholastica, speculativa, practica,* 4 vols. Ingolstadt, 1626.

Tschamser, Malachia. *Annales oder Jahrs-Geschichten der Baarfüeseren oder Minderen Brüdern zu Thann* (Thann, 1724), 2 vols., repr. ed. Colmar, 1864.

Undergerichtsordnung des Ertzstiffts Trier. Mainz, 1537.

Voltmer, Rita, and Karl Weisenstein, eds. *Das Hexenregister des Claudius Musiel. Ein Verzeichnis von hingerichteten und besagten Personen aus dem Trierer Land (1586–1594).* Trier, 1996.

Wahrhaffte und glaubwirdige Zeytung von hundert und vir und dreyssig Unholden, so umb ihrer Zaubery halben, diß verschinen LXXXII Jars zu Gefencknus gebracht. Strasbourg, 1583. Bayerische Staatsbibliothek München, Sign. Res. 4 Phys.m. 113/27.

Wahrhafftig geschicht und eigentliche Beschreibung von den Hexen Weybern, so man zu Rottenburg am Necker und in Westfahlen, Prißgew und anderstwo verbrand hat, dises 1596 Jar in Reimen weiß verfast. Innsbruck, 1596. Württembergische Landesbibliothek Stuttgart, Crim.R.qt K 46–19.

Wahrhafftige und ein erschröckliche Neuwe zeitung des grossen Wasserguß so den 15. May diß lauffenden 78. Jahrs zu Horb geschehen. Antwerp, 1578. Zentralbibliothek Zürich MSF 27.

Weyer, Johann. *De praestigiis daemonum* (Basel, 1583), ed. and trans. George Mora and H. C. Eric Midelfort as *Witches, Devils and Doctors in the Renaissance: Johann Weyer, De praestigiis daemonum.* Binghamton, N.Y., 1991.

Wyttenbach, Johann Hugo, and Michael Franz Josef Müller, eds. *Gesta Trevirorum,* 3 vols. Trier, 1838/39.

Zimmersche Chronik, 3 vols., ed. Karl August Barack. Freiburg, 1881.

Zwo Newe Zeittungen, was man Hexen oder Unholden verbrendt hat. N.p., 1580.

SECONDARY LITERATURE

Abel, Wilhelm. *Massenarmut und Hungerkrisen im vorindustriellen Europa.* Hamburg: Parey, 1974.

Abmeier, Karlies. *Der Trierer Kurfürst Philipp Christoph von Sötern und der westfälische Friede.* Münster: Aschendorff, 1986.

Ahrendt-Schulte, Ingrid. "Schadenzauber und Konflikte: Sozialgeschichte von Frauen im Spiegel der Hexenprozesse des 16. Jahrhunderts in der Grafschaft Lippe." In *Wandel der Geschlechterbeziehungen zu Beginn der Neuzeit,* ed. Heide Wunder and Christina Vanja, 198–228. Frankfurt am Main: Suhrkamp, 1991.

———. *Zauberinnen in der Stadt Horn (1554–1603).* Frankfurt am Main: Campus-Verlag, 1997.

Albert, Anna. "Die Verwaltung der Stadt Saarburg in kurfürstlicher Zeit." *Heimatbuch des Kreises Saarburg* 11 (1967): 10–14.

Ammann, Hartmann. "Der Innsbrucker Hexenprozess von 1485." *Zeitschrift des Ferdinandeums für Tirol und Vorarlberg* 34, no. 3 (1890): 1–91.

Anglo, Sidney, ed. *The Damned Art: Essays in the Literature of Witchcraft.* London: Routledge and Kegan Paul, 1977.

Ankarloo, Bengt. "Witch Trials in Northern Europe." In *Witchcraft and Magic in Europe: The Period of the Witch Trials,* ed. Bengt Ankarloo and Stuart Clark, 53–95. Philadelphia: Penn, 2002.

Antoni, Erhard. *Studien zur Agrargeschichte von Kurtrier.* Bonn: Röhrscheid, 1916.

Aubin, Herrmann. "Das Reich und die Territorien." In *Geschichte des Rheinlandes von der ältesten Zeit bis zur Gegenwart*, 2 vols., ed. Gesellschaft für rheinische Geschichtevols, 2:1–50. Essen: Baedecker, 1922.

Auer, Paul. *Geschichte der Stadt Günzburg*. Günzburg: Donau-Verlag, 1963.

Bächtold-Stäubli, Hanns. "Art. Hämmerlein." In *Handwörterbuch des deutschen Aberglaubens*, 10 vols., ed. Hanns Bächtold-Stäubli and Eduard Hoffmann-Krayer, 3:1376–78. Berlin: Walter de Gruyter, 1929–42.

Bahrdt, Hans Paul. *Schlüsselbegriffe der Soziologie*, 6th ed. Munich: Beck, 1994.

Barczyk, Michael. "Stadt Waldsee." In *Hexen und Hexenverfolgung im deutschen Südwesten, Aufsatzband*, ed. Sönke Lorenz, 253–56. Ostfildern: Cantz, 1994.

Barth, Jakob. *Geschichte der Stadt Stockach im Hegau bis zum Jahr 1850*. Stockach: Engler, 1894.

Bátori, Ingrid. "Schultheiß und Hexenausschuß in Rhens 1628–1632." In *Hexenglaube und Hexenprozesse im Raum Rhein-Mosel-Saar*, ed. Gunther Franz and Franz Irsigler, 195–224. Trierer Hexenprozesse 1. Trier: Spee, 1995.

Bauer, Joseph. *Philipp von Sötern, geistlicher Kurfürst zu Trier und seine Politik während des dreissigjährigen Krieges*, 2 vols. Speyer: Jäger, 1897/1914.

Baumgarten, Achim. *Hexenwahn und Hexenverfolgung im Naheraum*. Frankfurt am Main: Lang, 1987.

Beattie, John. *Other Cultures: Aims, Methods and Achievements in Social Anthropology*, 5th ed. London: Routledge, 1992.

Beck, Paul. *Ausgewählte Aufsätze zur Geschichte Oberschwabens*. Bad Buchau: Federsee-Verlag, 1985.

Becker, Thomas P. "Hexenverfolgung im Erzstift Köln." In *Hexenverfolgung im Rheinland. Ergebnisse neuerer Lokal- und Regionalstudien*, ed. Wolfgang Isenberg and Georg Mölich, 89–136. Bergisch Gladbach: Thomas-Morus-Akademie Bensberg, 1996.

Behringer, Wolfgang. "'Erhob sich das ganze Land zu ihrer Ausrottung,' Hexenprozesse und Hexenverfolgungen in Europa." In *Hexenwelten*, ed. Richard van Dülmen, 131–69. Frankfurt am Main: Fischer, 1987.

———. "Geschichte der Hexenforschung." In *Wider alle Hexerei und Teufelswerk*, ed. Sönke Lorenz and Jürgen Michael Schmidt, 485–668. Ostfildern: Thorbecke, 2004.

———. "Zur Haltung Adam Tanners in der Hexenfrage." In *"Vom Unfug des Hexen-Processes": Gegner der Hexenverfolgung von Johann Weyer bis Friedrich Spee*, ed. Hartmut Lehmann and Otto Ulbricht, 161–83. Wiesbaden: Harrassowitz, 1992.

———. *Hexen. Glaube, Verfolgung, Vermarktung*, 2nd ed. Munich: Beck, 2000.

———, ed. *Hexen und Hexenprozesse in Deutschland*, 5th ed. Munich: Deutscher Taschenbuch Verlag, 2001.

———. "Hexenverfolgungen im Spiegel zeitgenössischer Publizistik. Die 'Erweytterte Unholden Zeyttung' von 1590." *Oberbayerisches Archiv* 109 (1984): 339–60.

———. "Hochstift Augsburg." In *Wider alle Hexerei und Teufelswerk*, ed. Sönke Lorenz and Jürgen Michael Schmidt, 355–64. Ostfildern: Thorbecke, 2004.

———. "Kinderhexenprozesse." *Zeitschrift für Historische Forschung* 16 (1989): 31–47.

———. "Das 'reichskhündig Exempel' von Trier. Zur paradigmatischen Rolle einer Hexenverfolgung in Deutschland." In *Hexenglaube und Hexenprozesse im Raum*

Rhein-Mosel-Saar, Trierer Hexenprozesse, ed. Gunther Franz and Franz Irsigler, 1:436–47. Trier: Spee, 1995.

———. *Shaman of Oberstdorf: Chonrad Stoeckhlin and the Phantoms of the Night.* Charlottesville: University Press of Virginia, 1998.

———. *Witchcraft Persecutions in Bavaria.* Cambridge: Cambridge University Press, 1997.

———. *Witches and Witch-Hunts: A Global History.* Cambridge: Polity, 2004.

Bellinghausen, Hans, ed. *2000 Jahre Koblenz.* Boppard: Boldt, 1971.

Bender-Wittmann, Ursula. "Gender in der Hexenforschung: Ansätze und Perspektiven." In *Geschlecht, Magie und Hexenverfolgung, Hexenforschung,* ed. Ingrid Ahrendt-Schulte et al., 7:13–37. Bielefeld: Verlag für Regionalgeschichte, 2002.

———. "Hexenglaube als Lebensphilosophie. Informeller Hexereidiskurs und nachbarschaftliche Hexereikontrolle in Lemgo 1628–1637." In *Hexenverfolgung und Regionalgeschichte. Die Grafschaft Lippe im Vergleich,* ed. Jürgen Scheffler, Gerd Schwerhoff and Gisela Wilbertz, 107–35. Bielefeld: Verlag für Regionalgeschichte, 1994.

Berner, Herbert. "Die Landgrafschaft Nellenburg." In *Vorderösterreich,* 2nd ed., ed. Friedrich Metz, 613–36. Freiburg im Breisgau: Rombach, 1967.

———. "Die Landgrafschaft Nellenburg und die Reichsritterschaft des Kantons Hegau-Bodensee." *Hegau* 10 (1965): 57–86.

Bernheim, Ernst. *Lehrbuch der Historischen Methode und der Geschichtsphilosophie,* 6th ed. Leipzig: Dunker and Humblot, 1908.

Bettingen, Julius. *Geschichte der Stadt und des Amtes St. Wendel.* St. Wendel: Bettingen, 1865.

Bever, Eduard W. M. *Witchcraft in Early Modern Württemberg.* Princeton, N.J.: Princeton University Press, 1983.

Biedermann, Hans. *Knaurs Lexikon der Symbole.* Munich: Knaur, 1989.

Biener, Friedrich August. *Beiträge zur Geschichte des Inquisitionsprozesses und der Geschworenengerichte* (Leipzig, 1827), repr. ed. Aalen: Scientia, 1965.

Biesel, Elisabeth. *Hexenjustiz, Volksmagie und soziale Konflikte im lothringischen Raum.* Trierer Hexenprozesse 3. Trier: Spee, 1997.

———. "'Die Pfeifer seint alle uff den baumen gesessen.' Der Hexensabbat in der Vorstellungswelt einer ländlichen Bevölkerung." In *Methoden und Konzepte der historischen Hexenforschung,* ed. Gunther Franz and Franz Irsigler, 289–302. Trierer Hexenprozesse 4. Trier: Spee, 1998.

Birlinger, Anton. *Volksthümliches aus Schwaben,* 2 vols. Freiburg im Breisgau: Herder, 1861–62.

Bittmann, Markus. "Parteigänger—Indifferente—Opponenten. Der schwäbische Adel und das Haus Habsburg." In *Die Habsburger im deutschen Südwesten,* ed. Franz Quarthal and Gerhard Faix, 75–88. Stuttgart: Thorbecke, 2000.

Blauert, Andreas. *Frühe Hexenverfolgungen.* Hamburg: Junius, 1989.

Blickle, Peter. "Kommunalismus, Parlamentarismus, Republikanismus." *Historische Zeitschrift* 242 (1986): 529–56.

———. *Landschaften im Alten Reich.* Munich: Beck, 1973.

————. *Obedient Germans? A Rebuttal.* Charlottesville: University Press of Virginia, 1997.

————. "Die Reformation vor dem Hintergrund von Kommunalisierung und Christianisierung." In *Kommunalisierung und Christianisierung*, ed. Peter Blickle and Johannes Kunisch, 9–28. N.p.: n.p., 1989.

————. *Die Revolution von 1525.* Munich: Oldenburg, 1977.

Bloch, Marc. "Pour une histoire comparée des sociétés européennes." *Revue de Synthèse Historique* 46 (1928): 15–50.

Bodmann, Franz Joseph. *Rheingauische Alterhümer*, 2 vols. Mainz, 1819.

Bohl, Peter. *Die Stadt Stockach im 17. und 18. Jahrhundert, Strukturen und Funktionen einer Oberamtsstadt, Verwaltung-Wirtschaft-Gesellschaft-Bevölkerung.* Constance: Hartung-Gorre, 1987.

Bosl, Karl. "Eine Geschichte der deutschen Landgemeinde." *Zeitschrift für Agrargeschichte und Agrarsoziologie* 9 (1961): 129–42.

Bossier, Hans. "Genealogisches Exzerpt der Büchel-Chronik von Münstermaifeld." *Mitteilungen der westdeutschen Gesellschaft für Familienkunde* 67–68 (1979–80): 211–15.

Boyer, Paul, and Stephen Nissenbaum. *Salem Possessed: The Social Origins of Witchcraft.* Cambridge, Mass.: Harvard University Press, 1974.

Braembussche, Antoon van den. "Historical Explanation and Comparative Method. Towards a Theory of the History of Society." *Historisk Tidsskrift* 28 (1989): 1–24.

Braun, Rudolf, and David Gugleri. *Macht des Tanzes—Tanz der Mächtigen.* Munich: Beck, 1993.

Breisdorff, Nikolaus. "Die Hexenprozesse im Herzogtum Luxemburg." *Publications de la Section Historique* 16 (1860): 143–92.

Briggs, Robin. *Witches and Neighbours.* London: HarperCollins, 1996.

Broedel, Hans Peter. *The Malleus Maleficarum and the Construction of Witchcraft.* Manchester: Manchester University Press, 2003.

Brommer, Peter. *Kurtrier am Ende des Alten Reiches.* Mainz: Selbstverlag der Gesellschaft für mittelrheinische Kirchengeschichte, 2008.

Bücking, Jürgen. *Frühabsolutismus und Kirchenreform in Tirol (1565–1665).* Wiesbaden: Steiner, 1972.

Bumiller, Casimir. "'Ich bin des Teufels, wann er nur käm und holte mich!': Zur Geschichte der Hexenverfolgung in Hohenzollern," *Hohenzollerische Heimat* 33 (1983): 2–7.

Burgard, Friedhelm. "Auseinandersetzungen zwischen Stadtgemeinde und Erzbischof (1307–1500)." In *Trier im Mittelalter*, ed. Hans Hubert Anton and Alfred Haverkamp, 295–395. Trier: Spee, 1996.

Burke, Peter. "The Comparative Approach to European Witchcraft." In *Early Modern Witchcraft: Centres and Peripheries*, 2nd ed., ed. Bengt Ankarloo and Gustav Henningsen, 435–41. Oxford: Clarendon Press, 1993.

Burr, George Lincoln. "The Fate of Dietrich Flade." *Papers of the American Historical Association* 5 (1891): 189–243.

Byloff, Fritz. *Hexenglaube und Hexenverfolgung in den österreichischen Alpenländern.* Berlin: Walter de Gruyter, 1934.

———. *Volkskundliches aus Strafprozessen der Österreichischen Alpenländer mit besonderer Berücksichtigung der Zauberei- und Hexenprozesse 1455–1850*. Berlin: Walter de Gruyter, 1929.

Calo, Jeanne. *La création de la femme chez Michelet*. Paris: Nizet, 1975.

Caro Baroja, Julio. *Las brujas y so mundo*. Madrid: Revista de Occidente, 1961.

Clark, Stuart. *Thinking with Demons: The Idea of Witchcraft in Early Modern Europe*. Oxford: Clarendon Press, 1997.

Cohen, Deborah, and Maura O'Connor, eds. *Comparison and History: Europe in Cross-National Perspective*. New York: Routledge, 2004

———. "Introduction. Comparative History, Cross-National History, Transnational History—Definitions." In *Comparison and History: Europe in Cross-National Perspective*, ed. Deborah Cohen and Maura O'Connor, ix–xxiv. New York: Routledge, 2004.

Cohn, Norman. *Europe's Inner Demons*. New York: Basic Books, 1975.

Danckert, Werner. *Unehrliche Leute. Die verfemten Berufe*. Bern: Francke, 1963.

Daniel, Ute. "Clio unter Kulturschock. Zu den aktuellen Debatten der Geschichtswissenschaft." *Geschichte in Wissenschaft und Unterricht* 48 (1997): 195–218, 259–78.

Daum, Werner, et al. "Fallobst oder Steinschlag: Einleitende Überlegungen zum historischen Vergleich." In *Vergleichende Perspektiven—Perspektiven des Vergleichs. Studien zur europäischen Geschichte von der Spätantike bis ins 20. Jahrhundert*, ed. Helga Schnabel-Schüle, 1–21. Mainz: von Zabern, 1998.

Daxelmüller, Christoph. *Aberglaube, Hexenzauber, Höllenängste. Eine Geschichte der Magie*. Munich: Deutscher Taschenbuch-Verlag, 1996.

Decker, Rainer. "Teuflische Besessenheit und Hexenverfolgung. Paderborn, Rietberg und Reckenberg 1657–1660." In *Hexenverfolgung und Regionalgeschichte. Die Grafschaft Lippe im Vergleich*, ed. Jürgen Scheffler, Gerd Schwerhoff, and Gisela Wilbertz, 297–310. Bielefeld: Verlag für Regionalgeschichte, 1994.

Degn, Christian, et al., eds. *Hexenprozesse*. Studien zur Volkskunde und Kulturgeschichte 12. Neumünster: Wachholtz, 1983.

Delumeau, Jean. *Angst im Abendland*, 2 vols. Hamburg: Rowohlt, 1985.

Dienst, Heide. "Hexenprozesse auf dem Gebiet der heutigen Bundesländer Vorarlberg, Tirol (mit Südtirol), Salzburg, Nieder- und Oberösterreich sowie des Burgenlandes." In *Hexen und Zauberer*, ed. Helfried Valentinisch, 265–85. Graz: Leykam, 1987.

———. "Magische Vorstellungen und Hexenverfolgungen in den österreichischen Ländern (15. bis 18. Jahrhundert)." In *Wellen der Verfolgung in der österreichischen Geschichte*, ed. Erich Zöllner. Vienna: Österreichischer Bundesverlag, 1986.

Dillinger, Johannes. "Adam Tanner und Friedrich Spee." *Spee Jahrbuch* 6 (2000): 31–58.

———. "Austrian Western Territories, Witchcraft Trials." In *Encyclopedia of Witchcraft: The Western Tradition*, ed. Richard Golden, 1:75–76. Santa Barbara: ABC-Clio, 2006.

———. "Binsfeld, Peter." In *Encyclopedia of Witchcraft: The Western Tradition*, ed. Richard Golden, 1:122–25. Santa Barbara: ABC-Clio, 2006.

———. *"Böse Leute." Hexenverfolgungen in Schwäbisch-Österreich und Kurtrier im Vergleich*. Trier: Spee, 1999.

————. "Concerning Witches and Witch Busters: Interdisciplinary and International Cooperation." *Folklore* 108 (1997): 111–12.

————. "'Das Ewige Leben und fünfzehntausend Gulden.' Schatzgräberei in Württemberg 1606–1770." In *Zauberer—Selbstmörder—Schatzsucher. Magische Kultur und behördliche Kontrolle im frühneuzeitlichen Württemberg*, ed. Johannes Dillinger, 221–97. Trier: Kliomedia, 2003.

————. "Ein Fridinger Hexenprozeß." *Tuttlinger Heimatblätter, Neue Folge* 57 (1994): 133–38.

————. "Grafschaft Hohenberg." In *Hexen und Hexenverfolgung im deutschen Südwesten, Aufsatzband*, ed. Sönke Lorenz, 245–51. Ostfildern: Cantz, 1994.

————. *Hexen und Hexenprozesse in Fridingen*. Eigeltingen: Heimatkreis Fridingen, 1997.

————. "Hexen und Hexenverfolger in Obernau." In *Obernau 1145–1995*, ed. Karlheinz Geppert, 265–70. Rottenburg: Festausschuss 850-Jahrfeier Obernau, 1995.

————. *Hexen und Magie*, Historische Einführungen, vol. 3, ed. Andreas Gestrich et al. Frankfurt am Main: Campus, 2007.

————. "Der Hexenprozeß gegen Christina Rauscher." *Jahrbuch Landkreis Freudenstadt* (1994–95): 119–25.

————. *Hexenprozesse in Horb*, Veröffentlichungen des Kultur- und Museumsvereins Horb am Neckar e.V., vol. 11, ed. Joachim Lipp. Horb: Kultur- und Museumsverein, 1994.

————. "Die Hexenverfolgung in der Landvogtei Schwaben im 16. und 17. Jahrhundert." In *Frühe Hexenverfolgung in Ravensburg und am Bodensee*, ed. Andreas Schmauder, 125–47. Constance: Universitätsverlag Konstanz Verlags-Gesellschaft, 2001.

————. "Hexenverfolgung und Magie in geschlechtergeschichtlicher Perspektive." *Zeitschrift für Geschichtswissenschaft* 44 (1996): 717–19.

————. "Hexenverfolgungen in der Grafschaft Hohenberg." In *Zum Feuer verdammt*, ed. Johannes Dillinger, Thomas Fritz, and Wolfgang Mährle, 1–161. Hexenforschung 2. Stuttgart: Steiner, 1998.

————. "Hexenverfolgungen in Städten." In *Methoden und Konzepte der historischen Hexenforschung*, ed. Gunther Franz and Franz Irsigler, 129–65. Trierer Hexenprozesse 4. Trier: Spee, 1998.

————. "Der Hohenstaufen als Hexentanzplatz." *Hohenstaufen-Helfenstein* 4 (1994): 172–74.

————. "Die letzte Hexe. Hexen aus Weiler und Hexen auf der Weilerburg." In *Weiler 1244–1994, Rottenburg am Neckar*, ed. Karlheinz Geppert, 152–55. Weiler: Festausschuss 750-Jahrfeier Weiler, 1994.

————. "Das magische Gericht. Religion, Magie und Ideologie." In *Hexenprozesse und Gerichtspraxis*, ed. Herbert Eiden, 545–93. Trierer Hexenprozesse 6. Trier: Spee, 2002.

————. "Nemini non ad manus adesse deberet Cautio illa Criminalis. Eine frühe Spee-Rezeption in der dörflichen Prozeßpraxis Südwestdeutschlands." In *Methoden und Konzepte der historischen Hexenforschung*, ed. Gunther Franz and Franz Irsigler, 277–86. Trierer Hexenprozesse 4. Trier: Spee, 1998.

————. "Nichtseßhafte Frauen im Raum Horb-Freudenstadt um das Jahr 1600." *Jahrbuch Landkreis Freudenstadt* (1995–96): 145–50.

————. *Die politische Repräsentation der Landbevölkerung. Neuengland und Europa in der Frühen Neuzeit.* Stuttgart: Steiner, 2008.

————. "Procès de sorcellerie, torture, bûchers: Une approche pour comprendre l'étrange." In *Incubi succubi. Les sorcières et leurs bourreaux, hier et aujourd'hui,* ed. Rita Voltmer, 61–69. Luxemburg: Musée d'Histoire de la Ville, 2000.

————. "Richter als Angeklagte: Hexenprozesse gegen herrschaftliche Amtsträger in Kurtrier und Schwäbisch-Österreich." In *Vergleichende Perspektiven—Perspektiven des Vergleichs. Studien zur europäischen Geschichte von der Spätantike bis ins 20. Jahrhundert,* ed. Helga Schnabel-Schüle, 123–69. Mainz: von Zabern, 1998.

————. "Schwäbisch-Österreich." In *Wider alle Hexerei und Teufelswerk,* ed. Sönke Lorenz and Jürgen Michael Schmidt, 283–94. Ostfildern: Thorbecke, 2004.

————. "Terrorists and Witches: Popular Ideas of Evil in the Early Modern Period." *History of European Ideas* 30 (2004): 167–82.

————. "Town Meeting Republics." *Yearbook of German-American Studies* 37 (2002): 25–39.

————. "Tanner, Adam." In *Encyclopedia of Witchcraft: The Western Tradition,* ed. Richard Golden, 4:1106–7. Santa Barbara: ABC-Clio, 2006.

————. "Trier, Witchcraft Trials." In *Encyclopedia of Witchcraft: The Western Tradition,* ed. Richard Golden, 4:1135–36. Santa Barbara: ABC-Clio, 2006.

Dillinger, Johannes, and Petra Feld. "Treasure-Hunting: A Magical Motif in Law, Folklore, and Mentality. Württemberg, 1606–1770." *German History* 20 (2002): 161–84.

Dinges, Martin. *Der Maurermeister und der Finanzrichter. Ehre, Geld und soziale Kontrolle im Paris des 18. Jahrhunderts.* Göttingen: Vandenhoeck and Ruprecht, 1994.

Dirks, Maria. *Das Landrecht im Kurfürstentum Trier.* Saarbrücken: Heymann 1965.

Drechsler, Wolfgang. "The Use of Spectral Evidence in the Salem Witchcraft trials: A Miscarriage of Justice?" In *Die Salemer Hexenverfolgungen,* ed. Winfried Herget. Trier: Wissenschaftlicher Verlag Trier, 1994.

Droege, Georg. "Die kulturräumliche Stellung des Mosellandes in rechts- und verfassungsgeschichtlicher Sicht." In *Festschrift Matthias Zenders, Studien zur Volkskultur, Sprache und Sprachgeschichte,* 2 vols., ed. Edith Ennen and Günther Wiegelmann, 1:123–32. Bonn: Röhrscheid, 1972.

Duerr, Hans Peter. *Dreamtime: Concerning the Boundary between Wilderness and Civilization.* Oxford: Blackwell, 1985.

Duhr, Bernhard. *Geschichte der Jesuiten in den Ländern deutscher Zunge,* 4 vols. Freiburg im Breisgau: Herder, 1907–28.

————. *Die Stellung der Jesuiten in den deutschen Hexenprozessen.* Cologne: Bachem, 1900.

Dülmen, Richard van. "Die Dienerin des Bösen." *Zeitschrift für Historische Forschung* 18 (1991): 385–98.

————. ed. *Hexenwelten.* Frankfurt am Main: Fischer, 1987.

————. "Imaginationen des Teuflischen: Nächtliche Zusammenkünfte, Hexentänze,

Teufelssabbate." In *Hexenwelten,* ed. Richard van Dülmen, 94–130. Frankfurt am Main: Fischer, 1987.

———. *Kultur und Alltag in der Frühen Neuzeit,* 3 vols. Munich: Beck, 1990–94.

Dupont-Bouchat, Marie-Sylvie. "La répression de la sorcellerie dans le Duché de Luxembourg aux 16e et 17e siècles. Une analyse des structures de pouvoir et leur fonctionnement dans le cadre de la chasse aux sorcières." Ph.D. diss., Louvain, 1977.

Durkheim, Emile. *The Rules of Sociological Method* (Paris, 1895), trans. Basingstoke: Macmillan, 1992.

Eberl, Immo. *Geschichte des Benediktinerinnenklosters Ursprung bei Schelklingen 1127–1806.* Stuttgart: Müller und Gräff, 1978.

Ebert, Johann, and Ferdinand Ebert. "Ein Gang durch Montabaurs tausendjährige Geschichte." In *Montabaur und der Westerwald (930–1930),* ed. Stadtverwaltung Monatbaur, 28–88. Feudingen: Buchdruck- und Verlagsanstalt, 1930.

Eckstein, F. "Art. Brot." In *Handwörterbuch des deutschen Aberglaubens,* 10 vols., ed. Hanns Bächtold-Stäubli and Eduard Hoffmann-Krayer, 1:1590–1659. Berlin: Walter de Gruyter, 1929–42.

Eerden, P. C. van der. "Der Teufelspakt bei Petrus Binsfeld und Cornelius Loos." In *Hexenglaube und Hexenprozesse im Raum Rhein-Mosel-Saar,* ed. Gunther Franz and Franz Irsigler, 51–71. Trierer Hexenprozesse 1. Trier: Spee, 1995.

Ehrenreich, Barbara, and Deirdre English. *Witches, Midwives and Nurses,* 2nd ed. London: Compendium, 1974.

Eiler, Klaus. *Stadtfreiheit und Landesherrschaft in Koblenz.* Wiesbaden: Steiner, 1980.

Eitel, Peter. "Ravensburg und Vorderösterreich." In *Vorderösterreich in der frühen Neuzeit,* ed. Hans Maier and Volker Press, 263–70. Sigmaringen: Thorbecke, 1989.

Ellerhorst, Friedrich. "Karl Kaspar von der Leyen (1652–1676)." *Neues Trierisches Jahrbuch* (1976): 41–50.

Espagne, Michel. "Sur les limites du comparatisme en histoire culturelle." *Géneses* 17 (1994): 112–21.

Evans, Robert John Weston. *Rudolf II and His World: A Study in Intellectual History, 1576–1612.* Oxford: Clarendon Press, 1973.

Evans-Pritchard, Edward E. "The Morphology and Function of Magic: A Comparative Study of Trobriand and Zande Ritual and Spells." *American Anthropologist,* New Series 31 (1929): 616–41. Repr. in *Anthropological Studies of Witchcraft, Magic and Religion,* ed. Brian Levack, 203–25. New York: Garland, 1992.

———. *Witchcraft, Oracles and Magic among the Azande,* 2nd ed. Oxford: Clarendon, 1976.

Fabricius, Wilhelm. *Die Karte von 1789. Einteilung und Entwickelung der Territorien von 1600 bis 1794* (Bonn, 1898). Erläuterungen zum geschichtlichen Atlas der Rheinprovinz 2, repr. ed. Bonn: Hanstein, 1965.

Färber, Wolfgang. "Das österreichische Burgau." Ph.D. diss., Innsbruck, 1949.

Favret-Saada, Jeanne. *Die Wörter, der Zauber, der Tod. Der Hexenglaube im Hainland von Westfrankreich.* Frankfurt am Main: Suhrkamp, 1979.

Feld, Rudolf. *Das Städtewesen des Hunsrück-Nahe-Raumes im Spätmittelalter und in der Frühneuzeit.* Trier: Neu, 1972.

Fellner, Thomas, and Heinrich Kretschmar. *Die österreichische Zentralverwaltung,*

Abt. 1: Von Maximilian I. bis zur Vereinigung der österreichischen und böhmischen Hofkanzlei (1749). Vienna: Holzhausen, 1907.

Fichtner, Christian. *Das Horber Stadtrecht im Mittelalter.* Warendorf: Fahlbusch, 1990.

Fischer, Edda. "Die 'Disquisitionum magicarum libri sex' von Martin Delrio als gegenreformatorische Exempelquelle." Ph.D. diss., Frankfurt: Lang, 1975.

Fischer, Hermann. *Schwäbisches Wörterbuch,* 6 vols. Tübingen: Laupp, 1904–36.

Fischer, Joachim. "Das kaiserliche Landgericht Schwaben in der Neuzeit." *Zeitschrift für württembergische Landesgeschichte 43* (1984): 239–41.

Fisenne, Otto von. "Lucia Teimens, die 'Pesthexe' von Kell." *Heimat zwischen Hunsrück und Eifel, Beilage der Rhein-Zeitung für Schule und Elternhaus* 11, no. 10 (February 10, 1964): 5.

Foster, George. "Peasant Society and the Image of the Limited Good." In *Peasant Society,* ed. Jack M. Potter, 307–21. Boston: Little, Brown, 1967.

Fraikin, Jean. "Eine Seite der Geschichte der Hexerei in den Ardennen und im Moselraum. Die Affäre um Jean del Vaulx, Mönch in Stablo (1592–1597)." In *Hexenglaube und Hexenprozesse im Raum Rhein-Mosel-Saar,* ed. Gunther Franz and Franz Irsigler, 417–32. Trier: Spee, 1995.

Franken, Irene, and Ina Hoerner. *Hexen. Die Verfolgung von Frauen in Köln.* Cologne: Kölner Volksblatt-Verlag, 1987.

Franz, Gunther. "Ein 'dämonologischer Gang' durch Trier." In *Hexenglaube und Hexenprozesse im Raum Rhein-Mosel-Saar,* ed. Gunther Franz and Franz Irsigler, 485–517. Trier: Spee, 1995.

———. "Geistes- und Kulturgeschichte 1560–1794." In *Trier in der Neuzeit,* ed. Kurt Düwell and Franz Irsigler, 203–373. 2000 Jahre Trier 3. Trier: Spee, 1988.

———. "Die Hexenprozesse in der Stadt Trier und deren Umgebung." In *Hexenglaube und Hexenprozesse im Raum Rhein-Mosel-Saar,* ed. Gunther Franz and Franz Irsigler, 333–53. Trierer Hexenprozesse 1. Trier: Spee, 1995.

———. "Die Hexenverfolgung im Kurfürstentum Trier." In *Friedrich Spee. Dichter, Seelsorger, Bekämpfer des Hexenwahns,* ed. Gunther Franz, 59–77. Trier: Stadtbibliothek, 1991.

———. "'Der Malleus Judicum, Das ist: Gesetzhammer der unbarmhertzigen Hexenrichter' von Cornelius Pleier im Vergleich mit Friedrich Spees 'Cautio Criminalis.'" In *"Vom Unfug des Hexen-Processes": Gegner der Hexenverfolgung von Johann Weyer bis Friedrich Spee,* ed. Hartmut Lehmann and Otto Ulbricht, 199–222. Wiesbaden: Harrassowitz, 1992.

———. "Der 'Malleus Judicum, Das ist Gesetzhammer der unbarmherzigen Hexenrichter' von Cornelius Pleier und andere Gegner der Hexenprozesse bis Friedrich Spee." In *Die Salemer Hexenverfolgungen,* ed. Winfried Herget, 27–47. Trier: Wissenschaftlihcher Verlag Trier, 1994.

———. "Der Trierer Hexentanzplatz und das Verderben der Rieslingweinstöcke." In *2000 Jahre Weinkultur an Mosel-Saar-Ruwer,* ed. Rheinisches Landesmuseum Trier, 187–88. Trier: Selbstverlag des Rheinischen Landesmuseums, 1987.

Franz, Gunther, and Anita Hennen. "'Hauskreuze' (Teufelspeitschen) gegen Hexerei und Pest. Dämonenabwehr im Trierer Land des 18. Jahrhunderts." In *Hexenglaube und Hexenprozesse im Raum Rhein-Mosel-Saar,* ed. Gunther Franz and Franz Irsigler, 89–129. Trierer Hexenprozesse 1. Trier: Spee, 1995.

Franz, Gunther, Günter Gehl, and Franz Irsigler, eds. *Hexenprozesse und deren Gegner im trierisch-lothringischen Raum.* Weimar: Dadder, 1997.

Frazer, James George. *The Golden Bough,* 10th ed. London: Macmillan, 1978.

Frehsee, Detlev, et al., eds. *Konstruktion der Wirklichkeit durch Kriminalität und Strafe.* Baden-Baden: Nomos-Verlag-Gesellschaft, 1997.

Fritz, Thomas. "Hexenverfolgungen in der Reichsstadt Reutlingen." In *Zum Feuer verdammt,* ed. Johannes Dillinger, Thomas Fritz, and Wolfgang Mährle, 163–327. Hexenforschung 2. Stuttgart: Steiner, 1998.

———. "Reichsstadt Reutlingen." In *Wider alle Hexerei und Teufelswerk,* ed. Sönke Lorenz and Jürgen Michael Schmidt, 417–26. Ostfildern: Thorbecke, 2004.

Frueth, Eugen. "Berühmt durch Gewerbefleiß und Fastnacht: Oberndorf." In *Der Kreis Rottweil,* ed. Konrad Theiß and Hermann Baumhauer, 40–44. Aalen: Verlag Heimat und Wirtschaft, 1963.

Fuge, Boris. "Le roi des sorciers." In *Hexenprozesse und Gerichtspraxis,* ed. Herbert Eiden, 69–121. Trierer Hexenprozesse 6. Trier: Spee, 2002.

Füssel, Ronald. *Die Hexenverfolgungen im Thüringer Raum.* Hamburg: Verlag Dokumentation und Buch, 2003.

Gappenach, Hans. *Münstermaifeld.* Neuss: Gesellschaft für Buchdruckerei, 1980.

———. "Münstermaifelder Kriminaljustiz im Mittelalter nach Johann Büchel." In *Münstermaifelder Heimatbuch,* ed. Hans Gappenach, 56–57. Münstermaifeld: Fremdenverkehrs- und Amt für Wirtschaftsförderung, 1960.

Gareis, Iris. "Schamanen- und Hexenflug im präkolumbianischen und kolonialen Peru." In *Fliegen und Schweben. Annäherung an eine menschliche Sensation,* ed. Dieter Bauer and Wolfgang Behringer, 37–57. Munich: Deutscher Taschenbuch-Verlag, 1997.

———. *Religiöse Spezialisten des zentralen Andengebietes zur Zeit der Inka und während der spanischen Kolonialherrschaft.* Hohenschäftlarn: Renner, 1987.

Gaskill, Malcolm. "The Devil in the Shape of a Man: Witchcraft, Conflict and Belief in Jacobean England." *Historical Research* 71 (1998): 142–71.

Geary, Patrick. "Humiliation of Saints." In *Saints and Their Cults,* ed. Stephen Wilson, 123–40. Cambridge: Cambridge University Press, 1983.

Gehm, Britta. *Die Hexenverfolgung im Hochstift Bamberg und das Eingreifen des Reichshofrates zu ihrer Beendigung.* Hildesheim: Olms, 2000.

Geiger, Paul. "Art. Tod." In *Handwörterbuch des deutschen Aberglaubens,* 10 vols., ed. Hanns Bächtold-Stäubli and Eduard Hoffmann-Krayer, 8:970–85. Berlin: Walter de Gruyter, 1929–42.

Gemmel, Arthur. *Chronik von Schweich.* Trier: Arbeitsgemeinschaft für Landesgeschichte und Volkskunde des Trierer Raumes, 1960.

Geppert, Karl Heinz. *Kleiner Hirrlinger Geschichtskalender.* Hirrlingen: Gemeinde, 1991.

Gerteis, Klaus. "Frühneuzeitliche Stadtrevolten im sozialen und institutionellen Bedingungsrahmen." In *Die Städte Mitteleuropas im 17. und 18. Jahrhundert,* ed. Wilhelm Rausch, 43–58. Linz: Arbeitskreis für Stadtgeschichtsforschung, 1981.

————. "Die kurfürstliche Zeit." In *Heimatbuch der Gemeinde Beuren im Hochwald*, ed. Alfons Rosar, 31–92. Beuren: Selbstverlag der Gemeinde Beuren, 1988.

————. "Sozialgeschichte der Stadt Trier 1580–1794." In *Trier in der Neuzeit*, ed. Kurt Düwell and Franz Irsigler, 61–97. 2000 Jahre Trier 3. Trier: Spee, 1988.

Gestrich, Andreas. "Pietismus und Aberglaube. Zum Zusammenhang von popularem Pietismus und dem Ende der Hexenverfolgungen im 18. Jahrhundert." In *Das Ende der Hexenverfolgung*, ed. Dieter Bauer and Sönke Lorenz, 269–86. Hexenforschung 1. Stuttgart: Steiner, 1995.

Giefel, J. A. "Zur Geschichte der Hexenprozesse in Horb und Umgebung." *Reutlinger Geschichtsblätter* 13 (1902): 90–92.

————. "Zur Geschichte der Reformation und Gegenreformation." In *Beschreibung des Oberamts Rottenburg*, 2 vols., ed. Statistisches Landesamt, 1:379–414. Stuttgart: Kohlhammer, 1899.

————. "Zur Geschichte der Verfassung und Verwaltung der Grafschaft Hohenberg." In *Beschreibung des Oberamts Rottenburg*, 2 vols., ed. Statistisches Landesamt, 1:356–79. Stuttgart: Kohlhammer, 1899.

Ginzburg, Carlo. *Ecstasies*, 2nd ed. Chicago: Chicago University Press, 2004.

————. *The Night Battles: Witchcraft and Agrian Cults in the Sixteenth and Seventeenth Centuries*. New York: Penguin, 1985.

Girard, René. *Ausstoßung und Verfolgung: Eine historische Theorie des Sündenbocks*. Frankfurt: Fischer Taschenbuch-Verlag, 1992.

Godbeer, Richard. "Der Teufel in absentia: Hexerei in Salem im Jahre 1692." In *Die Salemer Hexenverfolgungen*, ed. Winfried Herget, 95–117. Trier: Wissenschaftlicher Verlag Trier, 1994.

Gönner, Eberhard, and Max Miller. "Die Landvogtei Schwaben." In *Vorderösterreich*, 2nd ed., ed. Friedrich Metz, 683–704. Freiburg im Breisgau: Rombach, 1967.

Göttmann, Frank. *Getreidemarkt am Bodensee*. St. Katharinen: Scripta-Mercaturae-Verlag, 1991.

Götz, Franz. *Kleine Geschichte des Landkreises Stockach*. Stockach: Bresto-Drucke, n.d.

Graf, Klaus. "Reichsstadt Schwäbisch Gmünd." In *Wider alle Hexerei und Teufelswerk*, ed. Sönke Lorenz and Jürgen Michael Schmidt, 437–42. Ostfildern: Thorbecke, 2004.

Green, Nancy. "The Comparative Method and Poststructural Structuralism." In *Migration, Migration History, History*, ed. Jan Lucassen and Leo Lucassen, 57–72. Bern: Lang, 1997.

Grinsell, Leslie Valentine. "Witchcraft at Some Prehistoric Sites." In *The Witch Figure, Festschrift Katharine Briggs*, ed. Venetia Newall, 72–79. London: Routledge and Paul, 1973.

Güntert, Hermann. "Art. Katze." In *Handwörterbuch des deutschen Aberglaubens*, 10 vols., ed. Hanns Bächtold-Stäubli and Eduard Hoffmann-Krayer, 4:1107–24. Berlin: Walter de Gruyter, 1929–42.

Gusfield, Joseph. "Moral Passage: The Symbolic Process in Public Designations of Deviance." *Social Problems* 15 (1967): 175–88.

Haag, Herbert. *Teufelsglaube*. Tübingen: Katzmann, 1980.

Haas, Emil. "Die kurtrierische Landgemeinde im 17. und 18. Jahrhundert." *Rheinische Vierteljahrsblätter* 2 (1932): 43–70.

———. "Die Zechen im ehemaligen kurtrierischen Amt Montabaur." *Rheinische Vierteljahrsblätter* 1 (1931): 118–28.

Habermas, Jürgen. *Theorie des kommunikativen Handelns*, 2 vols., 3rd ed. Frankfurt am Main: Suhrkamp, 1985.

Hacker, Werner. *Auswanderung aus dem nördlichen Bodenseeraum im 17. und 18. Jahrhundert*. Sigmaringen: Hegau-Geschichtsverein, 1975.

Hagemaier, Monika, and Sabine Holz, eds. *Krisenbewußtsein und Krisenbewältigung in der Frühen Neuzeit, Festschrift Hans-Christoph Rublack*. Frankfurt am Main: Lang, 1992.

Hämmerle, Georg. "Die Saulgauer Hexenprozesse." In *Aus der Geschichte der Stadt Saulgau*, vol. 1, ed. Georg Hämmerle. Saulgau: Stadtverwaltung, n.d.

Hammes, Manfred. *Hexenwahn und Hexenprozesse*, 4th ed. Frankfurt am Main: Fischer Taschenbuch-Verlag, 1981.

Hansen, Joseph. *Quellen und Untersuchungen zur Geschichte des Hexenwahns und der Hexenverfolgung im Mittelalter*. Bonn: Georgi, 1901.

———. *Zauberwahn, Inquisition und Hexenprozeß im Mittelalter und die Entstehung der großen Hexenverfolgung*. Leipzig: Oldenbourg, 1900.

Hartmann, Elisabeth. *Die Trollvorstellungen in den Sagen und Märchen der skandinavischen Völker*. Stuttgart: Kohlhammer, 1936.

Haßler, Ludwig Anton. *Materialien zur Geschichte des Landkapitels Rottweil*. Rottweil: Herder, 1808.

Haug, F. "Aus einer Anweisung für die Führung von Hexenprozessen." *Sülchgauer Scholle* 5 (1929): 26–27.

Haupt, Heinz-Gerhard. "Die Geschichte Europas als vergleichende Geschichtsschreibung." *Comparativ* 14 (2004): 83–97.

Haupt, Heinz-Gerhard, and Jürgen Kocka. "Comparative History: Methods, Aims, Problems." In *Comparison and History: Europe in Cross-National Perspective*, ed. Deborah Cohen and Maura O'Connor, 23–39. New York: Routledge, 2004.

———. "Historischer Vergleich: Methoden, Aufgaben, Probleme. Eine Einleitung." In *Geschichte und Vergleich. Ansätze und Ergebnisse international vergleichender Geschichtsschreibung*, ed. Heinz-Gerhard Haupt and Jürgen Kocka, 9–45. Frankfurt am Main: Campus-Verlag, 1996.

Hausmann, Jost. "Die Städte als integrierte Glieder des absoluten Staates im 17. und 18. Jahrhundert." In *700 Jahre Stadtrecht für sechs kurtrierische Städte 1291–1991*, ed. Dietmar Flach and Jost Hausmann, 63–70. Coblenz: Landeshauptarchiv, 1991.

Haxel, Edwin. "Verfassung und Verwaltung des Kurfürstentums Trier im 18. Jahrhundert." *Trierer Zeitschrift für Geschichte und Kunst* 5 (1903): 47–88.

Hegenbarth, Rainer. "Symbolische und instrumentelle Funktion moderner Gesetze." *Zeitschrift für Rechtspolitik* 14 (1981): 201–4.

Hehl, Ulrich von. "Hexenprozesse und Geschichtswissenschaft." *Historisches Jahrbuch* 107 (1987): 347–75.

Heinsohn, Gunnar, and Otto Steiger. *Die Vernichtung der weisen Frauen*, 6th ed. Herbstein: März-Verlag, 1985.

Heinz, Andreas. "'Bei den Trierern scheint der Böse Geist seinen Sitz aufgeschlagen zu haben.' Ein bisher unbekannter Bericht des Kölner Kartäuserpriors Johannes Reckschenkel (1526–1611) über Hexenverfolgungen in Trier." In *Hexenglaube und Hexenprozesse im Raum Rhein-Mosel-Saar*, ed. Gunther Franz and Franz Irsigler, 449–57. Trierer Hexenprozesse 1. Trier: Spee, 1995.

Heisterkamp, Hans. "Hexen auf dem Maifelde." *Eifel-Kalender* (1955): 69–70.

Henning, Friedrich Wilhelm. *Handbuch der Wirtschafts- und Sozialgeschichte Deutschlands*, vol. 1. Paderborn: Schöningh, 1991.

Herberhold, Franz. "Die österreichischen Donaustädte." In *Vorderösterreich*, 2nd ed., ed. Friedrich Metz, 705–28. Freiburg im Breisgau: Rombach, 1967.

Hettinger, Michael. *Das Fragerecht der Verteidigung im reformierten Inquisitionsprozeß.* Berlin: Duncker und Humblot, 1985.

Heuser, Peter. "Rezension zu Scheffler, Jürgen/Schwerhoff, Gerd/Wilbertz, Gisela, eds., Hexenverfolgung und Regionalgeschichte. Die Grafschaft Lippe im Vergleich." In *Annalen des Historischen Vereins für den Niederrhein* 198 (1995): 265–67.

Heyd, Wilhelm. *Bibliographie der Württembergischen Geschichte*, 2 vols. Stuttgart: Kohlhammer, 1895–96.

Hippel, Wolfgang von. "Bevölkerung und Wirtschaft im Zeitalter des Dreißigjährigen Krieges. Das Beispiel Württemberg." *Zeitschrift für Historische Forschung* 5 (1978): 413–48.

Hirn, Josef. *Erzherzog Ferdinand II. von Tirol*, 2 vols. Innsbruck: Wagner, 1885–88.

———. *Erzherzog Maximilian der Deutschmeister, Regent von Tirol* (Innsbruck, 1915), 2 vols., repr. ed. Bozen: Athesia-Buch, 1981.

Hobsbawm, Eric J. "The Crises of the 17th Century." In *Crisis in Europe, 1560–1660*, ed. Trevor Aston, 5–58. New York: Doubleday, 1967.

Hofacker, Hans-Georg. "Die Landvogtei Schwaben." In *Vorderösterreich in der frühen Neuzeit*, ed. Hans Maier and Volker Press, 57–74. Sigmaringen: Thorbecke, 1989.

———. *Die schwäbischen Reichslandvogteien im späten Mittelalter.* Stuttgart: Klett-Cotta, 1980.

Hoffmann-Krayer, Eduard. "Art. Zachariassegen." In *Handwörterbuch des deutschen Aberglaubens*, 10 vols., ed. Hanns Bächtold-Stäubli and Eduard Hoffmann-Krayer, 9:875–77. Berlin: Walter de Gruyter, 1929–42.

Hofmann, Hans Hubert. *Adelige Herrschaft und souveräner Staat.* Munich: Kommission für bayerische Landesgeschichte, 1962.

Hollmann, Michael. "Die Städte zwischen landständischer Autonomie und landesherrlicher Souveränität im 15. und 16. Jahrhundert." In *700 Jahre Stadtrecht für sechs kurtrierische Städte 1291–1991*, ed. Dietmar Flach and Jost Hausmann, 51–61. Coblenz: Landeshauptarchiv, 1991.

Hölz, Thomas. "Abt Johann Christoph Raittner (1575–1586) und das Heilige Blut." In *900 Jahre Heilig-Blut-Verehrung in Weingarten 1094–1994*, 3 vols., ed. Norbert Kruse and Hans-Ulrich Rudolf, 1:137–43. Sigmaringen: Thorbecke, 1994.

Holzherr, Carl. *Geschichte der Reichsfreiherrn von Ehingen.* Stuttgart, 1884.

Honegger, Claudia, ed. *Die Hexen der Neuzeit.* Frankfurt am Main: Suhrkamp, 1978.

Hoppstädter, Kurt. "Hexenprozesse im saarländischen Raum." *Zeitschrift für die Geschichte der Saargegend* 9 (1959): 210–67.

Horsley, Richard. "Who Were the Witches?" *Journal of Interdisciplinary History* 9, no. 4 (1979): 689–715.

Horton, Robin, and Ruth Finnegan, eds. *Modes of Thought.* London: Faber and Faber, 1973.

Hummel, Karl-Martin, and Christian Schwarz. "Zur Geschichte." In *Der Kreis Freudenstadt,* ed. Gerhard Mauer. Aalen: Theiss, 1978.

Hünnerkopf, K. "Art. Gold." In *Handwörterbuch des deutschen Aberglaubens,* 10 vols., ed. Hanns Bächtold-Stäubli and Eduard Hoffmann-Krayer, 3:918–26. Berlin: Walter de Gruyter, 1929–42.

Huter, Franz. "Zur Frage der Gemeindebildung in Tirol." In *Die Anfänge der Landgemeinde und ihr Wesen,* ed. Konstanzer Arbeitskreis, 7:223–35. Vorträge und Forschungen 7–8. Stuttgart: Thorbecke, 1964.

Irsigler, Franz. "Aspekte von Angst und Massenhysterie im Mittelalter und in der Frühen Neuzeit." *Trierer Beiträge* 21 (1991): 37–45.

———. *Herrschaftsgebiete im Jahr 1789.* Cologne: Rheinland-Verlag, 1982.

———. "Hexenverfolgungen im 15.–17. Jahrhundert." In *Hexenprozesse und deren Gegner im trierisch-lothringischen Raum,* ed. Gunther Franz et al., 9–24. Weimar: Dadder, 1997.

———. "Raumkonzepte in der historischen Forschung." In *Zwischen Gallia und Germania, Frankreich und Deutschland: Konstanz und Wandel raumbestimmender Kräfte, Vorträge auf dem 36. Deutschen Historikertag in Trier,* ed. Alfred Heit, 11–27. Trier: Verlag Trierer Historische Forschungen, 1987.

———. "Räumliche Aspekte in der historischen Hexenforschung." In *Methoden und Konzepte der historischen Hexenforschung,* ed. Franz Irsigler and Gunther Franz, 43–52. Trier: Spee, 1998.

———. "Wirtschaftsgeschichte der Stadt Trier 1580–1794." In *Trier in der Neuzeit,* ed. Kurt Düwell and Franz Irsigler, 99–201. 2000 Jahre Trier 3. Trier: Spee, 1988.

———. "Zauberei- und Hexenprozesse in Köln, 15.–17. Jahrhundert." In *Hexenglaube und Hexenprozesse im Raum Rhein-Mosel-Saar,* ed. Gunther Franz and Franz Irsigler, 169–79. Trier: Spee, 1995.

Isenberg, Wolfgang, and Georg Mölich, eds. *Hexenverfolgung im Rheinland. Ergebnisse neuerer Lokal- und Regionalstudien.* Bergisch Gladbach: Thomas-Morus-Akademie Bensberg, 1996.

Jäckel, Eberhard. "Die zweifache Vergangenheit. Zum Vergleich politischer Systeme." In *Gesprächskreis Geschichte.* vol. 2, ed. Dieter Dowe. Bonn: Historisches Forschungszentrum, 1992.

Jakoby, A. "Art. Hochschulen der Zauberei." In *Handwörterbuch des deutschen Aberglaubens,* 10 vols., ed. Hanns Bächtold-Stäubli and Eduard Hoffmann-Krayer, 4:140–48, 144. Berlin: Walter de Gruyter, 1929–42.

———. "Art. Benediktussegen." In *Handwörterbuch des deutschen Aberglaubens,* 10 vols., ed. Hanns Bächtold-Stäubli and Eduard Hoffmann-Krayer, 1:1035–40. Berlin: Walter de Gruyter, 1929–42.

———. "Art. Caravacakreuz." In *Handwörterbuch des deutschen Aberglaubens,* 10 vols., ed. Hanns Bächtold-Stäubli and Eduard Hoffmann-Krayer, 2:7–8. Berlin: Walter de Gruyter, 1929–42.

Jänichen, Hans. "Zur Geschichte des Landgerichts im Hegau und im Madach anhand eines neuentdeckten Auszugs aus dem Achtbuch." *Hegau* 13 (1968): 7–24.

Janssen, Franz Roman. *Kurtrier in seinen Ämtern vornehmlich im 16. Jahrhundert. Studien zur Entwicklung frühmoderner Staatlichkeit.* Bonn: Röhrscheid, 1985.

Janssen, Johannes. *Culturzustände des deutschen Volkes seit dem Ausgang des Mittelalters bis zum Beginn des dreißigjährigen Krieges,* ed. Ludwig Pastor. Freiburg in Breisgau: Herder, 1888–94.

Jerouschek, Günter. *Die Hexen und ihr Prozeß. Die Hexenverfolgung in der Reichsstadt Esslingen.* Esslinger Studien 1. Esslingen: Stadtarchiv, 1992.

Johansen, Jens Christian. "Als die Fischer den Teufel ins Netz bekamen. . . . Eine Analyse der Zeugenaussagen aus Städten und Landbezirken in den jütischen Zaubereiprozessen des 17. Jahrhunderts." In *Hexenprozesse. Deutsche und skandinavische Beiträge,* ed. Christian Degn, Hartmut Lehmann, and Dagmar Unverhau, 159–66. Neumünster: Wachholtz, 1983.

Johler, E. *Geschichtlich-topographische Beschreibung des katholischen Landkreises Horb.* Horb, 1825.

Jungbauer, Gustav. "Art. Sonntagskind." In *Handwörterbuch des deutschen Aberglaubens,* 10 vols., ed. Hanns Bächtold-Stäubli and Eduard Hoffmann-Krayer, 8:114–20. Berlin: Walter de Gruyter, 1929–42.

Jungwirth, G. "Art. Jagd." In *Handwörterbuch des deutschen Aberglaubens,* 10 vols., ed. Hanns Bächtold-Stäubli and Eduard Hoffmann-Krayer, 4:575–93. Berlin: Walter de Gruyter, 1929–42.

Junk, J. "Aus der Hexenzeit eines Moseldörfchens." *Trierische Heimat* 11 (1935): 135–39.

Jütte, Robert. "Sprachliches Handeln und kommunikative Situation." In *Kommunikation und Alltag in Spätmittelalter und früher Neuzeit, Internationaler Kongress Krems 1990,* ed. Herwig Wolfram, 159–81. Vienna: Verlag der Österreichischen Akademie der Wissenschaften, 1992.

Kaelble, Hartmut, and Jürgen Schriewer, eds. *Vergleich und Transfer. Komparatistik in den Sozial-, Geschichts- und Kulturwissenschaften.* Frankfurt am Main: Campus-Verlag, 2003.

Kamen, Henry. *The Iron Century.* London: Weidenfeld and Nicolson, 1971.

Karle, Bernhard. "Art. Hostie." In *Handwörterbuch des deutschen Aberglaubens,* 10 vols., ed. Hanns Bächtold-Stäubli and Eduard Hoffmann-Krayer, 3:412–22. Berlin: Walter de Gruyter, 1929–42.

Karlsen, Carol. *The Devil in the Shape of a Woman.* New York: W. W. Norton, 1987.

Kempf, Karl. "'Allerhand defect, mengel vnd müßbreich': Sittenschilderungen aus Rottenburg in nach- und gegenreformatorischer Zeit." *Der Sülchgau* 27 (1983): 13–25.

———. *Die Chronik des Christoph Lutz von Lutzenhardt aus Rottenburg am Neckar.* Vaihingen: Melchior, 1986.

———. "Die Hexenverfolgung im Raum Rottenburg." *Der Sülchgau* 28 (1984): 35–52.

———. "Hexenverfolgung in Rottenburg." In *Hexenverfolgung,* ed. Sönke Lorenz und Dieter R. Bauer, 159–202. Würzburg: Königshausen und Neumann, 1995.

Kentenich, Gottfried. "Das alte kurtrierische Amt Wittlich." *Trierische Chronik, Neue Folge* 9 (1913): 179–89, 10 (1914): 21–26, 57–60, 117–22, 178–84, 10 (1914): 183–84.

————. "Das Amt Saarburg beim Ausgang der kurfürstlichen Zeit." *Trierische Chronik, Neue Folge* 11 (1915): 161–73.

————. "Beiträge zur Geschichte des Landkreises Trier." *Trierische Chronik, Neue Folge* 8 (1912): 33–59, 83–88, 133–37, 177–80, 9 (1913): 79–90.

————. "Beiträge zur Geschichte des Weinbaus und Weinhandels im Mosellande I." *Trierische Chronik* 7 (1911): 149–54.

————. *Geschichte der Stadt Trier von ihrer Gründung bis zur Gegenwart* (Trier, 1915), repr. ed. Trier: Akademische Buchhandlung Interbook, 1979.

————. "Triers Statthalter 1580–1797." *Trierische Heimat* 1 (1924–25): 3–5, 18–21, 32–33, 105–9, 159–60, 2 (1925–26): 49–55, 84–88, 113–16, 129–32, 161–65, 177–82.

Kerber, Dieter. *Herrschaftsmittelpunkte im Erzstift Trier. Hof und Residenz im späten Mittelalter,* ed. Residenzenkommission der Göttinger Akademie der Wissenschaften. Residenzenforschung 4. Sigmaringen: Thorbecke, 1995.

Kettel, Adolf. "Hexenglaube heute." In *Hexenglaube und Hexenprozesse im Raum Rhein-Mosel-Saar,* ed. Gunther Franz and Franz Irsigler, 143–50. Trierer Hexenprozesse 1. Trier: Spee, 1995.

————. "Hexenprozesse in der Eifel." In *Hexenprozesse und deren Gegner im trierisch-lothringischen Raum,* ed. Gunther Franz, Günter Gehl, and Franz Irsigler, 69–98. Weimar: Dadder, 1997.

————. "Hexenprozesse in der Grafschaft Gerolstein und in den angrenzenden kurtrierischen Ämtern Prüm und Hillesheim." In *Hexenglaube und Hexenprozesse im Raum Rhein-Mosel-Saar,* ed. Gunther Franz and Franz Irsigler, 355–88. Trierer Hexenprozesse 1. Trier: Spee, 1995.

————. *Von Hexen und Unholden. Hexenprozesse in der West- und Zentraleifel.* Prüm: Geschichtsverein "Prümer Land," 1988.

Kieckheffer, Richard. *European Witch Trials.* London: Routledge Kegan Paul, 1976.

————. *Magic in the Middle Ages,* 2nd ed. Cambridge: Cambridge University Press, 2000.

Kimminich, Eva. "Hexe gesucht. Bemerkungen zum historischen Erscheinungsbild europäischer Fastnachtsbräuche." In *Die Fasnethex, Akademie der Diözese Rottenburg-Stuttgart, Materialien.* 8:27–54. N.p.: Akademie der Diözese, 1989.

Kindermann, Harald. "Symbolische Gesetzgebung." In *Gesetzgebungstheorie und Rechtspolitik,* ed. Dieter Grimm and Werner Maihofer, 222–45. Jahrbuch für Rechtssoziologie und Rechtstheorie 13. Opladen: Westdeutscher Verlag, 1988.

Klaits, Joseph. *Servants of Satan. The Age of Witch Hunts.* Bloomington: Indiana University Press, 1985.

Klaniczay, Gábor. *Heilige, Hexen, Vampire.* Berlin: Wagenbach, 1991.

Klein, Josef. *Geschichte von Boppard.* Boppard: Keil, 1909.

Klein, Kurt. "Die Bevölkerung Österreichs vom Beginn des 16. bis zur Mitte des 18. Jahrhunderts." In *Beiträge zur Bevölkerungs- und Sozialgeschichte Österreichs,* ed. Heimold Helczmanowski, 47–112. Munich: Oldenbourg, 1973.

Kleinheyer, Gerd. *Zur Rechtsgestalt von Akkusationsverfahren und peinlicher Frage im frühen 17. Jahrhundert.* Opladen: Westdeutscher Verlag, 1971.

Köhler, August Friedrich. *Oberndorf am Neckar.* Sulz: 1836. Reprint ed. Oberndorf: Stadtverwaltung, 1967.

Köhler, Joachim. "Zeiten des Umbruchs. Reformation, Bauernkrieg und Täuferbewegung." In *600 Jahre Stiftskirche Heilig-Kreuz in Horb*, ed. Joachim Köhler. Horb: Geiger, 1987.

Kommission für geschichtliche Landeskunde in Baden-Württemberg and Landesvermessungsamt Baden-Württemberg, eds. *Historischer Atlas von Baden-Württemberg*, 4 vols. Stuttgart: Landesvermessungsamt Baden-Württemberg, 1972–88.

Koppenburg, Ingo. "Die soziale Funktion städtischer Hexenprozesse. Die lippische Residenzstadt Detmold 1599–1669." In *Hexenverfolgung und Regionalgeschichte: Die Grafschaft Lippe im Vergleich*, ed. Jürgen Scheffler, Gerd Schwerhoff, and Gisela Wilbertz, 183–99. Bielefeld: Verlag für Regionalgeschichte, 1994.

Koppenhöfer, Johanna. *Die mitleidlose Gesellschaft. Studien zu Verdachtsgenese, Ausgrenzungsverhalten und Prozeßproblematik im frühneuzeitlichen Hexenprozeß in der alten Grafschaft Nassau unter Johann VI. und der späteren Teilgrafschaft Nassau-Dillenburg (1559–1687).* Frankfurt: Lang, 1995.

Kramer, Wolfgang. "Die Landgrafschaft Nellenburg und ihre Hauptstadt Stockach." *Der Hegau* 51–52 (1994–95): 361–64.

———. *Kurtrierische Hexenprozesse im 16. und 17. Jahrhundert, vornehmlich an der unteren Mosel.* Munich: Scharl, 1959.

Krebs, Ernst. "Die Verfassung der Stadt Günzburg bis zur Mitte des 16. Jahrhunderts." *Das obere Schwaben* 7 (1963): 127–58.

Kreuter, Peter Mario. *Der Vampirglaube in Südosteuropa.* Berlin: Weidler, 2001.

Krezdorn, Siegfried. "Die Herren von Ehingen." *Sülchgauer Altertumsverein Rottenburg, Jahresgabe* (1964): 37–46.

———. "Hohenberg und seine Landeshauptstadt." *Sülchgauer Altertumsverein Rottenburg, Jahresgabe* (1961): 19–22.

———. "Johann Jakob Koller von Bochingen." *Sülchgauer Altertumsverein Rottenburg, Jahresgabe* (1960): 15–24.

———. "Wendler von Pregenroths Aufstieg und Fall." *Der Sülchgau* 10 (1966): 50–59.

———. "Zur Genealogie der Familie Precht." *Sülchgauer Altertumsverein Rottenburg, Jahresgabe* (1959): 3–17.

Kriedte, Peter. "Die Hexen und ihre Ankläger: Zu den lokalen Voraussetzungen der Hexenverfolgung in der frühen Neuzeit." *Zeitschrift für Historische Forschung* 14 (1987): 47–71.

Kruse, Norbert, et al., eds. *Weingarten. Von den Anfängen bis zur Gegenwart.* Biberach: Biberacher Verlagsdruckerei, 1992.

Kuhn-Rehfus, Maren. "Mit dem greulichen Laster der Hexerei angesteckte Kinder. Kinderhexenprozesse in Sigmaringen im 17. Jahrhundert." In *Aus südwestdeutscher Geschichte. Festschrift Hansmartin Maurer*, ed. Wolfgang Schmierer et al., 428–46. Stuttgart: Kohlhammer, 1994.

Kyll, Nikolaus. "Die Hagelfeier im alten Erzbistum Trier und seinen Randgebieten." *Rheinisches Jahrbuch für Volkskunde* 13–14 (1964): 113–71.

———. "Hagel- Wetter- und Prozessionskreuze im Trierer Lande." *Landeskundliche Vierteljahresblätter* 7 (1961): 159–68.

Kyll, Theo. "Reben wuchsen an Our und Kyll." *Heimatkalender für den Kreis Bitburg* (1955): 93–95.

Labouvie, Eva. "'Gott zur Ehr, den Unschuldigen zu Trost und Rettung . . .' Hexenverfolgungen im Saarraum und in den angrenzenden Gebieten." In *Hexenglaube und
Hexenprozesse im Raum Rhein-Mosel-Saar*, ed. Gunther Franz and Franz Irsigler,
389–403. Trierer Hexenprozesse 1. Trier: Spee, 1995.

———. "Hexenforschung und Regionalgeschichte. Probleme, Grenzen und neue Perspektiven." In *Hexenverfolgung und Regionalgeschichte. Die Grafschaft Lippe im Vergleich*, ed. Jürgen Scheffler, Gerd Schwerhoff, and Gisela Wilbertz, 45–60. Bielefeld:
Verlag für Regionalgeschichte, 1994.

———. "Hexenspuk und Hexenabwehr." In *Hexenwelten*, ed. Richard van Dülmen,
49–93. Frankfurt am Main: Fischer-Taschenbuch-Verlag, 1987.

———. "Männer im Hexenprozeß." *Geschichte und Gesellschaft* 16, no. 1 (1990):
56–78.

———. "Rekonstruktion einer Verfolgung. Hexenprozesse und ihr Verlauf im Saar-
Pfalz-Raum und der Baillage d'Allemagne (1520–1690)." In *Hexenprozesse und deren
Gegner im trierisch-lothringischen Raum*, ed. Gunther Franz et al., 43–58. Weimar:
Dadder, 1997.

———. *Verbotene Künste. Volksmagie und ländlicher Aberglaube in den Dorfgemein-
den des Saarraumes (16.–19. Jahrhundert)*. St. Ingbert: Röhrig, 1992.

———. *Zauberei und Hexenwerk: Ländlicher Hexenglaube in der frühen Neuzeit*.
Frankfurt am Main: Fischer, 1991.

Laer, Annette von. "Die spätmittelalterlichen Hexenprozesse in Konstanz und Umgebung." *Schriften des Vereins für Geschichte des Bodensees u. seiner Umgebung* 106
(1988): 13–27.

Lager, Johann Christian. "Eine statistische Aufnahme der volkswirtschaftlichen
Zustände im Amt Saarburg vor und nach dem 30jährigen Krieg." *Trierisches Archiv*
9 (1907): 42–56.

Lamb, Hubert H. *Climate, History and the Modern World*, 2nd ed. London: Routledge,
1995.

Lambrecht, Karen. *Hexenverfolgungen und Zaubereiprozesse in den schlesischen Territorien*. Cologne: Böhlau, 1995.

Lauer, Dittmar. *Hexenverfolgung im Hochwald*. Hochwälder Hefte für Heimatgeschichte
8. Nonnweiler: Verein für Heimatkunde, 1988.

———. "Philipp Christoph von Sötern." *Hochwälder Geschichtsblätter* 9 (1997):
18–46.

Laufer, Wolfgang. *Die Sozialstruktur der Stadt Trier in der frühen Neuzeit*. Bonn:
Röhrscheid, 1973.

Laufner, Richard. "Dr. Dietrich Flade und seine Welt." *Landeskundliche Vierteljahresblätter* 8 (1962): 43–63.

———. "Die Gefangennahme des Trierer Erzbischofs und Kurfürsten Philipp Christoph von Sötern." *Der Kreis Trier-Saarburg* (1985): 176–80.

———. "Das Inventar des Fladeschen Hauses in Trier." In *Bericht über die Tagung
des Arbeitskreises für deutsche Hausforschung e.V. in Trier vom 8. bis 11. September
1966*, ed. Arbeitskreis für deutsche Hausforschung, 7–17. Münster: Arbeitskreis für
deutsche Hausforschung, 1967.

———. "Politische Geschichte, Verfassungs- und Verwaltungsgeschichte. 1580–1794."

In *Trier in der Neuzeit,* ed. Kurt Düwell and Franz Irsigler, 3–60. 2000 Jahre Trier 3. Trier: Spee, 1988.

————. "Triers Ringen um die Stadtherrschaft vom Anfang des 12. bis zum ausgehenden 16. Jahrhundert." In *Trier. Ein Zentrum abendländischer Kultur (Rheinischer Verein für Denkmalpflege und Heimatschutz)* 2 (1952): 151–74.

————. "Wein, Weinbau, Weingenuß und Weinhandel im Trierer Land vom Jahre 1000 bis 1814." In *2000 Jahre Weinkultur an Mosel-Saar-Ruwer,* ed. Rheinisches Landesmuseum Trier, 49–72. Trier: Selbstverlag des Rheinischen Landesmuseums, 1987.

Laven, Hermann. "Die Hexenprozesse in Trier und Umgebung." *Trierische Chronik, Neue Folge* 4 (1907–8): 113–35.

Lea, Henry Charles. *Materials toward a History of Witchcraft* (Philadelphia, 1939), 3 vols., repr. ed. New York: Yoseloff, 1986.

Lehmann, Hartmut. "Hexenverfolgung und Hexenprozesse im Alten Reich zwischen Reformation und Aufklärung." *Jahrbuch des Instituts für Deutsche Geschichte* 7 (1978): 13–70.

Leonardy, Johann. *Geschichte des Trierischen Landes und Volkes* (Trier, 1877), 2nd ed., repr. ed. Trier: Akademische Buchhandlung Interbook, 1982.

Le Roy Ladurie, Emmanuel. *The Peasants of Languedoc.* Urbana: Illinois University Press, 1974.

Levack, Brian, ed. *Articles on Witchcraft, Magic, and Demonology,* 12 vols. New York: Garland, 1992.

Liel, Anselm. "Die Verfolgung der Zauberer und Hexen in dem Kurfürstentum Trier." *Archiv für Rheinische Geschichte* 1 (1835): 17–80.

Lohr, Sabine. "Der Rottenburger Hexenprozeß gegen den Spitalvater Michael Pusper." *Der Sülchgau* 40 (1996): 131–46.

Lorenz, Chris. *Konstruktion der Vergangenheit. Eine Einführung in die Geschichtstheorie,* ed. Jörn Rüsen. Beiträge zur Geschichtskultur 3. Cologne: Böhlau, 1997.

Lorenz, Sönke. *Aktenversendung und Hexenprozeß. Dargestellt am Beispiel der Juristenfakultäten Rostock und Greifswald (1570/82–1630),* 2 vols. Frankfurt am Main: Lang, 1982–83.

————. "Einführung und Forschungsstand." In *Wider alle Hexerei und Teufelswerk,* ed. Sönke Lorenz and Jürgen Michael Schmidt, 195–212. Ostfildern: Thorbecke, 2004.

————. "Der Hexenprozeß." In *Wider alle Hexerei und Teufelswerk,* ed. Sönke Lorenz and Jürgen Michael Schmidt, 131–54. Ostfildern: Thorbecke, 2004.

————. "Die Rechtsauskunftstätigkeit der Tübinger Juristenfakultät in Hexenprozessen (ca. 1552–1602)." In *Hexenverfolgung,* ed. Sönke Lorenz und Dieter R. Bauer, 241–320. Würzburg: Königshausen und Neumann, 1995.

————. "Die Rezeption der Cautio Criminalis in der Rechtswissenschaft zur Zeit der Hexenverfolgung." In *Friedrich Spee: Düsseldorfer Symposion zum 400. Geburtstag,* ed. Theo G. M. van Oorschot, 130–53. Bielefeld: Aisthesis-Verlag, 1993.

Lorenz, Sönke, et al., eds. *Himmlers Hexenkartothek.* Hexenforschung 4. Bielefeld: Verlag für Regionalgeschichte, 1999.

Lott, Arno. *Die Todesstrafen im Kurfürstentum Trier in der frühen Neuzeit.* Frankfurt am Main: Lang, 1998.

Luck, Georg. *Hexen und Zauberei in der römischen Dichtung.* Zurich: Artemis, 1962.

Macfarlane, Alan. *The Origins of Individualism*. Oxford: Blackwell, 1978.

———. *Witchcraft in Tudor and Stuart England* (London, 1970), repr. ed. Prospect Hights, Ill.: Waveland Press, 1991.

Mährle, Wolfgang. "Fürstpropstei Ellwangen." In *Wider alle Hexerei und Teufelswerk*, ed. Sönke Lorenz and Jürgen Michael Schmidt, 377–86. Ostfildern: Thorbecke, 2004.

Malinowski, Bronislaw. "Magic, Science and Religion." In *Science, Religion and Reality*, ed. Joseph Needham, 19–84. London, 1925. Repr. in Bronislaw Malinowski. *Magic, Science and Religion and Other Essays*, 2nd ed., 17–92. London: Souvenir Press, 1982.

Manz, Dieter. *Kleine Rottenburger Stadtgeschichte*. Rottenburg: Stadt Rottenburg, 1988.

———. "Der Rottenburger Stadtbrand vom 4. März 1735." *Der Sülchgau* 28 (1984): 53–58.

Marx, Jakob. *Geschichte des Erzstifts Trier als Kurfürstentum und Erzdiözese von den ältesten Zeiten bis zum Jahre 1816*, 5 vols. Trier: Lintz, 1858–64.

Marzell, Heinrich. "Art. Farn." In *Handwörterbuch des deutschen Aberglaubens*, 10 vols., ed. Hanns Bächtold-Stäubli and Eduard Hoffmann-Krayer, 2:1215–29. Berlin: Walter de Gruyter, 1929–42.

Mauss, Marcel. *A General Theory of Magic*, 3rd ed. London: Routledge, 2001.

Meier, Ernst. *Deutsche Sagen, Sitten und Gebräuche aus Schwaben*. Stuttgart: Metzler, 1852.

Mengis, Carl. "Art. Geist." In *Handwörterbuch des deutschen Aberglaubens*, 10 vols., ed. Hanns Bächtold-Stäubli and Eduard Hoffmann-Krayer, 3:472–510. Berlin: Walter de Gruyter, 1929–42.

———. "Art. Geistermahl." In *Handwörterbuch des deutschen Aberglaubens*, 10 vols., ed. Hanns Bächtold-Stäubli and Eduard Hoffmann-Krayer, 3:535–36. Berlin: Walter de Gruyter, 1929–42.

———. "Art. Geisterort." In *Handwörterbuch des deutschen Aberglaubens*, 10 vols., ed. Hanns Bächtold-Stäubli and Eduard Hoffmann-Krayer, 3:541–43. Berlin: Walter de Gruyter, 1929–42.

———. "Art. Geistertanz." In *Handwörterbuch des deutschen Aberglaubens*, 10 vols., ed. Hanns Bächtold-Stäubli and Eduard Hoffmann-Krayer, 3:556–57. Berlin: Walter de Gruyter, 1929–42.

———. "Art. Grau." In *Handwörterbuch des deutschen Aberglaubens*, 10 vols., ed. Hanns Bächtold-Stäubli and Eduard Hoffmann-Krayer, 3:1123–25. Berlin: Walter de Gruyter, 1929–42.

———. "Art. Grün." In *Handwörterbuch des deutschen Aberglaubens*, 10 vols., ed. Hanns Bächtold-Stäubli and Eduard Hoffmann-Krayer, 3:1180–86. Berlin: Walter de Gruyter, 1929–42.

Mertes, Erich. "Hexenprozesse in der Eifel—eine zusammenfassende Übersicht." *Eifel-Jahrbuch* (1989): 94–99.

Michel, Fritz. *Geschichte der Stadt Niederlahnstein*. Niederlahnstein, 1954. Repr. in *Geschichte der Stadt Lahnstein*, ed. Franz-Josef Heyen, 385–484. Lahnstein: Stadt Lahnstein, 1982.

Middell, Matthias. "Forschungen zum Kulturtransfer. Frankreich und Deutschland." *Grenzgänge. Beiträge zur modernen Romanistik* 1 (1994): 107–22.

———. "Kulturtransfer und Historische Komparatistik—Thesen zu ihrem Verhältnis." *Comparativ* 10 (2000): 7–41.

Midelfort, H. C. Erik. *Exorcism and Enlightenment.* New Haven, Conn.: Yale University Press, 2005.

———. "Recent Witch Hunting Research, or Where Do We Go from Here?" *Papers of the Bibliographical Society of America* 62 (1968): 373–540.

———. *Witch Hunting in Southwestern Germany.* Stanford, Calif.: Stanford University Press, 1972.

Mitterauer, Michael. "Familiengröße—Familientypen—Familienzyklus. Probleme quantitativer Auswertung von österreichischem Quellenmaterial." *Geschichte und Gesellschaft* 1 (1975): 226–55.

———. "Der Mythos von der vorindustriellen Großfamilie." In *Seminar: Familie und Gesellschaftsstruktur,* ed. Heidi Rosenbaum, 128–51. Frankfurt am Main: Suhrkamp, 1978.

Mohr, Nikolaus. "Hexen und Hexenwahn in Ehrang und Umgebung." *Ehranger Heimat* 2 (1933–36): 1–9, 32–35, 41–44, 61–67.

Monter, William, ed. *European Witchcraft.* New York: Wiley, 1969.

———. "Scandinavian Witchcraft in Anglo-American Perspective." In *Early Modern Witchcraft: Centres and Peripheries,* 2nd ed., ed. Bengt Ankarloo and Gustav Henningsen, 425–34. Oxford: Clarendon Press, 1993.

———. *Witchcraft in France and Switzerland.* Ithaca, N.Y.: 1976.

———. "Witch Trials in Continental Europe, 1560–1660." In *Witchcraft and Magic in Europe: The Period of the Witch Trials,* ed. Bengt Ankarloo and Stuart Clark, 1–52. Philadelphia: Penn, 2002.

Moser-Rath, Elfriede. *Dem Kirchenvolk die Leviten gelesen: Alltag im Spiegel süddeutscher Barockpredigten.* Stuttgart: Metzler, 1991.

Muchembled, Robert. "L'autre côté du miroir: Mythes sataniques et réalités culturelles aux XVIe et XVIIe siècles." *Annales* 40 (1985): 288–305, 298–99.

———. *Popular Culture and Elite Culture in France, 1400–1750.* Baton Rouge: Louisiana State University Press, 1985.

Müller, Albert. "Mobilität—Interaktion—Kommunikation. Sozial- und alltagsgeschichtliche Bemerkungen anhand von Beispielen aus dem spätmittelalterlichen und frühneuzeitlichen Österreich." In *Kommunikation und Alltag in Spätmittelalter und früher Neuzeit, internationaler Kongress Krems 1990,* ed. Herwig Wolfram, 219–49. Vienna: Verlag der Österreichischen Akademie der Wissenschaften, 1992.

Müller, Hans Peter. "Geschichte der Stadt Oberndorf und ihrer Stadtteile von 782 bis 1805." In *Geschichte der Stadt Oberndorf,* ed. Stadt Oberndorf, 97–488. Oberndorf: Stadt Oberndorf, 1982.

———. "Horb am Ausgang des Mittelalters." In *Veit Stoß,* ed. Franz Geßler, 20–32. Horb: Kultur- und Museumsverein, 1983.

———. "Vom Mittelalter bis zum Ende Vorderösterreichs." In *Weiler 1244–1994,* eds. Karl Heinz Geppert and Festausschuß Weiler, 35–78. Rottenburg: Festausschuss "750-Jahrfeier Weiler," 1994.

———. "Ortsgeschichte Spaichingen 791–1805." In *Spaichinger Stadtchronik*, ed. Stadt Spaichingen, 56–218. Spaichingen: Stadt Spaichingen, 1990.

———. "Die Ortsgeschichte vom Hochmittelalter bis 1805." In *1200 Jahre Altheim*, ed. Ortschaftsverwaltung Altheim, 69–136. Horb: Geiger, 1991.

Müller, Karl Otto. "Heinrich Institoris, der Verfasser des Hexenhammers und seine Tätigkeit als Hexeninquisitor in Ravensburg im Herbst 1484." *Württembergische Vierteljahrshefte für Landesgeschichte, Neue Folge* 19 (1910): 397–417.

———. "Die Musterregister der Grafschaft der Grafschaft Hohenberg." *Württembergische Jahrbücher für Statistik und Landeskunde* (1915): 135–79.

Müller, Max. *Die Geschichte der Stadt St. Wendel von ihren Anfängen bis zum Weltkriege*. St. Wendel: Verlag der Stadt, 1927.

Müller, Michael Franz Joseph. *Kleiner Beitrag zur Geschichte des Hexenwesens im XVI. Jahrhundert, aus authentischen Akten ausgehoben*. Trier: Blattau, 1830.

Müller-Bergström, Walther. "Art. Zwerge und Riesen." In *Handwörterbuch des deutschen Aberglaubens*, 10 vols., ed. Hanns Bächtold-Stäubli and Eduard Hoffmann-Krayer, 9:1008–1138. Berlin: Walter de Gruyter, 1929–42.

Mündnich, Joseph. *Das Hospital zu Coblenz*. Coblenz: Selbstverlag der Stadt, 1905.

Nagel, Adalbert. "Altdorf-Weingarten im Wandel der Zeiten." In *Altdorf Weingarten*, ed. Stadt Weingarten, 49–123. Weingarten: Stadt Weingarten, 1960.

———. "Das Heilige Blut Christi." In *Festschrift zur 900 Jahr-Feier des Klosters 1056–1956*, ed. Gebhard Spahr, 188–229. Weingarten: Selbstverlag, 1956.

Nahl, Rudolf van. *Zauberglaube und Hexenwahn im Gebiet von Rhein und Maas. Spätmittelalterlicher Volksglaube im Werk Johann Weyers (1515–1588)*. Bonn: Röhrscheid, 1983.

Nebinger, Gerhart, and Norbert Schuster. "Das Burgauer Feuerstattguldenregister." *Das obere Schwaben* 7 (1963): 77–124.

Neher, J. *Personal-Katalog der seit 1813 ordinierten und in der Seelsorge verwendeten Geistlichen des Bistums Rottenburg*. Rottenburg: Bader, 1885.

Neugebauer-Wölk, Monika. "Wege aus dem Dschungel. Betrachtungen zur Hexenforschung." In *Geschichte und Gesellschaft* 29 (2003): 316–47

Niessen, Josef. "Hexenprozesse in der Westeifel." *Eifelvereinsblatt* 32 (1931): 73–75.

Nikolay-Panter, Marlene. *Entstehung und Entwicklung der Landgemeinde im Trierer Raum*. Bonn: Röhrscheid, 1976.

Noflatscher, Heinz. *Maximilian der Deutschmeister (1558–1618)*. Marburg: Elwert, 1987.

Nowosadtko, Jutta. "Betrachtungen über den Erwerb von Unehre. Vom Widerspruch moderner und 'traditionaler' Ehren- und Unehrenkonzepten in der frühneuzeitlichen Ständegesellschaft." In *Ehre—Archaische Momente in der Moderne*, ed. Ludgera Vogt and Arnold Zingerle, 230–48. Frankfurt am Main: Suhrkamp, 1994.

———. "Meister zahlreicher Hexenprozesse. Die Scharfrichter Johann Volmair und Christoph Hiert aus Biberach." In *Wider alle Hexerei und Teufelswerk*, ed. Sönke Lorenz and Jürgen Michael Schmidt, 464–83. Ostfildern: Thorbecke, 2004.

Oestmann, Peter. *Hexenprozesse am Reichskammergericht*. Cologne: Böhlau, 1997.

Olbrich, Karl. "Art. Trudenstein." In *Handwörterbuch des deutschen Aberglaubens*, 10 vols., ed. Hanns Bächtold-Stäubli and Eduard Hoffmann-Krayer, 8:1174–76. Berlin: Walter de Gruyter, 1929–42.

Ortner, Michael. *Geschichte der Markgrafschaft Burgau.* Burgau: Konrad, 1911.

Ostorero, Martine, et al., eds. *L'imaginaire du sabbat.* Lausanne: Université de Lausanne, 1999.

Ott, Josef. *Chronik der Stadt Spaichingen.* N.p.: Stadt Spaichingen, 1953.

Palme, Rudolf. "Frühe Neuzeit." In *Geschichte des Landes Tirol,* 3 vols., ed. Josef Fontana et al., 2:3–287. Bozen: Verlag-Anstalt Athesia, 1986.

Pauly, Ferdinand. "Geschichte der Stadt Boppard." In *Boppard am Rhein,* ed. Alexander Stollenwerk. Boppard: Stadtverwaltung, 1977.

Perkmann, Adelgard. "Art. Läuten." In *Handwörterbuch des deutschen Aberglaubens,* 10 vols., ed. Hanns Bächtold-Stäubli and Eduard Hoffmann-Krayer, 5:938–49. Berlin: Walter de Gruyter, 1929–42.

Petzold, Leander, ed. *Magie und Religion.* Darmstadt: Wissenschaftliche Buchgesellschaft, 1978.

Peuckert, Will-Erich "Art. Festmachen II." In *Handwörterbuch des deutschen Aberglaubens,* 10 vols., ed. Hanns Bächtold-Stäubli and Eduard Hoffmann-Krayer, 2:1353–68. Berlin: Walter de Gruyter, 1929–42.

———. "Art. Josaphat, Tal." In *Handwörterbuch des deutschen Aberglaubens,* 10 vols., ed. Hanns Bächtold-Stäubli and Eduard Hoffmann-Krayer, 4: 770–74. Berlin: Walter de Gruyter, 1929–42.

Pfaff, F. "Die Weinpreise in Rottenburg am Neckar 1545–1620." *Alemannia* 19 (1892): 167–68.

Pohl, Herbert. "Hexenverfolgungen im Kurfürstentum Mainz." In *Hexenglaube und Hexenprozesse im Raum Rhein-Mosel-Saar,* ed. Gunther Franz and Franz Irsigler, 225–54. Trierer Hexenprozesse 1. Trier: Spee, 1995.

Press, Volker. "Herrschaft, Landschaft und 'gemeiner Mann' in Oberdeutschland vom 15. bis zum frühen 19. Jahrhundert." *Zeitschrift für die Geschichte des Oberrheins* 123 (1975): 169–214.

———. "Die Reichsritterschaft im Reich der frühen Neuzeit." *Nassauische Annalen* 87 (1976): 101–22.

Puhle, Hans-Jürgen. "Theorien in der Praxis des vergleichenden Historikers." In *Theorie und Erzählung in der Geschichte,* ed. Jürgen Kocka and Thomas Nipperdey, 119–36. Munich: Deutscher Taschenbuch-Verlag, 1979.

Quarthal, Franz. "Absolutismus und Provinz." Habilitation thesis, Tübingen, 1981.

———. "Die 'Fridingische Unruhe' 1672–1677." *Tuttlinger Heimatblätter* (1972): 33–52.

———. *Landstände und landständisches Steuerwesen in Schwäbisch-Österreich.* Stuttgart: Müller und Gräff, 1980.

———. "Die Verfassungsänderungen in den Städten Vorderösterreichs im Rahmen der Staatsreformen Maria Theresias." In *Stadtverfassung-Verfassungsstaat-Pressepolitik, Festschrift Eberhard Naujoks,* eds. Franz Quarthal and Wilfried Setzler, 121–38. Sigmaringen: Thorbecke, 1980.

———. "Vorderösterreich in der Geschichte Südwestdeutschlands." In *Vorderöster-*

reich. Nur die Schwanzfeder des Kaiseradlers? ed. Württembergisches Landesmuseum Stuttgart. Stuttgart: Württembergisches Landesmuseum, 1999.

———. "Zur Wirtschaftsgeschichte der österreichischen Städte am oberen Neckar." In *Zwischen Schwarzwald und Schwäbischer Alb,* ed. Franz Quarthal, 393–446. Sigmaringen: Thorbecke, 1984.

Quarthal, Franz, and Georg Wieland. *Die Behördenorganisation Vorderösterreichs von 1753–1805.* Bühl: Verlag Konkordia, 1977.

Raith, Anita. "Herzogtum Württemberg." In *Wider alle Hexerei und Teufelswerk,* ed. Sönke Lorenz and Jürgen Michael Schmidt, 225–36. Ostfildern: Thorbecke, 2004.

Ranke, Friedrich. "Art. Aufhocker." In *Handwörterbuch des deutschen Aberglaubens,* 10 vols., ed. Hanns Bächtold-Stäubli and Eduard Hoffmann-Krayer, 1:675–77. Berlin: Walter de Gruyter, 1929–42.

———. "Art. Alp." In *Handwörterbuch des deutschen Aberglaubens,* 10 vols., ed. Hanns Bächtold-Stäubli and Eduard Hoffmann-Krayer, 1:281–305. Berlin: Walter de Gruyter, 1929–42.

———. "Art. Pfaffenkellerin." In *Handwörterbuch des deutschen Aberglaubens,* 10 vols., ed. Hanns Bächtold-Stäubli and Eduard Hoffmann-Krayer, 6:1544–47. Berlin: Walter de Gruyter, 1929–42.

———. "Art. Trude." In *Handwörterbuch des deutschen Aberglaubens,* 10 vols., ed. Hanns Bächtold-Stäubli and Eduard Hoffmann-Krayer, 8:1173–74. Berlin: Walter de Gruyter, 1929–42.

Rapp, Ludwig. *Die Hexenprozesse und ihre Gegner aus Tirol.* Innsbruck: Wagner, 1874.

Rau, R. "Zur Herkunft der Familie Precht." *Sülchgauer Altertumsverein Rottenburg, Jahresgabe* (1960): 71–75.

Reif, Karl-Heinz. *Kurtrierisches Ämterbuch des 16. und 17. Jahrhunderts.* Coblenz: Westdeutsche Gesellschaft für Familienkunde, 1984.

Reifart, Ernst. "Der Kirchenstaat Trier und das Staatskirchentum." Ph.D. diss., Freiburg im Breisgau, 1951.

Reinhardt, Rudolf. *Restauration, Visitation, Inspiration: Die Reformbestrebungen in der Benediktinerabtei Weingarten von 1567–1627.* Stuttgart: Kohlhammer, 1960.

Reißenauer, Franz. *Münzstätte Günzburg 1764–1805.* Günzburg: Volksbank Günzburg, 1982.

Reiter, Josef. *Die Gemeindearchive des Kreises Horb.* Stuttgart: Kohlhammer, 1974.

———. *Das Spitalarchiv in Horb.* Stuttgart: Kohlhammer, 1950.

Renczes, Andrea. *Wie löscht man eine Familie aus? Eine Analyse Bamberger Hexenprozesse.* Pfaffenweiler: Centaurus, 1990.

Rettinger, Elmar. *Historisches Ortslexikon Rheinland-Pfalz, Volume 1: Ehemaliger Landkreis Cochem.* Stuttgart: Steiner-Verlag-Wiesbaden, 1985.

Richel, Artur. *Zwei Hexenprozesse aus dem 16. Jahrhundert.* Weimar: Felber, 1898.

Richter, Paul. Die kurtrierische Kanzlei im späteren Mittelalter. *Mitteilungen der königlich preussischen Archivverwaltung,* vol. 17. Leipzig: Hirzel, 1911.

Riegler, R. "Art. Ungeziefer." In *Handwörterbuch des deutschen Aberglaubens,* 10 vols., ed. Hanns Bächtold-Stäubli and Eduard Hoffmann-Krayer, 8:1419–25. Berlin: Walter de Gruyter, 1929–42.

———. "Art. Maus." In *Handwörterbuch des deutschen Aberglaubens,* 10 vols., ed.

Hanns Bächtold-Stäubli and Eduard Hoffmann-Krayer, 6:31–60. Berlin: Walter de Gruyter, 1929–42.

Riezler, Sigmund. *Geschichte der Hexenprozesse in Bayern* (Stuttgart, 1896), repr. ed. Aalen: Scientia-Verlag, 1968.

Roeck, Bernd. "Christlicher Idealstaat und Hexenwahn." *Historisches Jahrbuch* 108 (1988): 379–405.

Roecken, Sully, and Carolina Brauckmann. *Margaretha Jedefrau.* Freiburg im Breisgau: Kore, 1989.

Röhm, Helmut. *Die Vererbung des landwirtschaftlichen Grundeigentums in Baden-Württemberg.* Remagen: Verlag der Bundesanstalt für Landeskunde, 1957.

Röhrich, Lutz. *Sage und Märchen.* Freiburg im Breisgau: Herder, 1976.

Roper, Lyndal. *Oedipus and the Devil.* London: Routledge, 1994.

———. Witch Craze. Terror and Fantasy in Baroque Germany. New Haven: Yale University Press, 2004.

Roth, R. "Die Universität Tübingen im Jahr 1577." *Württembergische Jahrbücher für Statistik und Landeskunde* (1871; Stuttgart, 1873): 280–95.

Roth von Schreckenstein, Karl Heinrich. "Der sogenannte Hegauer Vertrag zwischen der Landgrafschaft Nellenburg, dem Deutschorden und der Reichsritterschaft." *Zeitschrift für die Geschichte des Oberrheins* 34 (1882): 1–30.

Rowland, Robert. "'Fantasticall and Devilishe Persons': European Witch-Beliefs in Comparative Perspective." In *Early Modern European Witchcraft—Centres and Peripheries,* 2nd ed., ed. Bengt Ankarloo and Gustav Henningsen, 161–90. Oxford: Clarendon Press, 1993.

Rückert, Georg. "Der Hexenwahn, ein Kulturbild aus Lauingens Vergangenheit." *Alt-Lauingen* 2 (1907): 25–27, 34–36, 41–43, 49–54, 57–59, 69–71, 73–77.

Rudolf, Hans Ulrich. "Die Geschichte des Blutritts im Überblick." In *900 Jahre Heilig-Blut-Verehrung in Weingarten 1094–1994,* 3 vols., ed. Norbert Kruse and Hans-Ulrich Rudolf, 2:701–57. Sigmaringen: Thorbecke, 1994.

———. "Heilig Blut—Brauchtum im Überblick." In *900 Jahre Heilig-Blut-Verehrung in Weingarten 1094–1994,* 3 vols., ed. Norbert Kruse and Hans-Ulrich Rudolf, 2:553–698. Sigmaringen: Thorbecke, 1994.

Rummel, Walter. "Die Anfänge der Hexenverfolgung im Trierer Land." *Landeskundliche Vierteljahresblätter* 36 (1990): 121–33.

———. *Bauern, Herren und Hexen.* Göttingen: Vandenhoeck und Ruprecht, 1991.

———. "'Exorbitantien und Ungerechtigten.' Skandalerfahrung und ordnungspolitische Motive im Abbruch der kurtrierischen und sponheimischen Hexenprozesse 1653/1660." In *Das Ende der Hexenverfolgung,* ed. Dieter Bauer and Sönke Lorenz, 37–53. Hexenforschung 2. Stuttgart: Steiner, 1995.

———. "Friedrich Spee und das Ende der kurtrierischen Hexenverfolgungen." *Jahrbuch für westdeutsche Landesgeschichte* 15 (1989): 105–16.

———. "Gutenberg, der Teufel und die Mutter Gottes von Eberhardsklausen. Erste Hexenverfolgungen im Trierer Land." In *Ketzer, Zauberer, Hexen. Die Anfänge der europäischen Hexenverfolgungen,* ed. Andreas Blauert, 91–117. Frankfurt am Main: Suhrkamp, 1990.

———. "Hexenprozesse im Raum von Untermosel und Hunsrück. Raumkulturelle und soziokulturelle Dimensionen." In *Sobernheimer Gespräche I.: Prozesse im Raum,* ed. Klaus Freckmann, 83–92. Cologne: Rheinland-Verlag, 1993.

———. "Hexenprozesse als Karrieremöglichkeit." *Kurtrierisches Jahrbuch* 25 (1985): 181–90.

———. "Phasen und Träger kurtrierischer und sponheimischer Hexenverfolgungen." In *Hexenglaube und Hexenprozesse im Raum Rhein-Mosel-Saar,* ed. Gunther Franz and Franz Irsigler, 255–332. Trierer Hexenprozesse 1. Trier: Spee, 1995.

———. "Soziale Dynamik und herrschaftliche Problematik der kurtrierischen Hexenverfolgungen. Das Beispiel der Stadt Cochem (1593–1595)." *Geschichte und Gesellschaft* 6 (1990): 26–55.

Sannwald, Wolfgang. *Spitäler in Pest und Krieg.* Gomaringen: Gomaringer Verlag, 1993.

Sauter, Johann. *Zur Hexenbulle 1484.* Ulm: Ebner, 1884.

Savigny, Friedrich Carl von. *Geschichte des römischen Rechts im Mittelalter* (Heidelberg, 1833–51), 7 vols., 2nd ed., repr. ed. Bad Homburg, 1961.

Schaefgen, Heinz. "Die Strafrechtspflege im Niedererzstift des Kurfürstentums Trier." Ph.D. diss., Mainz, 1957.

Schäfers, Bernhard. "Gesellschaft." In *Grundbegriffe der Soziologie,* 4th ed., ed. Bernhard Schäfers. Opladen: Leske und Budrich, 1995.

Scheffler, Jürgen, Gerd Schwerhoff, and Gisela Wilbertz. "Umrisse und Themen der Hexenforschung in der Region." In *Hexenverfolgung und Regionalgeschichte. Die Grafschaft Lippe im Vergleich,* ed. Jürgen Scheffler, Gerd Schwerhoff, and Gisela Wilbertz, 9–25. Bielefeld: Verlag für Regionalgeschichte, 1994.

Schewe, Harry. "Art. Blau." In *Handwörterbuch des deutschen Aberglaubens,* 10 vols., ed. Hanns Bächtold-Stäubli and Eduard Hoffmann-Krayer, 1:1366–86. Berlin: Walter de Gruyter, 1929–42.

Schieder, Theodor. "Möglichkeiten und Grenzen vergleichender Methoden in der Geschichtswissenschaft." In *Geschichte als Wissenschaft,* ed. Theodor Schieder, 187–211. Munich: Oldenbourg, 1965.

Schild, Wolfgang. *Alte Gerichtsbarkeit. Vom Gottesurteil bis zum Beginn der modernen Rechtsprechung.* Munich: Callwey, 1980.

———. "Die Dimensionen der Hexerei." In *Wider alle Hexerei und Teufelswerk,* ed. Sönke Lorenz and Jürgen Michael Schmidt, 1–104. Ostfildern: Thorbecke, 2004.

Schindler, Norbert. "Die Entstehung der Unbarmherzigkeit." In *Widerspenstige Leute. Studien zur Volkskultur in der frühen Neuzeit,* ed. Norbert Schindler, 258–314. Frankfurt am Main: Fischer-Taschenbuch-Verlag, 1992.

Schindling, Anton. "Die katholische Bildungsreform zwischen Humanismus und Barock. Dillingen, Dole, Freiburg, Molsheim und Salzburg: Die Vorlande und die benachbarten Universitäten." In *Vorderösterreich in der frühen Neuzeit,* ed. Hans Maier and Volker Press, 137–75. Sigmaringen: Thorbecke, 1989.

Schlaier, Bernd. "Reichsstadt Ulm." In *Wider alle Hexerei und Teufelswerk,* ed. Sönke Lorenz and Jürgen Michael Schmidt, 453–64. Ostfildern: Thorbecke, 2004.

Schleichert, Sabine. "Vorderösterreich: Elsaß, Breisgau, Hagenau und Ortenau." In *Wider alle Hexerei und Teufelswerk,* ed. Sönke Lorenz and Jürgen Michael Schmidt, 253–66. Ostfildern: Thorbecke, 2004.

Schmid, Manfred. "Behörden und Verwaltungsorganisation Tirols unter Erzherzog Ferdinand II. in den Jahren 1564–1585." Ph.D. diss., Innsbruck, 1972.

Schmid, Martina. "Die Biberacher Scharfrichter." In *Hexen und Hexenverfolgung im deutschen Südwesten, Aufsatzband,* ed. Sönke Lorenz, 411–15. Ostfildern: Cantz, 1994.

Schmidt, Aloys. *Heimatchronik der Stadt und des Landkreises Koblenz.* Cologne: Archiv für deutsche Heimatpflege, 1955.

Schmidt, Jürgen Michael. *Glaube und Skepsis. Die Kurpfalz und die abendländische Hexenverfolgung 1446–1685.* Hexenforschung 5. Bielefeld: Verlag für Regionalgeschichte, 2000.

————. "Die Kurpfalz." In *Wider alle Hexerei und Teufelswerk,* ed. Sönke Lorenz and Jürgen Michael Schmidt, 237–52. Ostfildern: Thorbecke, 2004.

Schmidt, Leopold. *Volksglaube und Volksbrauch.* Berlin: Schmidt, 1966.

Schmitt, Franz. *Bernkastel im Wandel der Zeiten.* Bernkastel-Kues: Stadt Bernkastel-Kues, 1985.

Schmitt, Philipp. *Die Kirche des heiligen Paulinus bei Trier, ihre Geschichte und ihre Heiligthümer.* Trier: Grach, 1853.

Schnabel-Schüle, Helga. "Distanz und Nähe." *Rottenburger Jahrbuch für Kirchengeschichte* 5 (1986): 339–48.

————. "Herrmann und Siemann. Zur Hierarchie der Geschlechterbeziehungen in historischer Sicht." *Der Bürger im Staat* 43 (1993): 161–65.

————. "Institutionelle und gesellschaftliche Rahmenbedingungen der Strafgerichtsbarkeit in Territorien des Reichs." In *Vorträge zur Justizforschung. Geschichte und Theorie,* 2 vols., ed. Heinz Mohnhaupt and Dieter Simon, 2:147–73. Frankfurt am Main: Klostermann, 1993.

————. "Kirchenzucht als Verbrechensprävention." In *Kirchenzucht und Sozialdisziplinierung im frühneuzeitlichen Europa,* ed. Heinz Schilling, 49–64. Berlin: Dunker and Humblot, 1994.

————. "Die Menschen in Herdwangen-Schönaich im Spannungsfeld von Besitz und Herrschaft." In *Herdwangen-Schönaich: Heimatbuch zur Geschichte der Gemeinde und des nördlichen Linzgau,* ed. Gemeinde Herdwangen-Schönaich, 27–46. Herdwangen-Schönach: Gemeinde Herdwangen-Schönach, 1994.

————. "Das Majestätsverbrechen als Herrschaftsschutz und Herrschaftskritik." In *Staatsschutz,* ed. Dietmar Willoweit, 29–47. Hamburg: Meiner, 1994.

————. "Die Strafe des Landesverweises in der Frühen Neuzeit." In *Ausweisung und Deportation. Formen der Zwangsmigration in der Geschichte,* ed. Andreas Gestrich et al., 73–82. Stuttgarter Beiträge zur Historischen Migrationsforschung 2. Stuttgart: Steiner, 1995.

————. *Überwachen und Strafen im Territorialstaat. Bedingungen und Auswirkungen des Systems strafrechtlicher Sanktionen im frühneuzeitlichen Württemberg.* Cologne: Böhlau, 1997.

Schneider, Eugen. "Das Koster Weingarten und die Landvogtei." *Württembergische Vierteljahrshefte für Landesgeschichte, Neue Folge* 9 (1900): 421–37.

Schnell, Martin. *Fridingen—Lebensbild einer kleinen Stadt.* Tuttlingen: Bofinger, 1963.

Schnelling, Ingeborg. *Die Archive der kurtrierischen Verwaltungsbehörden 1768–1832.* Trier: Paulinus-Verlag, 1991.

Schoenemann, Thomas. "The Witch Hunt as a Culture Change Phenomenon." *Ethos* 3 (1975): 529–54. Repr. in *Anthropological Studies of Witchcraft, Magic and Religion*, ed. Brian Levack, 337–62. New York: Garland, 1992.

Scholer, Othon. "Die Trierer und Luxemburger Hexenprozesse in der dämonologischen Literatur." In *Hexenprozesse und deren Gegner im trierisch-lothringischen Raum*, ed. Gunther Franz, Günter Gehl, and Franz Irsigler, 99–116. Weimar: Dadder, 1997.

Schön, Theodor. *Geschichte der Familie von Ow*. Munich: Kastner und Callwey, 1910.

————. "Geschlechter der Stadt Rottenburg." In *Beschreibung des Oberamts Rottenburg*, 2 vols., ed. Statistisches Landesamt, 41–58. Stuttgart: Kohlhammer, 1899–1900.

Schormann, Gerhard. "Die Fuldaer Hexenprozesse und die Würzburger Juristenfakultät." In *Hexenverfolgung und Regionalgeschichte. Die Grafschaft Lippe im Vergleich*, ed. Jürgen Scheffler, Gerd Schwerhoff, and Gisela Wilbertz, 311–23. Bielefeld: Verlag für Regionalgeschichte, 1994.

————. "Die Hexenprozesse im Kurfürstentum Köln." In *Hexenglaube und Hexenprozesse im Raum Rhein-Mosel-Saar*, ed. Gunther Franz and Franz Irsigler, 181–93. Trierer Hexenprozesse 1. Trier: Spee, 1995.

————. *Hexenprozesse in Deutschland*, 2nd ed. Göttingen: Vandenhoeck und Ruprecht, 1986.

————. *Hexenprozesse in Nordwestdeutschland*. Hildesheim: Lax, 1977.

Schorp, E. "Der Nachlaß des letzten Scharfrichters von Rottenburg." *Sülchgauer Altertumsverein Rottenburg, Jahresgabe* (1961): 16–18.

Schuhmann, Helmut. "Krankhafte Färbungen der Gemütslage in den schwäbischen Hexenprozessen." In *Kriminologische Wegzeichen, FS Hans von Hentig*, ed. Herbert Schäfer, 41–52. Hamburg: Kriminalistik Verlag, 1967.

————. *Der Scharfrichter. Seine Gestalt—seine Funktion*. Kempten: Verlag für Heimatpflege, 1964.

Schulte, Rolf. *Hexenmeister. Die Verfolgung von Männern im Rahmen der Hexenverfolgung*. Frankfurt am Main: Lang, 2000.

Schurer, Paul. *Die selige gute Betha von Reute*, 5th ed. Reute: Katholisches Pfarramt, 1981.

Schusser, Marianne. "Art. Beschwörung." In *Handwörterbuch des deutschen Aberglaubens*, 10 vols., ed. Hanns Bächtold-Stäubli and Eduard Hoffmann-Krayer, 1:1109–29. Berlin: Walter de Gruyter, 1929–42.

Schuster, Hans-Joachim. *Agrarverfassung, Wirtschaft und Sozialstruktur der nellenburgischen Kamerallandschaft im 17., 18. und frühen 19. Jahrhundert*. Singen: Verein für die Geschichte des Hegaus, 1990.

————. "Fridingen und Spaichingen." In *Vorderösterreich*, ed. Andreas Zekorn et al., 111–24. Constance: Universitätsverlag Konstanz, 2002.

————. "Das Musterregister der Landgrafschaft Nellenburg von 1615." *Hegau* 43 (1986): 55–134.

Schuster, Sieglinde. "Das Jesuitenkollegium Rottenburg und seine Bibliothek." Staatsexamen thesis, Tübingen, 1979.

Schwerhoff, Gerd. "Hexenverfolgung in einer frühneuzeitlichen Großstadt—das Beispiel der Stadt Köln." In *Hexenverfolgung im Rheinland. Ergebnisse neuerer Lokal-*

und Regionalstudien, ed. Wolfgang Isenberg and Georg Mölich. Bergisch Gladbach: Thomas-Morus-Akademie Bensberg, 1996.

———. "Hexerei, Geschlecht und Regionalgeschichte." In *Hexenverfolgung und Region-algeschichte. Die Grafschaft Lippe im Vergleich,* ed. Jürgen Scheffler, Gerd Schwerhoff, and Gisela Wilbertz, 325–53. Bielefeld: Verlag für Regionalgeschichte, 1994.

Schwillus, Harald. *Kleriker im Hexenprozeß.* Würzburg: Echter-Verlag, 1992.

Sebald, Hans. "Hexengeständnisse. Stereotype Struktur und lokale Farbe." *Spirita. Zeitschrift für Religionswissenschaft* 1 (1990): 27–38.

Seger, Otto. *Hexenprozesse in Liechtenstein.* St. Johann im Schongau: Österreichischer Kunst- und Kulturverlag, 1987.

Selig, Thedor. "Ein Hexenprozeß aus dem Jahr 1619." *Der Bussen* 3 (1932): 39–42.

Sellert, Wolfgang and Hinrich Rüping. *Studien- und Quellenbuch zur Geschichte der deutschen Strafrechtspflege,* 2 vols. Aalen: Scientia-Verlag, 1989–94.

Setzler, Wilfried. "Die Geschichte." In *Der Kreis Tübingen,* ed. Wilhelm Gförer, 99–133. Stuttgart: Theiss, 1988.

Sick, Wolf-Dieter. "Oberschwaben als Wirtschaftsraum." In *Oberschwaben,* ed. Hans-Georg Wehling, 45–72. Stuttgart: Kohlhammer, 1995.

Siebel, Friedrich Wilhelm. *Die Hexenverfolgung in Köln.* Bonn: Rheinische Friedrich-Wilhelms-Universität, 1959.

Siebs, Theodor. "Art. Geldmännlein." In *Handwörterbuch des deutschen Aberglaubens,* 10 vols., ed. Hanns Bächtold-Stäubli and Eduard Hoffmann-Krayer, 3:625–26. Berlin: Walter de Gruyter, 1929–42.

———. "Art. Hecketaler." In *Handwörterbuch des deutschen Aberglaubens,* 10 vols., ed. Hanns Bächtold-Stäubli and Eduard Hoffmann-Krayer, 3:1613–24. Berlin: Wallter de Gruyter, 1929–42.

Skocpol, Theda, and Margaret Somers. "The Uses of Comparative History in Macrosocial Inquiry." *Comparative Studies in Society and History* 22 (1980): 174–97.

Soldan, Wilhelm Gottlieb, and Heinrich Heppe. *Geschichte der Hexenprozesse,* 2 vols. Stuttgart: Cotta, 1880.

Soldan, Wilhelm Gottlieb, Heinrich Heppe, and Max Bauer. *Geschichte der Hexenprozesse,* 2 vols. Munich: Müller, 1911.

Soldan, Wilhelm Gottlieb, Heinrich Heppe, and S. Ries. *Geschichte der Hexenprozesse,* 2 vols. Kettwig: Magnus-Verlag, 1986.

Spahr, Eduard. *Kreuz und Blut Christi in der Kunst Weingartens.* Constance: Thorbecke, 1962.

———. "Geschichte des Weinbaus im Bodenseeraum." In *Der Bodensee. Landschaft, Geschichte, Kultur,* ed. Helmut Maurer, 189–229. Sigmaringen: Thorbecke, 1982.

Spies, Heinz. *Burg, Schloß und Amt Blieskastel.* Homburg: Ermer, 1977.

Stegemann, Victor. "Art. Hagel, Hagelzauber." In *Handwörterbuch des deutschen Aberglaubens,* 10 vols., ed. Hanns Bächtold-Stäubli and Eduard Hoffmann-Krayer, 3:1304–20. Berlin: Walter de Gruyter, 1929–42.

Steim, Martin. "Die Herkunft und Familie des Fürstabts Martin Gerbert." In *Fürstabt Martin Gerbert,* ed. Joachim Lipp, 17–44. Horb am Neckar: Kultur- und Museumsverein, 1993.

Steinert, Heinz. "Über symbolisches und instrumentelles Strafrecht." In *Konstruktion der Wirklichkeit durch Kriminalität und Strafe,* ed. Detlev Frehsee et al., 101–16. Baden-Baden: Nomos-Verlag-Gesellschaft, 1997.

Steinruck, Josef. "Zauberei, Hexen- und Dämonenglaube im Sendhandbuch des Regino von Prüm." In *Hexenglaube und Hexenprozesse im Raum Rhein-Mosel-Saar,* ed. Gunther Franz and Franz Irsigler, 3–18. Trierer Hexenprozesse 1. Trier: Spee, 1995.

Steller, Walter. "Art. Pferd." In *Handwörterbuch des deutschen Aberglaubens,* 10 vols., ed. Hanns Bächtold-Stäubli and Eduard Hoffmann-Krayer, 5: 1598–1652. Berlin: Walter de Gruyter, 1929–42.

Stemmler, Eugen. "Die Grafschaft Hohenberg." In *Vorderösterreich,* 2nd ed., ed. F. Metz, 579–601. Freiburg im Breisgau: Rombach, 1967.

———. *Die Grafschaft Hohenberg und ihr Übergang an Württemberg 1806.* Stuttgart: Kohlhammer, 1950.

Stolz, Eugen. *Die Urbansbruderschaft in Rottenburg a. N.* Rottenburg: Bader, 1913.

Stolz, Otto. *Geschichte und Bestände des staatlichen Archives (jetzt Landesregierungs-Archives) zu Innsbruck.* Vienna: Holzhauens Nachf., 1938.

———. *Geschichtliche Beschreibung der ober- und vorderösterreichischen Lande.* Karlsruhe: Südwestdeutsche Druck- u. Verlagsgesellschaft, 1943.

Ströbele, Ute. "Leben im Spital." Staatsexamen thesis, Tübingen, 1986.

Syré, Willi. *Bendorfer Chronik von dem Jahre 400 bis 1700.* Bendorf: W. Syré, 1985.

Tantsch, Werner. "Deutsche Teufels- und Hexennamen aus Urgichten des XV.–XVIII. Jahrhunderts." Ph.D. diss., Heidelberg, 1956.

Taylor, Talbot. *Mutual Misunderstanding. Sceptizism and the Theorizing of Language and Interpretation.* London: Routledge, 1992.

Theil, Bernhard. *Rottenburg und die österreichische Grafschaft Hohenberg.* Stuttgart: Hauptstaatsarchiv, 1981.

Thomas, Keith. "History and Anthropology." *Past and Present* 24 (1963): 3–24.

———. *Religion and the Decline of Magic* (London, 1971), 4th ed. Harmondsworth: Penguin Books, 1991.

Thompson, Edward P. "Anthropology and the Discipline of Historical Context." *Midland History* 1 (1972): 41–55.

Thompson, Stith. *Motif-Index of Folk-Literature,* 6 vols., 2nd ed. Copenhagen: Rosenkilde and Bagger, 1955–58.

Thorndike, Lynn. *A History of Magic and Experimental Science,* 8 vols. New York: Columbia University Press, 1923–58.

Tilly, Charles. *Big Structures, Large Processes, Huge Comparisons.* New York: Russell Sage Foundation, 1984.

Traut, Monika. "Die Hetzerather Heide." *Jahrbuch für den Kreis Bernkastel-Wittlich* (1994): 159–62.

Trevor-Roper, Hugh. *The European Witch-Craze of the 16th and 17th Centuries,* 4th ed. London: Penguin Books, 1988.

Trusen, Winfried. "Rechtliche Grundlagen der Hexenprozesse und ihrer Beendigung." In *Das Ende der Hexenverfolgung,* ed. Dieter Bauer and Sönke Lorenz, 203–26. Hexenforschung 2. Stuttgart: Steiner, 1995.

Tschaikner, Manfred. *"Damit das Böse ausgerottet werde": Hexenverfolgung in Vorarlberg im 16. und 17. Jahrhundert.* Bregenz: Vorarlberger Autoren-Gesellschaft, 1992.

————. "Die Zauberer- und Hexenverfolgung in Tirol von 1637 bis 1645." *Tiroler Heimat* 66 (2002): 81–112.

Tüchle, Hermann, and August Willburger. *Geschichte der katholischen Kirche in Württemberg.* Rottenburg: Bader, 1954.

Tumbült, Georg. "Die Landgrafschaft Nellenburg." *Schriften des Vereins für Geschichte des Bodensees u. seiner Umgebung* 24 (1895): 13–18.

Tylor, Edward B. *Primitive Culture,* 2 vols. London: Murray, 1871.

Unverhau, Dagmar. *Von Toverschen und Kunstfruwen in Schleswig 1548–1557.* Schlewig: Schleswiger Druck- und Verlagshaus, 1980.

Valentinisch, Helfried, ed. *Hexen und Zauberer.* Graz: Leykam, 1987.

Vater, Andrea. "Hexenverfolgungen in nassauischen Grafschaften im 16.und 17. Jahrhundert." Ph.D. diss., Marburg, 1988.

Voges, Dietmar. "Reichsstadt Nördlingen." In *Hexen und Hexenverfolgung im deutschen Südwesten, Aufsatzband,* ed. Sönke Lorenz, 361–69. Ostfildern: Cantz, 1994.

Vöhringer-Rubröder, Gisela. "Reichstadt Esslingen." In *Wider alle Hexerei und Teufelswer.* ed. Sönke Lorenz and Jürgen Michael Schmidt, 403–16. Ostfildern: Thorbecke, 2004.

Völk, Josef. "Ein Günzburger Hexenprozeß." *Schwäbische Heimat, Beilage zum Günz- und Mindelboten* 8–9 (1928), n.p.

Voltmer, Rita. "Claudius Musiel oder die Karrier eines Hexenrichters." In *Methoden und Konzepte der historischen Hexenforschung,* ed. Gunther Franz and Franz Irsigler, 211–54. Trierer Hexenprozesse 4. Trier: Spee, 1998.

————. "Gott ist tot und der Teufel ist jetzt Meister!" *Kurtrierisches Jahrbuch* 39 (1999): 175–223.

————. "Monopole, Ausschüsse, Formalparteien." In *Hexenprozesse und Gerichtspraxis, Trierer,* ed. Herbert Eiden, 5–67. Hexenprozesse 6. Trier: Spee, 2002.

————. "Zwischen Herrschaftskrise, Wirtschaftsdepression und Jesuitenpropaganda." *Jahrbuch für westdeutsche Landesgeschichte* 27 (2001): 37–107.

Waardt, Hans de. *Toverij en Samenleving. Holland 1500–1800.* The Hague: Stichting Hollandse Historische Reeks, 1991.

Wagner, Hans. *Aus Stockachs Vergangenheit.* 2nd ed. Constance: Druckerei und Verlagsanst. Konstanz, 1981.

Waldmann, Peter. "Gewaltsamer Separatismus. Westeuropäische Nationalitätenkonflikte in vergleichender Perspektive." In *Nationalismus, Nationalitäten, Supranationalität,* ed. Heinrich August Winkler and Hartmut Kaelble, 82–107. Stuttgart: Klett-Cotta, 1993.

Walter, Ronald. "Signs of the Times: Clifford Geertz and Historians." *Social Research* 47 (1980): 537–56.

Walz, Rainer. *Hexenglaube und magische Kommunikation im Dorf der frühen Neuzeit.* Paderborn: Schöningh, 1993.

Weber, Hartwig. *Kinderhexenprozesse.* Frankfurt am Main: Insel-Verlag, 1991.

Weiler, J. "Die Gerichtsbarkeit im Mittelalter." In *Münstermaifelder Heimatbuch,* ed. Hans Gappenach, 57–59. Münstermaifeld: Fremdenverkehrs- und Amt für Wirtschaftsförderung, 1960.

Weisenstein, Karl. "Zaubereiprozesse in der Stadt Trier." In *Hexenglaube und Hexen-*

prozesse im Raum Rhein-Mosel-Saar, ed. Gunther Franz and Franz Irsigler, 469–84. Trierer Hexenprozesse 1. Trier: Spee, 1995.

Weiß, Elmar. "Grafschaft Wertheim." In *Wider alle Hexerei und Teufelswerk*, ed. Sönke Lorenz and Jürgen Michael Schmidt, 339–54. Ostfildern: Thorbecke, 2004.

Weiter-Matysiak, Barbara. *Weinbau im Mittelalter*. Cologne: Rheinland-Verlag, 1985.

Welskopp, Thomas. "Stolpersteine auf dem Königsweg. Methodenkritische Anmerkungen zum internationalen Vergleich in der Gesellschaftsgeschichte." *Archiv für Sozialgeschichte* 35 (1995): 339–67.

Widmoser, E. "Markgraf Karl von Burgau (1560–1618)." In *Lebensbilder aus dem Bayerischen Schwaben*, 14 vols., ed. Götz von Pölnitz et al., 3:269–84. Munich: Hueber, 1952.

Wieland, Georg. "Das leitende Personal der Landvogtei Schwaben von 1486 bis 1806." In *Die Habsburger im deutschen Südwesten*, ed. Franz Quarthal and Gerhard Faix, 341–64. Stuttgart: Thorbecke, 2000.

———. "Personalschematismus der vorderösterreichischen Oberämter Altdorf und Tettnang, der Zollämter Altdorf und Gebrazhofen und des Landgerichts Altdorf 1773–1797." Typewritten ms., Tübingen, 1975.

Willburger, August. "Hexenverfolgung in Württemberg." *Rottenburger Monatsschrift für praktische Theologie* 13 (1929–30): 135–45, 167–73.

Wolpert, Wolfgang. "Fünfhundert Jahre Kreuzweg in Ediger an der Mosel." In *Hexenglaube und Hexenprozesse im Raum Rhein-Mosel-Saar*, ed. Gunther Franz and Franz Irsigler, 19–34. Trierer Hexenprozesse 1. Trier: Spee, 1995.

Wrede, Adam. "Art. Benedikt." In *Handwörterbuch des deutschen Aberglaubens*, 10 vols., ed. Hanns Bächtold-Stäubli and Eduard Hoffmann-Krayer, 1:1031–35. Berlin: Walter de Gruyter, 1929–42.

Wunder, Heide: *"Er ist die Sonn, sie ist der Mond": Frauen in der frühen Neuzeit*. Munich: Beck, 1992.

Wüst, Wolfgang. "Historische Einleitung." In *Landkreis Günzburg 1—Stadt Günzburg*, ed. Klaus Kraft, 1–49. Munich: Oldenbourg, 1993.

———. *Günzburg, Historischer Atlas von Bayern, Teil Schwaben, Heft 13*. Munich: Kommission für Bayerische Landesgeschichte, 1983.

———. "'Ius superioritatis territorialis': Prinzipien und Zielsetzungen im habsburgisch-insässischen Rechtsstreit um die Markgrafschaft Burgau." In *Vorderösterreich in der frühen Neuzeit*, ed. Hans Maier and Volker Press, 209–28. Sigmaringen: Thorbecke, 1989.

Wyttenbach, Johann Hugo. "Abermaliger Beytrag zur Geschichte der Hexen-Processe." *Trierische Chronik* 10 (1825): 108–16, 124–26

———. "Noch ein höchst merkwürdiger Hexen-Proceß." *Trierische Chronik* 10 (1825): 196–209, 221–34, 245–57.

Zeck, Mario. "Reichsstadt Rottweil." In *Wider alle Hexerei und Teufelswerk*, ed. Sönke Lorenz and Jürgen Michael Schmidt, 427–36. Ostfildern: Thorbecke, 2004.

Zender, Matthias. "Glaube und Brauch. Fest und Spiel." In *Volkskunde. Eine Einführung*, ed. Günther Wiegelmann et al., 132–97. Berlin: Schmidt, 1977.

Zenz, Emil. "Cornelius Loos—ein Vorläufer Friedrich von Spees im Kampf gegen den Hexenwahn." *Kurtrierisches Jahrbuch* 21 (1981): 146–53.

———. "Dr. Dietrich Flade, ein Opfer des Hexenwahns." *Kurtrierisches Jahrbuch* 2 (1962): 41–69.

———. "Die weltliche Kriminalgerichtsbarkeit im Trierer Land im 17. und 18. Jahrhundert." *Jahrbuch für den Kreis Trier-Saarburg* (1991): 186–202.

Zimmermann, Wolfgang. "Hochstift Konstanz." In *Wider alle Hexerei und Teufelswerk,* ed. Sönke Lorenz and Jürgen Michael Schmidt, 365–76. Ostfildern: Thorbecke, 2004.

———. "Teufelsglaube und Hexenverfolgung in Konstanz 1546–1548." *Schriften des Vereins für Geschichte des Bodensees und seiner Umgebung* 106 (1988): 29–56.

Zingeler, D. "Ein Hexenprozeß zu Freudenstadt aus dem 17. Jahrhundert." *Württembergische Vierteljahrshefte für Landesgeschichte* 9 (1886): 148–53.

Zoepfl, Friedrich. "Hexenwahn und Hexenverfolgung in Dillingen." *Zeitschrift für bayerische Landesgeschichte* 27 (1964): 235–44.

Zorn, Wolfgang. *Handels- und Industriegeschichte Bayerisch-Schwabens 1648–1870.* Augsburg: Verlag der schwäbischen Forschungsgemeinschaft, 1961.

———. "Vorderösterreich als Karrieresprungbrett: Beobachtungen zur Sozialgeschichte des Beamtentums." In *Vorderösterreich in der frühen Neuzeit,* ed. Hans Maier and Volker Press, 43–56. Sigmaringen: Thorbecke, 1989.

Zürn, Martin. "Abseits und verfolgt? Die Hexen vom Bussen." In *Minderheiten in der Geschichte Südwestdeutschlands,* ed. Otto Borst, 35–72. Stuttgarter Symposion 3. Tübingen: Silberburg-Verlag 1996.

———. *"Ir aigen libertet." Waldburg, Habsburg und der bäuerliche Widerstand an der oberen Donau 1590–1790.* Tübingen: Bibliotheca-Academica-Verlag, 1998.

Index